HIMALAYAN FRONTIERS

Also by Dorothy Woodman

THE MAKING OF BURMA
THE REPUBLIC OF INDONESIA

DOROTHY WOODMAN

HIMALAYAN FRONTIERS

A POLITICAL REVIEW OF
BRITISH, CHINESE, INDIAN
AND RUSSIAN RIVALRIES

FREDERICK A. PRAEGER, *Publishers*
New York · Washington

BOOKS THAT MATTER
Published in the United States of America in 1969
by Frederick A. Praeger, Inc., Publishers
111 Fourth Avenue, New York, N.Y. 10003

© 1969 by Dorothy Woodman

Library of Congress Catalog Card Number: 70-85494

Printed in Great Britain

Contents

Maps

      [This map was supplied by the Government
of India, and the reference number which
appears on it has no relevance to the book.]

Preface

In a hundred ages of the Gods,
I could not tell you of all the
Glories of the Himalaya

So wrote an old Sanskrit poet. I have often shared his feelings while wandering along the frontiers of Bhutan, Burma, China, India, Pakistan, Nepal and Sikkim. But I am a political writer. *Himalayan Frontiers* is a political book which reviews the influence of the Himalayas on the Indian sub-continent, where they symbolized the abode of those gods and the centre of the universe. No other country has had this affinity with the Himalayas. It continues to this day, though the people who haunt them are ordinary humans, and peaceful ranges are smouldering volcanoes.

For years merchants crossed these high mountains looking for trade while religious men travelled to and from India and China seeking enlightenment on the Buddhist scriptures. Centuries later the frontier idea was introduced when the East India Company's expansion up to, and then beyond the Himalayas precipitated rivalries between Britain, China and Russia. In this book I follow the chain of events from the days when little piles of stones were enough to tell the traveller where he might be asked to pay a small tax on silk or shawl wool until the present day when unimaginative strategists see the Himalayas as a vast radar screen.

The Himalayas have dominated the Asian policy of Britain, China and Russia. And since geographical factors remain to a large extent constant, they still determine the shape of policy adopted by China, India, Pakistan and the Soviet Union as well as that of the smaller states which are on the Himalayan periphery. In the age of the nuclear bomb, America joins the Himalayan complex.

This is a controversial book. In the political tangles of the second half of the nineteenth century and the first half of the twentieth, allegiances changed as nations reached the limits of strategically safe expansion. Thus China was treated as an ally of Britain when British rulers were impressed by Russia's threat to India. But China became a rival when her troops threatened the plains of Assam, and by that time Russia and Britain had agreed to observe their respective spheres of influence in Tibet, Persia and Afghanistan.

The victory of communism, first in the Soviet Union, and then in China, and the withdrawal of Britain from the Indian sub-continent revolutionised the political outlook of the main participants in this story of Himalayan rivalry. It did not change the basic facts of their geography. Until the Sino–Soviet dispute developed, first in the secret sessions of the communist hierarchy, and then in communist parties everywhere, their common ideology was interpreted as the basis of a formidable threat to the western world. Today, the monolith of communism is shattered and the role of China, unhappily still outside the United Nations, is uncertain. America and Russia collaborate in, and dominate the Himalayan scene. They encourage India and Pakistan to adopt a more realistic policy towards one another in Kashmir.

Nationalism, contrary to the normal thinking of my generation, has proved more emotive, more provocative and more menacing to world stability than ideology. The area of maximum danger might now shift to the long frontier between communist China and communist Russia.

But I have not attempted prophecy. I have tried to draw the outlines of that struggle for the Himalayas which has not yet ended, selecting those facts which seemed essential for any evaluation of big power rivalry. This has involved studying the geographical background and the recapitulation of a wide area of historical data, some of it already covered by more distinguished writers, some of it by Indian and Chinese officials to establish their respective cases. I have also intimately followed the contemporary scene, not only from the outpost of London, once the centre that dictated it, but from frequent visits to Asian countries since 1948. I have also had the very great privilege of personal talks with many of the leading participants, above all with Pandit Nehru. He and the Labour Government's greatly under-estimated Prime Minister, Clement Attlee, laid solid foundations for Britain's honourable relinquishment of her Asian empire. Regrettably no comparable discussions with their Chinese counterparts were practicable.

No book written during times of such fluctuations and disarray can claim to be up-to-date. Official records are still only available till 1938. Access to Chinese records is ruled out, not only by language but by the breakdown of cultural bridges. Books and autobiographies proliferate, especially in India.

Himalayan Frontiers could not have been written without access to the Indian Office Library. I am indebted to Mr Stanley C. Sutton, Librarian and Keeper of the Records, who has so imaginatively transferred its wealth of documentation from the sedate precincts of Whitehall to the pedestrian hub-hub of Blackfriars Road. *A Guide to Lists and Catalogues of the India Office Records* by his Assistant Keeper of the Records, Miss Joan C. Lancaster, now eliminates many hours of difficult search. I owe a special debt to Mr Martin Moir and to Dr Richard Bingle, Research Assistants, who have given immeasurable and friendly help for many years. Miss K. Thompson has long given the Library an intimacy which is widely appreciated. The five Library Assistants, Ernest Brewster, Charles Flaskett, Alfred Pike, Walter Williams and George Martin, continue to produce books and records with efficiency, speed and a valued good humour. I am also indebted to the London Library, the Senate Library, the Library of the Royal Geographical Society, the Royal Institute of International Affairs (especially to its unrivalled Press Cuttings Library), and to the National Archives in New Delhi.

I have been extremely fortunate to have had discussions with Dr S. Gopal, who, as the then Head of the Historical Division of the Ministry of External Affairs in India, was primarily responsible for the most able documentation of the Indian section of the *Officials' Report*; with Dr Alastair Lamb, whose scholarly books on Himalayan frontiers and frontier problems are indispensable for anyone who wishes to make a careful study of this arena; with Sir Olaf Caroe, who, as ex-Deputy Secretary in the Government of India, played a vital part in the history of the McMahon Line; and with Neville Maxwell, who was *The Times* correspondent in India from 1959–1967. His forthcoming book on the Sino–Indian dispute, based on first-hand accounts will certainly add to our knowledge of this controversy.

Not one of these experts is wholly in agreement with what I have written, and none of them may be held responsible for my conclusions.

I want to thank Christopher MacLehose who, as Editor, has smoothed out many jagged edges and given so generously of his time in the transformation of a troublesome manuscript into the present book.

Finally, I can never adequately express my gratitude to Kingsley Martin whose encouragement and assistance have meant so much in the writing of this, as of my other, books. And no more would he endorse all that I have written and he is in no way responsible for it.

[He was never to see *Himalayan Frontiers* as a finished book. On February 16 his heart stopped. We were on Indian territory – at the home of Apa Pant, the Indian Ambassador, and his wife Dr. Nalini Pant, on the banks of the Nile in Cairo.]

D.W.
April, 1969

Acknowledgements

The following acknowledgements are made:

MAPS

1, 2 to Joseph Needham; 10 to India Office Library; 9, 17 to Royal Geographical Society; 12, 18, 19, 28, 29, 30 to Alastair Lamb; 8 to G. Alder; 3, 4, 5, 6, 7, 13, 14, 15, 20, 22, 23, 24, 25, 26, 27 to Ministry of External Affairs, Government of India; 11 to Public Record Office; 16 to Foreign Languages Press, Peking; 21 to Hsinhua News Agency.

DOCUMENTS

Documents, as listed in the References, have been published by permission of the following:

The Public Record Office, London.
The India Office Library.

I am also indebted to Mr E. D. Reid for permission to see the Papers of his father, the late Sir Robert Reid, Governor of Assam, 1937–1941.

HIMALAYAN FRONTIERS

India and China in Asia

CENTURIES OF UNEVENTFUL CO-EXIST-
ENCE; THE INDIAN NATIONAL CON-
GRESS AND SOLIDARITY WITH CHINA;
THE BONDS GROW STRONGER

On August 25, 1959, a cloud fell over the Himalayas which has not yet lifted. On that morning, Chinese and Indian troops exchanged fire on the border south of Migytun. The Himalayas, peaceful and remote, became an area of controversy and menace.

China and India were assumed to be models of co-existence, their good relations almost ostentatiously demonstrated to the world. A belief that the cold war halted at the Himalayan ranges had not before been challenged.

When the first White Paper was laid on the table of the Lok Sabha in September 1959, many unsuspected items were brought to light. They proved that while national leaders were chanting the Panch Shila, controversial Notes were passing between the Foreign Office of Delhi and Peking. Acid Indian protests against Chinese maps met with evasive replies from Peking. While Indian and Chinese crowds were shouting 'Hindi-Chini bhai-bhai' (India and China are friends) Indian complaints and Chinese non-committal replies were being exchanged on the intrusions of aircraft over Indian territory, on the condition of Tibetan emigrés in Kalimpong and on disturbances in Tibet. These subjects were new to the Indian masses, and, more surprisingly, to most journalists.

Chinese propaganda now called India a hostile neighbour, and Nehru grew the horns of a fascist monster. India's first reaction, one of sorrow rather than anger, was soon expressed in the harsh tones of a betrayed friend. Bewilderment followed on bewilderment. Men who had been Gandhi's closest associates talked in terms of national honour and sovereign rights. The 'Hindi-Chini bhai-bhai' slogan lapsed. Charges of Chinese aggression appeared in all but the Communist press, and that omission arose not so much from sympathy with China as from a division among Indian Communists. Nehru was extravagantly criticised by Right and Left for glossing over China's behaviour and for failing to meet its challenge. In terms unthinkable a year or two earlier, he told the Lok Sabha (on September 12, 1959): 'What we have to face today is a great and powerful nation which is aggressive. It might be aggressive minus Communism or plus Communism. Either way it might be there. That is a fact that you have to face.'

Thus the course of Indian history was violently changed in 1959.

CENTURIES OF UNEVENTFUL CO-EXISTENCE

The great arc of the Himalayas had shut off, or enclosed within its folds, the countries of Asia. The word Himalayas has a Sanskrit origin: *Hima* snow and *alaya* home. This home of snow does not only mean the mountains which feed the great rivers of the Ganges, Jumna, Gogra, Gandaki and Kosi; it is a primary source of Indian mythology, of Hindu and Buddhist ideas and has had a profound influence on poetry and art. 'All Indian poetry and mythology,' E. B. Havell, the orientalist, wrote, 'point to the Himalayas as the centre of the world, and as the throne of the great gods. . . . The Hindu regards the Himalayas, not from the point of view of the mountaineering sportsman or of the scientist, but as the Muhammadan thinks of Mecca and the Christian of Jerusalem'.[1]

The Himalayas have dominated the life, the culture and the religion of India. The *Vishnu Purana*, an early Sanskrit text, suggests that they were always the shield of India. The country south of the Himalayas and north of the Ocean is called *Bharat*, and all people who are born in this land are called Bharatiyas or Indians. The *Rig Veda*, two centuries before Christ, and the *Upanishads*, some centuries later, were composed by men who felt themselves part of the Himalayas. The Hindu gods were the mountains and the symbol. The heroes and heroines of *Mahabharata* and the *Ramayana* came from the world of the Himalayas, the abode of the gods. In the 5th Century A.D., Kalidasa's popular dance drama, *Kumarasambhava*, which is still frequently performed in India, begins with an invocation to the Himalayas, describing them as 'a measuring-rod spanning the wide land from the east to the western sea'.

Whereas the Himalayas were the Olympus of Hindu and Buddhist culture, they played no part in the early civilisation of China. They are not even a feature in any of the early Chinese maps, as Maps I and II demonstrate. They form a natural barrier between these two great Asian civilisations, so divergent in almost every aspect.

There is no more dramatic illustration of this early divergence than a comparison of Asoka's Edicts carved on stone pillars over an area including Afghanistan and Baluchistan with the rock inscriptions of Shih-huang, who unified China for the first time, made at just about the same time, in the 3rd Century B.C. Asoka, after exhausting his enthusiasm for conquest, became a Buddhist and his inscriptions were mainly moral exhortations. The Tai-chang pillar characteristically described Shih-huang ti: 'For the first time he has united the world,' and another claimed: 'The Sovereign Emperor has pacified in turn the four ends of the earth.' In the first naturalistic geographical survey made by Yu-Kung, the cosmology of the world was classified as royal domains, princes' domains, pacification zone, allied barbarism and cultureless savagery.

The attitude of China towards her western neighbours was dictated then, as it is now, by geography. Dr Joseph Needham in the first volume of his monumental *Science and Civilisation in China* quotes an influential high official as advising his prime minister that 'friendly intercourse with barbarian nations is advisable only where communications are reasonably easy'.[2] Less materialistic considerations inspired the early exchange of ideas. From about the middle of the 4th Century A.D. Indian scholar monks visited China to preach Buddhism and many more Chinese scholar monks made pilgrimages to India to study Buddhist scriptures. Prominent among the latter was Hiuan Tsang, one of the most endearing travellers of all times. In spite of official disapproval he left China secretly in 629, and according to his own moving Memorial written to the Tang Emperor on his return in 645 'traversed over vast plains of shifting sand, scaled precipitous mountain crags clad with snow, found my way through the scarped passes of the iron gates, passed along by the tumultuous waves of the hot sea'. He described the Himalayan borderlands of Assam, Nepal and Kashmir as being ruled by Hindu kings, and his description of sixteen years travel in India

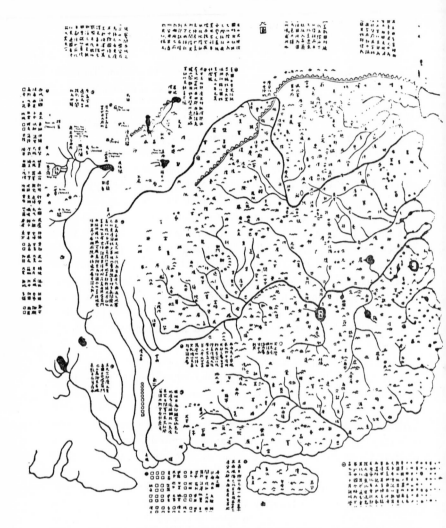

MAP 1. *The Hua I Thu* (Map of China and the Barbarian Countries), one of the two most important monuments of medieval Chinese cartography, carved in stone in + 1137 but probably dating from about + 1040 (from Chavannes). The size of the original (which bears a fuller explanatory text), which is now in the Pei Lin Museum at Sian, is about 3 ft square. The name of the geographer is not known.

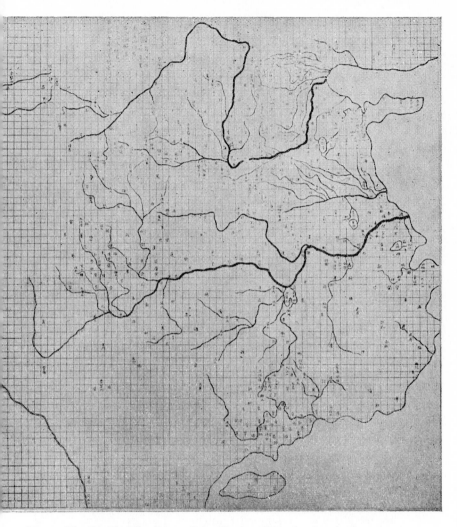

MAP 2. *The Yü Chi Thu* (Map of the Tracks of Yü the Great), the most remarkable cartographic work of its age in any culture, carved in stone in +1137 but probably dating from before +1100 (from Chavannes). The scale of the grid is 100 *li* to the division. The coastal outline is relatively firm and the precision of the network of river systems extraordinary. The size of the original, which is now in the Pei Lin Museum at Sian, is about 3 ft square. The name of the geographer is not known.

remains the most vivid account of the country of that period. He made many Indian friends and wrote to his co-religionist, the monk Jnanaprabha in 654: 'I returned ten years ago. The frontiers of the two countries are far away from each other. I had no news from you. My anxiety went on increasing.' 3

In Delhi, in the days when 'Hindi-Chini bhai-bhai' was a popular slogan, I saw an excellent documentary film about Hiuan Tsang produced by the Indian Ministry of Information. The theme was a thousand years of friendship between India and China. It was an imaginative political gambit, applauded by intellectuals and masses. The documentation was inevitably thin since the close personal contacts in the 7th Century were not to find a parallel until India was an independent country and China was under Communist rule. Hiuang Tsang was quickly forgotten when Chinese soldiers marched through Himalayan passes, and presumably today the dust of some official pigeonhole covers this discarded exercise in goodwill.

During those centuries of separation, the role of the Himalayas as India's frontier was not in question. An Indian scholar, P. C. Bagchi, Director of Research Studies in Santineketan, dedicated his book *India and China*, in 1944, 'To Friends in China'. It was a romantic study of more than 1000 years of Sino-Indian friendship. He wrote: 'The roads connecting these two countries had lost themselves in the desert sands or in tropical forests, uncared for; the footprints of the ancient messengers had been effaced by the ravages of time and the old literature had become a sealed book.' 4 It was the constant claim, not only of Bagchi, but of Nehru, Panikkar, Majumdar, Chakravarti and other historians that the two great civilisations of India and China, spreading as they did over Asia until they met in Indo-China, enjoyed an uneventful co-existence. That there should be boundary lines between them was a purely western notion.

There had never been war between India and China. They were both the victims of western imperial ambitions. The boundary idea was one product of western occupation and western strategy and, more particularly, of the British occupation of India.

Curzon, as a geographer who had explored the Pamirs and the Karakorum, described them as a barrier between India and Czarist Russia. In a memorable phrase he observed: 'Frontiers are indeed the razor's edge on which hang suspended the modern issues of war or peace, of life or death to nations. . . . The holders of the mountains', he appreciated, had an 'immense advantage ... against the occupants of the plains.' He advocated a scientific frontier to counteract that advant- age, 'i.e. a Frontier which unites natural and strategical strength, and by placing both the entrance and the exit of the passes in the hands of the defending Power, compels the enemy to conquer the approach before he can use the passage'. He realised that as far as Asia was concerned, the idea of a demarcated frontier was 'an essentially modern conception. ... It would be true to say that demarcation has never taken place except under European pressure and by the intervention of European agents.' 5

At the end of the 19th Century, Sir Thomas Holdich, Surveyor- General of India, described the Himalayas as the natural and accepted frontier. 'It is the finest natural combination of boundary and barrier that exists in the world. It stands alone. For the greater part of its length only the Himalayan eagle can trace it. It lies amidst the eternal silence of vast snowfields and icebound peaks. ... Could you stand on the summit of one of the lower and outer ranges in Kashmir, or in Garwhal, or Nepal, or at Darjiling, and watch on some clear day the white out- line of the distant snowy range, you would realise then that never was there such a God-given boundary set to such a vast, impressive and stupendous frontier.' 6

Nothing could have been further from Nehru's mind when sover- eignty was transferred to India in 1947. Whatever changes might take place in Asia, and 'the winds of change', as he described them, were blowing over the whole continent, Sino-Indian friendship seemed one of the few stable factors. The drama of a thousand years of contact between the two countries was one of his favourite themes. 'Probably China was more influenced by India than India by China,' he had earlier written in *The Discovery of India*, 'which is a pity, for India could well have received, with profit to herself, some of the sound common sense of the Chinese, and, with its aid, checked her own extravagant fancies. China took much from India, but she was always strong and self-confident enough to take it in her own way and fit it in somewhere in her own texture of life.' 7 China and India were cut off from each other for several centuries, and then, as Nehru describes it, they were 'brought by some strange fate under the influence of the British East India Company. India had to endure this for long; in China the contact was brief, but even so it brought opium and war'. He was writing in Ahmadnagar Fort prison camp somewhen between August 9, 1942, and March 28, 1945. '... The wheel of fate has turned full circle and again

India and China look towards each other and past memories crowd in
their minds; again pilgrims of a new kind cross or fly over the mountains that separate them, bringing their messages of cheer and goodwill
and creating fresh bonds of a friendship that will endure.' [8]

THE INDIAN NATIONAL CONGRESS AND
SOLIDARITY WITH CHINA

Nehru's admiration for and solidarity with China were more than a
personal matter. They were a dominating factor in the foreign policy
of the Indian National Congress, for which he was largely responsible
from 1927 onwards.

The National Congress was founded in 1885 – the same year that
Britain annexed Upper Burma – and although its founders included
retired British members of the Indian Civil Service it was an Indian
organisation, and as such it could not be indifferent to British annexation of a neighbouring country. It was a Party in a colonial country,
but it nevertheless expressed views which implicitly or explicitly
criticised the ruling power. At its first session, in December 1885, P. M.
Mehta moved a resolution describing annexation as unwise, unjust and
immoral. His criticism was based on a fundamental opposition to
imperial conquest and on the likelihood that Indian tax-payers would
be asked to help pay the bill. Mr Mehta did not refer to China, though
the pressure of British business interests to open up the country through
the back door of Burma was no secret, least of all in India. But there
was a separate resolution deprecating the annexation of Upper Burma.
And when the National Congress met in 1891, Dinshaw Wacha accused
the Government of trying to expand beyond India's eastern frontiers
'in obedience to the call of pious Manchester for the sale of the products
of its spindles and looms'.[9]

This was abundantly true. The factor which was largely overlooked
at the time and underestimated by most historians was China's acquiescence in the annexation of Upper Burma. The Anglo-Chinese Treaty
of 1886 amounted to an understanding by which China agreed that 'in
all matters whatsoever appertaining to the authority and rule which
England is now exercising in Burma, England shall be free to do whatsoever she deems fit and proper'.[10] Britain, in return, countermanded
the Trade Mission then in Peking, which was trying to open up relations
with Tibet. China aimed at an outpost on the Irrawaddy. It was a major

objective of British policy to prevent Chinese expansion. An official
document expressed it: 'To permit the Chinese to cross the mountain
ranges which separate the river systems of the Irrawaddy and the Upper
Salween, and to occupy the higher basin of the former river, would be
inconvenient to the Government of India, and would complicate their
action in that part of the country.' [11] Britain, with the power of the
Indian Army behind her, was strong enough to hold her own in Upper
Burma, though China's challenge remained the major factor in her
Burmese policy. Throughout this period British imperialism was a
subject for continuous criticism by the Indian National Congress; many
resolutions referred to British policy on China's eastern seaboard. That
China too had an expansionist policy in Tibet and in Burma was
scarcely taken into consideration.

British policy on the North-West Frontier was attacked as 'unwise
and aggressive', and as aiming at the extension of frontiers under the
pretext of defending the Empire. In 1895 and 1897, after the occupation
of Chitral, Congress urged the British Government to stop this aggressive policy, and added that if these expeditions were found necessary,
then they should be charged to the British Exchequer. Banerjee told the
11th Congress in 1895 that where domestic reforms were involved India
was found to be poor, but if a subsidy to some frontier expedition was
involved, or entertainment for the Princely families on the frontier, then
the Government was 'as rich as the richest Government in the world'.[12]

Although the Indian National Congress seemed to overlook Chinese
expansion, it was extremely outspoken against Curzon's policy. Sir
Henry Cotton, the President of the 19th meeting in 1903, described it as
'a monstrous thing, an outrage and a blunder through and through'.[13]
At the next meeting H. A. Waidya condemned it in equally strong
terms. He maintained that there was no evidence of any fresh provoca-
tion by Russia in Tibet or in Central Asia, and that even if there were
this was not India's concern.

The First World War and the Russian Revolution had far-reaching
results in the policy of Congress. Politically conscious Indians now had
no doubts that India would win freedom from British rule. The July
1921 meeting of the All India Congress Committee passed a resolution
that neighbouring and other non-Indian states should be informed:

(i) that the present Government of India in no way
represents Indian opinion and that their policy has been

traditionally guided by considerations more of holding India in subjection than of protecting her borders;

(ii) that India as a self-governing country can have nothing to fear from the neighbouring states or any state as her people have no designs upon any of them, and hence no intention of establishing any trade relations hostile to or not desired by the people of such states;

(iii) that the people of India regard most treaties entered into with the Imperial Government by neighbouring states as mainly designed by the latter to perpetuate the exploitation of India by the Imperial power, and would therefore urge the states having no ill-will against the people of India, and having no desire to injure her interests, to refrain from entering into any treaty with the Imperial power. The Committee wishes also to assure the foreign states that when India has attained self-government, her foreign policy will naturally be always guided so as to respect their religious obligations'.[14]

Three years later when Indian troops were used in China to put down the national movement, the A.I.C.C. openly condemned British policy and conveyed their sympathy to the Chinese people. The idea of an Asian federation now featured in the writings of Gandhi and in resolutions passed by the 37th, 38th and 41st meetings of the A.I.C.C.

Rabindranath Tagore's visit to China in 1924 produced many expressions of friendship in both countries, as well as in Rangoon, Penang, Kuala Lumpur, Singapore and Hongkong, where the Chinese communities welcomed him as he and his party passed through. Dr Sun Yat Sen sent friends to invite him to visit Canton, but Sun's sudden death prevented a meeting.

'No event in recent years has aroused so much interest in Chinese intellectual circles as the visit of Rabindranath Tagore' the *North China Standard* wrote. 'What is the explanation? It is because Dr Tagore belongs to the East and in honouring him the Chinese intellectuals are honouring the civilisation of the East.' The European attitude was expressed in the *Far Eastern Times*: 'He (Tagore) sees in the mechanics of the West and its destructive influence on the East, the real enemy. Against this enemy he bids Asia and Africa – Africa as well as Asia, for he thinks of the Dark Continent very frequently – gird up their loins,

not in a spirit of hate but in a spirit of race-consciousness of Freedom.'
Tagore was demonstrably pleased by the reception he received almost
everywhere in China. He was already known as a critic of the opium
policy of certain European powers and for a most perceptive appreciation of Chinese life and ideals in his review of Lowes Dickinson's
Letters to John Chinaman. His *Gitanjali* had been translated into Chinese.

Leonard K. Elmhirst, who acted as Secretary to the Indian delegation
in 1924, added an interesting point to the story of the tour. 'Tagore
used to say before we left India that it was vitally necessary for Indians
to try and discover the aspirations of modern China. He refused to
visit ancient buildings not because he was not interested in them, but
because time was short and he had brought a team of Indian specialists
with him, an artist, a Sanskrit scholar and a historian to study every
aspect of China's past. Meanwhile he determined to devote all his
energy to trying to meet and fathom the mind and aspirations of
modern China, of her students, her professors, her writers, her living
painters, singers and musicians.' [15]

One result of Tagore's visit was the establishment of a Chinese Hall
and Library in Santineketan some years later. The moving spirit was
Professor Tan Yun-shan, who met Tagore in Singapore and was so
much impressed by him that he raised most of the funds himself in
China.

Nehru shared Tagore's interest in China. He was struck by the
quality of the Chinese delegation to the League against Imperialism
Conference in Belgium in 1927 and wrote in his report to the A.I.C.C.:
'I suppose the Chinese representatives were the natural products of a
revolution and I was led regretfully to wish that we in India might
also develop some of this energy and driving force, at the expense, if
need be, of some of our intellectuality.' He described them as 'very
young and full of energy and enthusiasm . . . with a great deal of driving
force' and quite unlike the 'traditional notion of the placid and tranquil
Chinese'.[16] The Chinese and Indian delegations made a joint declaration
which today sounds unhappily ironical:

> For more than three thousand years the people of India and
> China were united by the most intimate cultural ties. From the
> days of Buddha to the end of the Mughal period and the
> beginning of British domination in India this friendly inter-
> course continued uninterrupted.

After the East India Company had, by intrigue and force, secured its firm hold on the greater part of India, the English began looking for new sources of revenue and new markets. They not only introduced poppy cultivation into areas where food had previously been grown, but also thrust Indian opium on the unwilling Chinese people by force of arms. Since that infamous Opium War of 1840–1844 Indian mercenary troops have been sent again and again to China in support of British capitalist brigandage in that country. For 87 years Indian troops have been permanently stationed as policemen in Hongkong, Shanghai, etc. Time and again they have been used to shoot down Chinese workers and have thus created ill will in China against the people of India. Even as we make this declaration Indian troops are again on their way to China in an attempt to crush the Chinese revolution.

With the strengthening of British imperialism, India was cut off more and more from intercourse with China, and in their cultural and intellectual isolation, the Indian people have now become completely ignorant of the condition of China.

It is this extreme ignorance that makes it difficult today to organise effective means of preventing India's money and manpower being used for the enslavement of the Chinese people. We think it urgent and essential that active propaganda should be carried on in India to educate the people regarding China and to arouse them to the necessity of immediate action.

We must now resume the ancient personal, cultural and political relations between the two peoples. British imperialism which in the past has kept us apart and done us so much injury, is now the very force that is uniting us in a common endeavour to overthrow it.

We trust that the leaders of the Indian movement will do all in their power to co-ordinate their struggle with that of the Chinese people so that by simultaneously engaging British imperialism on two of its most vital fronts, China may receive active support in her present struggle and the final victory of both peoples may be secured.[17]

Chinese affairs dominated Nehru's own report. He quoted in full the declaration of the British, Indian and Chinese delegates. It had been drafted by the British delegation – George Lansbury, Fenner Brockway, S. O. Davies, John Becket, Ellen Wilkinson, Harry Pollitt, Reginald Bridgeman, Arthur McManus, Helen Crawford, William Rust and J. Stokes.

Nehru and the Chinese signatory, H. Liau, both felt that as Britain 'was the chief sinner in regard to India and China it would be desirable if they prepared a statement as to what they proposed doing'. Their programme of action was a demand for the immediate withdrawal of all armed forces from Chinese territory and waters; strikes and embargoes to prevent the movement of munitions and troops either to India or China and from India to China; an agreement to vote against war estimates and to recognise the National Government; a demand for the abolition of all unequal treaties and extra-territorial rights. Edo Fimmen, who presided over the Congress, cabled it to the I.N.C. and the National Government of China.

Nehru emphasised the need for closer relations between the Chinese and the I.N.C. 'Nothing would please them more than to have a visit from representatives of the A.I.C.C. to study the Chinese situation on the spot. For students they are prepared to afford every facility, and even now, as is well-known, many of the records of ancient Indian culture can only be found in China.' [18] News of China was derived almost exclusively through English official sources. He felt that it was tainted, and he wanted first-hand information.

Nehru, as President of Congress in 1936, warned his audience: 'In the Far East also war hovers on the horizon and we see an eastern imperialism advancing methodically and pitilessly over ancient China and dreaming of world empire. Imperialism shows its claws wherever it may be, in the West or in the East.' [19]

He described 'Japanese imperialism continuing its aggression in North China and Mongolia; British Imperialism piously objecting to other countries misbehaving, yet carrying on in much the same way in India and the Frontier; and behind it all a decaying economic order which intensifies these conflicts'.[20]

Early in the same year Nehru spoke in London under the auspices of the Indian Conciliation Group. He was asked about Japan's potential threat to India, once China was defeated. He answered: 'One cannot go easily over the Himalayan mountains and the various deserts and other tracts of China. Therefore you must realise that India is not very easily accessible to Japan if Japan goes through China, so Japan has to come by a fairly intricate route through the Singapore Straits, and any hostile fleet could make it difficult for the Japanese to approach India.' He believed that even if China were conquered it would still be a problem 'and something which will really absorb the energies of Japan, and probably bring about its downfall'. He considered China weak 'because some of her rulers were weak, Chiang Kai-shek and others. . . . In any event, Japan would have a hostile China to deal with whether it was subjugated or not'.[21]

When the Chinese Hall was inaugurated in Sankineketan in 1937, Nehru, who was prevented by illness from being present, sent this message:

> What a long past that has been of friendly contacts and mutual influences, untroubled by political conflict and aggression. We have traded in ideas, in art, in culture, and grown richer in our own inheritance by the other's offering. Political subjection came to both of us in varying forms and stagnation and decay, and at the same time new forces and ideas from the West to wake us out of our torpor. . . . China and India, sister nations from the dawn of history, with their long tradition of culture and peaceful development of ideas, have to play a leading part in this world drama, in which they themselves are so deeply involved.[22]

The same theme was touched on by Professor Tan Yun-shan, the moving spirit of the Sino-Indian Cultural Society: 'India and China are naturally a pair of sister countries. Their similarities and their associations are great, numerous and intimate. Looking over the geography and history of all the nations of the world, we find there are not any other two nations that can be compared to our two countries. . . . The powers of Europe and America have come to the end of their wits in the labyrinth; it is then urgently necessary for the Easterner, especially Indians and Chinese, to shoulder this duty of human salvation,' threatened as it was, he claimed, by the 'misuse of science and materialism'.[23]

Japan's attack on China that same year moved Tagore to write to the Japanese poet Noguchi, deploring their militarism and extolling China's resistance. 'Faced by the borrowed science of Japanese militarism which is crudely western in character, China's stand reveals an inherently superior moral stature.'[24]

The second stage of Japan's war had already begun when Congress met for the 51st session in 1938. After expressing its 'deepest sympathy' with the Chinese people 'in their great ordeal' and its 'admiration for the heroic struggle they are conducting to maintain their freedom and integrity',[25] Congress assured China 'of the solidarity of the Indian people and as a mark of India's sympathy called upon the people of India to refrain from purchasing Japanese goods'. Other practical demonstrations of Congress support were made at meetings; Congress and Chinese flags were unfurled together; Dr M. Atal took out an ambulance unit to China.

THE BONDS GROW STRONGER

When Nehru visited China in 1939 he again showed his deep affection for the people and his faith in Indo-Chinese friendship. 'I chose to go,' he wrote, 'because while I hesitated, loving and comradely hands beckoned to me from China and distant memories of ages past urged me to go. The long perspective of history rose up before me, the agonies and triumphs of India and China, and the troubles of today "folded their tents like the Arabs and as silently stole away". The present will pass and merge into the future, and India will remain and China will remain, and the two will work together for their own good and the good of the world.' [26]

Mao Tse-tung and Chu Teh seemed no less emotional in their response. They praised Dr Atal's work with the Eighth Route Army. 'The great Indian people and the Chinese have a common destiny,' they declared, 'We, the Indian people and the Chinese combined, compose almost half of mankind. We are the two peoples who have been suffering longest imperial oppression and slavery, and we both have the glorious tradition of fighting for liberty and freedom. Our emancipation, the emancipation of the Indian people and the Chinese, will be the signal of the emancipation of all the down-trodden and oppressed.' [27]

When Generalissimo and Madame Chiang Kai-shek visited India in 1942, they were given a truly warm welcome, and won a good deal of praise in some circles for their appeal to the British Government to give real political power to the Indian people, and to the people of

India to join with the Big Four (China, Great Britain, the U.S.A. and the U.S.S.R.) in defending the free world. Characteristically, Nehru wrote: 'The bonds that tied Indian and China grew stronger and so did the desire to line up with China and other nations against the common adversary.' [28] The Chiang Kai-sheks made generous donations to the Midnapore Relief Fund and to the Santiniketan venture.

Six months later Singapore had fallen and China's position was alarming. Ties between Indian and China were so strong that the 'Quit India' resolution specifically expressed its desire 'not to embarrass in any way the defence of China or Russia, whose freedom is precious and must be preserved, or to jeopardise the defensive capacity of the United Nations'. Gandhi wrote personally to Chiang Kai-shek: 'I look forward to the day when a free India and a free China will co-operate together in friendship and brotherhood for their own good and for the good of Asia and the world.' [29] Nehru sent a personal message to the Chinese assuring them that India would keep faith with China. 'Whatever we do now, constrained by circumstances, is aimed at the achievement of India's independence so that we may fight with all our strength and will against the aggressor in India and China.' [30] Each country closely observed the vicissitudes of the other. The Chinese Consul-General in Calcutta, Dr J. C. Pao, passed over a handsome contribution for famine relief in Bengal in 1943, and, later, China Aid Committees in various parts of India donated gifts for Madame Chiang Kai-shek's relief fund.

When Dr S. Radhakrishnan visited China in 1944, giving philosophical rather than political lectures, he often referred to Gandhi's assertion that any recommendation he might make would 'be governed by the consideration that it should not injure China or encourage Japanese aggression against India or China'. His visit coincided with fratricidal struggles between Communists and Kuomintang, which he described as 'impeding the force of Chinese resistance'. One observation he made illustrates his a-political shrewdness: 'The Chinese Communists are not strict followers of the Russian creed. Their fatherland is China and not the Soviet Union. They are nationalists first and foremost and are fighting the battles of China against Japan, and not those of the Comintern.' [31]

Although China was at war, Radhakrishnan was greeted with banquets and orations. The Abbot Tai Hsu recalled: 'For centuries Buddhism permeated China. Today Confucian and Hindu thought interflow.' The Minister of Education, Chen Li-Fu, composed a poem 'to wish the interflow of the cultures of India and China, as long and perpetual as the Ganges and the Yangtse. . . . We have had intercourse for two thousand years, our hearts are one'.[32]

The Second World War nominally ended within a few months of Radhakrishnan's visit. The last and most violent stage of civil war began in China. In September 1946, Nehru, then Vice-President of the Interim National Government of India, broadcast: 'China, that mighty country with a mighty past, our neighbour, has been our friend through the ages and that friendship will endure and grow. We earnestly hope that her present troubles will end soon and a united and democratic China will emerge, playing a great part in the furtherance of world peace and progress.' [33] Nehru's most cherished vision of Sino-Indian partnership in an Asia freed from colonialism was not materially affected by the victory of Chinese communism.

The Frontier that was Assumed

INDIA'S FRONTIER WITH TIBET: LADAKH;
THE EXPLOITS OF WILLIAM MOORCROFT;
THE ROAD TO THE SHIPKI PASS; GULAB
SINGH AND THE SIKH EXPANSION; THE
1847 BOUNDARY COMMISSION

INDIA'S FRONTIER WITH TIBET: LADAKH

On the basis of good will between India and China there was no problem of frontiers between them which could not be a matter of adjustment. There was no cause in 1947 for the paraphernalia of boundary commissions along virtually inaccessible mountains and bleak plateaux. Elsewhere, along tracks dictated by geographical features, a traditional line existed and was accepted. And, most important, Imperialist Britain's policy of regarding Tibet as a legitimate sphere of political interest was not one which Nehru was prepared to assume for an independent India.

The case of Ladakh, at the present time the most sensitive area in the Sino-Indian dispute, is a perfect illustration of the role geography plays in international relations. At the beginning of the 19th Century it was important for two reasons. First, tracks along its river valleys, across its salt plains and through high Himalayan passes led to the back door of China, then regarded by the East India Company as a kind of Eldorado. Second, a Russian invasion of India, then believed inevitable, would have required to traverse Ladakh before it reached the plains of the Punjab. In the terms of Britain's Central Asian policy Ladakh acquired temporarily a significance which was matched only when Communist China challenged what India had regarded as her traditional and customary boundaries, and claimed 14,000 square miles of its territory.

The early history of the country is told in the Ladakhi chronicles (translated by such famous authorities as A. H. Francke, Z. Ahmad and Luciano Petech). Chinese and Indian officials each quoted them in such lights as served their separate ends. Indian experts quoting Italian and German scholars drew a very clear outline of the role Ladakh had played in the course of Chinese imperialism in the T'ang dynasty (A.D. 618–907). For nearly three centuries, China's efforts to control Turkestan involved the countries round its periphery; Kashmir, Baltistan, Ladakh and West Tibet. The struggle was between China and Tibet, with buffer countries such as Baltistan being subject to one or to the other according to the fortunes of war. Chinese armies, then assisting Baltistan chieftains against the Tibetans, reached Gilgit in 747. When they in turn were defeated by invading Arabs, they were forced to withdraw and once again Tibetans were in control of Baltistan. Tibetan rule, resting mainly on religious sanction, came to an end at the death of Kyi-de-ma-gon in 930. His territories were divided among his three sons. The boundaries of those given to his eldest son were defined. Ladakh became an independent state, though religious ties remained strong between Lhasa and Leh.

There is general agreement among experts as to the boundary of Ladakh, which the eldest son inherited. Chinese officials, during their talks with Indians in 1960, described the allocation of territory as that of 'feudal estates under the unified rule' of Kyi-de Nyi-ma-gon ('a local prince of China's Tibet'), though as Fisher, Rose and Huttenback, authors of *Himalayan Battleground*, point out, 'even the most exuberant Chinese historians have never claimed that Tibet was part of China in the 10th Century'.[1]

A new pattern of relationships between Himalayan states emerged during the period of Muslim invasions. With the establishment of an Islamic dynasty in Kashmir in 1339, Timur's invading armies through Afghanistan at the end of the 14th Century, and the sacking of Jammu and Kangra, the situation in Ladakh was uncertain, unstable and violent. Its imperial ambitions were threatened by the Moghuls who recognised then, as Indians do today, the strategic position of Ladakh in relation to Kashmir. When Aurungzeb visited Kashmir in 1663, the King of Leh saw the implied threat to his own kingdom of Ladakh. He had good reason, for in the following year Aurungzeb sent an emissary to Leh to enforce two agreements made with him. The King of Ladakh was obliged to embrace Islam and to build a mosque in his capital. Meanwhile hostilities continued between Ladakh and Tibet, based primarily on rivalry between the Red Sect and Yellow Sect of Lamas. Between 1639 and 1684 Tibetan forces captured Leh and Basgo twenty miles north-west. The King of Ladakh then turned to the Moghuls for help. The Tibetans were defeated and forced to withdraw to Tashigong, the accepted frontier point. After a period of stalemate, the Tibetans and Ladakhis signed the Treaty of Tingmosgang in 1684, which fixed the border at the Lha-ri stream, flowing into the Indus five miles south-west of Demchok. The Ladakhis obtained trading monopoly of the export of shawl wool from West Tibet, while the Dalai Lama received a monopoly of the brick tea trade with Ladakh. In the present Sino-Indian dispute the Chinese question the validity of this Treaty, though it has been accepted by historians of international repute for nearly three hundred years.

China now entered the arena. In 1720 her armies helped the Tibetans to drive out Dsungar Mongol invaders. The price of Chinese support was soon revealed. Peking benefited to the extent of appointing two Ambans or representatives in Lhasa who in due course achieved paramount influence in Tibet. In 1724 a Ladakhi Mission was in Peking. Discussions were held based on a common aim of holding the Mongols in check; Ladakh was a potential base of operations against Tibet and controlled the main passes between Tibet and Turkestan. Ladakh held on to her *de facto* independence, while exploiting Chinese goodwill to protect her own interests against both Mongols and Kashmiri. She observed a nominal political allegiance to Kashmir and she continued to enjoy steady commercial relations with Tibet.

The Western World had not yet impinged on the Himalayan states. The first contacts were through the Catholic missionaries who from the 16th Century onwards wrote extensively about the countries whose 'heathen' peoples they believed they could convert to their own faith. The most interesting of them was Ippolito Desideri of Pistoia who, at the beginning of the 18th Century, walked from his mission in Agra to Ladakh across snow and ice. He and his companions had to travel single file 'up the sides of very high and terrible mountains' where 'the guide would go in front and cut a step the size of a man's foot with his axe, and giving me his left hand help me to put my foot into the step while he excavated another until we again struck the narrow path'. The King of Leh received them and, when he was convinced they were only interested in missionary work, gave them every assistance in buying horses, giving them passports to the Governors under him, and special letters of introduction to the Lama, the Governor and the Castellan of a town called Trescij-Khang (Tashigong).

Tashigong is today claimed by both China and India. But in August 1715 Desideri had no doubts and wrote in his diary: 'On the seventh of September we arrived at Trescij-Khang, or "Abode of Mirth", a town on the frontier between Second and Third Tibet, defended by strong walls and a deep ditch with drawbridges. The Castellan and the Governor live in the fortress with a strong garrison, it being the frontier; but especially to guard against the Giongara (Dzungarians), Tartars of Independent High Tartary, ambitious, untrustworthy and treacherous men. Thanks to our letters from the King of Second Tibet we were most honourably received by the Lama, Governor and Castellan of Trescij-Khang.' [2]

An important development occurred in 1792 when Chinese troops helped Lhasa to defeat the Gurkhas and the opportunity was taken to impose Chinese rule on Tibet. The Company believed that Britain too might benefit by playing off Gurkhas against Tibetans and Chinese, since Gurkhas had asked for assistance, and Tibetans and Chinese had asked for neutrality. They therefore offered mediation to both sides, while secretly hinting to the Gurkhas that armed assistance would be forthcoming in return for a commercial treaty opening up Nepal to British trade. This policy served only to alienate both sides.

A Chinese historian, Tieh Tseng-li, describes it thus: 'The Emperor of China found the time was ripe to reform the whole administration of Tibet and to take effective control of the reins of government in order to preclude the need of further repetition of expensive expeditions.' Residents, who were appointed and given the same ranks as the Dalai Lama and the Panchen Lama, 'were made responsible also for frontier defences and the efficiency of native levies . . . Besides 1,000 Mongolian and 1,000 Chinese troops were stationed in Tibet'.[3] In the view of Sir John Davis, the first British Minister to China, the Manchu Minister Resident at Lhasa from now onwards 'in fact ruled Tibet on the part of the Chinese Emperor'.[4] British and Chinese policy now became more opportunist, equivocal, and invariably aimed at avoiding trouble while each took advantage of the other's misfortunes or ambitions.

B

THE EXPLOITS OF WILLIAM MOORCROFT

A century after Desideri's extraordinary journey little had changed along the tracks he covered. William Moorcroft said that 'Europeans in general have had no other knowledge of the nature of the road between Kashmir and Leh than derived from the relation of P. Desideri' and that it was in the same state when he himself saw it in 1822.[5]

Moorcroft remains a legendary, if not widely known, character.* He was the first European to cross the Himalayas, when in 1811 he walked over the Niti Pass. He described his life in Leh from 1820 to 1822 in long discursive letters, mainly to the East India Company. He frequently referred to traditional boundaries and the balance of power between Britain, China and Russia in Central Asia. Sir Alexander Cunningham, who, twenty years later, wrote the definitive history of Ladakh, described Moorcroft's accounts as 'marked by great shrewdness of observation, and by the most scrupulous accuracy'.

* William Moorcroft was studying medicine in Liverpool at the end of the 18th Century when an outbreak of cattle-plague in Derbyshire stimulated his interest in veterinary work. There was no veterinary college in England at the time and he continued his studies in Paris. When he returned to London he established a successful practice as a veterinary surgeon in Oxford Street. He later lost the bulk of his relatively large earnings in a venture designed to obtain patents for machine-made horseshoes. At that moment the East India Company offered him a job as veterinary surgeon to the Bengal Army and supervisor of their stud near Cawnpore. He left England in May 1806.

Travels in the Himalayan Provinces of Hindustan and the Punjab, published in two volumes in 1841, is a heavily edited selection of the hundreds of letters written by Moorcroft, the originals of which are in the India Office Library in London. H. H. Wilson, the official colonial historian, was as cautious in his choice as he was puritanical. Most of the letters treating of strategic problems are omitted and nothing remains to indicate the tempestuous nature of Moorcroft's personal life, or to illustrate his romantic adventures or to record his lively if untrained appreciation of the paintings and sculptures he came across on his journeys.

To evaluate his wanderings, directed by political as well as commercial considerations, his letters must be studied in the original. They are sometimes shrewd, often artless, invariably compiled in meticulous detail though they were frequently scrawled on odd pieces of paper, stained with tea or tougher beverages, scribbled over and occasionally fading to a close as he fell asleep in his tent in the Karakorum. The cause of his death in Northern Afghanistan in 1825 is still a mystery.

The illustration on the opposite page indicates how carefully he set out the routes which no European had previously visited.

FACSIMILE FROM MOORCROFT'S DIARIES

Thogjeechenmo to Chukkshung the Burjick
to Burkshu —
to Latch before mentioned —
to the place of Chukkshung — 7 Kos So 20 Eastly —
the pass of Pilloo Gongka is ascended but instead of
going towards Pookka the road turns to the right
keeping in the hills to a distance of 1½ Kos from
its crest —

thence the Village of Koomchog on the head of the Lake 4 Kos the bearing
more to the South — this merely consists of a Lummai & two or three
other small houses — a little Shirokh is grown there — Toomorearee
is about a Kos broad — its water is sweet & the washing shore of
it is 10 Kos from Chukkshung —

From Mooth to Choomuk Goorgoor —

To the Surai of Tegazoong 11 Kos S 15 W up the left bank of
a small rivulet the bed of which is dry before it joins the
Gongka Lake but it rises close to a fold & some land formerly
cultivated to the left of the road & not far from the end of the
march — the place is called Choomuk Gooloa or 108 springs
to the opposite Surai or across two passes between which
a valley intervenes — Tegazoong (Tega pass — joong a place between)
signifies a pass containing a narrow place — dist.
8 Kos
To Choomuk Goorgoor 5 Kos South 15 West — no wood grows here —
Kyangs are frequently at pasture on the plain in large numbers
— the road in the first & last marches is thanks good but in
the second is uneven — in some places & crooked

From Hanley to Choomuk Goorgoor

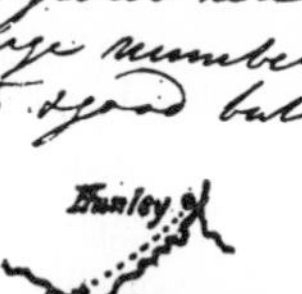

To the Surai at the foot of the Lanak pass 8 Kos the
road straight & good following the whole way the left bank
of a rivulet which close to the eastward of Hanley joins
another from the Choomoortee road — it rises close to
Tegazoong which in summer may be ascended by
traversing its course —
To the other side the Lanak pass the summit of
which is but a Kos distant from the morning's Camp & bearing
as before So 30 W — thence the road turns to So 25 E keeping that
in that direction as far as Choomuk Goorgoor — the march 6 Kos —
Choomuk Goorgoor 6 Kos
Note — either the last bearing of this route or the one preceding
it is incorrect — but this is perhaps most so — I make no alteration —

Moorcroft's letters reveal a wide range of interests. He was veterinary surgeon, botanist, wool merchant, linguist, historian, and, in his own way, politician and empire builder. He was tough, adventurous and ambitious. He feared neither bad climate nor robbers. He had an imaginative, if not always astute, head for business. He went to Ladakh because it was on the route to Yarkand, where he intended purchasing Turkman stallions to improve the cavalry horse of India. But he realised that here was a centre from which he might establish commercial contacts between the East India Company and trans-Himalayan traders. He reflected the dual policy of the Company by assuming that trade and the struggle for power between Russia, China and Britain in Central Asia were closely interwoven, that the best guarantee for British interests was gained by playing off Russia and China against each other. Ladakh was the springboard, strategically and commercially. He therefore suggested to Swinton, Secretary of the Political Department, that Britain might strike a useful bargain with Ladakh. 'Such an ascendancy,' he said, 'cannot fail to result from accepting the allegiance of Ladakh not only as the key to the western provinces of China but even to the capital itself, and in relation to the possession of the British Indian Empire, as now existing, commanding a commercial route by land both to the Southern and to the Northern frontier of the Chinese dominions.' 6

From Ladakh's point of view such a treaty of allegiance would assure her an increase of revenue which she was unlikely to obtain through her own efforts. If, as Moorcroft hoped, the Chinese would allow British merchandise and merchants 'under certain restrictions' to follow the old line of trade from Hindoostan through Khotan to Yarkand through Lhasa to Siling, then Ladakh would certainly reap the benefits.7 Moorcroft never questioned the right of Ladakh to make a treaty with the East India Company. 'It is a curious, if not an interesting fact,' he wrote, 'that the County of Ladakh, a territory larger, it would seem, than the whole of England, proves to be a Fief of Delhi.' 8 'China', he wrote to the Political Secretary, 'has shown herself somewhat desirous to protect but has assumed no power or claim of rights and with Yarkand, Ladakh has commercial rights only. Thus Ladakh continues to maintain her independence.'

Moorcroft was so convinced by his own arguments and so impressed by the willingness of Ladakh rulers to sign a treaty of allegiance that he acted on his own initiative, as if he were the political representative of the East India Company instead of the chief of its Indian Stud. [Text of his Engagement in Appendix 1]. He explained to the Political Department that 'first, such an agreement did not deal with a country which passed the natural boundary; second it did not involve the Company in the risk of war; third, it did not disturb the existing commercial relations with China, since that country never had nor ever has made a claim of a political nature upon Ladakh'.[9] A few days earlier he had seen a letter from the Emperor of China to the Raja of Ladakh, sealed with the Imperial signet, requesting that if the Raja should hear any news of the military movements of the Khaja of Kashgar he would be pleased to forward details of it to Lhasa. Accompanying presents of silk, lapis lazuli and jasper proved to Moorcroft 'the esteem and importance in which Ladakh was held by the proudest of all Governments'.[10]

The Company rejected Moorcroft's proposed agreement; they were not yet alive to the potentialities of trade with the Himalayan countries. They were not as convinced as he was that Russian activities, whether political or commercial, were a threat to India, and they were not prepared to risk involvement with China which might complicate their trade, or their plans for trade with the coastal towns of China. The Company's hesitations did not deter him. He was acting in a dual capacity. He was commissioned by the Company to purchase Turkman horses, and by the merchants of Calcutta to tap the trade in Kashmir shawl wool and also to explore the markets for British goods in Central Asia. The Company stood to gain in both cases. During the two-year stay in Ladakh he made many journeys from Leh, and, since he always hoped to get Chinese permission to travel to Yarkand, he was particularly careful to observe where their authority began and ended; he was, in short, constantly watching for signs of the frontier.

Moorcroft did not envisage serious rivalry with China; he believed that she would do nothing to risk difficulties in this remote part of her empire. He cited the interesting example of Changthang, which 'was traversed by the road on which commercial communication between Hindustan and Turkistan was conducted in the reign of Shah Jahan'. 'China,' he wrote, 'lost sight of her pretended aversion to innovation' [11] by shutting up the road to Hindustan and accepting Lhasa's usurption of Changthang, the valuable possession of the Raja of Ladakh. This was also some safeguard for her province of Khotan. But she did not go further and try to extend her influence by encouraging Lhasa to

occupy Ladakh and Balti. He believed that if the Ladakhi regained
Changthang the Honourable Company would benefit from access to
goldmines and to the source of a special kind of shawl wool.

Was Moorcroft only a trader-cum-veterinary surgeon? His letters
were always signed as Head of the Bengal Stud of the East India
Company. He told the Political Secretary: 'It appears that Russia is
very desirous to form a close connection with Ladakh and to obtain a
road across Kokohan or Ferghana as the Chinese Empire interposes
directly between Russia and Ladakh. Whether the motives of Russia
be political or commercial or both you will judge on seeing the document.' 12 The frequency of his correspondence with the Political Secretary suggests that the Company were prepared to make use of him when
it suited British purposes but were content to disown him if he created
embarrassment. Which is, after all, the character of political intelligence.

He saw Russia as a rival. 'If the unjust invasion of the political rights
of a nation should place Great Britain and Russia in relations of
hostility, certain schemes may be worked out by Emperor Paul's
successor.'13 His first concern, however, was trade with China.

> I must express a doubt as to the existence of the slightest
> degree of risk endangering our commerce by sea through
> accepting the allegiance of Ladakh or even by the more
> questionable measure of preferring claims on her behalf. This
> doubt is founded on a view of the following facts embracing
> some repetition. China has no claim nor shadow of claim upon
> the Government of Ladakh. She can show no plea to contro-
> vert the right of Ladakh to retain her independence or to
> commute it for protection with whatever power she may
> prefer. China has given no check to the trade of Kiakta in
> consequence of the late aggression and of the encroachment
> of the Russians as herein reported. *Formerly* China *stopped* the
> convenient communications between the two nations on the
> mere emigration of a horde of Tartars from her country to
> Russia; *now* she *utters* not a single complaint whilst Russia
> receives not the simple allegiance of such a horde but actually
> takes possession of the district they inhabit lying within the
> Empire of China. Nor does her own conduct under circum-
> stances of direct aggression formerly practised contrast
> strongly with that of the present day.14

Moorcroft travelled frequently and widely in Ladakh. Some of his journeys covered areas which are now disputed by China and India, notably the one to the Pangong Lake:

> Beginning at Leh I lately traced the route of the Kalmak Army, which invaded Ladakh, first up the right bank of the River Singh Kha but past the Town and Monastery of Chimres, the Fortress of Sukhtee ruined by the invaders, up the Valley of Tughus across the pass of Chung Lha and after a journey of nine rather short marches found myself at the head of the long but somewhat narrow lake of Pangkoong which divides the District of Rudokh in the country of Changthang from the Principality of Ladakh. Ruins of fortified towns, dry stone walls stretching across valleys and a fortified gorge designated the more early part of the route and thenceforward lateral outlet was tendered impracticable by unbroken lines of high mountains flanking a narrow valley along which the road continued until it reached the head of the Lake, where it divided into two branches leading in opposite directions.
>
> That going to the NE skirted the right bank of a River which rising in the Mountains some days journey distant from the town of Pangkoong runs close past it and flows into the head of the Lake. Of the other, it need here only be observed that trending to the SE it was followed by my party for two days along the right bank of the lake, in progress towards the valley of Phagjoung. The former was pointed out to me as that by which the Kalmaks came from Khotan. The tradition of a fact connected as this is with an event of such magnitude as the complete though temporary conquest of this country and occurring so lately as within the last two hundred years is in itself entitled to credit were it not supported by other circumstances of proof which communicate to it the features of certainty.
>
> Soon after the Kalmak invasion the road to Khotan was blocked by the order of the Government of Ladakh a little above the town of Pangkoong and has continued to be prohibited ever since. But accounts whispered by peasants of that neighbourhood who had pursued its probable direction in their search for strayed cattle describe the country as

comparatively open and level and presenting few obstacles to travellers. And some time ago persons entrusted with treasure intended to be remitted from Rudokh to Leh pursuing this deserted route fell in with the road to Yarkand and escaped with their booty to that city. In reference to this road in a military view, I must observe that the portion pursued by me was somewhat difficult in parts but if followed in a suitable season it offers no material difficulties, except in the transport of artillery which may be overcome by the aid of Pioneers and of the robust Porters of Kashmeer and of Balteem.[15]

Moorcroft had Russia in mind when he referred to the strategic value of this road. He also envisaged Russia invading Chinese territory, especially in view of the 'factious commotions, the ill-organised state of the military force at Yarkand indicative too probably of imperfect arrangements in the larger masses of soldiers with the disaffection of the Moosulman if not of the Kalmuk population of which latter the Chinese army is principally composed'. He had views too about the defence of Ladakh:

> No military science is required to defend defiles fortified by nature like those of Ladakh and no military genius however great originally however perfected by experience, aided by all the projectiles of ancient and of modern warfare and accompanied by the best appointed army of chosen veterans could force a passage through them in opposition to the efforts of a band of the hardy Natives of the Country under the orders of a few European individuals possessing courage and commonsense.

But Moorcroft did not consider British interests in Ladakh threatened by China.

> The policy of China in respect to the defence of the frontier adjoining this country, Tibet, seems influenced by severity and clemency, each available under different situations and circumstances. It would appear that Tibet forms a band that extends from Yarkand to Lhasa, at each of which cities, the extreme points of this long line, there is a considerable Chinese Military

force, – and from each a road runs to Peking viz. from Lhasa by Leling, from Yarkand by Turfan and Kumalee.

But there does not seem to be any Chinese force in this vast extent of Tibet, nor is it clear that there is any in that frontier of China which it joins, nor have political circumstances for a very long period rendered it necessary, and under the usual condition of the country, police severity has effectually supplied its place and saved the expense of its maintenance. Nor have I been able to ascertain that there exists any communication between Tibet and the frontier of China except by the road first mentioned.[16]

Moorcroft was able to establish a good deal about Changthang, the province which, he wrote, 'formerly belonged to Ladakh, now an appendage and extending almost the whole of the northern frontier of the recently acquired British possessions'.[17] He was primarily interested in its extensive flocks and described the goats and sheep of Rudokh as producing the finest wool in the whole of the province. Travellers often told him stories of Chinese monopoly and strictness. 'Death is the punishment, with which any inhabitant of Khotan or Tibet is threatened who shall dare to cross the range, forbidden to the footsteps of men and accorded only to the wild quadrupeds on each side, viz. horses, apes, camels, a great variety of goats and sheep and as it is probable also of Llamas. . . . Whether the excessive severity attending a breach of the prohibitions imply a desire to conceal a weakness of frontier, either natural or artificial through economy and a wish to confine a formidable military force to each extremity of the Tibetan frontier out of economy or aside from other motives, I cannot determine, but the separating chain of mountains is said to be low.' [18]

Moorcroft's description of the road from Leh to Rudokh is important to-day as it establishes the then accepted boundary:

The road is principally even and along plains save in the passage of jungle and a short way between Soongoongma and Chochool – from the southern side the jungle ghat or rivulet runs into the Indus and passes through Suktee and Chummree – the road over the mountain is closed in winter. Doorgookh stands on the left bank of a river which is drained from it and joins the Shayook on the Yarkand road but a short distance from this village – Meerut is on the same bank and rises at the small pass in the neighbourhood of Soongoongma and on the march to Choochool two or three streams from North and South contribute to it – from the opposite side, the Ghat, flows another rivulet which running through Choochool turns northwards and empties itself into the large lake of Pangkoon, the wider end of which is about 8 ks. north of the village – the boundary of Ladakh is a little west of Punjoor just within the Rudokh territory, and the road from thence to Sinzoong is either on the northern or southern bank of the Tsoorol Lake.[19]

The boundary he describes conforms to India's present alignment. Chusul is one of the military outposts India built in 1959. Indians and Chinese now regard each other as enemies along the banks of the Pangong Lake. When Moorcroft was there a century and a half ago he was thinking in terms of a Russian invasion of India. He invariably assumed the Chinese to be a potential ally against a common rival. Further, he was convinced that the Russians were making headway in trade with Tibet, where their merchants were already welcomed at the annual fair in Gartok. Should the people of Central Asia and Tibet, he asked, be clothed in Russian or English broadcloth? Should they cook in pewter, copper and iron pots from Birmingham or from St Petersburg? [20]

He was well ahead of his time in believing that the Company could expand their interests in the areas which linked them with Tibet and Central Asia. Years before his visit to Leh, he had travelled along tracks not hitherto known by the Company. He had reached Lake Manasarowar. Now, during his stay in Leh, his own pioneering journey was followed up by Major Lloyd and Captain Gerard.

THE ROAD TO THE SHIPKI PASS

Lloyd and Gerard kept detailed diaries of geographical and meteorological observations. Their chief purpose was to find a way to Gartok, the main centre of Western Tibet, thence to Lhasa. Although far away from the centre of power, British activities were carefully watched by Chinese officials who were not satisfied that sporting or scientific obsessions of British officers provided a complete explanation for their visits to the Sutlej valley or the mountain passes of Kumaon. They knew about Moor-croft, and the companion of his first journey in the Himalayas, one Hearsey. Their suspicions were such that shortly thereafter two pilgrims who piously walked round Lake Manasarowar were arrested at Shipki because they were suspected of being Europeans in disguise.

Like Moorcroft, Gerard and Lloyd were always on the look out for points where Chinese officials were posted. Take the case of the village of Bekhur, commanding the Langzing or Khampa valley to the Niti Pass in the south-east and to Gartok in the north-east. They imagined an easy journey down the valley, but their grape-vine soon told them that on hearing of their movements, 'the Chinese were instantly in agitation, and people from Chubrung and Thooling had assembled at Bekhur to stop us.' Gerard and Lloyd took the precaution of sending a letter to the Garpon of Gartok, one to the Zongpon of Chubrung and 'the third to the Chinese officer of Murmokh, the district containing Bekhur'. They were all suitably wrapped in silk scarves and 'some pyramids of sugar, a few almonds and dates in cloth bags sealed and directed, accompanied the letters, agreeably to the established custom'.[21]

Soon after crossing the Keobrung Pass, at the foot of which Bekhur stood, Gerard met three Koonawaree shepherds laden with salt and wool 'who said that the Chinese were quite close, and would not allow me to advance beyond their post'. Here, only two miles from Bekhur, Gerard arranged for the despatch of his letters, but as it was clear that no replies would be received quickly, and as he had supplies for only four days, he had no alternative but to return. He climbed pass after pass from Nisung, taking readings from barometer and thermometer, observing fauna and flora, or their absence, and marched to Shipki.

At the Peeming Pass, from which the road descended to Shipki, he observed: 'This is the line of separation between Busahir and Chinese Tartary, and there could scarcely be a better-defined natural bound-ary'.[22] The harvest festival was being celebrated at Shipki. At sunset, the chief person of the village told him 'that orders had been received from Lahassa, some months ago, to make no friends of Europeans, and to furnish them neither with food nor firewood'. Then a reply from the Garpon of Gartok arrived. It was most unhelpful. The Garpon said how alarmed the Lhasa Court had been by the earlier visit of Moor-croft, and how 'in consequence had directed him to give orders at all the frontier posts to prevent European gentlemen from passing the boundary, and if they entered the country unobserved, to stop them at the first village and afford no supplies'. He added that he was 'so completely under the authority of the Lama of Ouchang, that to hear was to obey, and in future he could neither receive nor answer letters from Europeans; and must return them unopened'.[23] Again and again as Captain Gerard proceeded, sextant, barometer and thermometer in hand, he came to a village or a bundle of stones where someone would inform him that beyond – three or four miles – the Chinese were waiting for him, to turn him back.

He was turned back from Bekhur, and took the road to Shipki, recording that 'the villages between Nisung and Shipki once belonged to the Chinese, but were given to Busahir many years ago, for the support of Tusheegung Thakoordwara, on the right bank of the Sutluj, opposite Numgea'.[24] They, together with Nungrung, were now included in Koonawur. Gerard was doubtful about being able to take the road to Leh via Dankur, because Spiti was 'tributary to the Chinese'. Later, the Commandant at Dankur told Gerard that his 'authority over Peeno was purely nominal, and he had no concern with the place beyond receiving the tribute for Ladakh'. In other words, the 'tributary' position implied the payment of a given sum to the Chinese authorities but not an acknowledgment of Chinese sovereignty. Later, Gerard describes Spiti as a 'Purgunna, containing about thirty villages, and lies between Busahir, Kooloo, Ludak and Chinese Tartary. It has occasionally been under the authority of each state; and about fifty-five years ago, Dankur Fort was in the possession of Busahir, for two years. These border districts have frequently been the scene of war; but their contests were neither bloody nor protracted, and resembled the frays amongst the Scottish clans of old time, confined to the seizure of cattle, and sometimes setting fire to a village. The revenue is now chiefly shared between Ludak and Chinese Tartary; but there is an annual present of thirty punkhees or blankets to Busahir, and as many to Kooloo'.[25]

The chief man of Peeno, in this controversial area which dominates the Spiti valley, told Gerard that his 'allegiance to Kooloo and Ludak was nominal and the annual tribute they required was a few blankets and some wool. He was entirely under the control of the Chinese at Tooling or Ling, a large town two koss south west of Chubrung, on the left bank of the Sutluj'. If Gerard tried to pass that way, then this chief 'would do his duty by detaching people to different points of the road who would repeat his orders'. Gerard also failed to persuade the Lafa (chief person) of Peeno to give him permission to pursue the route by the Taree Pass to Wangpo. But neither gifts in the form of dates, sugar and tobacco, nor silk scarves, could persuade him. He assured Gerard that 'his order against the intrusion of foreigners could not be infringed; and that no lucrative incitement, however great, would have any effect upon his resolution'.

On October 12, 1818, Gerard had already made this march along the nine miles from Numgeea to Shipki Pass. The last stream he crossed was the Oopsung, and from there 'the road was a tiresome and rocky ascent, to the pass which separates Koonawur from the Chinese dominions, 13,518 feet above the level of the sea'. He described the village of Shipki as 'large ... under the Governor of Chubrung a town, or rather collection of tents, on the left bank of the Sutluj, eight marches to the eastward ...'. More than eighty of the people of Shipki went out to meet Gerard and his companions, 'the first Europeans they had ever seen'.[26] Just how closely the Chinese watched every movement along the frontier is indicated by Gerard's story about his brother who 'took a walk of about a mile towards Keookh with the perambulator and pocket compass'. He had not gone very far before two horsemen followed him and insisted that he should go no further. Subsequently, the principal officer of Shipki showed him a long piece of parchment written in what he supposed were Chinese characters. This was presumed to be an 'express order from the Garpan of Garco, under whose authority the Debas are, prohibiting strangers from entering the country; he, at the same time, said we had so many people with us (having nearly 100) that he could not oppose our progress, but it would cost him his head if he gave us the means of going on, so he would not supply us with provisions, which was the most effectual mode he could have adopted to stop us.' The party therefore failed in going to Gartok, and continued the track to the north, crossing the Sutlej at Shealkur fort 'situated on the confines of Ludak and the Chinese dominions ... in a ruinous state, but the position is commanding; the village is a poor place'.[27] And here Gerard and his party decided to turn back to Rampoor. Leh, they calculated was sixteen days ahead, with a choice of two roads. There was also a road to Gartok from Shealkur, but they made no further efforts to travel along it.

Gerard's observation that the Shipki Pass was the traditional

boundary was confirmed by a distinguished traveller, Dr Gutzlaff, who
told the Royal Geographical Society in February 1849: 'Proceeding
about 20 geographical miles further (from Deba) to the N.W. we
arrive at Shipki, in Lat. 31°49, Long. 78°44 E on the banks of the
Satadra (Sutlej) and the first place after crossing Kanawar over high
passes exceeding 15,000 ft. on the frontier of Hindostan.' [28] To sum up:
In the early part of the 19th Century the traditional boundary line
between Tibet and India was known by custom. It was not
a defined line as we understand it today, but obvious geographical
features could and did provide the basis of a satisfactory working
arrangement.

GULAB SINGH AND THE SIKH EXPANSION

Gulab Singh now enters the picture. He was a dependant of the Sikh
kingdom of Lahore, and Lahore was an ally of Britain, He was an
ambitious man, and his general Zorawar Singh, an energetic strategist.
By 1841 he had occupied all the land up to Lakes Rakastal and Manasarowar, including the important trading towns Rudok and Gartok. The
Company was not indifferent to his military prowess. But it was very
important to evaluate Chinese intentions before actively encouraging him, and B. H. Hodgson, the then British Representative in
Kathmandu, proved an effective listening-post. He informed the
Political Agent:

> Over Ladakh the Chinese Viceroy at Lassa has himself just
> declared (what indeed was priorly known) that he neither
> claims nor desires any sort of authority. But over the districts
> immediately East and South of Ladakh, as Garoo for
> example – China it is understood has always asserted more or
> less of dominion and may hence be presumed to deem herself
> learned to protect them. How far China by reason of her rela-
> tions with that quarter seems called on de jure or is likely de
> facto, to exert herself for its protection whether against
> Sikhs or Goorkhas is what I desire to have the means of con-
> jecture anticipatively and therefore wish to hear more
> accurately the limits and the nature of Chinese authority in the
> Easternmost parts of Tibet.[29]

Hodgson believed that the Company's interests would be best served by preventing Gulab Singh from taking any further steps which would provoke China. He hoped that the Government might 'find it convenient to put a stop' to Gulab Singh's plans 'before the lazy and reluctant Chinese have been compelled by shame to repel it forcefully, for if the din of arms once resound on this frontier there is no saying where the plague may spread to'.[30]

Gulab Singh was determined to stretch his territories as far as possible without provoking either Chinese action or British restraint. His general, Zorawar Singh, like all generals, wanted a maximum military victory with minimum political consequences. But Chinese authorities in Tibet had reached the end of their 'wait and see' policy and Chinese and Tibetan troops cut off Zorawar Singh's army in December 1841. His defeat was so conclusive that 4000 out of his 5000 men were killed and he himself was wounded and died before Captain J. D. Cunningham could give him the benefit of the Company's advice to retreat while there was still time. Gulab Singh himself did not accept defeat, and in spite of a revolt by Ladakhis he raised another army.

Tibetan troops therefore marched on to Leh, whereupon Gulab Singh asked for British help. In this classic situation of checks and balances British neutrality was the only solution. Gulab Singh had not played the British game. The Company could not afford to challenge China on the frontiers of India when it was already fighting her on her eastern seaboard.

The complex Sino-Tibetan-Ladakhi triangle has recently been revealed in documents translated for the first time into any western language by Margaret Fisher, Leo Rose and Robert Huttenback.[31] They are the reports made by Meng Pao, Imperial Resident at Lhasa from 1839 to 1844, either written by himself or passed through his hands. Meng Pao sent 5000 Tibetan troops to help the Ladakhi, who were supposed to ask for them against the Dogra garrison at Leh. The garrison, reinforced by other Dogra forces outside Leh, drove them back along the Indus river towards the Pangong Lake area (the scene of fiercest fighting between India and China in 1962). The defeated Tibetans then signed an agreement with Gulab Singh on about September 15, 1842, in Leh. It took the form of an exchange of documents which were in Persian and Tibetan. The existing situation was recognised; the Dogras were accepted as the legitimate authority in Ladakh, while Gulab Singh surrendered all claims to West Tibet. The 'old established frontiers' were reaffirmed. The Ladakh King and his family were given the right to live in Ladakh as long as they refrained from intrigue against the Dogra rulers. The King could continue to send Lapchak (annual gifts) to the Dalai Lama without any political implications. Both signatories agreed 'to have nothing to do with the countries bordering on the frontier of Ladakh . . . to carry on the trade in Shawl, Pasham and Tea as before by way of Ladakh', and if anyone of the Shri Rajah's enemies attempted to win over either of the two signatories, neither of them would 'listen to him' nor 'allow him to remain in our country'. Almost immediately afterwards, according to Panikkar, since this treaty 'did not bind the suzerains of both', a supplementary treaty was signed, this time 'on behalf of the Government of Lahore and the Emperor of China' [Text in Appendix 2]. After pledging eternal friendship, without 'any deviation even by a hair's breadth' it stated:

> 'We shall remain in possession of the limits of the boundaries of Ladakh and the neighbourhood subordinate to it, in accordance with the old customs, and there shall be no transgression and no interference in the countries beyond the old-established frontiers.' [32]

Three years later, the pattern of relations between these Himalayan regions was again changed. A war between Britain and the Sikhs led, as such wars tended to do in India, to the extension of British influence. Gulab Singh, an astute politician, saw that neutrality would pay him high dividends. When the Sikh army was defeated at Sobraon, the British Government annexed all the Sikh hill possessions between the Sutlej and the Indus, including Jammu, Kashmir and Ladakh, legalising this occupation in the Treaty of Lahore of March 9, 1846. One clause said that 'in consideration of the services rendered by Raja Gulab Singh of Jammu', in facilitating the signing of the treaty, and of his 'good conduct', the British Government 'agrees to recognise his independence' in these territories 'and to admit him to the privilege of a separate Treaty'. Accordingly, a week later, Gulab Singh signed the Treaty of Amritsar [Text in Appendix 2a], by which the British Government made over to him and his family the territories of Jammu, Kashmir and Ladakh. Since this Treaty is highly relevant to the present Sino-Indian dispute, several of its articles are worth quoting in full.

Article 2 stated: 'The eastern boundary . . . shall be laid down by the Commissioners appointed by the British Government and Maharajah Gulab Singh respectively for that purpose and shall be defined in a separate engagement after survey.' Article 4 stated: 'The limits of the territories shall not be at any time changed without concurrence of the British Government.' By Article 6 Gulab Singh engaged 'for himself and his heirs to join, with the whole of his Military Forces, the British troops, when employed within the hills or in the territories adjoining his possessions', and by Article 7 he engaged 'never to take or retain in his service any British subject nor the subject of any European or American State without the consent of the British Government'. In Article 9 the British Government pledged itself 'to give its aid to Maharajah Gulab Singh in protecting his territories from external enemies'.[33]

THE 1847 BOUNDARY COMMISSION

Four months after the treaty was signed British authorities settled down to implement Article 2, which concerned the boundary with China. Experience had shown that an unsettled boundary was, as Cunningham described it, 'the most common of all disputes in the East'. It was possible, he pointed out, 'that out peaceful relations with the Chinese Emperor might be considerably embarrassed by His Celestial Majesty's ignorance of any distinction between the rulers of India and the rulers of Kashmir.' [34]

The result was that two officials, P. A. Vans Agnew and Captain Alexander Cunningham, were sent to the Tibetan frontier of Ladakh to ascertain the ancient boundaries and to lay down the boundary ceded by the Treaty of Lahore. This was the last occasion on which any boundary line was laid down. The instructions on the boundary and on trade relations with China issued by Sir Henry Lawrence in Lahore indicate the importance attached to the frontier mission.

> Keeping the above objects in view and avoiding as much as possible all cause of offence to Maharajah Golab Singh and his people or to the Chinese authorities, you will quietly and unostentatiously make enquiries as to the lines of trade between Central Asia and the Punjab, and you will explain to any Chinese or Tibet authorities that you may fall in with, as

also to any traders you may meet, that no duty will be levied
on shawl wool or other commodities that may be brought
by them into the British territory.[35]

Cunningham and Vans Agnew spent the summer of 1846 travelling
from Simla to the Bara Lacha Pass, just beyond the boundary stone
between Lahul and the Zanskar district of Ladakh. As a result of an
exchange of territory with Gulab Singh Spiti became part of the
British dominions. This meant that the trade route between Gartok
and Rampur was under British control. From the Zanskar district to
the Tshomoriri Lake Cunningham mapped in the British boundary.
Lord Hardinge, the Governor-General, paved the way for the territory
beyond by writing to the Vizier of Lhasa Gartok and the authorities
in Tibet.

> I have to express my hope that Your Excellency will see
> fitting to depute confidential agents to point out to my
> officers the exact limits of the Chinese Frontier in order that
> no interference may thro' ignorance be exercised with the
> territories of your high and esteemed Government. As by the
> Fourth Article of the Treaty with the Government of Lahore
> the entire rights and interests of the Durbar in the territory
> now ceded to Maharajah Goolab Singh were transferred to
> the British Government I have deemed it expedient that
> certain portions of the Treaty between the Chinese authorities
> and those of Lahore should be cancelled as these were in their
> nature highly injurious to the interests of the British Govern-
> ment and its Departments. I have accordingly determined
> that the Second Article of the Treaty aforesaid by which it
> was provided that the entire trade should pass through Ladakh
> should be cancelled and that the Third Article should be
> modified and run as follows: 'Such persons as may in future
> proceed from China to Ladakh or to the British territory or its
> dependencies to China are not to be obstructed on the road.' [36]

The year 1847 was decisive in the history of the frontier with China.
The boundaries of Lahul and Spiti had been settled by Cunningham
and Vans Agnew [text of Vans Agnew's summary in Appendix 3].
Would a combined approach to China via Lhasa or via Hong Kong

lead to a settlement with China? Lawrence believed that it might, and in 1847, when the snows had melted, he sent out a second Boundary Commission. It consisted of Alexander Cunningham in command, Lt Henry Strachey, whose earlier journey to Lake Manasarowar was one of the great explorations of that period, and Dr Thomas Thomson, Assistant-Surgeon on The Bengal Establishment and Commissioner of Tibet* [text of Lord Hardinge's letter to his Directors explaining in detail the background to the Boundary Commission in Appendix 4.] Sir Henry Lawrence told Cunningham:

> The boundary is the great object of your mission; and freedom to trade with security of person, and the abolishing of all imposts on importation which will of themselves 'place on a more satisfactory footing than at present the commercial relations between Tibet and the Provinces of British India'.
>
> I need hardly impress on the Commission, that the permanent and willing observations of the boundary they lay down will depend on the perfect impartiality and friendly spirit with which they consult and listen to the representations of the Chinese and Jummoo deputies. With regard to the Chinese and deputies in particular, it is essential that they should not misunderstand the objects of the mission. If they once imagine that it is intended to spy into China, your real and avowed purpose will be altogether defeated. Let me request you, therefore, and the two other gentlemen who are associated with you, not to let the curiosity and spirit of enquiry which is so laudable in travellers and men of science, carry you a mile further than is necessary to ascertain the boundary.[37]

* Aside from their work on the Boundary Commission of 1847, each of these three earned distinction as explorers. Cunningham was the first to observe the Zaskar Range's continuity and to distinguish it from the axis of the Great Himalayas. His book *Ladakh, Physical, Statistical and Historical* remains the definitive work on the area. It was published in 1854. Henry Strachey and his brother Richard (the grandfather of Lytton Strachey) described a variety of routes in the Karakorum. Richard explored the Kumaun Himalayas and first determined their height in 1848. Henry reached Lake Manasarowar and Rakas Tal in 1846, and after completing his work on the Boundary Commission explored the Changchenmo valley. Dr Thomson, who was a distinguished naturalist, later explored the road to Yarkand. Extracts from his record of one of the most valuable pioneering journeys of the period, undertaken in 1848, are quoted at the end of Chapter Two.

China was under no obligation to co-operate with this Boundary Commission, which had been set up by the Company 'for the purpose of laying down the boundary between the territories of Maharajah Goolab Singh and the Emperor of China'.[38] Her unwillingness to do so arose in part from recent happenings on her eastern seaboard.

In 1842, by the Treaty of Nanking which ended the first Opium War against China, Britain secured Hong Kong, an indemnity of 21 million dollars, the opening up of four ports to foreign trade, and the end of the Chinese monopoly. Thus, when in November 1846 Sir John F. Davis requested Peking's consent to discuss frontiers and trade, the Chinese High Commissioner in Hong Kong replied two months later that the Treaty of Nanking, 'sanctioned by the vermilion pencil of the Great Emperor' and 'ratified by the signature of the Sovereign of your Honourable Country', had limited trade to Canton, Foochow, Ningpo and Shanghai. He asserted:

> You now request to have commercial intercourse with Tibet which would be establishing a mart besides those five ports in opposition to the provisions of both treaties.
>
> Respecting the frontiers, I beg to remark, that the borders of those territories have been sufficiently and distinctly fixed, so that it will be best to adhere to this ancient arrangement, and it will prove far more convenient to abstain from any additional measures for fixing them.[39]

This was a subtle request to keep out of China's way in Central Asia. Davis at once pushed the matter a stage further:

> With regard to the frontiers it surely was not to affix any new boundaries, but merely to ascertain old ones that Commissioners were sent to Lhasa. The Governor-General expressly declares his wish that the 'exact limits of the Tibetan frontier may be pointed out with the view of preventing any encroachment'. The Viceroy of Lhasa will doubtless be more willing to make known these ancient limits than to incur the chances of future misunderstanding by leaving the point uncertain.
>
> If the British Government in India were not to be informed of the ancient boundaries would it be possible to prevent mistakes and encroachments? Your Excellency by supposing

that it was intended to fix new boundaries instead of ascertaining the ancient ones, has entirely misapprehended the object of His Excellency the Governor-General.[40]

Such a reply clearly indicated that there was a generally recognised boundary, and that the Company wanted to make a joint recognition by demarcating it with the Chinese. Davis tried to allay Chinese suspicions, not only about the frontier, but about trade. He pointed out that the Governor-General had already despatched Commissioners to Lhasa, and that, on such an important issue, Keying, the High Commissioner should take up the matter with the Emperor. The High Commissioner's answer was prompt, shrewd, diplomatic and evasive:

> In regard to your question, whether this matter has been reported to the Emperor, I beg to remark that you, the Hon. Envoy in your former correspondence, referred to the distinct settlement of the boundaries and the wish of the English merchants to trade with Tibet. Since, however, that territory has its ancient frontiers it was needless to establish any other. The trading with Tibet would not be in conformity with the Maritime Treaty, as it is not included in the five ports. I, the Great Minister, therefore wrote you in reply (to that effect) and would not venture hastily to submit the request to the throne.[41]

The Indian assumption today is that the Chinese answer did imply the existence of a frontier. Davis was not misled by this exchange of letters; he did not assume that either Peking or Lhasa would give any assistance to the Boundary Commission and he went ahead.

Intelligence reports soon reached him that Chinese chiefs expected to visit Gartok in the autumn of 1847. He instructed the Commission to meet them, but warned the Court of Directors that it was 'not improbable that these Chinese may have been sent as much for the purpose of preventing our Commission from crossing the boundary, as for defining it,' and added, 'I am not too sanguine respecting this information'. He took the precaution of equipping the Commission with surveying instruments and medicines which would enable them to go beyond the boundary. If possible they 'should winter beyond the Karakorum range. If they can obtain the permission of the Chinese

Commissioners to proceed to Yarkand, or even to Khoten, nothing could be more satisfactory. In the event of their not being able to pass the Karakorum to the North, Rohdokh on the borders of the great desert (where all is at present unknown) would be their best resting-place, and it is to be hoped that the Chinese Commissioners may not object to their going there'.[42]

British hopes about the Commission were not fulfilled. Gulab Singh was less than co-operative. There was no meeting with Chinese officials.

The frontier laid down by the Boundary Commission in 1847 was unilateral. Cunningham and Strachey defined it themselves, and it has existed until the present time. They did not simply imagine a line and transfer it to maps, as Chou En-lai suggested a century later. They found that a frontier was usually known by custom and tradition, as Mr. Nehru often pointed out, and they recognised existing frontier posts. Cunningham describes the Karakorum 'or Trans-Tibetan chain' as forming the natural boundary of Ladakh. He admitted that 'nothing whatever is known of this range to the eastward of the Upper Shayok river, and of the northern portion we know but little'. He wrote at great length about the relations between Ladakh and surrounding countries, and concluded that the difficulty of crossing the Karakorum mountains 'prevented the Chinese governors of Yarkand and Kotan from attempting [its conquest] . . . and the poverty of the country offered no temptation to the Mahomedan rulers of Kashmir. The Ladahki relations with these states were therefore friendly'. Ladakh's relations with surrounding states, he wrote, 'were few . . . simple and easy . . . and chiefly confined to political relations with Balti and Rudok; to commercial ties with Yarkand and Kashmir; and to the religious connection with Lhasa'.

> With Rudok on the east there has been a long peace. The boundary is well-defined by piles of stones, which were set up after the last expulsion of the Sokpo or Mongol hordes, in A.D. 1687, when the Ladakis received considerable assistance from Kashmir.[43]

Cunningham observes: 'A large stone was then set up as a permanent boundary between the two countries, the line of demarcation being drawn from the village of Dechhog to the hill of Karbonas.' Dechhog is now known as Demchok, and today it is claimed by both India and China. Another illustration Cunningham gives of the existence of a definite boundary refers to the incident in 1842, when the Tibetans, having been pushed back from Leh, settled down to winter in Rudok. The Lhasan commander was made a prisoner. Then, Cunningham writes: 'The strong position of the Tibetans was shortly afterwards turned; and the Lhasan Vazir was glad to be permitted to retire on the single condition that the old boundary between Ladakh and China should be re-established.' [44]

Dr Thomas Thomson made a pioneering journey to the Karakorum Pass in 1848 with the expressed intention 'to visit the highest part of the mountain range lying between Ladakh and Yarkand'. He chose the road which was 'followed by the merchants who trade between these two countries, who are the only travellers on this route, Yarkand being subject to the Chinese government, whose system of seclusion is there in full force'. Moorcroft's failure to get Chinese permission to visit Yarkand just over twenty-eight years before suggested to Thomson that he too would be unlikely to reach it. He travelled up to the Nubra Valley and crossed over the Sasser Pass into that of the Shayok River. The road to Yarkand, he wrote, 'till ten years ago, when it was blocked by glaciers, lay up the Shayok'. He therefore had to follow a more circuitous route. After crossing the Shayok, he climbed a low pass, and after three days following a valley and making 'a short, steep ascent up a gravelly ravine . . . emerged upon a wide, open, somewhat un-dulating, gravelly plain, extending eight or ten miles'. To the south he 'perceived a continuous range of lofty snow mountains, extending uninterruptedly as far as the eye could reach E. and W.' Beyond was a plain, the northern part of which he presumed was 'the highest flat plain on the globe'. He encamped on the edge of the plain and then a day later proceeded to the top of the pass.

> To the E. a small stream, commencing just below the pass, could be traced for about half a mile . . . Along this small stream I was informed the road to Yarkand lay, but through an absolutely desert country, so that I had determined for this and other reasons not to attempt to go farther. First, this portion of the country was thoroughly barren, and I knew that on the edge of the habitable portion was a Chinese post, where I should have been stopped, if not seized. Secondly,

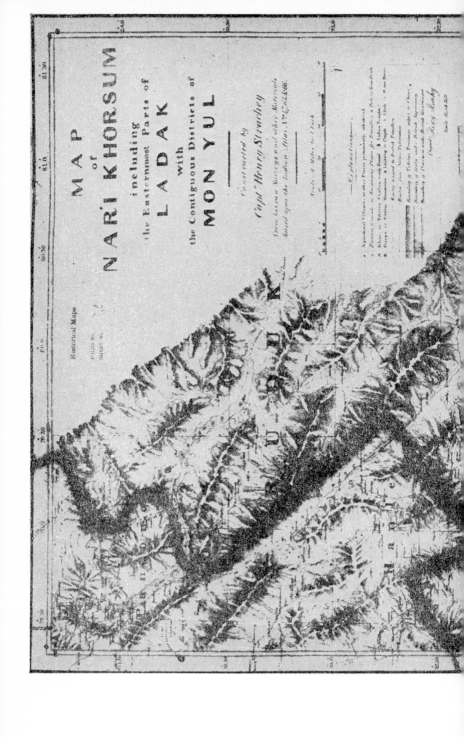

MAP
of
NARI KHORSUM
including
the Easternmost Parts of
LADAK
with
the Contiguous Districts of
MON YUL

Constructed by
Capt.ʳ Henry Strachey

from his own Surveys and other Materials
based upon the Indian Atlas 1846 & 1847.

Scale 8 Miles to 1 Inch

— Explanations —

Historical Maps
FOLIO No.
SHEET No.

MAP 3. *Nari Khorsum including the Easternmost Parts of Ladak*. This map was made by Capt Strachey in March 1851, covering the areas that he visited. It shows the boundary from the Changchenmo Valley down to the Lipu Lekh Pass in Uttar Pradesh more or less as it is shown in Indian maps today.

from Nubra there is no subsistence for man or beast, and even fuel is barely procurable above 17,000 feet . . . I think I have determined the points of most interest both geographically and botanically. The remainder will be done some day from Yarkand, but cannot till the Russians take it from the Chinese.[45]

Lt Henry Strachey, who was also a member of the 1847 Boundary Commission, made another tour through areas hitherto unknown to British explorers. He followed the road to the Chang Chenmo valley, which is today a hinge of Indian and Chinese strategy. His Diary is a remarkable document, precise and detailed. It shows that alignment made by the Indians in 1960 was known and accepted nearly a century before. He was never challenged by the Chinese and his report ends:

I mentioned above, that I had completed my survey of the Tibetan boundary. As I have now less reason than ever for expecting the LASSAN authorities to deviate from the system prescribed to them by their Chinese masters at the mere suggestion of an individual Foreigner I take my leave of attempts to open intercourse with them. I shall return to India when the Passes are open next spring, availing myself of the intermediate time to add to my stock of information regarding this country, and of my journey thither to survey some other of its districts.[46]

These reports indicate two points which are highly significant within the context of the present Sino-Indian dispute. The first is that there existed plenty of evidence of a boundary line observed by custom and tradition, that is to say by the traders who looked on it purely from the point of view of when and where taxes had to be paid. The second is that instructions given to the Commission were emphatic that no risks whatever were to be incurred in challenging the Chinese.

3

Where Three Empires Met

LT MONTGOMERIE AND THE TRIANGULA-
TION OF KASHMIR; SHAHIDULLA AND
THE ROAD TO YARKAND; THE SECOND
YARKAND MISSION; CHINA AND THE
VACUUM; THE CHANGCHENMO VALLEY;
LANAK LA AND RUDOK; AKSAI CHIN
AND THE LINGZITHANG; THE THREAT OF
RUSSIAN EXPANSION AND THE KASHGAR
CONFERENCE; DIFFERENCES WITH CHINA
UNRESOLVED

LT MONTGOMERIE AND THE TRIANGULATION OF KASHMIR

In 1847 Britain and China were neighbours. Their frontier was not demarcated, but throughout the centuries, village people and traders had known the extent of Chinese influence; an armed guard, a tax collector or merely odd piles of stones on a mountain side had been accepted as a signal of overlordship. The limits of Russian or British control were as familiar. As British imperialism consolidated its power in India and the East India Company saw opportunities for extending their trade beyond the Karakorum, explorers and surveyors on the spot and officials in Whitehall and Simla recognised the need to observe and record those points beyond which China or Russia was in control.

With Kashmir as a base, the Company pushed forward in two directions: into Central Asia and into Tibet. The roads to Yarkand and Lhasa now figured in every Himalayan exploration. Eight years after Cunningham, Strachey and Thomson had recorded the boundary

lines, Lt T. G. Montgomerie started the triangulation of Kashmir.*
He and his team worked on the whole tract of mountains between the
British frontier and Chinese Turkestan and by 1865 the limits of
Ladakh had been reconnoitred and mapped.[1] They carried a 14-inch
theodolite and other equipment over immense mountain ranges,
through perpetual snow, in conditions so severe they sometimes had
to melt snow to slake lime for mortar in setting up triangulation
station pillars.

Montgomerie was not only interested in the contours of Kashmir;
he wanted to investigate countries north of the Mustagh or Karakorum
ranges. Any European wandering in those remote areas would have
excited suspicions. In 1869 he persuaded an intelligent Moonshee called
Mahomed-i-Hameed to spy out the land. Hameed started from
Yarkand 'making his observations by night', returned over the mountain
passes in the following spring; his return being hastened by the threats
of suspicious Chinese authorities. Unhappily, this Moonshee fell sick
and died within a short distance of one of Montgomerie's surveying
stations. But all his papers were intact, and his personal description of
the march across the mountains 'to the watershed dividing India from
Turkestan' provides one of the earliest eye-witness accounts of the vast
scale of the Himalayas. No European had yet set foot in Yarkand and
the details of fifty-one days of hard travel that he had recorded excited
the interest of the Indian Survey and then of the Royal Geographical
Society. Montgomerie lectured about him to a R.G.S. audience. Sir
Andrew Waugh, Surveyor-General of India was present. He spoke of
the Moonshee's fate as 'untimely and most touching' and explained:
'There might be some wonder felt that there was so much uncertainty
about places situated at so short a distance from an Indian frontier. The
reason was, that the intermediate region was mountainous, the climate

---

* Lt T. G. Montgomerie, Royal Engineers, made a preliminary reconnaissance of the Great Himalaya. He was a brilliant triangulator and was responsible
for the planning and the organisation of the survey of Kashmir. In 1857, during
the Mutiny, he was an unofficial political adviser to Gulab Singh. The Maharaja
died in the same year, but Montgomerie's personal influence with his successor,
Ranjit Singh, maintained continuity for the work of the Great Trigonometrical
Survey. Montgomerie trained Indian explorers in reconnaissance and route
surveys and taught them to count and record their paces and keep accurate
notes. In a variety of guises his students passed unnoticed where Europeans
would have excited immediate suspicion. The most valuable of these assistants
was the ill-fated Mahomed-i-Hameed.

excessively severe, and the people were fanatics, among whom it was difficult to travel. The Government of India would not allow any enterprising officers to explore the country, however much they desired to do so. The plan adopted by the author (namely of using local people) was the only one by which the exploration under existing conditions could be made.' [2]

Montgomerie and his successors were continually on the alert for any evidence of existing boundary posts between India and China. By telling the story of selected places, it is possible to show how often they endorse Indian statements that there was a customary and traditional frontier. Long before 1846 which we may take as the beginning of British rule in these frontier regions, Indian and Chinese traders had their own methods of deciding where the writ of one country began and where that of the other ended. Given goodwill today, there is abundant data on which to determine a Sino-Indian border.

SHAHIDULLA AND THE ROAD TO YARKAND

The Chinese, the Kashmiris, and, later, the British recognised the particular importance of Shahidulla in the Kuenlun range. In 1865, when the Chinese were pre-occupied with the Muslim rebellion, the Maharaja of Kashmir built a fort there which enabled him to extend his control over trade between India and Eastern Turkestan for a short time until Yaqub Beg's Turkestan troops occupied it. G. W. Hayward arrived there in 1868, intending to reach the Pamir steppe, and made this observation about the local boundaries:

> The Maharajah of Kashmir, it is believed, considered his territory to extend up to the Kilian range, north of Shadula, doubtless from the fact of . . . having a fort built there; but the last habitation now met with in his territory is at the head of the Nubra valley, in Ladakh. The boundary line is given on the latest map of Turkistan as extending up to Kathaitum, in the Kilian Valley; but not only this valley but the valleys of the Yarkand and Karakash rivers are frequented by the Kirghiz, who all pay tribute to the ruler of Turkistan.
>
> The natural boundary of Eastern Turkistan to the south is the main chain of the Karakorum; and the line extending along the east of this range from the Muztagh to the

Karakorum, and from the Karakorum to the Changchenmo passes, may be definitely fixed in its geographical and political bearing as constituting the limit of the Maharajah of Kashmir's dominions to the north.[3]*

Hayward's ambition was to get permission to travel beyond Shahidulla. To his surprise he found another Englishman already in this border area – Robert Shaw, who had also travelled up the Changchenmo route with a large caravan of tea and other gifts intended for the ruler of Yarkand. The Yarkandees were most suspicious. 'The simultaneous arrival of two Englishmen on the southern frontier,' Hayward wrote, 'with the avowed intention of penetrating to Yarkand, where no Englishman had ever been before, added to the doubts and alarms excited at the prospect of their being brought into contact with Europeans.'[4] Faced with the uncomfortable prospect of spending a winter in Ladakh, Hayward managed to escape the vigilance of his Turki sipahis, reached the Kuen Lun, discovered the sources of the Yarkand River, and explored more than 300 miles of mountainous country. His contribution to geographical knowledge was that the Karakorum and the Kuen Lun, hitherto marked on maps as one and the same chain, were separated by a distinct watershed of the Yarkand and Karakash rivers. The Royal Geographical Society, which had given their blessing to his expedition, presented him with a Founder's medal to mark his success.

Robert Shaw had also made a pioneering journey.† He reached Shahidulla on November 13, 1868, via the Pangong Lake, the Changchenmo valley, the Lingzithang plain and the Karakash valley. He expected to receive permission from the King of Yarkand to visit his country. Shahidulla he described as 'merely a camping ground on the regular route between Ladakh and Yarkand' and the first place where he would hit that route. He considered that the fort belonged to the Atalik-Ghazee, not to the Maharaja of Kashmir:

* Lt G. W. Hayward crossed the Lingzetang plains in 1868 and followed the Karakash valley as far as Shahidulla. He later reached Yarkand, and in 1869 he explored the sources of the Yarkand River near the Karakorum Pass. He was murdered in 1870 by warring Chitral factions while on an expedition to the Darket Pass in the Pamirs.

† Robert B. Shaw was a tea planter by profession who saw the strategic as well as the commercial potentialities of Eastern Turkestan. In 1869 he charted the route the Russians might take in the event of their invading India. He

Four years ago, while the troubles were still going on in Toorkistan, the Maharaja of Cashmeer sent a few soldiers and workmen across the Karakorum range (his real boundary), and built a small fort at Shahidoola. This fort his troops occupied during two summers; but last year, when matters became settled, and the whole country united under the King of Yarkand, these troops were withdrawn. In reality the Maharaja has no more right to Shahidoola than I have. He has never had any rights on a river which flows north through Toorkistan, nor over the pastures of the Kirghiz, who pay taxes to Yarkand. It is the more astonishing that our most recent maps have given effect to his now abandoned claim, and have included within his frontier a tract where he does not possess a yard of ground, and whose inhabitants are the subjects of another State.[5]

On his return journey from Kashgar, Robert Shaw again wrote about Shahidulla. 'The Yoozbashee', he recorded, 'talking about Shahidoola Fort, says that the Atalik-Ghazee was very angry about it as it was distinctly in his dominions, the Kirghiz paying him tribute. I told him that the Lord Sahib would be very angry on hearing that the Maharaja had advanced beyond his boundary. The Yoozbashee said it was at first thought that this invasion was done by the English, but since my arrival they now knew better.' [6]

Shaw returned over the Suget Pass of the Tien Shan range, and reached the Sasser Pass of the Karakorum. For eight hours he marched by compass, since his guide was struck with snow blindness. 'We had here arrived in the British dependencies,' he wrote, 'having crossed the Karakorum and Sasser Passes, first explored by Dr Thomson. The country beyond this is known to our surveyors and our sportsmen, though the latter seldom penetrate to the Karakorum.' Here at last having 'crossed that imaginary *red line*,' he felt that he had almost reached home. The 'imaginary red line' he saw as starting 'modestly

believed this to be inevitable. He was with Hayward on his last journey, investigating the eastern approaches to the Pamirs. He was appointed an officer on special duty in Kashgar to develop trade over the Changchenmo route and in 1877 was made Joint Commercial and Political Agent at Leh. He was the uncle of F. E. Younghusband and inspired his early ambition to be an explorer.

surrounding a few factories on the coast' and 'reaching its furthermost
extension among the snows and high plateaux of the Karakorum, the
watershed between India and Central Asia'.[7]

Shaw was versed in strategy as well as in trade. On his return he
wrote two Memoranda. One dealt with potential trade routes between
British India and Yarkand; the other described 'Russian advances in
Asia'.[8] He concluded:

> It is thus not impossible for Russia if ready to make sufficient
> sacrifices of men and money, to place a small army with
> artillery in Cashmere at a time of year when the British
> troops in India could have no means of moving up to
> oppose it, and during the season when no Englishman is
> allowed to remain in the territories of the Maharajah, who
> might get news of the movement in time. Cashmere is also
> well adapted for defence against attacks from India.[9]

That Shahidulla was the frontier town was again recognised by the
second Mission to Yarkand led by Sir T. Douglas Forsyth in 1873.[*]
This was the most important mission of the period, determining the
direction of British trade with Central Asia until the end of the
century. 'At Shahidulla,' he stated, 'we were met by Yuzbasi Zareef
Khan, a Captain of the Amir's army, who had been deputed with some
soldiers to await our arrival, and who gave us a hearty welcome . . .
After a halt of four days at Shahidullah, during which time Captain
Trotter and his subordinates explored the surrounding country,
Lieutenant-Col. Gordon moved on with the chief part of the camp to
Sanju, the nearest village in the Yarkand Plain.' [10]

---

* Sir T. Douglas Forsyth played a significant role in the official evaluation of
trade and strategy in the 1870's. He organised a Fair at Palampur in the Kangra
Valley in 1867 to attract merchants from Yarkand. His First Mission to Kashgar
(1870) and his Mission to Yarkand (1873–1874) gave an exaggerated view of
trading potentialities with Eastern Turkestan. Explorers and scientists attached
to his Second Mission added geographical and strategic information of great
importance. He believed Russians would invade India across the Pamirs and
through the lower passes into Hunza, Yasin and Chitral. He believed that the
Kashmir boundary should be pushed up from the Karakorum to the Kuenlun
Range. In 1875 he was sent as Envoy to Burma.

THE SECOND YARKAND MISSION

The Yarkand Mission, consisting of '300 souls and 400 animals', made the journey of 240 miles from Leh to Yarkand in 15 marches. Forsyth's long and fascinating report includes photographs with such titles as; 'Camp at Shahidulla Khivoja, the frontier outpost of Yarkand territory towards Kashmir 22nd. October 1873'; 'Camp at the frontier outpost of H.H. the Maharajah of Jummoo and Kashmir. Shahidulla Khivoja, October 1873' [11]; Forsyth's map places the Kashmir boundary far to the east, but he made this reservation; The Boundaries laid down on this map are approximate only, and are not to be considered authoritative', He was specific on the southern limits of Yarkand; 'The limits of the State are, along the southern frontier, Sanju to Shahidulla, Kilyan to Kunjit.' [12] This conforms to the present Indian alignment.

Optimism about the potential trade expansion with Yarkand was shortlived. Captain Molloy, British Joint Commissioner in Leh, who shared Forsyth's enthusiasm, recorded in his report for 1874: 'This year witnessed the first direct introduction of the fabrics of Manchester to the markets of Central Asia, an enterprising English merchant having piloted himself within the year a considerable caravan of goods from England to Tukestan.' [13] He was referring to Mr Russell of the Central Asian Trading Company who travelled via the snowswept Changchenmo valley to Shahidulla Khoja which he described as 'the borders of Yarkand' and 'on the borders of Chinese territory'. The significance of Shahidulla, for all intending traders, was that it was at this point that the Chinese imposed customs duties.

The Yarkand Mission was the last of its kind. By 1878 trade was negligible, the Chinese regained power in Sinkiang and the Ladakh routes were closed. Forsyth had already appreciated its impracticbility. On his return journey from Yarkand he had used an old route which Hayward had discovered crossing the Kuenlun by a single pass instead of two much higher and more difficult ones on the customary Karakorum track.

Forsyth's Report was vital, not only because it caused the British Indian Government to make a reappraisal of its trading policy with Central Asia but because experts made explorations along the route which suggested strategic potentialities. Col. Gordon, for example, alerted the India Office to the lower passes of Hunza, Yasin and Chitral which the Russians might take in the event of their advance across the Pamirs.

c

CHINA AND THE VACUUM

Shahidulla dropped out of the picture as a trading centre on the road to Yarkand. But as political rivalries in Central Asia became fiercer, it retained a certain significance. In 1891, Q.M.G. Intelligence Branch asked the Resident of Kashmir to provide a pass to Lt H. J. Coningham 'to enable him to cross the Karakorum on military route-sketching duty'. The Resident replied; 'The Government of India have lately recognised the Karakorum Pass as the frontier between Kashmir and Chinese territory, on the road where Lt Coningham proposes to travel. Strictly therefore, a Chinese pass would be needed for him to cross the pass; but in practice he would, at least, be able to proceed as far as Suget, near Shahidulla without any pass being required'. The Foreign Department of the Government of India, when consulted, wrote: 'No objection to Coningham crossing Karakorum without Chinese passport but he should not go beyond Suget.' [14]

By this date the Chinese were active on the frontier. They pulled down their fort in 1890 and eight miles further south, near the summit of the Suget Pass, they built one to take its place. Then, in 1893, the Foreign Department suddenly heard that they had put up an immense board on the Karakorum Pass on which was written in large characters: 'This board is under the sway of the Emperor of China.' One of the pillars supporting it was on the crest, the other some 50 feet down the descent towards Ladakh.

The Wazir Wazarat of Ladakh, complained to the Vice-President of the Jammu-Kashmir State Council of the Chinese Amban who had constructed the pillar. The Wazir said that as far as he had been able to ascertain his own frontier was considered up to Shahidulla, 16 stages from Ladakh, where one of his predecessors had built a fort which was still standing. This proved, he added, that 'the State frontier extends to that place'. The Foreign Department's Note of December 1892 was equivocal.

> We are not in a position to commit ourselves definitely as to the position of the boundary between the territories of Kashmir and of China and the vicinity of the Karakorum. H.M.G. is, I understand, endeavouring to bring about a settlement of the frontier questions between Russia, China and ourselves. In the meanwhile, all we can say is that we are not

sorry to notice indications of activity on the part of the Chinese. We have always hoped that they would assert effectively their claims to Shahid-ulla and the tract between Kuen Luen and Karakorum range. We encouraged them to do this in 1890 at the time of Captain Younghusband's Mission. But I don't know that we should go to the length of saying now that we admit unreservedly their right to claim up to the very summit of the Karakorum. It will be best to say that we see no occasion to remonstrate with the Chinese on account of the erection of those boundary pillars (provided they are not on this side of the summit), but that it must be clearly understood that no boundary marks will be regarded as having any international value, unless they have been erected with the concurrence of both powers. We can say this to the President and tell him that on principle we favour the idea of getting the 'No Man's Land filled up by the Chinese, subject to future delimitation of boundaries. . . .' [15]

The Earl of Dunmore visited the new Chinese fort in Shahidulla in 1892. He had crossed the Karakorum in good weather, met a blinding snowstorm over the Suget Pass, walked up the nearly dry bed of the Suget river, and then reached a high plateau four miles beyond from which he could look down over the Karakash river. He expected to see some form of habitation, but through his field-glasses saw only the Chinese fort. A scurrying of figures suggested he might have trouble. His party rode up to the fort 'in martial order'. On the way they saw 'a board wedged in between two stones, on which was printed in large Chinese characters and also in Hindustani: "Anyone crossing the Chinese Frontier without reporting himself at this fort will be imprisoned" '. The Chinese asked them many questions, but as Dunmore intended stealing 'quietly off to the Pamirs from Shahidullah, six miles north' he was uncommunicative, merely saying they were on the way to Yarkand. When they arrived at Yarkand an impressive escort of Chinese officials met them anxious to know only 'where were they going from Yarkand'. This time they admitted that their real objective was the Pamirs. Dunmore wrote that Shahidulla was no longer the frontier between China and Ladakh, 'the Chinese claiming up to the watershed of the Karakorum', and he added that 'their claim has been allowed by the Indian Government'.[16] The simple fact was the inaccessible and practically uninhabited area between the Karakorum and Kuenlun ranges was of interest to the Indian government only in terms of the Russian threat. Lansdowne had considered it was desirable

> to encourage the Chinese to take it, if they showed any inclination to do so. This would be better than leaving a no-man's land between our frontier and that of China. Moreover, the stronger we can make China at this point, and the more we can induce her to hold her own over the whole Kashgar-Yarkand region, the more useful will she be to us as an obstacle to Russian advance along this line.[17]

As the Russian threat to India receded, Shahidulla again ceased to have any significance in the struggle between the three Empires. According to the Chinese officials during talks in 1960, the Governor of Sinkiang had proposed in 1927 that Shahidulla should be made a bureau of administration. Peking approved, but there is no evidence that it was ever set up. Shahidulla was not a factor in the Sino-Indian border dispute and Chinese claims to the area have not been disputed by Kashmir, Britain or India.

THE CHANGCHENMO VALLEY

The word Changchenmo means literally a large plain. Local traders were familiar with the Changchenmo valley as the road from Yarkand to Leh which passed through it was easier than that over the Karakorum Pass. In 1857, Adolph Schlagintweit, one of three German brothers who did intelligence work for the East India Company, travelled up the valley and then crossed the watershed to the east of the Karakorum.* He shared the fate of several other political agents whose activities in the Himalayas created suspicion – he was murdered in mysterious circumstances on his return journey. But he had given good value to his Company employers, and his last letter written in the Changchenmo valley provided data about this alternative way to Yarkand.[18] Surveyors followed up this information. Captain H. Strachey

---

* The de Schlagintweit brothers, Hermann, Adolphe, and Robert, were employed by the East India Company as explorers between 1854 and 1858. Robert crossed the Tibetan frontier in disguise in 1856, and penetrated as far as Gartok. Hermann and Robert were the first Europeans to cross the chains of the Karakorum and the Kuenlun. In about 1850 they explored the Kumaun

remarked at the time that 'so long as the Chinese were in the ascendant, Adolph Schlagintweit would have had little chance of penetrating the inhabited country to so great a distance, as they have outposts on all the roads across the frontier, and from the rarity of population and traffic, individuals are easily marked and moreover would hardly have been able to disguise himself enough to bear scrutiny'.[19]

G. W. Hayward had established the existence of three well-known routes to the Karakorum range, the most easterly of which had been discovered by Adolph Schlagintweit's. He described this Chang-chenmo route as

> the easiest of all the passes leading across the Karakorum and Hindu Kush ranges. It is quite practicable for laden horses and camels, would offer no great impediment to the passage of artillery; indeed the ground is so favourable, that a little labour expended on the construction of a road up the Chang-chenmo valley to the pass would render it practicable for two-wheeled carts and conveyances.
>
> Geographically, the pass is remarkable as being across the main range of the Karakorum, forming the watershed between the Indus and the Turkistan rivers, and constituting the natural boundary of the Maharajah of Kashmir's dominions to the north.[20]

Efforts were made to establish this as the most practical route to Yarkand. During the second Yarkand Mission Captain Biddulph had followed it and continued across the Lingzithang plains. Opinions differed on the question. Captain Trotter, for instance, believed that the summer route (via the Karakorum and Sanju Passes) and the winter route (via the Karakorum and Kujiar Passes) would continue to be used not only because they were shorter, but because their extreme elevation caused casualties among the pack animals. Dr Cayley, the then Resident at Ladakh, favoured the Changchenmo route. He

Himalayas. Nain Singh and Mani Singh travelled with them before they were trained as explorers by Montgomerie. Adolphe was murdered in 1857. Henry Strachey believed that he had passed the winter of 1857/58 at the foot of the Kuenlun on the border of Khotan on this side of the Chinese outposts. *Scientific Mission to India and High Asia* by the three brothers Schlagintweit is an important document of the period.

was responsible for building supply depots at Tankse and Gogra and several caravans of camels came that way from Yarkand to Leh as a result. Robert Shaw also favoured the Changchenmo route and believed that traders would 'take to it' once it was 'properly laid out'.

Frederick Drew, Governor of Ladakh and a geographer and geologist, travelled widely in the area under his administration and wrote a definitive book on Ladakh. He visited the Changchenmo valley, referring to Phobrang 'some five miles above Lukung' as 'the last in Ladakh in this direction'. In his *Jummoo and Kashmir Territories* he outlined a boundary line, adding that there were areas where it was uncertain. His description of the boundary line is the clearest expression of the then existing information by the man ideally placed to evaluate facts.

> We now come to the Yarkand territory, under the rule of the Amir of Kashgar. As to the boundary with this, from the Mustagh Pass to the Karakorum Pass, there is no doubt whatever. A great watershed range divides the two territories. But it will be observed that from the Karakorum Pass eastward to past the meridian of 80′, the line is more finely dotted. This has been done to denote that here the boundary is not defined. There has been no authoritative demarcation of it at all; and as the country is quite uninhabited for more than a hundred miles east and west and north and south, I cannot apply the principle of representing the actual state of occupation. I have by the dotted boundary only represented my own opinion of what would be defined were the powers interested to attempt to agree on a boundary. At the same time this dotted line does not go against any actual facts of occupation.
>
> These last remarks apply also to the next section, from the Kuen Lun Mountains southwards to the head of the Changchenmo Valley; for that distance the boundary between the Maharajah's country and Chinese Tibet is equally doubtful.
>
> From the Pass at the head of the Changchenmo Valley southwards the boundary line is again made stronger. Here it represents actual occupation so far that it divides pasturelands frequented in summer by the Maharaja's subjects from those occupied by the subjects of Lhasa. It is true that with respect to the neighbourhood of Pangong Lake, there have

been boundary disputes which now may be said to be latent. There has never been any formal agreement on the subject. I myself do not pretend to decide as to the matter of right, but here again I can vouch that the boundary marked accurately represents the present state. For this part my information dates from 1871, when I was Governor of Ladakh. This applies to all the rest of the boundary between the Maharaja's and the Chinese territories.[21]

LANAK LA AND RUDOK

In its earliest days the Company recognised the importance of Rudok as a trading centre for the high quality wool of the Changthang area. Later surveyors believed that a road might be made from the northern plains of India to Khotan through Rudok, which would avoid Leh and the taxes levied there by the Maharajah. Punjab traders according to W. H. Johnson (see p. 67) would go 'via the Hindostan and Tibet road, up to the Chinese boundary, after which they would pass over the Chumurti plains to the Indus, and thence to Rudok, without touching on the Maharajah's territories'.[22] The boundary between the territories of the Maharajah and China were generally accepted. When Capt. H. H. Godwin-Austen, working for the Topographical Survey, visited the Pangong Lake area, he noticed an ancient fortified post at Tuggu Nuggu.* He followed the lake for about half a mile, rounded a large bay, only to find another one which was called Phursool. He noted: 'This forms the boundary between the Kashmir Rajah's territory

* H. H. Godwin-Austen was an officer in the 24th Foot, later the South Wales Borderers, who served in the 2nd Anglo-Burmese war in 1852. He joined Montgomerie at a survey station in Kashmir in 1857. During the Mutiny he was an unofficial political adviser. He continued the survey of the Kaj Nag range in southern Kashmir, and was the first to put Gulmarg on the map. In 1858–1859 he surveyed in eastern Kashmir and Jammu. In 1861 he crossed the Skoro La, and was the first to ascend the great glaciers of Chogo Lungma, Biafo and Baltoro. In 1862 and 1863 he sketched the upper Changchenmo and northern border of the Pangong district in eastern Ladakh, up to the Tibetan frontier near Rudok. The same year he surveyed the country between Darjeeling and Punaka and elsewhere with the Bhutan Field Force. He also made quick reconnaissances on the north-east frontier.

He was reckoned as one of the greatest mountaineers of the day. He was immensely brave and had great powers of endurance. He was also a considerable artist and illustrated his original surveys of the glaciers.

and the Chinese district of Rudok.' [23] He learnt that certain areas
round the lake, notably Ote and the plain behind it, were disputed
areas. The men of the Pangong district claimed it, but he observed:
'judging by the site of an old fort standing on a low rock on the north-
western side of the plain, I should say it undoubtedly belongs to the
Shassan authorities, by whom it was built years ago: proximity of
Leh and greater part of Thanander there places it in the Kashmir
Rajah's territory.' [24]

Godwin-Austen hoped that he could get through to Rudok. But he
failed. The Zimskang of Rudok pitched his tent on the opposite side of
the stream at Pal and delivered a letter from the Governor with a white
scarf, bricks of tea, and goats. The letter Godwin-Austen reported 'was
to the effect that it was not in his power to give me leave to visit
Rudok, as he had strict orders from his superiors in Lhassa to prevent
foreigners crossing the frontier, and that it would eventually be known
if he permitted it. He added that he could not use force to prevent my
further progress, but he trusted I would not lose him his appointment
by so doing, and that I would accept the presents as a sign of friendship.'
Godwin-Austen explained; 'Having received orders not to bring on
any collision with the Chinese officials, I had to give up the idea of
seeing Rudok.'

He assumed the frontier was at Pal, and the Zimskang of Rudok
obviously accepted that assumption. This is an interesting point, since
Strachey, nearly twenty years earlier, in drawing what he thought to
be a frontier line, had placed it some miles to the west of Pal, Pal being
in Rudok territory.

The Chinese precautions against foreigners in Rudok were again
reflected in the experience of Captain M. S. Wellby, who in May 1896
left Leh bound for Tibet, and hoping one day to find the road to
Peking. Just as he left the gate of his compound, a long-awaited Chinese
passport one-and-a-half-feet square and Chinese visiting cards five
inches broad and ten inches long were delivered to him. The passport
gave him permission to travel through Kansu, Shansi, and Shensi to
Peking and through the New Dominion without paying taxes. Six
days later he arrived at Shushal, 'back against the hills, five miles or so
from the Pangong Lake, which is not even in sight'.

The first thing for us to find out was the shortest and best
way over the frontier. We learnt that the ordinary route over

the Marsemik into Chang Chenmo was closed by snow . . .
With the exception of this road and another one that went to
Rudok, nobody knew of any other, or more correctly speaking, would own that there was another road. Rudok lies at the
south-east corner of the Pangong Lake, and we knew that at
Rudok a large Tibetan guard was maintained, who jealously
guarded the main road to Lhasa, under the condition that
should they allow any foreigners to pass that way, they would
have to pay for the negligence with the loss of their heads.[25]

And in that particular year apparently 'they were more than ever
prepared to oppose any attempt at crossing the frontier in that direction', the result, Wellby calculated, of the Littledale expedition the
year before which had camped for several days within 50 miles of the
capital.* So he made other plans. The headman of Shushal denied any
knowledge of any other crossing over a narrow strip of the Pangong
Lake to the village of Pal, and Wellby thereupon sent his servant Esau
and a companion to ride out to this stream twenty miles away to see
whether it was fordable. On the way they were stopped by twenty
armed men who said there would be trouble if Wellby tried to travel
by this route. They had heard of Wellby's departure from Leh, they
knew that he was waiting in Shushal and, as Wellby writes, 'were
prepared to oppose any attempt we might make to cross the frontier
in that direction'.[26]
Shushal was thus clearly inside Indian territory, as the Indian
Government maintain today. Wellby left Leh and headed north-west
along the shore of the Pangong Lake and on to Niagzu before he was
turned back by men from Rudok and Rundore, Tibetans, in fact, from
the other side of the frontier. One of Wellby's party, a Lt Malcolm,
recorded the incident in a letter to his father.

> We sent our caravan ahead of us from Leh, and followed it
> on May 4th, catching it up at Shushal, whence we intended to
> cross the frontier by Lanak-La as Bower did. Finding, how-
> ever, that a pass called the Marsemik-La (18,300 ft.) was still
> closed by snow, we had to take a rather circuitous route and
> cross the Wapu-La (18,434 ft.). Unluckily, the Tibetan officials

* The story of Mr and Mrs Littledale's expedition across the plateau of
Northern Tibet is told by Sir T. Holdich in *Tibet the Mysterious*, pp. 281–284.

at Rudok had heard of us, and came post haste to stop us; so, finding that neither persuasion nor threats had any effect, there was nothing for it but to retrace our steps across the pass. The Tibetans gave us guides to show us the way to the east side of the Lanak-La (our frontier) and there we arrived on May 30th. That night our guides disappeared, so that we were left to find our way across Tibet without any.[27]

Wellby mentions the Lanak La as the then accepted border between Ladakh and Tibet. A. D. Carey made the same point in the diary he kept of his journey in 1885: 'August 21. 1885. Gentle ascent to head of Lanak La Pass, From top of this pass slight descent into valley with wood, water, and a little grass. At 5th. mile a grassy swamp crossed . . . Route now lies in independent Tibet.' [28]

Carey left Simla in May, 1885, to spend two years travelling on the frontiers of northern Tibet. His journey was officially blessed. He had a passport to visit Turkestan, China proper and Tibet. His companions included Ney Elias, the then British Commissioner in Ladakh. Their objective was the road which linked Polu and Rudok. It had been discovered by Kishen Singh, a member of the Yarkand Mission. He had found his way back to India along this road via Polu, Noh and the Pangong Lake. It ran from one and a half to two degrees to the east of the most easterly route, namely that which W. H. Johnson discovered on his journey to Khotan in 1865. Carey's idea was to reach Turkestan by this more easterly road, travelling 'through the uninhabited tract of Tibet lying between Rudokh and Polu, which is now rarely if ever used'. He struck the road at the Mangtza Lake, and found Kishen Singh's observations so accurate, he could use them as an informed guide. He followed it along the eastern side of the Aksai Chin and since this area, a century later, is crossed by roads newly built by China, the observations Carey made when he arrived at Kiria are highly relevant.

The existence of the Polu road from India was entirely unknown to the Chinese authorities at Kiria, and the news of our arrival appears to have caused some consternation. We were informed that the garrison was called out at midnight, and 200 men sent half-way to Polu, while the commanding officer, with a smaller body of men and several Mahomedan officials, came to Polu on the evening of the 10th. having marched more than 50 miles during the day.

The next morning they paid me a visit, saw the passport, and were very cordial and profuse in offers of assistance. The Chinamen spent a day in exploring the road by which we had come down, and before returning to Kiria instructed the villagers, that all our wants were to be supplied.

I do not think that the Chinese regime in Turkestan compares unfavourably with other Asiatic governments such, e.g. as those of many Native States in India. In spite of their absurd self-conceit and other peculiarities, the Chinese appeared to me to be by no means altogether wanting in the better characteristics of a ruling class, and to be quite the superiors of the Turks in decision, moderation, intelligence, and the other qualities which fit men for positions of authority.[29]

He thought their military strength was not great, and although there was good raw material among the soldiers they were 'undisciplined and poorly armed, while the officers are utterly inefficient and often addicted to opium'. China he concluded,

is an unaggressive and not unfriendly neighbour, and our good wishes may therefore go with her efforts to maintain and consolidate her authority.[30]

The next British traveller to cross the Lanak La was Captain Hamilton Bower. In 1890 he was in Chinese Turkestan. The following year – 'thoroughly bitten with the love of travel that seems to come to everybody who has once experienced the charm of wandering amongst the peaks, passes and glaciers of the Himalayas' – his thoughts turned to the then unexplored Tibet. The Viceroy sanctioned this idea, and Bower set out from Leh on June 14, 1891, with Dr W. G. Thorold of the Indian Medical Service, armed with thermometers, theodolites, compasses and other surveying instruments as well as material for the collection of natural history specimens. The party arrived in the Changchenmo valley a fortnight later. Fortunately, a Ladakhi who arrived with hired animals at Pamzal 'acknowledged that he had been across the frontier to a place five marches distant to get salt, and on being promised a reward offered to show the road. Under his direction the party travelled towards Lanak La, crossing two small easy passes *en route.*' Bower's diary for July 3, 1891, reads: 'Crossed the frontier at Lanak La, and after marching 24 miles, which took us nine hours, camped. The pass is easy, and there was no snow on it.' [31]

The frontier was known then. The Ladakhi guide seemed to have 'great dread of the Khamba people' but 'would not confess that he had been inside their country'. The reference is interesting, since it was a Khamba revolt in 1956 that caused the Chinese to build the road across the Aksai Chin, as a short cut for the garrison from Yarkand, which was used to suppress it.

The other small pass which Captain Bower mentions must have been the Kongka Pass, well inside Indian territory, where 17 Indian soldiers were killed by Chinese troops in October 1959. With the remainder of his journey beyond Lanak La, we are not concerned, since this was indisputably Tibetan territory. But it is very interesting to have Captain Bower's evidence of the frontier post.

Captain H. H. P. Deasy, a distinguished name in the history of the Survey of India, succeeded in travelling much further east than did Wellby. In May 1896, following the now well-known road from Leh to Lanak La, he reached the 'wretched village of Fobrang, not far from the Pangong Lake, where his remaining stock of barley, suttoo, etc. was obtained through the good offices of the Wazir of Ladakh. Fobrang, he wrote 'was the last village we were destined to see until our return to British territory in about five months' time'.[32] Three years later, Deasy described in considerable detail to members of the Royal Geographical Society his amazing journey to Yeshil Kul through mainly uninhabited parts of Western Tibet. Part of the way was over mountain ranges which Captain Bower had crossed before him. He was more fortunate than Wellby in that he approached Rudok territory from the east. But he found, even as Wellby did, that he excited suspicion. Orders had been sent from Lhasa every fortnight warning people 'to look out for about 20 British officers and 3000 soldiers, who were invading Tibet from Ladak, to promptly turn them back, and report to Lhasa'.[33]

That a customary boundary line existed is indicated by an incident at the small village of Gerge where Deasy was unable to get 'fresh transport and more supplies . . . without an order from the Rudok authorities'. He found the officials adamant; the headman said that Deasy's advance 'could only be made over the dead bodies of himself and all the Gerge people, who considered being killed by us quite as good as being executed in Lhasa for allowing us to proceed'.[34] Up to this point Deasy had found his own way over about 460 miles of unknown, almost uninhabited country. But in the face of such opposition from the people of Gerge, he had no alternative than to promise to go back to Ladakh by the route which he was shown. His animals were tired out – only one survived the return journey – and he was uncertain about finding water and grass. Tibetan guides led them to Rudok, over the Napu La, earlier reached by Wellby, to Rundor and into Ladakh. Once more a British surveyor had observed the recognition of a customary boundary by local people and one which corresponds to India's present alignment.

Captain C. G. Rawling and Sven Hedin are two of a number of European travellers of the present century who crossed over the Lanak La Pass and noted it as the frontier mark. In 1902, Rawling had entered the Changchenmo valley and made a number of expeditions on over the Lanak La 'for the sake of sport'. His second journey, which started from Leh in May 1903 had the support of the Surveyor General, Col. St G. Gore, who seconded to him a sub-surveyor. The Foreign Office gave him permission 'to cross the frontier into Tibet'.

His book, *The Great Plateau*, added considerably to existing geographical knowledge. He records in an entry for June 11:

> A four miles' march brought us to the Lanak La, 18,000 feet high. The ascent was easy. So the tents were pitched that night but a few feet below the summit of the pass and about seven miles beyond the boundary pillar between Ladak and Tibet.[35]

Three years later Sven Hedin, an agent in the pay of more than one government, was less fortunate. He had taken the familiar road from Leh-Tikse, Tankse, Probang – to Pamsal in the Chengchenmo valley. But he only saw the Lanak La in the distance because, he explains, it 'was closed to him by the Anglo-Indian Government'.[36]

AKSAI CHIN AND THE LINGZITHANG

Up to this point we have seen that observations made by responsible people demonstrate the existence of a customary boundary which provided the basis of frontiers marked on official maps. British explorers usually only confirmed existing boundaries. Indeed, their instructions invariably contained a warning not to trespass into any areas claimed by the Chinese.

The Aksai Chin appeared to be of little commercial or strategic significance and was rarely visited. Such data as was culled before the middle of the 19th Century was scanty and often contradictory. The area, often termed the Soda Plains, provided the Ladakhis with salt and with rather unappetising pasture for their goats, sheep and yaks. Its strategic importance lies in the fact that there the frontiers of Tibet, Sinkiang and Ladakh march together. In November 1717, Dsungar Mongols marched over the Aksai Chin, then over the Lanak La into Rundok and on to Lhasa. Two centuries later, Chinese troops used the same tracks, first to occupy Tibet, and second, to put down a Khamba rising.

One of the first Europeans to visit this dreary plateau was an Italian, Roero du Cortanze. He stayed in the territories of the Maharaja of Kashmir from 1853–1875, during which time he travelled to Baltistan and into Ladakh as far as the desert and almost unknown plateau of Changchenmo and Aksai Chin, east of the Shayok valley. Dr Cayley, Resident in Ladakh, in 1870 commented on reports from travellers:

> There extends the high plateau, sometimes called the Aksai Chin, which is reached by a pass of 19,400 feet and itself varies from 19,000 and 18,000 feet in elevation at the level of the plain. For the first three days the ground is absolutely bare and the horses are entirely dependent on the corn which travellers carry with them. Beyond this, a scant herbiage exists at intervals, but the corn is indispensable as an adjunct. [37]

But for its inaccessibility, Aksai Chin might have been used as an alternative route for traders who would have thereby escaped the high duties imposed by the Maharaja of Kashmir. The Kashmir authorities maintained two caravan routes right up to the traditional boundary. One, from Pamzal, known as the Eastern Changchenmo route, passed through Nischu, Lingzi Tang, Lak Tsung, Thaldat, Khitai Pass, Haji Langar, along the Karakash valley to Shahidulla. Police outposts were placed along these routes to protect traders from Kirghiz marauders who roamed the Aksai Chin after Yaqub Beg's rebellion against the Chinese (1864–1878).

One of the earliest detailed reports of the Aksai Chin was written by W. H. Johnson, Civil Assistant of the Trigonometrical Survey of India.* In July 1865, he was instructed to explore the country of Khotan. According to his own account the Khan Badsha had invited him to visit his country and to stay in Ilchi, its capital [Ilchi is now called Khotan and is described as such throughout this book].

Johnson calculated that its acceptance might provide 'information of value . . . as regards those provinces of Central Asia, which are at present almost unknown to Europeans, and also of the movements of the Russian forces in those parts of the world'. He followed the familiar route from Leh as far as Kyam, and then broke new ground by marching in a northerly direction. He travelled through Nischu, Huzakhar and Yangpa, describing these isolated places in the Aksai Chin in great detail. He was the first European to cross the Yangi Diwan pass between Tash and Khushlaslangar, and to take a route which Juma Khan, Ambassador from Khotan to the British Government, had travelled some time before.

He waited at the source of the Karakash for someone to receive him at the first village on the northern side of the Kuen Lun. On the twentieth day his patience was rewarded; a bearer came from the Badsha of Khotan saying 'he had dispatched his wazeer, Sarfulla Khoja, to meet me at Brinjga, the first encampment beyond the Ladakh boundary, for the purpose of escorting me to Khotan'. Three miles from Khotan, Khan's two sons were waiting to welcome him. The Khan had a great deal to say. Four years before he had visited Mecca and on his return he was made the Chief Kazi of Khotan. 'Within a month,' he said, 'he succeeded in raising a rebellion against the Chinese, which resulted in their massacre, and his election by the inhabitants of the country to be their Khan Badshan, or ruler.' When the Chinese were defeated in Khotan, Yarkand, Kashgar and other places in Central Asia, Yaqub Beg set up an independent Muslim country which survived until 1877 when Chinese troops recaptured Kashgar.

* W. H. Johnson was an extremely energetic member of the Great Trigonometrical Survey. In 1854 he placed a triangulation station in the Great Himalayas at a height of 19,069 feet, a quarter of a mile east of the Nela Pass. He worked for the G.T.S. in Kashmir, 1857–1863, making triangulations which for sixty years were the highest stations in the world. He resigned after a dispute over funds he had accepted from the local ruler in Khotan, in whose service he subsequently derived financial benefit. His later survey work in the neighbourhood of the Karakorum Pass was exposed to serious criticism.

Certain important points about the frontier were established by Johnson's surveys. Brinja was in his view the frontier post (a few miles south-east of Karangutah). This implied that the northern boundary lay along the Kuenlun range. Johnson's findings demonstrated that the whole of the Qara Tash valley was part of Kashmir territory. He noted where the Chinese boundary post was accepted. At Yangi Langar, three marches from Khotan, he noted that there were a few fruit trees and cultivation at this place which originally was a post or guard house of the Chinese.

> The last portion of the route to Shadulla is particularly pleasant, being the whole way up the Karakash valley which is wide and even, and shut in on either side by rugged mountains. On this route I noticed numerous extensive plateaux near the river, covered with wood and long grass. These being within the territory of the Maharajah of Kashmir, could easily be brought under cultivation by Ladakhees and others, if they could be induced and encouraged to do so by the Kashmeer Government. The establishment of villages and habitations on this river would be important in many points of view, but chiefly in keeping the route open from the attacks of the Khergiz robbers.[38]

The Indian Government rebuked him officially for having crossed the British frontier, but he was enthusiastically acclaimed by the Royal Geographical Society, which awarded him a medal for his contribution to geographical knowledge.

Johnson was a highly controversial explorer who was much admired by Sir A. S. Waugh for his earlier surveys. His report as Surveyor-General in 1861 reads: 'To W. H. Johnson belongs the merit of having ascended, camped at, and observed, from higher elevations than has before been achieved (19,989 ft.), and he has continued to distinguish himself by his ability in connection with the great triangulation. My thanks are specially due to this able Civil Assistant, whose conduct and cheerful zeal are alike honorable to himself and to the survey department.'[39] But Colonel Walker, who was Surveyor-General in 1867, placed it on record of Johnson that:

> When he came back from Khotan, he wrote a report which has had to be entirely rewritten in my office; he brought a map

which has had to be recast, and reductions of astronomical observations which have had to be reduced. In their original state, all three were unfit for publication. He had made an error in projecting one of his Trigonometrical Stations, which threw out the whole of his map; his observations for determining the latitude of Ilchi Khotan by the pole star were really reliable, but his production of them was erroneous to a degree.[40]

Walker insisted that the map as published was far different from Johnson's original. He had sat down with Johnson, collected all information from him and helped him to correct the map. 'His report', Walker wrote, 'would have been ridiculed, and would have brought discredit on the Department, had it been published as it came from his pen. His map would have done more harm than good to the cause of geography.' [41] Walker's severe criticisms were subsequently repeated by Mason, Wood, Stein and, most recently, by Alastair Lamb. But it is the Johnson map which is important, and that, as we have seen, was corrected by the Surveyor General.

Eight years after Johnson's journeys, Dr F. Stolicza, Geographical Surveyor attached to the Mission to Yarkand, crossed the Changchenmo valley to Gogra and then made an intensive geological study along the road to Kizil Jilga and northwest to Aktagh. The results were published in the Report of the Mission to Yarkand and prove that he travelled without any undue difficulties over the Lingzithang, the western half of the Aksai Chin. Routes across the Aksai Chin were studied by other members of the Mission who moved freely wherever they chose. The fact was that Aksai Chin was too cold, too high and too inhospitable to tempt anyone but the most hardened explorer and the most enthusiastic hunter. Forsyth had believed that a route across the western part might be developed for trade between Leh and Yarkand, but the idea was abandoned in 1884 when a caravan of ponies lost its way and only reached Kizil-Jilga after considerable suffering and many losses.

In 1898, Captain H. H. P. Deasy travelled from Khotan to Polu hoping to triangulate two high peaks in the Tekelik Tagh. His passport covered the Aksai Chin. The Amban of Keria, who several times informed him that the Aksai Chin was a part of the province of Sinkiang, refused to let him use the Polu route, or indeed to obtain

MAP

illustrating the routes taken by

M.ᴿ JOHNSON CIVIL ASSIS.ᵀ G.T. SURVEY

in travelling from LEH to KHOTAN and back

in 1865

SCALE 16 MILES = 1 INCH

Notes

*The Country to the South of the Karakoram
and Kuen Lun Ranges is taken from the Maps
of the G.T. Survey of Kashmir and Ladak.*

———— *M.ᴿ Johnson's Route.*

—·—·— *Boundary of Maharajah of Kashmir.*

△ K_2 28278

△ K_6 25119

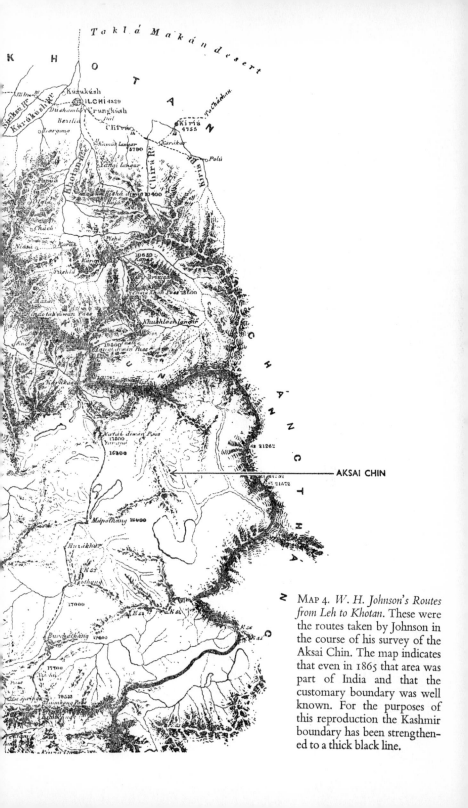

AKSAI CHIN

MAP 4. *W. H. Johnson's Routes from Leh to Khotan*. These were the routes taken by Johnson in the course of his survey of the Aksai Chin. The map indicates that even in 1865 that area was part of India and that the customary boundary was well known. For the purposes of this reproduction the Kashmir boundary has been strengthened to a thick black line.

supplies at Polu. He was therefore forced to take a much longer route and went via the Keria river and the north side of Yeshi Kul to extend the triangulation he had made two years earlier. On returning to his camp at Aksu, he found that the Amban of Keria had 'established a temporary post apparently for the purposes of making it plain to me that the Aksai Chin, at least the part I was in, was under his jurisdiction'.[42] It was only a few hundred yards from his own camp. When Chinese and Indian officials discussed their relative claims to the Aksai Chin in 1960, the Chinese produced a report from Pan Chen, Commissioner of Hotien, dated May 23, 1898, saying:

> To the south-west of the Polu Mountain there is a road leading to Tiaopaiti [Ladakh] of Britain. This mountain road is rugged and has long been severed and closed. And sentinels have been despatched to guard it.[43]

The road described by Deasy and Commissioner Pan Chen was the Sinkiang-Tibet route in territory which the Indians today accept as Chinese.

THE THREAT OF RUSSIAN EXPANSION AND THE KASHGAR CONFERENCE

In the late 1880's the Government of India was alarmed at Russian advances in Central Asia. When Captain Grombchevsky reached Hunza in 1888 via a gap between the Pamirs and Sinkiang, Durand, the experienced frontier expert, commented: 'The game had begun.' It was a triangular game, since the controversial areas were on the fringes of three Empires. For the first time the Aksai Chin was the subject of direct talks between British and Chinese officials in Kashgar in 1896. Peking had a powerful advocate in George Macartney, British representative in Kashgar. His father, Sir Halliday Macartney, was adviser to the Chinese Legation in London and his mother a Chinese. From 1890 until he retired in 1918, George Macartney sympathised as much with Chinese aims as he mistrusted those of Russia. In the struggle which developed between Russia and China for the control of Sinkiang, his influence was decisively in China's favour.

[British, Chinese and Russian representatives studied a variety of maps, many of them to be produced again as evidence in the Sino-

Indian talks of 1960. Most of them did not show any boundary of the Aksai Chin. The chief item they had in common was the south-west boundary of Sinkiang along the Karakorum. This was the case, for example, in a "General Map of Sinkiang" (1821) in *Chin ting hsin Chiang chih lueh*; in a "Map of India" (1840) by the Cartographer Royal, James Wyld; in the definitive work on "Ladakh" by Major Cunningham (1854); and in "Northern Frontier of British India" (1862) by the Surveyor General, Calcutta. Drew's "The Jummoo and Kashmir territories" (1875) was based partly on the Kashmir Survey, completed in 1868, partly on his own surveys. But the map which stimulated controversy over the Aksai Chin was in Keith Johnston's *Atlas* of 1894. Sir William Hunter, Editor of the *Imperial Gazetteer*, wrote an introduction and the *Atlas* was given official approval. It showed an alignment running along the Kuen Lun range to a point east of 80° Longitude, and Aksai Chin as belonging to Kashmir. When Russian officials showed it to the Chinese Taotai of Kashgar in 1896, the Taotai made a verbal representation to Macartney to the effect that Aksai Chin belonged entirely to China. Macartney, always anxious to meet China's case, described the Aksai Chin as 'a general name for an ill-defined and very elevated table land at the north-east of Ladakh', adding that 'it was probably the case that part was in Chinese and part in British territory'.⁴⁴ The same view was expressed by E. H. S. Clarke of the Foreign Department in an official Note, dated December 15, 1896; 'The region is partly in Chinese and partly in British Kashmir territory.' ⁴⁵ Clarke added that a Chinese map drawn by Hung Ta-chen, Minister in St Petersburg, confirmed the Johnson alignment showing West Aksai Chin as within British (Kashmir) territory. Macartney would have chosen to make some specific agreement with China about the boundaries of Aksai Chin. The Government of India were against any such proposal, believing 'that it would certainly bring us into trouble with China besides probably precipitating the active interference of Russia in Kashgaria'.

The Director of Military Intelligence, Sir John Ardagh, did not share Macartney's trust in China as an ally, and her collapse in the Sino-Japanese war only confirmed his views that she would be 'equally useless as a buffer between Russia and the Northern frontier of India'. In the frontier he proposed on January 1, 1897, he included the Aksai Chin in British territory, following approximately the line laid down by W. H. Johnson. But the Ardagh proposals [text in Appendix 5] were turned down, and, for the time being, the Aksai Chin remained open to discussion.

Within a year, Russian and Chinese officials in St Petersburg were reported to be in conference to settle the frontier between their possessions in Eastern Turkestan. The Foreign Office believed that these discussions might result in decisions such as would 'place Her Majesty's Government at a disadvantage when our frontier with China came to be defined'. The Government of India decided: 'It would be of great advantage to obtain a demarcation of the Chinese frontier between China and Kashmir, Hunza and Afghanistan.' [46] Attention was focused on the area west of the Karakorum, the subject of the next chapter.

The required boundary east of the Karakorum was described by Elgin:

> From the Karakorum Pass the crests of the range run nearly east for about half a degree, and then turn south to a little below the 35th parallel of North Latitude. Rounding them what in our maps is shown as the source of the Karakash, the line of hills to be followed runs north-east to a point east of Kizil Jilga and from there, in a south-easterly direction, follows the Lak Tsung Range until that meets the spur running south from the Kuen Lun Range which has hitherto been shown on our maps as the eastern boundary of Ladakh. This is a little east of 80° East Longitude. We regret that we have no map to show the whole line either accurately or on a large scale. [47]

This line, involving the Aksai Chin, was included in a Note of March 14, 1899, which Sir Claude Macdonald addressed to the Tsung-li Yamen [Text in Appendix 7]. They passed it on to the Titai and Taotai in Kashgar who reported in favour of the proposed frontier to the Governor of the New Dominion. But China never answered the Note.

The Aksai Chin was not specifically mentioned in the correspondence. Indians claim it was approximately the same as the Johnson alignment, and that of Hung Ta-jen's map, produced in 1893. No survey had been made of the area, and the boundary line proposed was not then, and has never since been, precisely laid down. Macdonald overcame the problem of precise definition by saying

> It will not be necessary to mark out the frontier. The natural frontier is the crest of a range of mighty mountains, a great part of which is quite inaccessible. It will be sufficient if the two Governments will enter into an agreement to recognise the frontier as laid down by its clearly marked geographical features. [Appendix 7] 48

Once again, the Foreign Office, still calculating that maximum concessions to China would ensure maximum support for Britain's Sinkiang policy, pointed out in the last paragraph of Macdonald's letter:

> Your Highness and Your Excellencies will see by examining this line that a large tract of country to the north of the great dividing line shown on Hung Chun's map as outside the Chinese boundary will be recognised as Chinese territory.49

In short, the Aksai Chin was expendable, and had the Chinese accepted the Macdonald proposals, the Aksai Chin would have been within their jurisdiction.

DIFFERENCES WITH CHINA UNRESOLVED

The northern boundary of Kashmir was discussed again in 1907. Dane wrote to Ritchie on July 4 of that year:

> ... for the time being, we had followed the old maps and gazetteers and had shown the boundary as following the Kuenlun range from the north eastward of the Gusherbrun Pass. ... We are afraid that the boundary must be withdrawn from the Kuenlun range to the line detailed in par. 10 of the attached Note, this being boundary indicated to the Home Government in 1898 and to the Chinese authorities in 1899, and unless there is any objection this will now be done.
> We hope, however to be able to keep Aksai Chin in Tibet in order to adhere to the Kuenlun boundary for that country

INDEX MAP

TO

ROUTES REFERRED TO

IN THE

GAZETTEER OF KASHMIR & LADAK

(Compiled and drawn in the I. B., Simla, 1891.)

Scale 1 Inch = 32 Miles.

MAP 5. *Routes in Kashmir and Ladak.* The eastern boundary of Ladakh as
delineated in this map approximates closely to the traditional boundary so as to
include Aksai Chin in India.

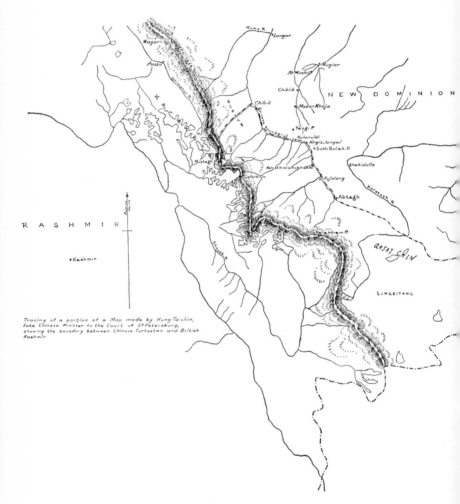

Tracing of a portion of a Map made by Hung Ta-chin,
late Chinese Minister to the Court of St Petersburg,
showing the boundary between Chinese Turkestan and British
Kashmir

MAP 6. *Hung Ta-chen's Map*. This is the tracing of a map given officially by
Hung Ta-chen, a senior Chinese official, to the British Indian Consul at Kashgar
in 1893. It clearly shows Aksai Chin and Lingzithang in India.

as far as possible, and we are having enquiries instituted with a
view to determining, if possible, the southernmost marks of
Chinese jurisdiction in the neighbourhood of the Kuenlun
Range.[50]

The situation about Aksai Chin was clearly outlined in par. 12 of the
*Note on the history of the boundary of Kashmir between Ladakh and
Kashgaria* attached to Dane's letter.

> It will appear ... that prior to 1898 no definite boundary
> was recognised as existing between Ladakh and Kashgar, but
> that since that date we have been consistent (except with
> reference to the trivial alteration near Shamshal) in recog-
> nising one definite boundary line, which has twice been
> described in detail to the Secretary of State and once to the
> Chinese authorities. At the same time, the Chinese have
> never accepted our proposed boundary, so that we cannot be
> held to be committed to abide by it. In regard to the Chinese,
> it will be seen that their ideas as to the boundary are extremely
> vague, though it is probable that, in view of the boundary
> pillar and notice board, they would make every effort to avoid
> having it pushed back beyond the Karakorum.[51]

This implies that between 1899 and 1907, the official assumption of
the boundary was the Macdonald alignment. It was shown as such in the
Indian Foreign Department map of 1908, prepared for use in the 1909
edition of Aitchison's *Collection of Treaties*. Whereas the *Gazetteer of
Kashmir and Ladakh* in 1890 discussed the use of Aksai Chin and
Lingzithang for the collection of food and fodder, the Ladakh Settlement Report of 1908 included both these areas in Ladakh.

The Chinese Revolution in 1911 prompted a re-evaluation of the
northern frontier of Kashmir. Viceroy Hardinge wrote to the Secretary
of State for India, on September 12, 1912:

> There are serious objections on political grounds which
> must not be overlooked or underestimated, to occupation of
> New Dominion (Sinkiang) and Kashgar by Russia, even
> though such occupation may be inevitable and may entail no
> specific military danger. Russia would be brought thereby

within 300 miles of Simla and 150 miles of Srinagar, and new
and undesirable political conditions would inevitably be introduced by this propinquity in spite of difficulties of intervening
country. Russian occupation, moreover, would stifle our
trade on this side, which, though small, is increasing with
improvements in trade route; while our trade with Tibet
will be decreased if old route into that country via Khotan
is reopened with Russia.

Further, suzerainty over Hunza Nagar is claimed by China;
the claim is harmless in Chinese hands, but it will prove
embarrassing if transferred to Russia. We deprecate on these
grounds any diplomatic action calculated to facilitate occupation by Russia.

But first essential, in the event of this being forced on us, is
to demand that a boundary line placing Raskam, Aksai Chin,
Shahidulla, and Taghdumbash inside our territory, and outside that of Russia, should be recognised as a preliminary to
negotiations. This object will be obtained by line similar to
that which was proposed in 1897 by Sir John Ardagh, see
Gov. of India's letter of 23rd. December 1897. Reference is
invited to map prepared by Survey of India in 1891 to
illustrate explorations of Capt. Younghusband. The following
would be a good line:

From Baiyik peak, where line would start, eastwards to
Chang pass, Dehde and Taghdumbash being left on our side;
thence through Sargon pass along crest of range, and so to
crest of Kuen Lun range north of Raskam after crossing
Yarkand river; thence along crest of Kuen Lun range to Sanju
or Grim pass via the passes named in the map of 1891, viz:
Kukahang, Dozaki, Yargi, and Kilik; thence along Kuen Lun
watershed to frontier of Tibet crossing Karakash river, the
plain of Aksai Chin being left on our side of the frontier. With
regard to possibility that compensation might be found in
Tibet, we are generally of opinion that entanglement in Tibet
affairs should as far as possible be avoided. Renunciation by
Russia of all interests in Tibet, subject to our recognition of
religious connection between Tibetan lamas and Russian
Buddhists, and to guarantee on our part not to violate integrity
of Tibet, except possibly by occupying Chumbi valley,

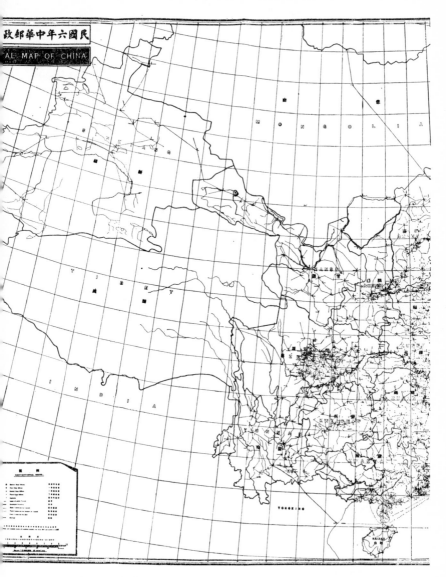

政郵華中年六國民

AL MAP OF CHINA

MAP 7. *Postal Map of China*. A Map published by the Government of China in Peking in 1917. It shows the whole northern boundary of India more or less according to the traditional Indian alignment.

should this be forced on us for maintenance of order and protection of our interests, would be the ideal compensation . . .

We consider that the disadvantages of occupation of New Dominion by Russia outweigh these concessions, even if they are obtained in full, and that we should contend if we are forced to accept occupation that a balance to be settled elsewhere remains to our credit.[52]

The Russian revolution in 1917 caused another shift in British policy, though no new agreements were made either with her or with China. The boundary line drawn up in Hardinge's note, which envisaged a boundary almost identical to the Ardagh's, now became the assumed frontier. It was so drawn in "*The Times* Atlas" and "The Oxford Atlas" with the Aksai Chin included in British territory. In editions of the "Postal Atlas of China" from 1917 to 1933 this was shown as the boundary and China never challenged it. In 1918, according to the Chinese officials in their talks with Indians in 1960, the Cartographic Bureau of the General Staff of the Chinese Army drew up a map showing the whole of Aksai Chin in Chinese territory. It was never published and the Indians obviously doubted its *bona fides*. What these maps prove, Geoffrey Hudson points out, 'is an aspiration in Chinese military quarters from 1918 onwards for effective inclusion of the West Aksai Chin, if possible, within the frontiers of China, and the fact that this aspiration first comes to light in a document of the General Staff indicates that it had a strategic motive'.[53] That motive was the conquest of Tibet which China was not able to undertake till after the communists had come to power and provided a strong centralised government. But the intention was there, whether Chiang Kai-shek or Mao Tse-tung held the reins of power. The Bureau of Survey of the Chinese Ministry of National Defence was ostensibly providing plans for it when, in 1943, they drew up a map showing West Aksai Chin in China.

Aksai Chin was of little moment in the last phase of British rule. Neither China, weakened by internal and external factors, nor the Soviet Union, more concerned with affairs in Europe than in Asia, presented any challenge to Britain. In 1927 the Indian Government considered the adoption of most of its claims to a boundary north of the Karakorum watershed and the adoption of what was, in effect, the alignment proposed in MacDonald's letter to the Yamen in 1899 with certain modifications.

Aksai Chin was virtually unadministered during this period, and only rarely visited. Dr Emil Trinkler, a German geologist was there in 1927. He called it 'the westernmost Plateaux of Tibet' because, he writes, 'geographically the Lingzithang and Aksai-Chin are Tibetan, though politically they are situated in Ladakh.' His expedition was to investigate the former glaciation of these regions during the Ice Age, and he made a study of the belt of mountains separating the Lingzitang from the Aksai-Chin – the Lokzung. His journal reveals that there were no Chinese in this part of the country, and that it was indeed within the boundaries of India. 'I must confess', he wrote, 'that I have rarely seen such utterly barren and desolate mountains'.[54]

4

West of the Karakorum Pass: Triangular Diplomacy

CHINESE AMBITIONS IN HUNZA; CON-
FLICTING CLAIMS ON THE PAMIRS; THE
RUSSO-AFGHAN FRONTIER; THE THREAT
OF RUSSIAN AGGRESSION; THE DECLINE
OF CHINESE INFLUENCE

When Lord Lytton became Viceroy in 1876, he was already committed to an active policy in the North West, aimed primarily at countering Russian expansion which threatened to overflow the mountain ranges. He believed that the prevention of such a catastrophe was best achieved by buying off, subsidising or neutralising the tribal people who had hitherto lived on the fringes of the Himalayas, satisfying their martial spirit by inter-tribal disputes, or raiding occasional caravans en route for Kashgar.

Afghanistan had already been neutralised and Kashmir was under control. Lytton convinced the more cautious Salisbury that it was now necessary to occupy Yasin. This would cover the Iskoman and Barog-hill passes; the first one controlled a road from Wakham into the Indian plains via Chitral, Chilas and Torbela; the second one led to Chitral and on to Peshawar. Lytton suggested that the Maharajah of Kashmir should extend his authority to Yasin with the help of five thousand British rifles, and that in return he should permit a British agent in Gilgit. The Maharaja liked the first idea but not the second – a British representative in Kashmir and in Gilgit who would track his ambitions in Afghanistan. Eventually, the Chief of Chitral received a handsome annual stipend. A Kashmiri official amenable to British pressure was allowed in Chitral and Yasin. An agreement was signed by the Chief of

Chitral and the Maharaja of Kashmir by which the Chief agreed to signify his friendship with the Maharaja 'by presenting annually ... 2 horses, 2 hawks and 2 hunting dogs.' These tribal chiefs were unsophisticated but they knew who held the purse and who could supply the rifles. Yet, Dr Alder's meticulous study of this period led him to conclude that 'the subsidy which Aman received from Kashmir might as well have been thrown down in the Indus for all the good it did. As a guardian of the passes he was useless and, if war had come with the Russians in 1878–79 as it so nearly did, he would probably have joined a Russia supreme on the Upper Oxus and in alliance with Kabul'.[1]

Britain's Himalaya policy was built on bonds with Chiefs who controlled strategic zones between the British frontier and those passes which Lytton once described as 'the broad belt of independent barbarism'. The leaders of Missions to these areas were instructed to develop friendly relations with tribes beyond the Kashmir border, but on no account to interfere with the internal administration of the Maharaja's territories or to encourage complaints against his Government'.[2] Frontier diplomacy meant the discovery of a Chief's price and how much the other suitor was prepared to pay.

By 1879, Lytton had laid down the outline of a policy for Britain's Northern frontier in India.

> The natural boundary of India is formed by the convergence of the great mountain ranges of the Himalayas and of the Hindu Kush which here extend northwards up to their junction. .... Within the angle thus formed lie the territories of Chitral, Darel, Yasin, Hunza and other petty dependencies. From Hunza on the slopes of the Mustagh, westward to Chitral under the Hindu Kush, these States occupy the valleys which run up to the skirts of the ranges, and are drained by the uppermost tributaries of the Indus river system. And the only pass through these ranges from the Pamir are ... in the hands of these semi-independent Chiefs. If a strong, independent and hostile power were established on the north of these mountains, the passes might become lines of a demonstration ... which might at least be useful as a diversion to facilitate and support the flank of more serious operations in Afghanistan. If, on the other hand, we extend,

D

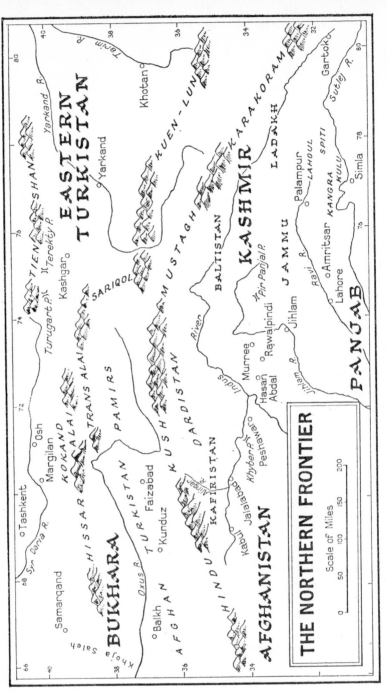

MAP 8. *The Northern Frontier.* This map illustrates the territories which surround the Northern Frontier of India and Pakistan.

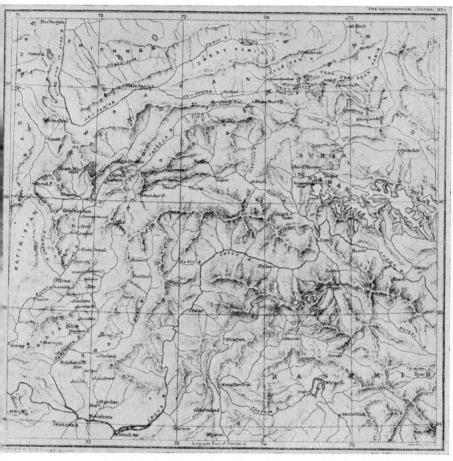

MAP 9. *Chitral and Adjacent Countries.* A map made to illustrate the paper on Chitral and adjacent countries by Capt Younghusband given to the Royal Geographical Society.

and by degrees, consolidate our influence over this country, and if we resolve that no foreign interference can be permitted on this side of the mountains, or within the drainage system of the Indus, we shall have laid down a natural line of frontier which is distinct, intelligible, and likely to be respected.[3]

By the time Lytton left India in 1880 Chinese troops had reoccupied Eastern Turkestan, calling it the New Dominion. In 1881, a treaty between Russia and China provided for complete freedom of commerce between the two territories and Russian caravans soon poured such large quantities of goods into Eastern Turkestan, that Indian exports could not compete with them. In the interests of trade and strategy, Captain F. E. Younghusband was sent to Kashgar to take stock of the situation.

> As regards the feelings towards ourselves, I am convinced that it is distinctly favourable. The Chinese officials, too, are favourably disposed to us, though when Russian and English interests clash, to prevent annoyance from the Russians, who have a consul at Kashgar, while we are unrepresented, they are inclined to side with the Russians rather than with us; and, though they look upon ourselves and the Russians as barbarians, I think they look upon us as the less barbaric of the two, and respect us as the conquerors of India.[4]

Lytton's successors, though not as committed as he was to a 'forward' policy, had no alternative but to adopt it. The situation in 1881 was outlined from Simla:

> The Chinese have now drawn their western and southern frontier in Turkestan. The western frontier extends to the Bolan mountains and follows this range in a southerly direction until it meets the northern spur of mountains that springs from the Hindu Kush. This northern spur runs in an east-south-east direction and joins the Kuen-luen range, taking in the Yengi-Dawan Pass via Kojiar, the Kilian Pass via Kilian, and the Sanju Pass via Sanju, and becomes the southern frontier.

The Chinese consider all to the south of the Sirikol district and the above-named three passes the territory of their friendly neighbour, the British.

Dalgleish, the author of the memorandum, carefully considered Chinese susceptibilities as he sought their alliance.

> The Chinese will not occupy Kunjut, though they desire the route to be opened out. It was solely on my strong recommendation that they occupied Sirikol, but they would not go south of the range that forms the northern boundary of Kunjut, and I was not anxious to press it, because had they so occupied it, then when Kashgaria falls into the hands of Russia as it inevitably must, failing counteraction on our part, Kunjut would have become part of Russian territory, and the Russians would have acquired a position far more threatening to us than if they occupied Herat or even Kabul – almost as threatening as if they held Kandahar.[5]

The belief that Russia might one day occupy Kashgar had caused Lytton and his successors to give priority to Gilgit, as well as to the Yasin passes. 'Kashmir has been called the northern bastion of India. Gilgit can be described as her farther outpost,' wrote E. F. Knight in *Where Three Empires Meet*, 'and hard by Gilgit it is that, in an undefined way, on the high Roof of the World – what more fitting place! – the three greatest Empires of the Earth meet – Great Britain, Russia and China.'[6] He saw the significance of Gilgit as commanding the Indus valley and the mouth of the Hunza river. So had Colonel Durand considered it, when, as Governor of the Punjab, he emphasised the need for the head of the Gilgit valley to be in the hands of Kashmir, thereby ensuring that an adequate force could hold the watershed between the Gilgit and Chitral valleys. Brigadier-General W. S. Lockart urged the need for a British Agency at Gilgit, where the British presence might help to keep the peace between the Chieftains of Hunza on the right bank of the Hunza river and Nagar on the left bank. Hunza, a small state sometimes called Kanjut, was in the northwest of Kashmir, marching in the north-east with the Sarikol district of Sinkiang. To the north it stretched up towards the junction of the

Mustagh and Hindu Kush ranges, divided only by a narrow wedge of
Afghan territory from the Russian Pamirs. Its importance in British
Indian strategy was obvious, but taking it under British control
presented complications. In April 1886, the reigning Thum Ghazan
told Lockart 'in an angry argument that he was subject to the King of
China and acknowledged no other master'.[7] Ney Elias (officiating
British Joint Commissioner at Ladakh) confirmed this. A year earlier
he had reported that 'the opportunity was taken of a dispute between
the people of Sarikol and the Kanjutis (people of Hunza) to send down
a Chinese official to the frontier to accept formally the allegiance of the
Hunza Khan'. The result was that at the time of his visit (1886) the
Chinese regarded Hunza 'as an outlying district of the New Dominion
(Sinkiang) and talked of incorporating it formally into the province'.[8]
They had successfully blocked a British mission to Hunza by persuading
the Hunza Khan to refuse permission. In short, Hunza was the object
of both British and Chinese imperial ambitions. It was essential that no
dispute should arise between them since they needed a common front
against Russian advance.

CHINESE AMBITIONS IN HUNZA

Chinese ambitions in Hunza were a recent development, stimulated
no doubt by British activities in Kashmir. Col. Prideaux, sent to
investigate Sino-Hunza relations, reported:

> It does not appear that there was any intercourse between
> Hunza and China until the insurrection of the seven Khojas
> in Yarkand in 1847, when Shah Ghazanpur Khan of Hunza
> rendered assistance to China in overcoming the rebellion. In
> return for his service a jagir was granted to him in the
> vicinity of Yarkand, and a brass tablet, inscribed with a
> record of the friendship of Hunza towards Pekin and its
> reward, was placed on the gates of the city. A fixed subsidy
> was paid by China to the Hunza Chief, who in return gave a
> nominal allegiance.[9]

When Yaqub Beg turned the Chinese out of Yarkand, the Hunza
Chief retained possession of his jagir. On Yaqub Beg's death the former
state of things was resumed.

A yearly tribute appears to have been paid by the Hunza Chief since 1878, consisting of an ounce and a half of gold dust, in return for which he receives a present of two rolls of satin.

Prideaux's research also covered Hunza's relations with Kashmir.

from early times a nominal allegiance was paid to the Trakhane rulers of Gilgit, which slackened as the power of these Chiefs grew weak. This allegiance was continued to the Sikh and Dogra successors of the ancient Gilgit Chiefs, but it is doubtful if it was ever enforced, and the actual relations between Kashmir and Hunza appear to have been uninterruptedly hostile, until the year 1869, when the late Chief Ghazan Khan consented to yield allegiance to Kashmir, and to pay a yearly tribute of two horses, two hounds and 20 ounces of gold, in return for which Kashmir engaged to pay an annual subsidy. The attitude of Hunza, however, has always been one of veiled contumacy; on several occasions the peace of the border has been seriously threatened, and in 1888 the combined forces of Hunza and Nagar ejected the garrison of Chalt and Chaprot, and peace was not restored until the Kashmir Durbar had undertaken active measures at a large expenditure of men and money.[10]

Nagar, on the opposite bank of the Hunza river, did not raise any of these problems. It had never professed allegiance to China. On the other hand, it stood on similar footing to that of Hunza in its relations with Kashmir. After 1868, Nagar paid an annual tribute of 20 tolas of gold and 2 baskets of apricots, receiving an annual subsidy in return.

When Durand re-established the Gilgit Agency, Safdar Ali Khan, ruler of Hunza, promised 'that there should be a cessation of interference on the part of Chinese officials in the internal affairs of his country, the Rajah merely pointing out that owing to the long connection of his country with China and to his having a jagir in Yarkand, some communication must still be carried on'.[11] Durand increased his subsidy. Safdar Ali Khan made the best of both worlds by a yearly visit to Kashgar where he was free to put up his price to the Chinese.

Durand's policy towards these tribal chieftains was clear cut. His first task was to counteract the Chinese and Russian attempts to establish an influence in these parts, to explain to the Chiefs the position of affairs, to acquaint them with the wishes of the Government and to offer them increased subsidies of Rs. 2000 per annum, conditional upon the cessation of raiding by the Kanjutis in the Shimshal Valley and elsewhere, and the grant of free access to their countries by British officers, whenever considered necessary.

Mixed loyalties, conflicts of interest, mutual exploitation of strategic positions combined to produce a complicated web of intrigue. The Nagar Chief reportedly considered his increased subsidy enough to buy his complacency. The Hunza Chief had to consider his jagir in Yarkand and also objected to being put on the same footing as the Nagar Chief. At first he thought he could afford a little rudeness to Durand, but had second thoughts. In a letter of apology he promised: 'I will never deviate from any engagement that I have entered into with you as long as I live. Should Sahibs come here through the Upper Pass, I will serve them, heart and soul, treat them with hospitality according to the means of my country, and make them reach Gilgit with safety'. [12] Such picturesque expressions of loyalty were not entirely convincing to Durand, who advised Simla: 'Possibly we can remain on good terms with him for a year or two . . . He has an inordinate idea of his own importance and strength, and he will most likely raid the Yarkand road as of yore. In this case there will be nothing left after stopping his subsidy, but to give him a sharp lesson for which the force at Gilgit will be amply sufficient'. [13]

Durand's diagnosis was accurate. The next year caravans on the Leh-Yarkand route were burgled by the Hunza Chief. But the commercial loss had its bright side for the Company. It provided the excuse for one of the most ambitious, far-reaching expeditions of the time. Francis Younghusband, who was to lead the more famous expedition to Lhasa a few years later, had demonstrated his courage and tenacity in 1887 when he reached the Mustagh Pass in a remarkable journey from Yarkand. In 1889, he started from Shahidulla, ostensibly to chase Hunza robbers from the Shimshal Pass, 190 miles away. He reached the Pass and took the opportunity to explore the country into Hunza. [14] Arriving at the Kulanargu River separating the two branches of the Kuenlun range, he found that the lower part of the river was inhabited by Turkis under Chinese jurisdiction though they received no protection from Kunjuti raids. The Chinese told them that 'they lived outside the frontier passes, and must therefore expect no assistance'.[15] Younghusband's reports were followed very closely by the British authorities and undoubtedly influenced all frontier decisions at the time. For instance it was highly probable that it was his information which caused Salisbury to inform the Chinese Minister in London in August 1891 'that Hunza lying entirely to the South of the Hindu Kush was held by Her Majesty's Government to be within the sphere of their influence'.

Younghusband, as he once described himself, was a political soul with interests more military and political than scientific. He realised that it was essential for his Government to control the Pamir passes by which a Russian army could march through to the plains of India. His reports are the most valuable of any official during this period of imperial expansion. He summarised the state of affairs:

> We have here in the centre of Central Asia four nations grouped round some desert mountains; the Afghans afraid of the Chinese, and the Chinese afraid of the Afghans; the English suspicious of the Russians advancing south, and the Russians suspicious of the English advancing north.[16]

His brief for the journey in 1889 had been quite explicit: 'the thorough exploration of the main range of the Mustagh Mountains from the Karakorum to the Kilik passes, and of the strip of almost uninhabited country which lies between the Karakorum and Kuenlun Mountains.' He took five months to carry out his instructions. The theme of co-existence with China recurs frequently in his Report. Russia was extremely active in the Pamirs at that time and a common front with China was explicit in many of his interviews. In September 1890, he talked with Pan Chen, Commissioner of Hotien, whom we last met making claims that Aksai Chin belonged to China.

> Captain Younghusband then proceeded to show the Amban a map of Kashmir in which the Karakorum and Kilian Passes were marked, and stated that His Excellency the Viceroy was anxious to come to an understanding with the Chinese Government with regard to the boundary between Kashmir and Yarkand . . .

Pan Ja-jeu expressed himself as being of the same opinion
as Captain Younghusband.

Captain Younghusband proceeded to state the Viceroy of
India had ever been of opinion that the best boundary between
Kashmir and Yarkand was that formed by the watershed of
the Karakorum range; but, last year, his Excellency had been
led to believe that the Chinese considered their frontier
extending only as far as the Kilian Pass and that the intervening
country was unoccupied by any Power, or in other words,
was a tract of no-man's land. This being an unsatisfactory
state of affairs and one that would afford opportunities for
lawless procedure on the part of the Kanjuts, his Excellency
was contemplating extending the Indian frontier to the
Kilian Pass and annexing all the country situated between it
and the watershed. He had since, however, learned that the
Chinese were undertaking the protection of the trade route,
and if he found this to be really the case, he will be unwilling
to extend the frontier beyond the Karakorum range.

Pan Ja-jeu, in reply, stated the Chinese had ever considered
the watershed which he defined as a natural (or literally in
Chinese) a Heaven made, boundary to the frontier between
Kashmir and Yarkand, and that the Chinese were prepared to
protect the trade route as far as that range.[17]

British policy west of the Karakorum was often to China's advantage.
Take the case of Wakhan, a tract intervening between the Russian
dominions and India. Lansdowne explained to Cross:

We have long been aware that both China and Afghanistan
laid claim to be in possession of certain tracts in or near the
Pamirs, and we hold that it should be our policy to encourage
China to assert her position, and at the same time safeguard
the interests of the Ameer, with the eventual object of recognising a definite occupation by one or the other of the entire
region, thus excluding all chance of encroachment by third
parties.[18]

Later, when a frontier line was being worked out on the basis of
Younghusband's information, the India Office added this caveat to
the Foreign Office:

Lord Lansdowne's Government explain that, though they wish to encourage Chinese occupation of territory on the Pamir up to Afghan and Russian limits, they would deprecate any steps being taken by Her Majesty's Imperial or Indian Governments to demarcate the line proposed.

Lord Cross concurs in this view, and recommends that, if the Chinese Government will recognise the frontier line proposed by the Government of India, they should be urged to make their occupation effective by the periodical deputation of Kashgar or Yarkand officials to the border of their dominion where it marches with Afghan and Russian territory.[19]

CONFLICTING CLAIMS ON THE PAMIRS

But China too had claims which might conflict with those of Britain at any moment, especially if Safdar Ali of Hunza showed signs of encouraging the Russians. The meeting place of three empires inevitably provides many opportunities for diplomacy by blackmail. When Safdar Ali received arms and ammunition from the Russians at their military outpost, Osh, Durand asked for and received permission to strengthen his outpost at Chalt which commanded the southern exit of Hunza and Nagar. Once so equipped, he sent an ultimatum to Safdar Ali in November 1891 insisting that 'the British Government claim the right of free access to his territory, and that of making roads therein for military purposes'. The Rajah did not take this ultimatum lying down. He wrote imaginatively defiant letters to his challenger. Why, he asked, had the British strayed thus into his country 'like camels without nose-rings'. He expressed contempt for the womanly English, as he hung upon the skirts of the manly Russians, and he warned Col Durand that he had given orders to his followers to bring him the Gilgit Agent's head on a platter'. Another letter dictated to the Court Munshi in forcible Persian read: 'I have been tributary to China for hundreds of years. Trespass into China if you dare. I will withstand you, if I have to use bullets of gold. If you venture here, be prepared to fight three nations – Hunza, China and Russia. We will cut your head off, Colonel Durand, and then report you to the Indian Government.' [20] They were brave words, but Durand had the stronger forces and marched on Hunza. Nagar was added to the British Empire by the campaign described by Durand in *The Making of a Frontier* and by E. F. Knight, who was with him, in *Where Three Empires Meet*.

Younghusband saw that the occupation of these romantic mountain villages would introduce a new element into Sino-British relations. When the campaign was first planned he told Cunningham that it would 'certainly greatly offend the Chinese and seriously jeopardise the friendly relations which, in spite of a few signs to the contrary, undoubtedly exist between us and the provincial authorities of Chinese Turkestan at present'. And, in a very odd proposal which could not have deceived the most amateur Chinese diplomat, he concluded: 'Perhaps therefore it would be well now to change round and assume a high and aggrieved tone. We can no longer profess friendly intentions when we deliberately attack a state which has been a tributary to China for centuries, and the ruler of which actually bears official rank granted him by the Emperor.' Younghusband's notion was that complaints should be made about China's insufficient protection of British subjects, and that Britain must therefore protect them herself. 'This much I think we can say to the Chinese, and I think we ought to do so before we get complaints from them regarding our action in Hunza. To be the first to complain is always an advantage.' [21]

The suggestion was not adopted. Durand's troops had scarcely settled down in the castle of Hunza before Chinese officials in Kashgar wanted to know why they were there. These enquiries were pursued in London and Peking and the Chinese sent an envoy to Hunza to keep in touch with events on the spot. But Britain could not afford to incur Chinese hostility at a time when Russian activities were threatening British designs along the whole line of the Hindu Kush, and the Pamirs became a potential battleground. Two officials dominated the scene: Macartney and Younghusband. George Macartney, 'our man' in Kashgar, knew the Chinese mind sufficiently well to take advantage of every move and Younghusband knew the Pamirs and the Hindu Kush intimately. He also understood the logistics of mountain warfare, and was determined to defeat Russian designs. After a thorough examination of the limits of Chinese jurisdiction, he spent the winter of 1890–91 in Kashgar persuading them 'to assert their authority in a manner sufficiently definite to prevent any cause for dispute'. When he was convinced that the Russians intended moving on the Pamirs, he 'warned the Taotai of this possibility, and pointed out to him how ill-defended his frontier was. The immediate effect . . . was that he sent men out to the Russian frontier to gain accurate information about the preparations going on, and on their return he despatched General Chang with thirty soldiers to Murghabi, at the junction of the Akbaital with the Aksu and to Somatash'. Younghusband calculated: 'Now that the Chinese had so definitely asserted their authority, I thought it improbable that the Russians would send any troops on to the Pamirs towards the Hindu Kush or Afghan frontiers.'

He left Kashgar in July 1891 to follow Russian movements on the Pamirs. He caught up with Colonel Yonoff at Bozai-Gumbaz and he asked him whether it was true, as the Kirghiz had told him, that he had annexed the Pamirs. The Russian replied that it was, and showed Younghusband a frontier-line marked on a new Map of the Pamirs, dated 1891, which had the northern boundary of Badakshan and Wakhan as a straight line from Victoria Lake to the junction of the Kojcha with the Oxus. The following day, August 14, Colonel Yonoff demanded Younghusband's withdrawal to the Tagh-dum-bash Pamir, refused to let him pass into Chitral territory and finally demanded his signature to a declaration that he would not return by any pass in a list he produced. Characteristically, Younghusband discovered a new pass not included in the list and used it when he returned to Gilgit in October. His report observed:

> Here is the point at which the three great Empires of Asia – England, Russia and China – meet. Speaking of the last first, my opinion is that the position of the Chinese is sufficiently secured against any attack of Asiatic, either from within or from without, but that they are quite unable to withstand an invasion from Russia.[22]

Younghusband considered that the Russians had been warned in time. A few years earlier they might easily have taken Gilgit. Now, they were more likely to send in small parties up to the Hindu Kush and persuade tribal peoples that they had more to offer than the British. He believed the position would be safeguarded if Britain were to cover certain strategic places and to encourage the Chinese to assert their claims to the extreme limit. The Chinese were told that Hunza was within the sphere of British influence but that they should advance to the extreme point of their claims on the Alichur Pamirs. Until the Pamirs settlement of 1893, British diplomacy was functioning on two fronts, Hunza and the Pamirs. Whitehall tried to keep the two issues separate; in the first case China was a potential rival, and, in the second, a potential ally. Peking, on the other hand, tried to deal with both issues at once, taking advantage of her usefulness to Britain on the Pamirs front to advance her claims on that of Hunza. Not for the first time, there were two trends in Britain's Asian policy. Lansdowne, the man on the spot, saw it through Indian eyes, while Salisbury was thinking in terms of trade with China. Peking, understanding the ambivalence of British calculations, warned London that she 'could not remain silent as to the British action in Hunza while challenging a Russian invasion of the Pamirs'.[23]

THE RUSSO-AFGHAN FRONTIER

Yet another problem faced Imperial frontier builders – that of Afghanistan. Britain needed a neutral Afghanistan, since China had claims here too. In 1892, Chinese and Afghan troops clashed near Somatash on the Alighur Pamir which was claimed by China. Peking protested to Whitehall on the grounds that Afghan's foreign policy was a British responsibility, and that some months previous to the incident, Younghusband had encouraged China's advance to Somatash as part of a countermove to that of Russia.

This Himalayan tangle was not without humour. Dr Alder relates the following incident. 'The Russians carried off the stone commemorating a Chinese victory at Somatash, the Afghans in turn destroyed Russian marks there, and the Chinese retaliated by carefully scratching out a Russian mark on a rock at Ak-tash which had reminded Younghusband of Mr Pickwick's "Bill Stump, his mark".' [24] Dr Alder is a skilful guide to the moves and countermoves in London, St Petersburg, Kabul and Peking during one of the most confused but formative periods of British policy.

As long as the frontiers with Afghanistan and Russia were undecided, every consideration was given to claims made by China. But meanwhile, Chinese diplomacy was active and ambivalent. She had to consider not only her complex relationships with Britain and with Russia, but the more direct threat from Japan, Macartney's diaries reflect his close liaison with the Taotai in Kashgar and provide a clue to the Chinese mind. In June 1893, Hung Ta-chen, late Chinese Minister to the Court of St Petersburg gave him two sections of a map; one showed the Russo-Chinese frontier on the Pamirs, the other has already been referred to in the last chapter on the Aksai Chin. Kashmir's boundary was 'somewhat to the north' of the watershed between the Indus and the Yarkand river valleys, following the Yarkand river which Younghusband had explored in 1889. Macartney argued:

> Whether there would be any advantage in an extending of our frontier to the northern side of the Karakorum range, is a question on which I am incompetent to express an opinion. But it has occurred to me that one day, when the Russians shall have taken possession of Sarikol and Ruskum we may have to consider the advisability from a strategic point of view, of either advancing or waiving the claims which Kunjut (Hunza) is said to have over certain places beyond its generally recognised boundary; and when such a contingency arises, we may find it in our interest to have all the evidence we can discover to show that the Chinese frontier never actually extended as far as the Karakorum range; and possibly this map of Hung Ta-chen may not be without its use.[25]

Macartney's reports from his Kashgar base carried considerate weight in Whitehall. His political and strategic calculations were formulated on the assumption of a Russian advance towards the Hindu Kush. After a series of complex diplomatic moves involving British and Russian efforts to win Afghanistan's support on the one hand and that of China on the other for their respective frontier aims, London and St Petersburg suddenly agreed to talk rather than to fight. A *modus vivendi* was achieved, mainly through the highly skilful diplomacy of Sir Mortimer Durand, the then Indian Foreign Secretary. The Agreement with Russia of March 11, 1895, arranging for the delimitation of the frontier between Russia and Afghanistan in the Pamirs contained the following article.

> 3. The Commission shall also be charged to report any facts which can be ascertained on the spot bearing on the situation of the Chinese frontier, with a view to enable the two Governments to come to an agreement with the Chinese Government as to the limits of Chinese territory in the vicinity of the line, in such manner as may be found most convenient.[26]

The official British view was that

> Taghdumbash Pamir is subject to concurrent rights of China
> and Kanjut. We do not propose to make any claim, however,
> on account of the latter, except for the purpose of precaution
> against China ceding it to Russia.[27]

The Taghdumbash Pamir is about 40 miles long and occupied by
Kirghiz nomads.

The Russo-Afghan frontier was delimited as far as the Povalosch-
veikovski, a point on the watershed of the Taghdumbash, where it
was declared to have reached the Mustagh range at Sarikol which was
considered as the actual Chinese frontier.

The Government of India's next move was to work out some
arrangement by which a definite limit would be drawn to Russia's
potential expansion towards the Mustagh and Karakorum mountains.
Their proposal was that 'it might be possible to stipulate that, if China
gave up control of the Taghdumbash, it should lapse to Hunza, and
they considered the time favourable for settling the Chinese frontier
with Kashmir, Hunza and Afghanistan'.[28] The idea was turned down
by the Foreign Office on the grounds that 'the condition of the Chinese
Government was such as to make it impolitic to bring these questions
before them'.[29] So the matter was left in abeyance.

The natural frontier between Hunza on the one side and Afghan and
Chinese territory on the other, was the main chains of the Hindu Kush
and the Mustagh moutains. But the actual frontier was not delimited and
Hunza laid claims to two territories outside this natural barrier: (i) the
Raskam and (ii) the Taghdumbash Pamir. These claims, described by the
Government of India as 'indefinite but rather extensive', were recognised
by the Chinese. At the same time, the Chinese claimed to exercise a
concurrent jurisdiction over Hunza itself, and because China's support
or at least neutrality in the Pamir crisis was necessary for British policy,
the Government of India had indirectly acknowledged these claims by
recognising the interchange of presents between Hunza and Chinese
authorities at Kashgar and by allowing Chinese envoys to be present
when the Mir of Hunza was installed in September 1892. Younghusband
and Durand had both agreed that China should be encouraged to recognise Hunza's claims since her help might prove decisive if Russia occupied
Sinkiang and had designs on the Taghdumbash.

The General Staff had a different approach; China's uncertainty in countering Russia's designs was a serious handicap. Sir John Ardagh's 1897 Memorandum included recognition of a basic military fact that the great mountain ranges to the north of Chitral, Hunza and Ladakh were too extensive, too high, too inaccessible and too sparsely populated to provide an acceptable defensive boundary which was easy to pass, and fairly dividing the peoples on either side. The highest watersheds were defective as a frontier; an enemy must be prevented from establishing himself on the glacis. This necessitated a boundary which left all longitudinal valleys in British possession or at least under their influence. In short, British control of the Kilik, Mintaka, Khunjerab, Shimshal, Mustagh and Karakorum passes. Ardagh concluded that if for some reasons of policy, the moment for communicating this proposal to China was inopportune, then British agents and officers 'adjacent to the frontier may arrange to procure the recognition of our supremacy and protection by the Chiefs of the local tribes, and to assert it by acts of sovereignty, annually exercised within the limits decided upon, and in this manner acquire a title by prescription'.[30] But the Ardagh proposals were rejected, as we have seen, and a few months later the Foreign Office learned that the Russians and Chinese were meeting to settle their Eastern Turkestan frontier.

THE THREAT OF RUSSIAN AGGRESSION

In Kashgar and Simla, officials began to press for a specific policy, one which dealt with Hunza, which was regarded as the crux of the problem. The Director Military Intelligence Kashgaria advised the Foreign Office on July 18, 1898:

> Before that province (Kashgaria) is absorbed by Russia, we should endeavour to secure a frontier which will keep her as far away as possible, lest when the time for actual demarcation arrives, we may find the Russians inconveniently near us on the Taghdumbash and Karakorum, as they are now on the north of Chitral.[31]

The Viceroy added his advice two days later:

> We think it expedient to settle with China the boundaries of Afghanistan, Hunza and Kashmir . . . We might claim rights

for Hunza over Taghdumbash and Raskam, but be prepared
to renounce them in exchange for Chinese renunciation of all
claims over Hunza. Our political control over Hunza and
Nagar is not relaxed.[32]

The India Office presented their case on October 27, 1898, to Lord
Salisbury in response to a request for precise information on the
demarcation of the Chinese frontier. Concurrent Chinese rights over
Hunza with Hunza's claims over Raskam and Taghdumbash were thus
explained: 'These Chinese rights within our borders would be embarrassing if they passed to Russia; while Hunza's counterclaims might
be valuable as a means of disentangling Hunza from the Chinese
claims.' They then proposed the following line of frontier:

> following the crest of the main watershed, except in respect of
> two tracts lying beyond it, which "there would be advantages
> in including within our sphere, viz. (a) Western end of the
> Taghdumbash Pamir because of its position between Hunza
> and the eastern extremity of Wakham, and at the entrance to
> the Kilik and Mintaka passes and (b) a small deviation from
> the main crest of the Mustagh, near the Shimshal pass to
> Darwaza, which is passable by cavalry. In 1889 a Kanjuti
> post was found at Darwaz, so this deviation was in accordance
> with the facts of occupation. The limits of these two tracts
> are clearly marked by natural features, and there would be no
> need for actual demarcation.[33]

This boundary was carefully worked out 'to get rid of the claims of
China over Hunza',[34] since it was assumed that at some future date
Russian would advance and succeed China. It was formulated in Sir
Claude Macdonald's Note to the Chinese Government on March 14,
1899.[35] (See Appendix). The Tsungli Yamen informed him on
April 7 that they had 'referred the question to the Governor of Chinese
Turkestan'[36] and would reply when they heard his views. Macartney
reported that the Governor favoured the proposal, but the Chinese
Government never replied to the Note, and British representatives in
the Legation were never instructed to press the matter. Yet the line
proposed by Macdonald gave China maximum claims. The proposed
boundary seems never to have been considered in the same form again
until Alastair Lamb revived it in 1964.[37]

The Ardagh boundary now became official policy. This is explained by the fact that once again in the story of India's northern frontier, the triangle of Britain-Russia-China was complicated by relations between Russia and China. The crux of the problem was the Raskam valley where China recognised Hunza's claims. Macartney telegraphed on April 16, 1899, that the Russians had threatened the Chinese that should they grant land in Raskam to Hunza, they (the Russians) would occupy Taghdarma in Sarikol and a place called Yegin, 12 miles inside the Chinese frontier from Irkeshtam.[38]

The Government of India challenged the right of Russia to make these threats. They had already sent a mission to Kashgar to forestall the Russians, and informed London:

> This district lies outside of frontier suggested by us in October last, and our claims are not, therefore, affected, but it is most desirable that Hunza should now be supported, and that Russian interference, which is animated by an unfriendly spirit towards England, and, if successful, will produce most unfortunate impression upon Hunza, should be discovered by Imperial Government, to whom it is probably unknown.[39]

Curzon, now Viceroy, advised Hamilton to support the Hunza claims, not because they 'have anything to do with our frontier – as a matter of fact they lie outside it; but because they are lands to which Hunza has a *bona fide* claim and over which China who exercises a sort of over-lordship in those districts has been willingly or voluntarily to admit her rights which she has occupied and cultivated more or less regularly for half a century; and which are essential to the expansion of her already much straitened population'.[40] It was not so much that Curzon favoured the Chinese but his imperial sense was offended by Russian behaviour. Of China's evocation of Hunza's freedom to cultivate the Raskam Valley, he wrote: 'That a bargain of this sort should be cancelled at the last moment owing to the bluster of Petrovoski at Kashgar, and to the threats of the Russian Minister at Peking, is, I think, quite inexcusable. Nor do I understand the reluctance of the Foreign Office to approach the Russian Government about an action so obviously unfriendly.'[41] Curzon and Hamilton were both anxious that the Hunza Mir should be supported. Unofficial protests were made in St Petersburg where Count Mouravieff replied 'that he was not aware that Russian agression had been threatened in Kashgar owing to the grant to Hunza'. In Peking, Bax-Ironside, after an interview with the Yamen reported to Salisbury that 'owing to the attitude of Russia, they could not carry out proposals to allow land in Raskam to be rented to Kanjutis. They had not settled their frontier with Russia, and any concession to India would be taken by the Russians as a pretext for making larger demands farther North'.[42]

Curzon continued to press the Hunza Mir's claims. The Hunza people, he said were causing no trouble to the British raj.

> Hence the necessity of converting into a permanent occupation, under the sanction of the Chinese authorities, the somewhat sporadic, though fairly continuous, settlements which they have hitherto effected in the valley of the Raskam River. Of all the tribes on the Hindu-Kush frontier the Hunza men are the most manly and the most loyal, and we must certainly stand by them in their trouble.[43]

The Russians suspected Curzon's concern for the Mir of Hunza. Their War Office held that the Mir's claims 'comprised lands in Sarikol extending in a northerly direction towards Taskurgan on the flank of the Taghdumbash Pamir'.

THE DECLINE OF CHINESE INFLUENCE

In March 1901, a Russian military post was established at Tashkurgan by agreement with the Chinese. Curzon described this as the 'first step to ultimate Russian claims over entire Taghdumbash and Sarikol'. China had 'ousted Hunza from Raskam' and he was 'prepared to send a British officer from time to time to Taghdumbash to vindicate our joint interests'.[44] Peking was diplomatically reproached and a great deal of shadow boxing took place as one Viceroy after another assumed that Russia would one day advance and China must be considered. The Curzon Government in 1904 decided that the connection between Hunza and China must be severed 'without delay'. The moment seemed opportune 'because the Mir of Hunza, owing to the increase of Russian influence in Chinese Turkestan, had grown sceptical as to the advantage of his connection with China, and had recently declared that, unless Raskam was to be included within the sphere of British influence, he would prefer to have nothing to do with the tract'. Curzon's plan was to make a formal notification to Peking that since they had been unable to fulfil their promises to the Mir, the British Government would now advise him 'to withdraw from all relations with China' and henceforth own suzerainty to the Kashmir State and the British Government alone'. The alternative was to tell China that since 'they had shown no grounds for dissenting from the proposals contained in Sir C. Macdonald's Note of the 14th March 1899, we should henceforth assumed Chinese concurrence and act accordingly'.[45] The Foreign Office did not approve, considering it inadvisable 'to make any communication to China on the subject of the boundary unless the Government of India were able to exercise effective control up to the frontier claimed'.[46] Instead they asked for information about how far Kanjutis had recently exercised rights in the western extremity of the Taghdumbash Pamir and what measures would be practicable 'for the effective assertion of Hunza rights in territory in question, in the event of China acting inconsistently with such rights' and 'for securing the observance of the frontier which it was proposed to treat as having been accepted by the Chinese'.[47]

The Government of India not only provided an answer to these questions, but proposed that China should be invited to forego all connection with Hunza and agree to the inclusion within the British frontier of a small projection beyond the watershed in the vicinity of the Shingshal Pass and Darwaza. In return, Britain would abandon all Hunza claims to Raskam and Taghdumbash, and, instead of pressing for the frontier embodied in the Macdonald letter, it would accept a frontier from peak Pavaloschveikovski following the watershed, except for the projection near Darwaza.[48] But the new Minister in Peking, Sir John Jordan, considered the proposed bargain as unacceptable to the Chinese. And he referred to the great difficulty of 'bringing the Chinese Government to agree to any rectification of frontiers in remote districts of which they have very imperfect geographical knowledge',[49] and once more, the Foreign Office turned down a proposal which might have offended China.

For the next three years the Hunza question was in abeyance. In 1911 Macartney reported that 'Russian dictatorship' was 'practically established' in Sarikol, when the Chinese gave way to Russian pressure to revise the Russo-Chinese Treaty of St Petersburg of 1881.[50] Russian troops were already mobilised on the northern frontier of Sinkiang. In the same year Archibald Rose, on retiring from his post as British Consul at Tengyueh, travelled home overland from India through Hunza and Kashgar. He too was willing to entertain any concessions to China which would strengthen her resistance to Russia. At Tash-kurgan he saw a 'tumble-down fort with 20 opium-sodden coolies in possession',[51] and learned of the Chinese Amban's desertion. There was a second fort, a Russian one, efficiently garrisoned by 35 Cossacks under a lively captain. His explanation that he was there to protect Russian trade was obviously unsatisfactory. Rose advocated action on behalf of the Mir of Hunza, and suggested that the Chinese should be given the Hpimaw district on the Burma-Yunnan border, but the suggestion was scotched by the 1911 Chinese Revolution. Outer Mongolia broke away and the Chinese were driven out of Tibet.

Now, it seemed to frontier strategists, was the opportunity for Russia to occupy Sinkiang and Kashgaria. China was no longer in a position to play Britain off against Russia and a settlement of the frontier was urgent. The India Office proposed (on July 12, 1912) that the whole question of Anglo-Russian relations should be reconsidered, and that 'H.M.G. should give Russia a free hand in Kashgar in return for ade-quate compensation elsewhere'[52] Lord Crewe suggested: 'This com-pensation might be found in Tibet.'[53] The India Office now outlined 'a new convention giving Russia a free hand in Chinese Turkestan, the New Dominion, and Outer Mongolia, and Great Britain a free hand in Tibet, and providing for the protection of Russian and British interests respectively should either Power eventually assume complete control of the districts in question'.[54]

In Kashgar Macartney predictably continued to maintain that the greatest danger was that the Russians would occupy Sinkiang and Kashmir. 'Russia would be brought thereby within 300 miles of Simla and 150 miles of Srinagar, and new and undesirable political conditions would inevitably be introduced by this propinquity in spite of difficult-ies of intervening country'.[55] If this should happen, the first essential, as the Government of India put it to Crewe in September 1912, was to 'demand that a boundary line placing Raskam, Aksai Chin, Shahi-dulla and Taghdumbash inside our territory and outside that of Russia' as a preliminary to negotiation. This was similar to the Ardagh Line. The idea of compensation being found in Tibet seemed to policy-makers in Kashgar an uncertain proposition since it might endanger relations with China.

But in the context of limiting Russian expansion the Ardagh boundary was accepted as the official one and was included as such in *The
Times* Atlas" and the "Oxford Atlas". The boundary west of the
Karakorum remained quiescent. In 1927, the Indian Government,
according to a report in *The Times**, 'decided that a claim of the Mir of
Kashmir that his dominions were bounded to the north by the northern
watershed of the Kuenlun ranges was insupportable' [56] and reverted to
a variant of the Macdonald-Macartney line. The Government of India
asked the Mir to abandon his grazing rights in the Taghdumbash area
and made a rectification of the resulting alignment in 1936.

The boundary west of the Karakorum was finally settled by China
and Pakistan on March 2, 1963 and marked on the ground for the first
time. But this runs ahead of the story.

* March 6, 1963.

China and Britain on the Frontier of India:
Britain Unchallenged

THE LOHIT VALLEY; THE DIHONG VALLEY;
THE MIRIS; THE DAPHLAS; THE AKAS; THE
MONPAS; BEYOND THE OUTER LINE;
CHALLENGE AND COUNTER-CHALLENGE;
CHINESE AND BRITISH ACTIVITIES IN THE
ASSAM HIMALAYAS; THE SECOND ABOR
EXPEDITION (1911); WEST OF THE SUBAN-
SIRI

The North-East frontier had played so insignificant a part in Britain's
Indian policy that Archibald Rose could describe it in 1911 as 'hazy in
its geographical limits, peaceful in its policies, and happy in the dull-
ness of its annals'. Assam had been added to the British Empire after
victory in the first Anglo-Burmese war (1824–1826). The area, though
undefined, included the Assam Himalaya. It was neither sufficiently
commercially attractive nor strategically relevant to warrant immediate
administration. Along the Himalayan foothills it was inhabited by
primitive tribal communities, separated from Tibetans on their high
plateau and from more sophisticated people in the plains of Assam.
Two main tracks connected them: one from Rima down through the
Lohit Valley, the other from Lhasa over the Se-La. The Lohit was the
more attractive; it was more readily accessible, it led to Rima, and
beyond to China. The track over the Se-La and through Tawang was
the most important link between Tibet and India.
    The tribal peoples of the North-East frontier of India – the Mishmis,
Abors, Daflas, Miris and Monpas – did not fit easily into any tidy
administrative scheme. It was easier to leave them alone in their

mountain fastnesses than to introduce them to the paraphernalia of imperial rule. Verrier Elwin describes the attitude of many Europeans who visited these tribal peoples as 'too often patronizing or scornful'. He quotes, most aptly, a leading article from *The Pioneer* in 1865: 'The only idea which most men had, with reference to the hills and forests (of Assam) was that they were the habitat of savage tribes, whose bloody raids and thieving forays threatened serious danger to the cause of tea.' [1]

Sir Thomas Holdich,* one of India's greatest surveyors, once described them as 'neither Tibetan nor Assamese; their origin and ethnographical extraction is conjectural, and they are in social ethics, in manners and customs, amongst the most irreclaimable savages in the world. . . . They are but half clothed aborigines of those jungles which they infest, and which they are determined to keep to themselves. Above all, they are profoundly impressed with the notion that we are afraid of them'.[2]

In 1875 the skeleton of an orderly administration was drawn up by applying to these tribal peoples the Bengal Eastern Frontier Regulations of 1873. This formalised the results of half a century of expansion stimulated in 1826. The Treaty of Yandabo which ended the first Anglo-Burmese War, had halted Burmese expansion and provided Britain with the springboard of Assam. People living in these newly-acquired territories had never before had contact with the Western world. The Mishmis, even those who lived nearest to British territories, were constantly in touch with Tibetans. The Abors had trade contacts with Tibet. Colonel Dalton,† an ethnologist, described them as

---

* Sir Thomas Holdich served on the NW Frontier with scarcely a break from 1878 till 1898. He accompanied frontier campaigns as well as the Afghan wars, surveying the borderland beyond the Indus. In 1896, the remainder of Russia's southern boundary on the Pamir was demarcated. Holdich mapped the country along the new boundary, planned in such a way that a small finger of Afghan territory in Wakhan was extended to join the province of Chinese Turkestan on the Taghdumbash Pamir.

† Edward T. Dalton was born in 1815, joined the Bengal Staff Corps, of which he became a colonel in 1872 and a major-general three years before he died in 1880.

In 1845 he visited the hills in the neighbourhood of the Subansiri river, and then went on to Membu in the Abor country in 1855. In 1851 he was Political Assistant Commissioner, and in 1855 became Principal Assistant to the Governor General's Agent in Assam. His 35 pages on the North-East Frontier in his classic *Descriptive Ethnology of Bengal* is the ablest document on the subject in the 19th century.

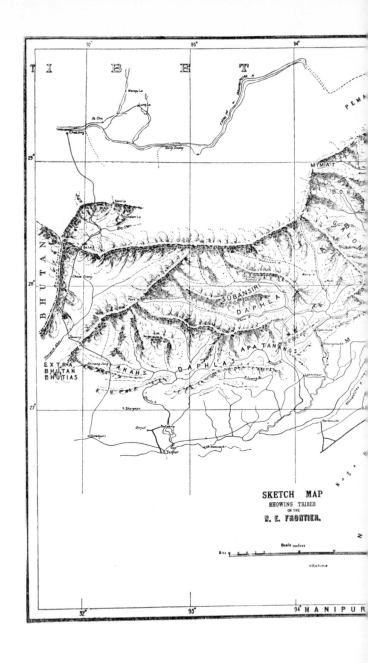

SKETCH MAP
SHOWING TRIBES
ON THE
N. E. FRONTIER.

Scale
Miles

MAP 10. *The Tribes on the North-East Frontier.*

'wearing coats, and possessing pipes of metal, vessels, swords, and beads, of Tibetan or of Chinese manufacture; but for some reason they throw a veil of mystery over their intercourse, and always repudiating direct trade with Tibetans, tell you of the existence of barbarous tribes on the high snowy ranges behind them; and you meet with no one of the clan who will acknowledge to have passed this barrier of savages'.[3] He wrote of the Daflas: 'They are in communication with the Tibetans as they possess many articles of Tibetan or Chinese manufacture, but like the Dihong Abors and Hill Miris, they tell wild stories of the savages between them and Tibet.' [4]

Mountains preserved the identities of these tribal groups; they came into touch with each other to fight, or when they had trekked down to the fairs at Udalgiri or Sadiya. In 1876, some 3600 tribesmen were at the Udalgiri Fair. They brought ponies, sheep, dogs, salt, a little gold, blankets, yak's tails, musk, chillies, spice, wax, madder, oranges and walnuts, and bought in exchange English and Assamese cloth, thread, rice, betel-nuts, iron and brass utensils and hoes. The Sadiya Fair attracted an equal, and later, a larger number, catering for the Abors, Miris, Mishmis, Singphos and Khamtis. Fireworks, elephants and dancing girls make it a colourful affair. Traders from all parts of Tibet and places east and west of the town were there, some of them wearing Chinese clothes and looking Chinese, as Tibetans would to an European eye.

THE LOHIT VALLEY

Explorations and expeditions had penetrated these tribal areas before the Bengal Eastern Frontier Regulations were applied to them. The distinction between exploration and expeditions is subtle. Explorers often combined curiosity about mountain and stream with a calculation about their value as boundary, while political agents invariably displayed the toughness and imagination of the explorer. When Assam was acquired by the Treaty of Yandabo, the large area of the Himalayas which we now know as the North East Frontier Agency, was open for exploration and promenade, the official term for punitive expeditions, or merely showing the flag. R. Wilcox was the first to explore the Lohit Valley, the most accessible track leading up from Sadiya to Rima, in Tibet, and beyond into China. Between 1825 and 1828 Wilcox made a number of surveys, reaching three quarters of the way up the valley towards Rima. His most sympathetic records about the Mishmis who live in that part of Assam appeared in *Asiatic Researches*.[5] at the time, and extracts from them nearly a century and a half later were included in Verrier Elwin's *India's North-East Frontier in the Nineteenth Century*.[6]

Dr William Griffith, a botanist, and Dr MacClelland, a geologist, took Assam in their stride. They were interested in developing the cultivation of tea, but they had an eye for much besides in the Mishmi Hills 'from the debouchment of the Lohit to about ten miles east of the Ghalums'. Dr Griffith's diary of travels in the Mishmi Hills – as well as those in Burma, Bhutan and Afghanistan – is a fascinating study of the fauna among these rich and varied landscapes.[7] E. A. Rowlatt made an expedition to the Mishmi Hills in 1845 and wrote about the people and their customs in the *Journal of the Asiatic Society of Bengal*,[8] and two years later John Butler, who lived in Assam for fourteen years described the Mishmis in his book on Assam, written, as he records, 'to make Assam better known, to remove some prejudices against it, and preserve the memory of many remarkable scenes.' [9] Finally, we must recall the exploits of Father Crick, who, with his friend Father Bourri, went on foot from Gauhati 'with his cross, his flute, sextant and medicine-chest' as far as Rima. They made the journey a second time, but in October 1854, in the Mishmi Hills, they were both murdered by a powerful Digaru Mishi Chief. Revenge was a frequent incentive in the spread of empire, Lord Dalhousie sent a small party of the Assam Light Infantry into the Mishmi country to exact it in the following year. They 'pressed on by forced marches, swinging across dangerous torrents on bridges of single canes, climbing for hours at a time without water and in better cold, till in the grey dawn of a misty morning' [10] this punitive expedition surprised the murderer chief, killed his two elder sons, scattered his people, destroyed his village and tried and hanged him in Dibrugarh jail, but not before he had killed two of his warders.

Two other travellers into the Mishmi Hills, before they were prescribed beyond the Outer Line, were Thomas Thronvill Cooper and William Robinson, Cooper, determined to reach China from India, since the Chinese refused him permission to reach India from China, left Sadiya in October 1869 and reached the village of Prun, twenty miles from Rima. He described his adventures and his forced return in *New Routes for Commerce*. Robinson belonged to the Gauhati Government Seminary. Unmoved by the prospect of extending the tea trade of Assam, but thinking that tea traders should be well informed, he wrote *Account of Assam*, which Verrier Elwin calls 'one of the first of the gazetteers'.[11] Many of his articles on the

languages of the Mishmis, as well as of other tribes of the North East
Frontier Agency, appeared in the *Journal of the Asiatic Society of Bengal*.

THE DIHONG VALLEY

On the east and west banks of the Dihong are the Abors; the word
Abor means independent, and the Abors, living on high mountain
ranges, densely forested, intersected with fast-flowing rivers, lived up
to that description. The original Abors were said to have come from
the high mountain ranges between Tibet and Assam and to have
spread from that area. They all claimed their right to hunt in the
forests and wash gold in the rivers at the foot of their hills, as well as
an 'absolute sovereignty over the Miris of the plains'.[12] This, as the
Government of Assam explained to the Government of India, 'necessarily brought them into conflict with British authority.' Until 1862
the history of British relations was 'an unprofitable list of raids and
depredations on their part and of expensive and ineffectual attempts at
reprisals on ours'.[13] There were differences of opinion about these
independent raiders. Military Intelligence called them the 'most ruthless savages on the whole of the northern frontier', but the Government
of East Bengal had 'a high opinion of their own strength and importance'.[14] On November 5, 1862, the Meyong Abors signed an agreement with the Government of Bengal at Camp Lalee Mukh, whereby
their acts of hostility 'towards the British Government, and for which
the assembled heads of villages have sued for pardon, are overlooked
and peace is re-established'. Major H. S. Bivar, Deputy Commissioner
Upper Assam, Agent to the Governor-General N. E. Frontier, signed
this agreement with 34 Meyong Abor Chiefs. If, in future, they met
him, they engaged, 'in earnest of their continued friendly feeling . . .
to make a tribute offering of a pig and fowls, in exchange for . . . usual
suitable acknowledgments'. The Deputy Commissioner, on his part,
agreed to provide yearly '100 iron-hoes, 30 maunds of salt, 80 bottles
of rum, 2 seers of Abkaree opium and 2 maunds of tobacco'. Important
clauses of this agreement laid down:

> 1. The limit of the British Territory which extends to the
>   foot of the hills is recognised by the Meyong Abors, who
>   hereby engage to respect it;
> 2. The British Government will take up positions on the

frontier in the plains, will establish stations, post guards, or construct forts, or open roads, as they may be deemed expedient, and the Meyong Abors will not take umbrage at such arrangements, or have any voice in such matters;

3. The Meyong Abors engage not to molest or to cross the frontier for the purpose of molesting residents in the British territory;

4. The Meyong Abors shall have access to markets and places of trade which they may think fit to resort to, and on such occasions they engage not to come armed with their spears and bows and arrows, but merely to carry their *daos*;

5. Any Meyong Abors desiring to settle, or occupy lands, in the British Territory, engage to pay such revenue to Government as may be fixed upon by the Deputy Commissioner, the demand, in the first instance, to be light.[15]

Other villages followed the example of the Meyong (or Minyong) Abors, and although some of them were reported to have eaten the treaty to show their contempt for it, they continued to appear regularly to receive their gifts.

THE MIRIS

The Miris, west and south-west of the Abors, with whom they had some kind of servile relationship, were 'quiet and inoffensive' people, and their backwardness was such that Colonel Dalton wrote of them, in his definitive work on the anthropology of tribal peoples, 'I suppose there are no people on the face of the earth more ignorant of arts and manufacture than the tribe I am treating of. They are decently clad, because they can exchange the wild produce of their hills for clothes, and they purchase clothes with the money received from Government as blackmail commutations; but they cannot make for themselves any article of clothing, unless the cane bands and bamboo crinolines can be so called.'[16] He thought that they seemed satisfied with an annual allowance of money, salt and rum which the British Government agreed to pay them.

THE DAPHLAS

North and west of the Miris, in country 60 miles from east to west and about 40 miles from north to south, were the Daphlas. From the beginning of the British occupation of Burma in 1826, 'the Daphlas gave much trouble to the local officers' who tried in vain to persuade them to give up the rights given them by the Assam Government in 1825 to collect from every ten houses 'one double cloth, one single cloth, one handkerchief, one dao, ten head of horned cattle, and four seers of salt'. The Daphlas had an unsavoury reputation; in the 17th Century they were described as alone refusing to 'place its feet in the skirt of obedience', people who, after carrying off a number of Assamese subjects, were said to be 'captured only if an elephant can enter into a rat-hole', and, later, in the 18th Century, as having the 'fierce and warlike spirit of the ancient Assamese', indulging 'in eating unclean food as much as the impure nations of China and Europe'.[17] By 1852, thr *posa* (gift) was finally commuted for a money payment. Until then tribal raids disturbed the peace of the Subansiri area and military posts were placed along the frontier. Once again in 1872, the Tagin Daphlas raided a village, killed two people, and captured forty-four others, believing that the plains people were responsible for an epidemic of smallpox. They were blockaded for their unwillingness to release the captives. When this had no effect, a military force was sent into their hills in 1874–5, and the captives were released.

THE AKAS

The Akas, living to the west of the Daphlas, in the hills in an angle formed by Assam and Bhutan, were difficult to reach. Expeditions were 'costly out of all proportion to the damage inflicted on the enemy'.[18] 'They are in two clans, (i) the Hazari-Khawa, or "eaters of a thousand hearths" and (ii) the Kapachoes, or "thieves who lurk amid the cotton plants".' The Hazari-Khawas, before Britain acquired Assam, were entitled to receive from their allotted household 'one portion of a female dress, one bundle of cotton thread, and one cotton hand-kerchief'.[19] The idea that these tribal people could collect their annual dues from the plains peoples upset the British administrative mind, and it was only in 1842, after a number of skirmishes, that the payment in kind was commuted, the Akas, in return, promising to keep the peace of the frontier. (They swore according to their customs by taking in their hands the skin of a tiger and a bear and elephant's dung, and by killing a fowl.) This agreement seems to have worked, as there were few disturbances from that time onwards. Their frontier line was demarcated with those tribes to the west of them in 1872–1873.

THE MONPAS

West and south of the Akas in the Tawang area were the Monpas, people of the same race as the Bhutanese but in 1875 still ecclesiastically subject to Tibet. To the east of Tawang Bhutias claimed independence both of Tibet and Bhutan. The Monpa monastery which paid dues to Tibet was the centre of their culture.

In 1875 these Monpas were relegated beyond what was called the Outer Line by the Bengal Eastern Frontier Regulation. It represented the 'external territorial frontier' which was demarcated that year as far east as the Baroi river. Beyond this point the boundary followed 'a readily recognisable line along the foot of the hills' as far as Nizamghat and was said to be 'throughout well recognised by usage'.[20] In that part which was Abor country the Treaty of Camp Lalee Mukh in 1862 acknowledged that 'the British territory which extends to the foot of the hills will be respected by the Abors'.[21] Beyond Nizamghat there was no defined territorial border; the only recognised frontier was 'the purely jurisdictional or administrative line' laid down by the Regulation of 1873. In short, there was no 'outer line' east of Nizamghat, dividing the administered areas of rich tea plantations in the plains and the underdeveloped stretches of poorer lands from which the tribal peoples might be tempted to make raids. They did not always resist such temptation. The Inner Line was in practice a boundary maintained at the Lieutenant-Governor's discretion. Beyond it British subjects were prohibited from crossing without a licence. It ran along the whole of the northern frontier of Darrang and Lakhimpur districts and represented 'the limits of the Deputy Commissioner's ordinary, as distinguished from his political jurisdiction'.[22] The area between the Outer and Inner Lines varied; it sometimes ran less than ten miles apart.

The Outer Line acquired a significance far beyond the expectations or indeed the plans of the 1870s. Between the Outer Line and the MacMahon Line in Alastair Lamb's map [12] the area is approximately that which was claimed by the Chinese in 1959. It is true that British rulers gradually extended a shadowy administration into this territory between 1873 and 1914 when it was formalised in the MacMahon Line. But it is not true as the Chinese claim today, that they were under their rule, or, with the exception of part of the Tawang tract, under that of Tibet. Alastair Lamb contends that the British considered these tribal areas, 'while not under British administration

E

in any sense of the word, as yet falling within the British sphere of influence. There was no need to define the question further, it was felt, because there was no other sphere of influence in the immediate neighbourhood into which they could fall. Was this true?' [23] We shall see that it was not.

BEYOND THE OUTER LINE

Beyond the Outer Line, where the country was largely unexplored, the Survey of India set in motion a systematic collection of geographical, commercial and strategic data by men some of whom were to become famous as explorers. Some combined the duties of Political Officer with the more romantic assignment of tracking streams to their sources, finding their way over mountain passes and tracks known before only to local tribesmen. The follow-up of geographical knowledge by military expeditions against tribal peoples, who neither invited them nor wished to change their customs, is a long story. It can be traced in the diaries and reports of British officers who assumed the right to plant the British flag wherever they chose, to occupy lands to which they had not the slightest claim, and to mark out frontiers along watersheds which were almost inaccessible.

Naturally enough the tribal people did not always welcome British intrusion. The Abors, overcrowded in their settlements in the high mountain ranges between Assam and Tibet, tried to move down into the valley of Assam through the gorge of the Dihong, and thence to spread out over the foothills where there was more room and better land. This did not suit the British administration then centred in Sadiya. Major G. W. Beresford was sent out with three hundred officers and men of the 43rd Assam Light Infantry to stop them, to build stockades at Bomjur and Nizamghat, but to avoid hostilities. This was only achieved with difficulty, and eventually a special officer was appointed to conduct British relations with the Abors in particular and with the tribes bordering on Sadiya. J. F. Needham of the Bengal Police was posted to Assam as Assistant Political Officer in Sadiya in 1882.* He remained there for 23 years, and made numerous expedi-

---

* J. F. Needham served in Sadiya for twenty-three years. He originally belonged to the Bengal Police. In 1885–6 he visited the Mishmi Hills and the next year the Hukong valley of Burma. He crossed the Patkoi Range to Burma in 1891, and two years later accompanied the military expedition into the Abor

tions to the Mishmi Hills, the Abor Hills and over the Patkoi Range
to Burma. The *Assam Gazetteer* credited him with having laid the
foundations of the modern North-East Frontier of Assam.

Between December 1885 and January 1886, J. F. Needham and Capt
E. H. Molesworth travelled from Sadiya up the course of the Brahma-
putra into the Zayul valley, where the river emerges into the plains of
Assam. They were the only two Europeans who had travelled this way
since 1855 when Lt. Eden had captured the murderers of the two
French missionaries Crick and Bourri. Needham and Molesworth, by
following the Brahmaputra along its whole course from Sadiya to
Rima established the fact that the Brahmaputra was identical with the
Zayul. This was to prove vitally important when, in 1893, Needham
acted as Political Officer with a military expedition into the Abor Hills,
a heavy-handed reprisal for the murder of three of his sepoys. One
point at issue was that Needham neither returned nor gave compensation for runaway slaves, and another was that he 'had gone himself
and taken other Sahibs shooting and fishing in the rivers'.[24] He maintained that this raised the question

> whether the country between the Brahmaputra and the hills
> is ours or theirs, and whether the Miris residing there and
> paying us revenue are British subjects or theirs. Both points
> are provided for in the treaty which was eaten.[25]

Needham was a ruthless Political Officer. He gained the reluctant
permission of the Chief Commissioner to take a party a long way up
the Yamne river in unknown country to punish the villages of Damroh
– a centre of sedition, as he saw it. The Chief Commissioner categorised
his punishments

> as severe as it is possible for an expeditionary force to inflict
> on the hill tribes on this frontier. We have now proved to the
> Abors for the first time that we can march throughout their
> country from one end to the other with the greatest ease, and
> destroy every village they have, their cattle, their household
> goods, and their crops.[26]

Hills. In this, as in the expedition against the Mishmis two years later he was
strongly criticised for his impulsive behaviour. He wrote many and detailed
reports of these expeditions and compiled outline grammars of the languages
spoken by the tribal people in this Sadiya area.

Six years later he realised that the wrong villages had been destroyed, and Needham led a second punitive expedition to punish the guilty ones. The blunders of this punitive expedition were such that Curzon recorded in a Minute that 'so far from regarding this expedition as having been satisfactory, either in its inception or in its results, I hold it to have been marked by a serious miscalculation from the start, by a sacrifice of life which ought, with reasonable precautions, to have been avoided, by an expenditure of money for which there has been no proportionate return and by political and scientific results that are all but worthless . . . Finally, to cap the whole story, the Bebejiyas, who were the objects of the expedition, who had hitherto been described "as a fierce race of cannibals, a very savage, bloodthirsty and dangerous race", were discovered by the Political Officer to be a petty community of only 3000 to 4000 souls (including not more than 1500 adult men) who are described by him as "on the whole a well behaved and inoffensive tribe, very desirous of being on friendly terms with us" '.[27] Needham admitted his mistake, but the harm was done.

These punitive expeditions, with which Needham's name was so closely associated, were well beyond the Outer Line laid down by the Bengal Eastern Frontier Regulation. They extended effective British political control into areas which were later to become the North East Frontier Agency. Meanwhile tension developed in the Upper Lohit Valley where China was making rival claims.

CHALLENGE AND COUNTER-CHALLENGE

Until the arrival of the Younghusband Mission in 1904 suggested a potential rival in Tibet, China had never shown any interest in the areas between the Outer Line and the Himalayan ranges. Louis King, writing from the excellent listening point of Tachienlu wrote:

> The action taken by the Indian Government in 1903–1904 would appear to have caused China to contemplate the possibility of a British protectorate over Tibet, and steps were at once taken to earmark as much territory on the western border of Szechuan as possible.[28]

Chinese suzerainty over Tibet dated from 1720, when Lhasa was first occupied, but

no attempt to administer any of the territory was made until
after the British expedition to Lhasa in 1903 had given China
cause to fear the responsibility of losing her paramount
position in Tibet.[29]

The Lohit Valley was an extension of this interest.

In a series of events which led one by one to the Simla Conference
China's first step was to incorporate the territory of the King
of Chala (Tachienlu was the capital) into the province of Szechuan.
Two years later, after helping to suppress a tribal revolt in the Marches,
Chao Erh-feng was appointed Warden of the Marches of Szechuan
and Yunnan. Three years' campaigning led by Chao Erh-feng brought
a large part of this territory under Chinese administration. In 1908 he
was ordered to march on Lhasa. The Dalai Lama, who had just returned to Lhasa – he had been in exile since the Younghusband expedition – saw the danger of Tibet's becoming a province of China,
and appealed to Britain to intervene with the Chinese to stop the despatch
of their troops. Peking said 'that the troops were only being sent to
police the trade routes as provided under the Trade Regulation',[30] and
the Amban in Lhasa gave similar assurances to the Tibetans. When the
Chinese troops appeared in spite of these assurances, they met with
practically no resistance and reached Lhasa in February 1910. The
Dalai Lama escaped to India. He stayed in Darjeeling until 1912 where
he formed an intimate relationship with Charles Bell which was to
prove decisive in Britain's Tibetan policy. Indeed, H. E. Richardson,
second only to Charles Bell in his profound knowledge and appreciation of Tibet's political and cultural background, describes 1910 as 'a
turning point in the relations between China and Tibet [marking] a
break with previous Chinese policy'.[31]

Chinese rule in Lhasa now seemed established. The Dalai Lama was
in exile. The Chinese government issued a proclamation deposing
him. Lien-yu, the Chinese Amban, took over the administration,
reducing the Tibetan officials to puppets. More than 3000 Chinese
troops 'hastily enlisted in Szechuan' were sent to Lhasa. Tieh-tseng Li
describes many of them as 'belonging to the Ko-lai-hui, a secret
society composed of both national revolutionaries and hoodlums'.[32]

British policy-makers did not remain indifferent to these indications
of a 'forward' policy which bade fair to challenge them along the whole
Tibetan frontier. Charles Bell warned:

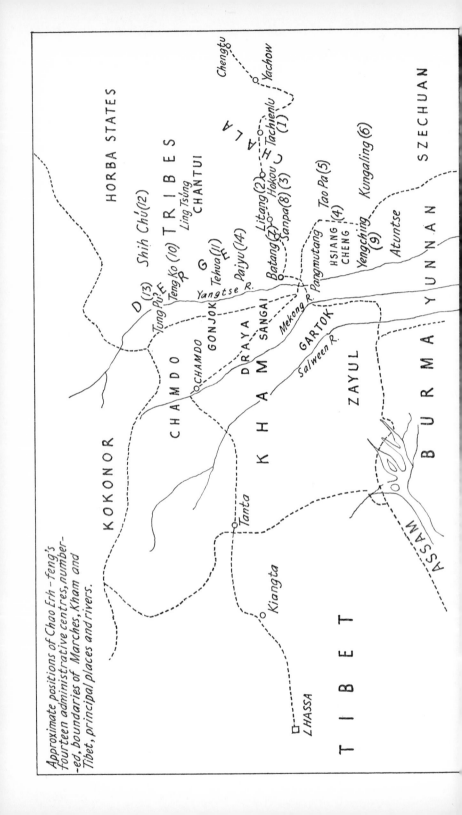

Approximate positions of Chao Erh-feng's fourteen administrative centres, number-ed, boundaries of Marches, Kham and Tibet, principal places and rivers.

HORBA STATES

KOKONOR

SZECHUAN

Chengtu

Yachow

TRIBES

Shih Chʻu (12)

Ling Tsung

CHANTUI

Tachienlu (1)

Litang (2)

Hokou (7)

Sanpa (8) (3)

Tao Pa (5)

HSIANG CHENG (4)

Yengching (9)

Kungaling (6)

Atuntse

YUNNAN

D (13)

Tengko (10)

Tehua (11)

Paiyu (14)

Tung Pu

Yangtse R.

Batang

Pangmutang

CHAMDO

GONJOK

DRAYA

SANGAI

Mekong R.

GARTOK

KHAM

Salween R.

CHAMDO

ZAYUL

BURMA

ASSAM

Tanta

Kiangta

TIBET

LHASSA

If the Chinese regain control over Tibet, later on they will pay special attention to the development and consolidation of the at present thinly populated but warm and fertile districts in the southwest of Tibet, which are not far from Assam and from which districts, when developed, a considerable army could be fed. The Tawang district borders directly on Assam. The Chinese are moreover likely to intrigue with Indians for the undermining of British rule in India.[33]

Not every report could be confirmed, and troop movements were almost certainly exaggerated, but J. E. Shuckburgh produced a Memorandum describing Chinese activities 'along the whole Tibetan frontier from Gartok in the West to Rima in the extreme East, and also along the entire length of the Yunnan border from the Khampti country in the North to Keng Tung in the South'.[34]

From his vantage point in Gangtok, Charles Bell reported that the Chinese were planning a new road from Batang to Lhasa, very near tribal territory. A 'very confidential' evaluation he wrote at this time puts the situation in perspective.

> Until the recent Tibet Mission, and the resulting growth of Chinese power in Tibet. . . . China had very little power and there were no signs of her being aggressive on the Indian frontier. . . . The position is now completely changed, China is becoming every year more formidable as a military Power. She has seized the power in Tibet and is increasing her military strength there more and more. Only a narrow stretch of territory intervenes between her conquests and the plains of India. And these conditions apply to 1,100 miles of frontier, i.e. from the north-west corner of Nepal to the north-east corner of Assam. Over 800 miles of this frontier we have but few troops.
>
> It is of vital importance to keep China and all foreign Powers out of this narrow stretch of territory. . . . Two things are essential as regards this zone. The first is to keep China out of it. The second is to keep British and Indian vested interests out of it as far as possible, and to avoid responsibilities in its internal administration.[35]

In the struggle that developed in this area between Britain and China the attitude of the border tribes was crucial. Their primitive villages were the point of contact of two expanding imperialisms. Charles Bell suggested that the most suitable policy for these tribal peoples would be control somewhat on the lines of the treaty he had recently concluded with Bhutan.

> This would prevent for ever the establishment of Chinese agents or the stationing of Chinese or Tibetan troops in these countries. It would in fine prevent any Chinese menace on this part of our frontier, a part, which in years to come is certain to be of much greater importance than at present.[36]

He was aware that much too little was known about these tribal people 'with whom fresh arrangements are desirable' and suggested that several points should be established about them: how far the territory of the tribe stretches in towards Tibet from the Indian frontier; how far the country was cultivable; to what extent the tribal territory would act as a barrier to invaders; 'whether the tribe has in any way recognised the suzerainty of Tibet or China. The claims of these countries to suzerainty are often so shadowy that it would be well to clear up the point as far as possible'[37]; and the possibility of inducing the tribe to sign such a treaty.

Bell reinforced his plea for a more active policy along the frontier by quoting from a military resumé dealing with the possibility of an actual invasion of Assam through the territory of these border tribes. It bluntly observed

> that Assam would ever stand the slightest chance of being invaded by a civilised military Power has never been contemplated, and consequently no strategic plan, no defences, no organisation whatever exists to repel a serious invasion.[38]

The pundits considered that 'the San-po valley with an advance base probably in the neighbourhood of Rima . . . and the Hukong valley as a base' were the vital points to secure in the event of an invasion of the North-East Frontier, and these, Bell specified, were 'precisely the places, in which the Chinese have of late pushed their intrigues most strongly. The boundary advocated by Military Intelligence ran 'approximately from the east of the wedge-shaped portion of Tibetan territory (Tawang district) which runs down to the British frontier north of Udalgiri, in a north-easterly direction to the Zayul Chu, as far east and as near Rima as possible; thence across the Zayul Chu – Irrawaddy divide: and then along that divide until it joins the Irrawaddy divide'.[39]

The dilemma of British frontier policy at the end of 1910 is reflected in the Viceroy's despatch to the Earl of Crewe, then Secretary of State for India.

> There was the danger on the one hand that, if the Chinese were permitted to advance to the foot of the hills bordering on the Brahmaputra, serious administrative inconvenience might result. On the other hand, it was felt that an extension of our territory right up to the Tibetan frontier might entail collision with hostile tribes and involve us in obligations which it would be inconvenient to assume.[40]

When Minto was Viceroy the Government finally arrived at the conclusion that 'the best means of safeguarding the frontier from Chinese aggression would be to push forward the present "outer line" so as to obtain a good strategical boundary under our control' and to make a further reassurance move by extracting agreements from the tribal peoples 'within or beyond the line binding them to have no relations or intercourse with any foreign Power than ourselves'. Such a policy was not immediately practicable; neither the areas nor the people who lived in them were well enough known to risk the strategic frontier envisaged without further exploration. The man on the spot, Sir Lancelot Hare, strongly advocated a forward policy to Lord Hardinge when they met in Calcutta on November 22, 1910. Hardinge deprecated any forward movement beyond the administrative frontier, believing that 'Chinese aggression would be met, not in the tribal territory bordering Assam, but by attack on the coast of China'.[41] So why, he held, should money be spent on creating strategic frontiers? Hare was not satisfied; a letter, following up the Calcutta discussion, put the strongest argument he could build to persuade Hardinge to think again.

> We only now claim suzerainty up to the foot of the hills. We have an inner line and an outer line. Up to the inner line

we administer in the ordinary way. Between the inner and the outer lines we only administer politically. That is, our Political Officer exercises a very loose jurisdiction, and to prevent troubles with frontier tribes passes are required for our subjects who want to cross the inner line. The country between the two lines is very sparsely inhabited and is mostly dense jungle.

Now should the Chinese establish themselves in strength or obtain complete control up to our outer line, they could attack us whenever they pleased and defence would be extremely difficult. . . . It seems to me, in view of the possibility of the Chinese pushing forward, that it would be a mistake not to put ourselves in a position to take up suitable strategic points of defence. It is true in any trial of strength between England and China the contest would not probably be decided on this frontier, but we should be bound to defend our valuable tea gardens, and unless we had suitable positions this would be extremely difficult, and we could very easily be greatly harrassed and put to great expense and have to maintain an unduly large force on this frontier.

He wanted the Viceroy to send out men who would tour the frontier villages, improve trade routes and give presents for friendly services and information. He concluded:

When we have already established ourselves by friendly relations, as in the country on extreme east up to Sati on the road from Sadiya to Rima, we should maintain our present standing and should forbid China stepping in. After all if China press forward, we must forbid further progress some day, and at this point of our frontier I do not think we can safely allow the Chinese to advance beyond Sati.[42]

The Viceroy was not convinced by the Lieutenant Governor's arguments. He asked Crewe to endorse his proposal to have Hare 'instruct his frontier officers that they should confine themselves as hitherto, cultivating friendly relations with the tribes beyond the "outer line" and punishing them for acts of hostility within our limits' He was in favour of explorations beyond the outer line if they were possible 'without risk of complications', but he deprecated 'any general increase of activity' or any sort of promise to the tribes that they could rely on Britain's support or protection in the event of Tibetan or Chinese aggression.

CHINESE AND BRITISH ACTIVITIES IN THE ASSAM HIMALAYAS

From now onwards both British and Chinese focused more attention on the Assam Himalayas. Chinese officials were sent to probe the loyalties of tribal peoples and British explorers, who acted as political agent whether or not they were on the payroll of Intelligence, collected a great deal of geographical and strategic data in the area. Capt F. M. Bailey was one of the most outstanding among them and a prolific writer. In four months he travelled from Peking to Kahap via Rima and Mishmi country, making careful observations which were to become the basis of several famous books. His official report outlined the points of tension in the Assam Himalayas.

1. The Chinese are in effectual occupation of the Upper waters of the Irrawaddy and Tara Wan rivers along my route. This country is inhabited by Tibetans.
2. The Chinese in South-eastern Tibet have not extended their influence down these rivers, south of my route, but the Chinese from Yunnan may have come from the east into the Irrawaddy valley south of my route.
3. The country called Chiu Tzu, which according to the maps extends from the Zayul Chu – Tara Wan watershed (east of Rima) on the west, to the frontier of Yunnan, on the east, has not been occupied by the Chinese in the western part, i.e. the valley of the Tara Wan.
4. The Chinese have been attempting to enter into relations with the Mishmis, but up to the present have not suc- ceeded.
5. This summer the Chinese have had considerable fighting in Pomed and are subduing that country.[43]

Bailey certainly exceeded his instructions, though Jordan, describing the journey to Grey, pointed out with relief, 'I have received no complaint from the Chinese Government and, little as I anticipated that Captain Bailey would make so hazardous a venture, I cannot but think that the experience, through which he has fortunately come, of a region particularly interesting to us and hitherto untraversed by a European, may be of great value to our administration in that part of the Empire'. But Bailey did not altogether escape censure; the Government of India wrote to him: 'Your proceedings were in contravention of the instructions given you by Sir John Jordan, and it is impossible that you should have been unaware of the stringent rule about exploration in tribal territory beyond the outer line of the Assam border; moreover it cannot be overlooked that your infringement of the rules referred to might have led to grave consequences.[44]

Bailey's intelligence reports were related to the strategically placed Lohit Valley, and to Rima, the Tibetan village which commanded it. When he passed through Rima on his way back to Sadiya, he had met two Mishmi headmen at Tini (two days south of Rima and three miles north of the Chinese boundary flags) who told him they were on their way to visit the Chinese official at Chikung, a Chinese military post 35 miles north-east of Rima. Apparently Chinese from Zayul (in which Rima and Chikung were situated) had sent a Tibetan messenger to them some months before, summoning them to make their submission at Chikung. They refused, with the result that they were threatened with military action if they disobeyed a second summons. This was why they were on their way to Chikung, but before actually going there they planned to attend a gathering of Mishmis to be held in Tini. Bailey advised them to consult the Political Officer at Sadiya before visiting Chikung, assuming, of course, that in the undeclared cold war between Britain and China in the Assam Himalayas these Mishmis would look to Britain. They did, in fact, turn back, and stayed with Captain Bailey until they reached their own villages. Bailey's growing suspicions of Chinese activities were confirmed by two Tibetans, who told him that a month before they had received orders to bring in Mishmi headmen to the Chinese official at Chikung within fifteen days, under pain of decapitation should they fail to do so. They had persuaded a few of them, but not within the time specified, and daily expected punishment.

Chinese activity on the Mishmi border was considered a serious enough threat to British intentions to warrant a Memorandum by the expert in the Political and Secret Department. Tibetans, he reported, had shown orders to the Chief of Pangum village received from Chinese officials, who ordered them to cut a track from Tibet to Assam broad enough for two horsemen to ride abreast. 'The Chief refused to obey, saying that he was a British subject, and that he declined to take orders from anyone except the Assistant Political Officer at Sadiya'. Again, a Miju Miri named Halam had reported to the Assistant Political Officer that 'the Chinese had established a firm control over Rima, and had planted flags near the River Yepuk, a tributary of the upper Lohit, but that they had not attempted to assert sovereignty beyond what might be argued to be the limits of Tibet'.[45]

The Chief of Pangum village was a source of very useful information when, in October 1911, Mr W. C. M. Dundas led a mission to the Mishmi country.* Only a month earlier, the Chief said, Tibetan lamas sent by the Chinese summoned him and his fellow headmen to go to Rima 'for a purpose to be disclosed on their arrival'. They refused, suspecting that the 'purpose' was to recruit them in the campaign against Pomed which the Chinese were known to be organising. Again, during the previous rainy season, a party of Chinese had turned up in the Taroan section of the Mishmi country, having travelled from the north via the Glei Dakhru pass. According to the headman of Taroa, they demanded that this and other villages should open the road down the Dilli river (a tributary of the Lohit) and allow them to use it. 'To this the tribesmen replied that the road was very bad and that the Chinese should use the Lohit road, which was the road the British also used. The Chinese then gave the Headman a piece of paper with some writing on it, which they said should be shown both to the Chinese and British; this the Taraons did not take. Next the Chinese produced a flag and ordered the tribesmen to set it up at the confluence of the Dilli and Lohit. This they also refused to do, replying that if the Chinese wished to plant flags they must do it themselves. The Chinese then produced nine loads of salt, which they gave to the villagers saying that they should eat Chinese salt as well as British. Mazanon stated that his

* W. C. M. Dundas belonged to the Police and was appointed an Assistant Political Officer to the Abor Expedition in 1911.

He was later in chief political control of the Mishmi Expedition. He led the Lohit Valley column which reached the Yepak river, $\frac{3}{4}$ mile north of flags set up at Menilkrai by the Chinese. After the Mishmi Mission, Dundas became Assistant Political Officer, Sadiya (1911–1912); then Political Officer, Central and Eastern section, North-East Frontier (1912–1919), and, finally, (1919–1920) Political Officer, Sadiya Frontier Tract.

people took the salt and ate half of it, leaving the other half in the village for fear of incurring our displeasure'.[46] The Chinese realised their attentions were less than welcome, and soon left over the Glei Dakhru in the Direction of Pomed.

Captain Hardcastle later toured up the Dilli valley. He confirmed the Dundas report and also found that the Chinese had been distributing 'passports'. 'Their purport was to the effect that (individually or on behalf of a village) having "tendered his submission, the said Minister (Chao Erh-feng) after due enquiry feels it incumbent on him to sanction the issue of a Warrant of Protection for his property".' The Chinese date on these 'passports' was February 1911. When a Chinese military officer dressed in black uniform and belt had produced these 'passports' he insisted that money was not his object but that in future the villagers 'must obey all the orders of the Chinese'.[47]

One other instance of these empire-building rivalries comes from the Yepuk river. In 1910, the Chinese, having established firm control over Rima, planted flags at Menilkrai village, near the Yepuk river, a tributary of the Upper Lohit. One was a red flag with a blue four-clawed dragon, the other a board with a roughly printed notification in Chinese and Tibetan: 'The Southern Frontier of Zayul on the borders of the Szechuan Province of the Chinese Empire.' [48] But the flags did not remain the only symbol of empire in that Himalayan village. When the Chinese revisited the village in 1912 they found a British camp on the Yepuk, and on a granite boulder were two inscriptions credited to 'the Sappers and Miners'. The Chinese promptly had further signs erected alongside, and to be protected by a thatch covering.

Peking and London, appreciating the strategic significance of the Lohit valley, followed each other's moves. The vernacular press in Szechuan carried articles which Consul-General Wilkinson in Chengtu considered sufficiently important to translate. The *Szechuan Kung-pao*, a semi-official paper (March 4 and 11, 1912) published an interview with the Director of a newly-established Officer for Frontier Arrangements at Chengtu, who observed:

What is . . . a real cause for anxiety is the country to the extreme south of Chiamdo, Tsa-yu (Za-yul) which is adjacent to the British territory of Assam, and is distant only a dozen days' journey from Chiamdo. From Tsa-yu to Chiang-ka

(Gartok) again, is not more than a dozen stages. Should an Anglo-Tibetan question arise, and one (British) Army proceed from Shigatse and another from Tsa-yu, the whole length and breadth of Tibet for hundreds of miles would be cut through. The Frontier Office is much alarmed, and as a first step troops are being sent to occupy Tsa-yu.[49]

The same paper followed up this interview, on March 17, 1912, by publishing a Memorandum submitted by political officers for the Affairs of the Szechuan-Tibet Marches to the Szechuan Government.

The English last winter moved forward a force by way of Tsa-yu (Za-yul). It is most urgent to despatch an experienced Political Officer thither, and to select persons, who can read and write English, to proceed to the spot as quickly as possible at the same time telegraphing to the Central Government to open direct negotiations with the British Government. [50]

Other Szechuan papers were less discreet. The *Kung-pao* reported that 'Two or three hundred men of a certain country (India) are moving about on the borders of Lo-yu, taking advantage of our troubles to peer and pry. Our rulers ought to ask for an explanation; for otherwise the savages in their ignorance may easily become suspicious, and some harm may result to the relations or our Republic.' [51] And in the *T'ien-min-pao*: 'It seems that in the country of Za-yul it was reported that English troops were furtively entering [ts'uan – snaking in as rats do] . . . The British pretend that they are avenging the murder of Englishmen by the savages, but it may be doubted whether this is not a pretext to pick a quarrel'.[52]

The murder was that of Noel Williamson. The troops were those of the Mishmi Mission, which had set up camp at the Yepuk river bounding the Menilkrai flats on the north, 1100 yards beyond the Chinese flags. Dundas's diary on January 4, 1912, observed:

A mile or so beyond our camp is a much better place Kali Tiiang (Miju-Kalet) but it is near Walong, a Tibetan village, paying tribute to China, and our presence in force, so near the village, might give cause for further alarm to the Chinese at Rima.

Our present position is open to objection. The land is neither Tibetan nor Miju, and there can be no question of our having gone past, and violated an impossible boundary in the fixing of which neither Government nor the people concerned were consulted.

I do not propose to erect a cairn here, because, in my opinion the boundary should run much further north. This is, however, a matter for future negotiations, and it is as well for the present not to bind Government in any way, or make it appear by erecting a cairn, that we acquiesce in the Chinese claims.[53]

This same Mishmi Mission visited Walong (which J. F. Needham had reached some years before and reported that within living memory it had never consisted of more than one house) and proclaimed it ideally provisioned for a post. On January 26, 1912, Dundas recorded:

Captain Gunter has mapped all the country up to a little beyond Sama on both sides of the Lohit. He was, however, very unfortunate in not seeing Rima, but can fix its position with fair accuracy on the map. Mr Morshead took a traverse 10 miles up the Thod Chu, and was able to determine approximately the source of that stream, as well as map in its source. This stream will, in my opinion, be our best boundary with Tibet.[54]

Chinese suspicions of the Mishmi Mission were such that three men, Kou Kuo Hua (Intendant of Zayul), Chiang Hung Hsi (Commander of troops in Rima) and his secretary Lu Pu Yun, visited the British camp at Yepuk, leaving a letter saying that 'the people were in a state of panic' at the sight of British troops, and why they had come?

The problem of communications had to be faced; how could the road to Rima be kept open? The country from Walong to Rima was 'a tangled mass of hills, thickly wooded and precipitous, with the Lohit running in a deep defile'. The track opened out at Kamlung Kanunig, then passed over a succession of flats varying from 200 yards to a mile in length. Between Minzong and Menilkrai, the valley narrowed again. Major Stansfield pointed out in *The Road to Rima* that 'a few men, well armed and well handled, could make it difficult for a force advancing from Sadiya to reach Menilkrai. The Chinese official who placed a boundary board at the south end of the Menulkrai flats in June 1912 evidently realised this, as he put his board at the southern edge of the open port of the valley'.[55]

The Walong Promenade led by T. P. M. O'Callaghan from January to March 1914, had as its objective to secure a base in Walong, O'Callaghan exchanged visits with Tibetan officials who were in charge in Rima following the Chinese withdrawal. At Menilkrai three miles south of Walong he removed the boundary pillars put up by the Chinese. O'Callaghan held strong views about a post at Walong, envisaging renewed Chinese interests in the area.

> A small force, operating from Walong, could occupy Rima and hold the Rong Tho and Zayul valleys in 24–30 hours and *vice versa*, a force moving from Rima can unopposed be in position on Menilkrai at within 36 hours and effectually prevent any advance up the Lohit Valley. Should delay be made, it is not impossible that in the years to come it may take much more than the resources which the local Administration will have at its immediate command, to assert our legitimate rights and claims, which the ready completion of the already sanctioned but uncompleted scheme for the Lohit Valley will confirm.[56]

If the Chinese could be kept out of Zayul – and at the moment O'Callaghan was visiting the area, MacMahon and the Lonchen Shatra were doing their best to ensure it – then expenditure on a road to Rima would no longer be a matter of prime urgency. He toured north of Walong and advised that the frontier should lie there, so that the Di Chu stream, a tributary of the Lohit, would be under British control. The banks of the Di Chu provided a possible route to the Diphu or Talok Pass leading into Burma.

Its importance was appreciated in 1963 when Chinese and Burmese officials left demarcation unsettled at this tri-junction of Burma, China and India.

In 1914, MacMahon drew his line north of the Di Chu stream, having received the report of the Walong Promenade in the middle of the Simla Conference, and the Lohit Valley was thereby then secured.

THE SECOND ABOR EXPEDITION (1911)

The Diang or Siang River, as the Tsangpo is called where it runs through Abor territory, was another relatively accessible river valley. Noel Williamson made an expedition up the Dihang River in 1911 which was to affect the whole future of Britain's China policy. He already had an astonishing record of exploration; in 1908 he had toured alone through the Pasi Minyong countrg, where no European hsd previously been; in 1909 he travelled up the Lohit, almost as far as Rima; and in the early part of 1911 he again penetrated the Mishmi Hills as far as Walong. He saw the Chinese flags at Menilkrai and reported the Chinese occupation of Rima.

At the end of March 1911, Williamson set out from Passighat to visit the Abor country. He was familiar with the rule that he must not go beyond the Outer Line, although he had gone forty miles beyond it on his first trip to the Abor country along the Dihang valley. On that occasion he found there was no Tibetan control in the tract; that the hillmen were friendly, that all the country up to the foot of the hills was British territory, and that the Abors were susceptible to financial benefits and therefore likely to consider making some pecuniary arrangements. But on this second visit he went further, and as he and his companion and an escort of 44 people approached the village of Komsing, they were attacked and all of them killed. The massacre had been planned by the Great Council of Abors. On the eve of the massacre, Williamson's own servant, Katoki, wrote to his wife: 'Have arrived at Pangighat. Here Kebong Abors forbid going further. Sahib insists on going on into the village. My impression is we shall never return.'

Williamson had taken too many risks in trying to find out how far Chinese had penetrated in their Po-med campaign. The Governor-General in Council, while regretting 'the untimely end of this zealous and gallant officer', declared that his report illustrated an unique experience of the tribes on the North-Eastern frontier and that his services had been of the greatest value to the Government of Eastern Bengal and Assam. But he felt it his duty to add that 'this sad incident could never have occurred but for Mr Williamson's breach of well-known standing orders, prohibiting the crossing of the Outer Line without permission'.[57]

Not for the first time the massacre of British officers and their escort resulted in a punitive expedition and an addition to the Empire.

Until the Abor massacre, the idea of a forward move in Assam did not find favour in London, nor, for that matter, in Simla. Sir Lancelot Hare, the Lieutenant-Governor, had advocated this policy in November 1910. 'In view of the possibility of the Chinese pushing forward,' he suggested, 'it would be a mistake not to put ourselves in a position to take up suitable strategic points of defence.' And in January 1911 Sir Arthur Hirtzel, of the Political and Secret Department in the India Office, warned that if anything went wrong in Assam 'there would be very voiceful public opinion against us ... Think of the howl the planters would let out, and the rise in the price of tea!' [58]

The Viceroy wrote to the Secretary of State:

> The primary objects of the [punitive] expedition, are the exaction of reparation for the murder of Mr Noel William-son and his party, and the establishment of our military superiority in the estimation of the Abor tribe ... It is of prime importance that we should take advantage of the opportunity afforded by the expedition to carry out such surveys and exploration as may be possible, in order that we may obtain the knowledge requisite for the determination of a suitable boundary between India and China in this locality, as to which at present we know practically nothing. Recent events on the frontier of Burma have shown the urgent necessity of coming to an understanding with China about our mutual frontier, of preventing Chinese intrigue within our limits, and of keeping her as far as possible re-moved from our present administered area. [59] [The text of McMahon's instructions to Major-General H. Bower, com-manding the expedition is contained in Appendix 8].

Nor was the expedition confined to the Dihang. Simultaneously a friendly mission was sent to the Mishmi country 'with the double object of checking any tendency on the part of the Mishmis to help the Abors, and of obtaining information for boundary purposes.' This step was taken in view of 'the advance of China to Rima'. [60]

The Abor expedition cost £150,000. It included 2350 troops in addition to a contingent of Military Police. 'A British officer was murdered in the Abor country,' the Hon. E. S. Montague, then Secretary of State, India Office, told a questioner in the House of

Commons, 'and the Indian Government is taking steps to demonstrate that it is impossible to murder a British officer without serious consequence.' 'That is the return to this country for the £150,000 that is being expended,' the M.P. retorted. But for £150,000, plus 1 officer wounded, 2 other ranks killed and 2 wounded, and 3 followers killed and 2 wounded, the murderers were punished, the Minyon tribe was crushed and its villages brought to submission, while the power of Kebang, 'which for years had terrorised its neighbours, was finally broken'.[61] The official account of the expedition took a different standpoint.

> The geographical results of the expedition, although not as full as had been expected, owing to the climate and physical difficulties of the country, were still of great value. Practically the whole of the country was surveyed accurately as far as latitude 28° 40′. The whole of the valley of the Yamne was surveyed up to the snow ranges, the Shimang river was mapped throughout its entire length; the course of the Siyom was roughly traced; and the valley of the Dihang was followed as far as Singging, Latitude 28° 52′ (approximate), a point within 25 or 30 miles of the most northern Abor village. The identity of the Dihang with the Tsangpo, though not absolutely proved, was at any rate practically established. . . .
>
> Although it was not possible to determine accurately the natural frontier between the Abor country and Tibet, a rough idea of its nature and position was obtained. Points on the great snow range to the north were definitely fixed and a way was paved for an accurate determination of the boundary in the future while the chances of Chinese aggression in this region were greatly reduced.[62]

The Abor expedition led to a series of others under the general supervision of Major-General Bower, who was also Chief Political Officer. His assistant A. H. W. Bentinck, returned to Komsing and then travelled northwards to Singging. Colonel D. C. F. McIntyre visited Damro. J. F. Needham went through Minyong villages on the right bank of the Dihang as far as Parong. Needham and Molesworth went up the Shimang valley to Yingku, and Captain Dunbar toured

⟩ Kombong. All these expeditions succeeded in providing data for McMahon's red line at the Simla Conference two years later.

While the Abor country was being explored and the Outer Line pushed northwards to include it, the Mishmi expedition visited thirty villages. It was organised in two columns one, the Dibang or Nizam-ghat Column, commanded by Captain Bally with Captain F. M. Bailey as Political Officer, the other, the Lohit Valley Column, commanded by Mr Dundas. Captain Bally's instructions were:

> To enter into friendly relations with the Mishmis; to inform the Mishmis that for the future they will be under British control exclusively and must accept no order except for the present from the Political Officer, Mishmi Mission and thereafter from the Assistant Political Officer, Sadiya; to inform them that, in return for the protection afforded, they must unhesitatingly obey orders and provide coolies for work on the track, which is about to be improved, between Nizam-ghat and Amili and to carry such loads for the column as they may be ordered.[63]

The British 'hawks' of the period, many of them having at one time accompanied expeditions in extraordinary conditions of terrain and climate, wanted to follow them up by military posts and mule-tracks which would enable them to face a Chinese challenge. The 'doves' mainly in Whitehall, were not anxious to add to the frustrations of an abortive diplomatic exchange with China. In fact, 'as regards Chinese influence' the Chief Commissioner of Assam reported that

> neither the Abor Expedition nor the Miri Mission found any trace of the Chinese in the country which they explored. Only in the extreme north of the Abor country was there some signs of Tibetan influence. The position in the Mishmi country was different and was such as, in the opinion of the Chief Commissioner, urgently to call for further survey and exploration.[64]

He warmly endorsed recommendations the General Staff had made ⟩ build a road up the Lohit Valley to Walong and the construction of Military Police posts at Walong, Minzang and near the mouth of the

Delei river. The General Staff left no doubt as to who was their poten
tial enemy. They wanted the posts to observe as well as to impres
Chinese who were said to be concentrating troops at Rima just at th
time of the Mishmi Mission.

The 'hawks' won the day. Orders issued by the Government o
India on October 16, 1912, met most of the demands. Six month
earlier, the Secretary of State had said that he 'would prefer even no
to keep a permanent post beyond the Inner Line'. In October he ordere
the 'despatch of exploring and survey parties, with sufficient escorts t
overcome any possible opposition, to the Doshung pass and the head
waters of the Siyom and Sigon rivers; . . . surveys to be made of th
Dibong valley . . . of the Dri river to its source; of all the inhabite
valleys leading into either the Dri or Dibong rivers; and of the Sisse
valley to connect with the Mishmi and Abor surveys of last season
This Dibong Survey and Exploration was in the field from Novembe
1912 till June 1913. Captain G. A. Nevill a Superintendent of Police o
the Assam List, was in charge and Captain F. M. Bailey served a
Intelligence Officer.* The entire country was surveyed.

An administrative pattern was now drawn up; the areas covered b
the Abor Expedition and the Mishmi Mission were divided int
Central, or Abor Section, based on Rotung; Eastern Section (Mishm
Hills and Bor Hkamti country) based on Sadiya. The Western Sectio
comprised the country between Tawang and the Subansiri rive
including the eastern watershed of that river.

WEST OF THE SUBANSIRI

The area west of the Subansiri was the least known territory beyon
the Outer Line which was later to be within the frontier of th
McMahon Line. For a short period in 1847 when the merits of a missio

---

* Capt. G. A. Nevill. In 1913, the Western Section of the North-East Frontie
was formed with Capt. G. A. Nevill of the Indian Police as its first Politic
Officer. In 1919 it became known as the Balipara Frontier Tract. Capt. Nevi
became its first Political Officer, and stayed there until he retired in 1928.

He was Transport Officer to the Miri Mission, and led the Aka Promenad
and the visit to Tawang in 1914.

In 1925 he again visited the Akas and put forward suggestions for a clos
political control and the placing of posts in the Hills. They were largely un
noticed since the importance of a skeleton administration was not seriousl
considered until just before the Second World War.

to Tibet were weighed, the idea arose of negotiating with the Tawang Rajah 'for a free intercourse between Assam and Tawang'. Writing from Gauhati, Major Jenkins, Agent to the Governor-General for the North-East Frontier, recommended a route 'from Lassa through the Tawang Rajah's country by Koreeaparah Doar to Tazpore'. The Government, he said, was 'aware that the Tawang Rajah is not under the Government of Bootan but is a feudatory of the Rajah or Governor of Lassa, and by this route the Tibetans (Kampa Booteahs) are now in the habit of visiting Assam for the purpose of traffic but, though all the inhabitants of the hills are perfectly free to visit Assam on any account whatever, and the objection is principally directed against the visits of European officers – the removal of the restriction on the intercourse of our people with the hills might perhaps not improperly be made the subject for the attention of the Mission'.[65]

Jenkins knew that the route via Tawang was 'the shortest between Lhasa and British dominions'. But the Seven Rajas of Tawang proved no more willing than the Tibetans to welcome British penetration, though in 1844 they had accepted an annual cash payment in return for British control of Kuriapara Duar of Assam. This arrangement did not work smoothly; the Seven Rajas had Tibetan masters also. Matters came to a head in 1852 when the leading Raja tried to hold on to the money instead of passing it as usual to the Tibetans. Once again a local dispute opened the door to territorial gains. Twenty years after the dispute had been settled, British and Tibetan officials marked out the boundary between British Assam and the Tawang Tract. It was, in fact, as Alastair Lamb points out, 'the only section of the boundary between British India and Tibet which, in the nineteenth century, had been jointly demarcated by British and Tibetan officials'.[66]

In 1903 Captain W. F. O'Connor, writing from his camp at Kamba Jong, described the Tawang Tract in his Report on Tibet as consisting

> of a strip of country which runs south between Bhutan and the Akah country and touches upon Assamese territory a little north of Odalguri. The whole district from the Kya Kya Pass to the plains is known as Mon-yul, or the law country, and the capital is Tawang or MenTawang. At Tawang is situated a large monastery whose monks and lamas were in former days the *de facto* rulers of the country, but latterly the Lhasan authorities are said to have asserted their influence and the

country is now governed in the recognised manner by Jong-
pons deputed from Lhasa. This strip of country is of importance as affording a high road through Tibetan territory
from the plains of India to the uplands of Tibet and may some
day become of great value as a commercial highway.[67]

However, it was the strategic rather than the commercial possibilities
of the area west of Subansiri which affected British policy. In 1912 in an
all-embracing and valuable Note on the North-East Frontier [full text
in Appendix 9] the Chief of the General Staff pointed out its significance:

> The direction of the frontier line about Tawang requires care-
> ful consideration. The present boundary (demarcated) is
> south of Tawang, running westward along the foothills from
> near Udalgiri to the southern Bhutan border, and thus a
> dangerous wedge of territory is thrust between the Miri
> country and Bhutan. A comparatively easy and much used
> trade route traverses this wedge from north to south, by which
> the Chinese would be able to exert influence or pressure on
> Bhutan, while we have no approach to this salient from a flank,
> as we have in the case of the Chumbi salient. . . . Rectification
> of the frontier here is therefore imperative, and an ideal line
> would appear to be one from the knot of mountains near
> Longitude 93° Latitude 28° 20′ to the border north of Chona
> Dzong in a direct east and west line with the northern frontier
> of Bhutan. There appears to be a convenient watershed for it
> to follow.[68]

In December 1913 an expedition known as The Aka Promenade was
mounted under the command of Captain Nevill, comprising a total of
1032 of all ranks. It started from Peinjulie on the Borelli river and
crossed the Se-La over deep snow, frozen hard (The Dalai Lama
travelled the same way in 1959, and the Chinese troops in 1962). Nevill
visited the chief of the Monba village of Dirang Dzong, south of the
pass, on March 30, 1914, and on April 1 reached Tawang, where he
received 'a most overwhelming welcome'. North of Se-La was the
'magnificent open valley of the Tawang-chu, well tilled and producing
quantities of barley, wheat, rice, onions, chilis, etc.' South of Se-La

was the Diraangchu, a well cultivated and well populated valley. But the people north of the Se-La pass were richer than those south, and Nevill accounted for the fact by explaining that between the Se-La and the Assam border, with the exception of the village of Sengedzong, the area was controlled by the monks of Tawang, who took more than their fair share in goods and taxation.

> The chief Tibetan influence is the monastery, in which 500 monks live, this monastery is an off-shoot of the Drepung monastery in Lhasa. Its abbot and the principal officials are also appointed from Lhasa.
>
> The country south of the Se-La is, with the exception of the village of Sengedzong, administered only by the monks of Tawang. There are two Zongpens at Kalaktang.[69]

Two thousand miles of previously unexplored country had been surveyed during the Aka promenade and the visit to Tawang. Captain Nevill had no compunction in making suggestions for its inclusion within British administration. He foresaw some resistance from the Tawang monks, who for a century had had complete control over the Tawang area, and suspected that 'this obstructive policy might perhaps be backed by the weight of the Drepung monastery, the largest of the three great religious houses in Lhasa, and from which the Tawang monastery had sprung'. And he saw many difficulties in administering the Tawang country north of the Se-La, and, to a lesser degree, south of this pass. Events overtook Captain Nevill; his detailed proposals were not forwarded to the Government of India until November 7, 1914, by which time the war in Europe overshadowed developments in Tawang, and the Government of India was 'averse from anything in the shape of a forward move upon the frontier'.[70]

But this did not prevent the Simla Conference from attaching some considerable degree of importance to Tawang, which was included in British territory as the result of an agreement signed in Simla by Sir A. H. McMahon and the Lonchen Shatra in March 1914.

North-East Frontier: Prelude to Simla

On February 10, 1910, the *Morning Post* reported: 'A great Empire, the future military strength of which no man can foresee, has suddenly appeared on the North-East of India. The problem of the North-West Frontier thus bids fair to be duplicated in the long run, and a double pressure placed on the defensive resources of the Indian Empire ... China, in a word, has come to the gates of India, and the fact has to be reckoned with.' Younghusband and Curzon enthusiastically endorsed these sentiments, and regarded them as vindicating their earlier Chinese policy. The area of conflict was the territory between the Himalayas and the Brahmaputra – approximately the North-East Frontier Agency of today. Chinese infiltration among the Assam hill tribes was regarded in Simla and London as proof that they planned a general offensive along the whole range of the Himalayas. We can only speculate today, as diplomats and strategists speculated in 1911, whether or not Chinese aims were to expand to the Brahmaputra.

In 1911 the extent of Chinese probing in the Assam Himalayas made a strong case for a more active military commitment. The argument was how much and when? Alastair Lamb maintains that her policy was probably 'not throwing down the gauntlet before the British Empire and challenging the Indian Government to hold its frontiers if it could! ... There was not, in these years 1919 to 1912, a single and concerted aggressive threat to the integrity of India's northern borders. There was not, indeed, at this period anything like a single and concerted

Chinese policy in Central Asia'. He acknowledges that China's aim in 1910 was the 'military domination of the Dalai Lama's dominions'.[1] Revolution brought Chao Erh-feng's expansionist campaign to a halt and he was murdered by his own troops. China's armies did not return to Central Tibet till 1951, but at no point between these two dates, Dr Lamb maintains, was her ambition to have one there diminished.

Chinese imperial policy was unequivocal, though diplomacy dictated the tempo at which it was implemented. British imperial policy was, by contrast, ambivalent; the Foreign Office always had to calculate its relations with Peking and the reactions on British investments concentrated in the Yangtse Valley. Too sharp a reaction to Chinese activities in Himalayan areas might provoke reprisals.

Chief among those who advocated an extension of the Outer Line to the water-shed of the Himalayas was Minto. He was prepared to accept the risks involved in pushing the edge of the Empire into areas where only tribal peoples had spread their control. (He found ready support in various commercial quarters, not least from timber contractors who had their eyes on the vast forests between the Inner Line and the Outer Line.) Under his administration the tribal peoples between the Lines became subject to poll-tax, in default of which they were expelled from the area. Even those who lived north of the Outer Line but were cultivating land to the South had to make their contribution to the Indian exchequer. The collection of the taxes laid the basis for a skeleton administration.

China was the only potential rival for territory between the Outer and Inner Lines and, beyond, for the crests of the Himalayas. Sir Charles Bell, one of the more persistent 'hawks' in the history of the North-East Frontier, sought throughout his long career in India, Sikkim and Tibet to strengthen British influence at the expense of the Chinese. But Morley, the Secretary of the India Office between 1906 and 1910 was a dove by temperament and conviction and feared that if Minto and the Army in India had their way there was the risk of a second Younghusband Mission. He cautioned Minto:

> China is awakening, and is beginning to have increased knowledge of, and interest in, the geography and conditions of her dependencies. So we have no right to be surprised if China seeks to render more effective that shadowy control that she always possessed in Tibet, and which we vehemently blamed

her for not exercising more effectually in practice.... Of course, if China were a decent place, we should settle the boundary by arbitration, joint commissions, and the other resources of civilisation; only these devices are not well suited to people who speak disdainfully of latitude and longitude, and work their oracle by forged maps.[2]

But Morley's non-intervention policy did not last and, in the years immediately following his departure from the India Office, China adopted a 'forward' policy in the Himalayan borders of the British Empire and General Chao Erh-feng's armies reached Rima.*

Ironically, it was not General Chao Erh-feng who startled Hardinge into an 'active' policy, but the murder of Noel Williamson, busily probing Chinese activities in the upper Dihang valley.

Foreign Office correspondence in the autumn of 1911 bears witness to some official uncertainty. Grey did not support the idea of 'sending expeditions into unadministered territory with a view to claiming a frontier and of subsequently withdrawing'. He did not agree with any proposal to demarcate a new frontier until he was 'satisfied that the Government of India are prepared to take adequate measures to protect any line which may eventually be selected from all risk of violation by the Chinese'. He questioned the wisdom of demarcating a frontier by boundary cairns and then retiring, since this policy would certainly lead to more and larger expeditions.... That the Chinese would advance upon the withdrawal of the expedition may ... be taken for granted in view of ... the "forward policy" now favoured by the Chinese Government in all frontier matters'.[3]

Statesmen in Simla showed neither ambivalence nor hesitation, while the military mind was already working out a boundary which would contain Chinese expansion and consolidate Britain's hold over

* Alastair Lamb provides a valuable study of this period in *The McMahon Line*, Volume 1; Morley, Minto and Non-Interference in Tibet. He makes an analogy between the events of 1910 and with Nehru's non-intervention policy in 1954. 'Had Morley's non-interference policy also contained a positive element, an expressed wish to see Tibet as Chinese, rather than as an unstable power vacuum ... then some Anglo-Chinese Treaty over Tibet might well have emerged in 1910 ... The existence of a Chinese Tibet between 1912 and 1950 might not have guaranteed friendly Sino-Indian relations today; it would certainly, however, have ensured for those relations a rather different history' (p. 234).

the tribal areas. Chinese claims had not yet been made to these North-East frontier areas; Chinese maps published at the end of the century make this point clear. In September 1911, when Chao Erh-feng was still advancing, the General Staff Branch prepared a Memorandum 'on the points which should be brought to the notice of Survey parties working in the tribal territory on the Assam-Tibet border in 1911–1912'. McMahon's instructions to Major-General Bower when he set out with the Abor Expedition (Appendix 8) 'to submit proposals for a suitable frontier line between India and Tibet in general conformity with the Memorandum' contained the injunction that:

> No boundary must, however, be settled on the ground without the orders of Government except in cases where the recognised limited of Tibetan-Chinese territory are found to conform approximately to the line indicated above, and to follow such prominent physical features as are essential to a satisfactory strategic and well-defined boundary line.[4]

He added:

> If during the course of the expedition Chinese officials or troops are met, endeavour should be made to maintain amicable relations. If, however, such officials or troops be met within the territory of tribes on this side of recognised Tibetan-Chinese limits, they should be invited to withdraw into recognised Tibetan-Chinese limits, and, if necessary, should be compelled to do so.[5]

The Indian Government also told officers on the Tibetan frontier that 'it is not desirable that matters regarding the Abors, Mishmis and other tribes on the North-East Frontier should be discussed with the Dalai Lama and his Ministers'.[6]

Sir Arthur Hirtzl detailed the ideal modus operandi, necessitated he explained 'solely by the advance of China', as follows:

> . . . a line suitable for a frontier with China has, if possible, to be found and eventually demarcated, and that between the administrative boundary and the new external frontier . . . our future policy should be one of loose political control,

having as its object the minimum of interference compatible with the necessity of protecting the tribesmen from un-provoked aggression, the responsibility for which we cannot avoid, and of preventing them from violating either our own or Chinese territory.[7]

Men on the spot did not delude themselves that they could wander through tribal territories without exciting Chinese antagonism. On the Burma-China frontier, after one British expedition had been withdrawn, the Chinese had sent in a party with the usual appointment orders and tokens for issue to village headsmen. Why should they not adopt a similar policy on the China-India frontier? In fact, a party of Chinese had appeared in the Aka country close to the administrative frontier of Assam; at Rima they had summoned Mishmi tribal heads-men to appear before them with a view to annexation, and in the Poyul and Pomed country in south-eastern Tibet, the Peking Govern-ment had sanctioned a force down the Dibong river towards the Abor country. Hardinge strongly advised a return to the policy originally put forward by Minto of securing 'as soon as possible a sound strategical boundary between China cum Tibet and the tribal territory from Bhutan up to and including the Mishmi country'.[8] This was, in effect, a line which represented 'roughly the limits of tribal territory on the Assam frontier which we desire to keep out of Chinese control'. Subject to any modifications which explorations and expeditions in the 1911–1912 season might necessitate, Hardinge proposed: 'We consider that line should be our approximate objective, up to which the existing Assam "outer line" should be advanced'. This policy of 'loose political control' between the Inner Line and the new, advanced Outer line implied, as Hardinge admitted, 'effective steps to prevent the violation of the new external boundary by the Chinese after the expedition and missions had been withdrawn'.[9]

The 1911–1912 season's activities in the Assam Himalayas unob-trusively extended the Indian Empire, and the military element were, as an official Minute commented, 'rewarded by a copious Honours list.' A General Staff Memorandum instructed the Survey parties on the Assam-Tibet border in 1911–1912:

A suitable military frontier should follow the principal water-sheds and include on our side the tributaries of the lower

Brahmaputra, the Lohit and Irrawaddy rivers. A mountain chain is from every point of view the most advantageous strategical frontier' ... other questions, such as the determination of the limits of habitation of tribes, originally under Tibet on the one hand, and independent frontier tribes on the other, will largely affect the question of our frontier *vis-a-vis* China, but the military aspect should be prominently kept in view.[10]

Survey parties were instructed to collect data about the Lohit: the Nagong Chu of Dihang; possibly the Yamne; the Tsangpo or Dihang; the Nia Chu or Kamla; the Tawang Chu or Dangma. On their reports the General Staff would 'determine the best military line under the circumstances'.[11] Chinese military authorities were naturally examining the same areas from the point of view of their own frontier, and despite Chao Erh-feng's death and the subsequent disarray of his army, Yuan Shih Kai's frontier policy was no less ambitious. He described the Marches and Tibet as being 'to Szechuan as the lips to the jaw'. Plans for a Chinese Survey Party in 1912, obtained by the Military Attaché Colonel Willoughby, included areas covered by the Abor Expedition, recently brought under effective British control; and which the Viceroy declared would be 'within the proposed new British borderline'. Similarly, the Chinese planned to visit the Mishmi country, where, as a result of the past winter's Mishmi Mission under Mr Dundas, (not to mention the previous influence of Mr Williamson and Mr Needham), they would find themselves in a region acknowledging British control'.[12] The Chief of the British General Staff was taking no risks. In his 1912 Memorandum he declared that:

> Throughout this note the assumption is made that the pertinacity of the Chinese will not long permit of their acquiescence in the present state of affairs in Tibet. Although their activity on our frontier may have received a temporary check on account of the Revolution, history proves that succeeding a Revolution, as a rule, a period of national vigour and expansion follows. . . . There is therefore no time to be lost in declaring to the Chinese in unmistakeable terms the line the frontier is to follow, in making our occupation of that line effective insofar as placing ourselves in positions whence we

can watch developments and prevent further encroachments is concerned, and in improving communications on our side [13] [full text in Appendix 9].

There remained the problem of reconciling diplomacy with the legalisation of strategic plans for a new frontier line. The Assam Himalayas were little known outside business circles, ex-officials of the Indian Services, and in learned Societies. A rare contemporary public statement was that of Sir Thomas Holdich to the Indian Section of the Royal Society of Arts.

> Politically, it is here [the North East Frontier of India] that a dividing line exists between the Chinese Empire and our own. Here is the hedge over which we may look, but which we may not pass; and here we may discern what the expansion of another great empire may effect in the matter of approach to our domains, and of control over a horde of Mongoloid peoples who have direct relations with ourselves and whose goodwill as frontier neighbours we cannot ignore. . . . The significance of Rima lies in the military post which China has recently planted there. We are politically on the edge of China wherever we touch Tibet, or the wild tribes that border Tibet; but nowhere is the practical advance of that irrepressible nation so distinctly marked as at Rima. What does it mean to us? What is the real significance of this apparition of a yellow face looking over the border hedge into a corner of Assam? [14]

Occasionally Parliamentary questions were asked of the Secretaries of State for India and the Foreign Office respectively. But expeditions were carried out in comparative secrecy. A Central News correspondent wanted to go on the Mishmi Expedition, but it was officially decided that it was inadvisable that such an expedition, and this was a peaceful endeavour, should be the subject of publicity. The official observer, Dundas, the Political Officer, recorded that:

> At the very worst, in villages which had never been visited before, the sentiment was one of indifference, which may in course of time be turned into active friendship. In such places,

more especially in the Delei and Dou villages, the people seemed indifferent as to whether Chinese or British influence should be paramount. They preferred to sit on the fence and let the British and Chinese fight it out between themselves. It must be remembered in this connection that the Chinese have taken active measures to win the confidence of the people. They encourage them to settle in Tibetan territory and treat them very favourably as compared with Tibetans, asking neither land revenue nor *begar* from them.[15]

Tribal peoples of the Assam Himalayas were involuntarily pawns in the power struggle between Britain and China. The Secretary of State instructed the Viceroy: 'Explanations to tribes regarding line laid down should be as noncommittal as possible at present, since it will be difficult to withdraw from it without loss of prestige and H.M.G. cannot finally commit themselves to any line until they have all the facts before them. Cairns should be as few as possible.' [16]

A skeleton of British administration already existed by the middle of 1912. Posts were set up where the likelihood of Chinese infiltration was greatest, and although the Foreign Office, and, to some extent, the India Office, showed occasional reluctance to extend the area of administration, the North-East Frontier was now divided into three sections, the Western, Central and Eastern Sections.

In August 1912, the time had come to set down Britain's Tibetan policy in unequivocal terms. This involved British-Russian diplomacy, not only because of the Anglo-Russian Agreement of 1907, but Russia was herself 'on the move' in Mongolia. 'What appears to be so essential', a Foreign Office Memorandum frankly stated,

> is that Tibet, while nominally retaining her position as an autonomous State under the suzerainty of China, should in reality be placed in a position of absolute dependence on the Indian Government, and that there should be set up an effective machinery for keeping out the Chinese on the one hand and the Russians on the other ... What is essential at present is that we should obtain a completely free hand both by an agreement with Russia and by an agreement with China.

The first step proposed was

F

to inform Russia of our desire to reverse the 1907 Agreement and thereby to obtain a free hand in Tibet, and then ask what her price is to be.[17]

The opportunity to find out arose when M. Sazonof, the Russian Foreign Minister, came to London to discuss relations with Persia. Grey mentioned the subject to Sazonof at Balmoral on September 24 and five days later Crewe pursued the matter in separate talks. The crux of the matter was what could Britain give Russia in return. Britain's hands had been tied by her undertaking to respect the territorial integrity of Tibet, to abstain from interference with its internal administration, to enter into no negotiations with Tibet except through the intermediary of the Chinese Government, and not to send representatives to Lhasa. As in most agreements, loopholes existed. In this case, the Anglo-Tibetan and Anglo-Chinese conventions of 1904 and 1906 respectively were expressly exempted from the operation of the clause relating to the Chinese Government. Crewe noted after his talks with the Russian:

> M. Sazonof said that if any definite change were made in the convention which would appear to be to our sole advantage, he would be seriously attacked at home . . . M. Sazonof said that our recent warning to China was now well-known in Russia, and if as a sequel to a Chinese advance we were to occupy the Chumbi valley, he did not believe that a word would be said. When I mentioned some rectification of the Nepal frontier, he said that this would be on a different footing, because it effected the subject-matter about which the convention was framed. On the whole, however, he thought it better to deal with any matter affecting Tibet as it naturally arose, and not to attempt a formal revision of any points. At the same time, if we were able to give material assistance in smoothing things with Afghanistan, he would be able to face opinion in Russia more easily in connection with other questions.[18]

Sazonof mentioned several facilities which Russia wanted in Afghanistan – the redistribution of water for irrigation, for example – but the Foreign Office believed that this only obscured his real intention, which amounted to a redivision of spheres of interest. The Crewe Hall talks had no concrete results, but behind this diplomatic fencing, Crewe assumed a green light to go ahead in Tibet. He told Grey that Sazonof was really implying 'that it does not matter what we do in Tibet, if only it is done *sub rosa*'.[19] The important point was that British policy must not openly seem to be revising the 1907 Agreement. Honour among diplomats was satisfied. British pressure was now applied to China to accept the August 17 Memorandum, and to Tibet to bargain her suzerainty for a British guarantee against further Chinese penetration. If Tibet and China could be persuaded or diplomatically blackmailed into attending a tri-partite conference, Russia being kept informed of some, if not all of the proceedings, then the British objective of a strategic frontier might be the result [See Appendix 10].

Meanwhile, China's acceptance of the August 17 Memorandum was an essential preliminary. Yuan Shih Kai was in no hurry. His troops were advancing, and his idea was now taking shape of a new province called Hsi-kang formed out of the Marches and the eastern portion of the Tibetan province of Kham. The India Office foresaw that if this advance continued, 'a situation of direct conflict' would arise between the British and Chinese Governments which it was 'desirable to avoid'. An ultimatum should therefore be given to Peking. 'If a refusal to recognise the Chinese Republic should, (as the Government of India apprehend), prove to be an insufficient threat to the Chinese Government'[20] then a three months' time limit should be given, and if this failed, then H.M.G. would consider itself free to break the Anglo-Chinese Agreement of 1906, to enter into direct negotiations with Tibet and to go to its assistance against China's advance. China's reply came on December 23, 1912. It denied any intention of converting Tibet into a province of China. As to the status of Tibet, it had already been defined in existing Treaties and no new one was required.

Military experts went ahead irrespective of diplomatic fencing, and worked out a boundary with which they could most easily contain China. The Government of India told Crewe on January 4, 1913:

We have information to show that formerly it was recognised that the boundary of Tibet proper, i.e., the country under temporal rule of Tibetans, included the Zayul, Markham, Draya, Chiamdo, Gyade and Nagchukha districts. Derge, Sanngai and Batang were not reckoned as within this boundary, though as regards religious administration they are under Tibet. Till they were brought under administration of China in 1910 by Chao-Erh-feng, Chiamdo and Draya districts remained under temporal administration of Tibet. We think it desirable that these districts should not be ceded to China, unless their cession is inevitable in view of the fact above stated and of their recent reconquest. For in these two districts there are about a dozen difficult passes, whereas, if they are ceded to China, Chinese will be dangerously close to Lhasa, with only three of passes of any difficulty intervening. Also, we are of opinion that Tibet proper should continue to include Markham as well as Zayul.[21]

China's military success in the Marches led Britain to pursue a tougher line. In January 1913 Grey told Jordan that the Chinese Minister had been instructed to ask for the withdrawal of the August Memorandum. He did not do so![22] A month later, the Foreign Minister, Lu-Cheng-hsiang, raised the question of Tibet with Jordan and 'expressed a desire to resume negotiations on the basis of the Memorandum of August 17'. And at the same time Bell was trying to convince the Dalai Lama that his interests would best be served by close relations with Britain, and Lu Hsing Chi, in Chinese Intelligence Calcutta, was trying to convince him that wisdom dictated friendship with China. Lu's telegrams were intercepted, and the Foreign Office was able to summarise Chinese policy:

1. Adoption of a concilatory policy towards people of Tibet.
2. Despatch to that country of secret agents with Tashi Wangdi (who is believed to be now in Lasa) at their head for purpose of winning over officials and populace, and inducing Dalai Lama and adherents to return Allegiance.
3. Major Peng of Cheng Tu to be appointed guardian of eastern frontier of Tibet.
4. Firm attitude to be adopted *vis-à-vis* British Minister at Peking, and pressure to be put upon him to settle the Tibetan question without delay.
5. Dalai Lama to be persuaded to state publicly in Western press that Tibet is an integral portion of the Republic of China; to withhold recognition from treaty between Tibet

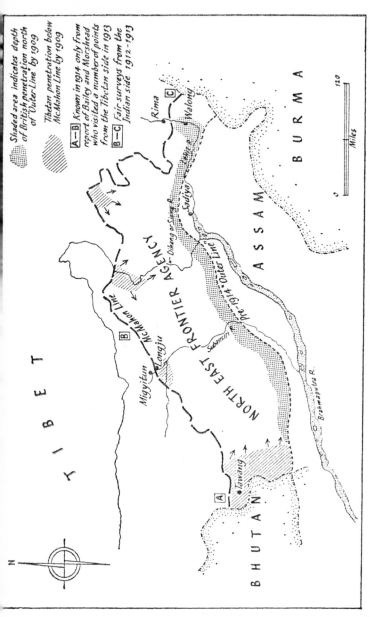

MAP 12. *British and Tibetan Penetration in the Assam Himalaya.*

and Mongolia, and to forbid Hutukhtu of Urga by telegram to continue rebellious attitude.[23]

On May 23, 1913, the Foreign Office invited the Chinese Government to take part in a 'joint conference in India with a view to settling
the Tibetan question by means of a tripartite agreement'. A similar
invitation was sent to the Tibetan Government and the Russians were
kept informed.

Peking's response was not immediately favourable. Exception was
taken to the idea of Tibetan participation. The Foreign Minister, as
Jordan reported to London, 'made a pointed reference to his former
contention that China's rights over Tibet were of a sovereign and
not of a suzerain character, the implication being that Tibet had no
treaty-making status'.[24] Chinese troops were again on the offensive,
and once more a Presidential mandate made claims to Tibetan territory
which Jordan described as 'of a much more extravagant character than
any which the Chinese Government have seriously put forward in the
past'.[25] They involved Chinese military occupation as far as Chiangta, only about 125 miles east of Lhasa. These were modified on June 2,
probably as the result of Jordan's verbal protest, by a mandate placing
the limit of advance 'for the time being at En-ta, some 75 miles west of
Chiamdo, or some 425 miles east of Chiangta'.[26]

The Tibetans also made extensive claims known to Sir Charles Bell
in Sikkim. These were:

> Firstly, that Tibet shall control administration of her domestic
> affairs. Secondly, as regards external matters, Tibet shall con-
> sult with Great Britain in important questions, but otherwise
> manage them herself. Thirdly, that Chinese traders only shall
> be allowed in Tibet, neither Chinese Ambans, nor officials nor
> soldiery being admitted. Fourthly, that in Tibet shall be
> included Litang, Batang, Derge and Nyarong, the whole area
> in fact in which population is Tibetan, i.e., as far east as
> Tachienlu.[27]

The Government of India considered these conditions 'so extensive as
practically to amount to a declaration of independence' which could
not be supported, for the time being, by not actually opposing either
Chinese or Tibetan claims. Britain's hands would be strengthened in
Simla by seeming to influence both claimants to reduce their demands.

Prevarication by all parties concerned delayed the opening of the Conference. Peking questioned the right of the Tibetan delegate to be treated as an equal. Alston telegraphed Grey from Peking in August; 'I was asked whether I could not devise some means for getting over Chinese objection to equality of status of Tibetan, and suggestion was made that China's face might be saved by separate negotiations between China and Tibet, to be followed by negotiations between China and ourselves.' Alston was not impressed and repeated once more that H.M.G. 'intended that delegates should go to the conference on a footing of equality'.[28] Finally, a Chinese Presidential order was signed appointing Ivan Chen special plenipotentiary for Tibetan negotiations. In view of subsequent developments, the wording is significant . . .

> It becomes the duty of this Government to order said plenipotentiary speedily to proceed to India, there to negotiate provisional treaty jointly with the plenipotentiary appointed by Great Britain and the Tibetan plenipotentiary, and to sign articles which may be agreed upon in order that all difficulties which have existed in the past may be dissolved.[29]

The Dalai Lama conferred equally precise authority on the Tibetan delegate. 'The Chief Minister, Shatra Paljor Dorje, is hereby authorised to decide on all questions which may benefit Tibet, and to seal all documents relating thereto.' [30] He carried with him the seals of the three monasteries, of the National Assembly and of the Lonchens, and, on Bell's advice, received later that of the Dalai Lama.

Before the delgations met in Simla, Tibetans intrigued with Chinese and British, from both of whom they hoped to gain or regain territory and increased autonomy. British and Chinese influence was exerted on Tibetans, both powers intending territorial gains and political concessions. Bell played his country's hand with the advantage of a sincere admiration for Tibet and an intimate friendship with the Dalai Lama. The Lonchen Shatra met Bell in Gyantze on his way to Simla. 'He showed me some letters from the Chinese officials in eastern Tibet', Bell wrote. 'They pressed the Dalai Lama and the Tibetan officials to negotiate with the Chinese officials at Cham-do, though they must have known that their Government had already accepted the invitation to the Conference in India.' [31] In May, Lu Hsing Chi telegraphed to the Dalai Lama asking him to send officers to escort him to Lhasa. He advised Peking; 'We must check the interference of the British and draw the Tibetan officials into closer connection with ourselves and dispel their tendency to rely on foreigners by revealing to them the oppressive nature of British administration. Thus we shall promote the solidarity of the people and later on we can gradually regain our sovereign rights.' [32]

Lu Hsing Chi walked a diplomatic tight-rope, advising Peking to occupy territory claimed by Lhasa while advising Lhasa to make no concessions to the Government of India. The Dalai Lama communicated with Lu in June 1913:

> In my reply to the President, I am pointing out that in Ta Mu [the 39 States], Chiang [Ka-Gartok], Cha' a [Chiamdo and Pa Hsu], the administration has been usurped by Chinese officials, although these localities have for long formed part of Tibet and have been provided with officers civil and military by the Tibetan 'Treasury'. This usurpation is the cause of the ill-feeling between Chinese and Tibetans. Many proposals for a conference at Chiamdo have been received from Wang Chin Ch'ing Staff officer of the troops; other letters suggest K'ang Pa, while you desire to come direct to Lhasa; but all these courses present difficulties because the misconduct of the troops has raised the suspicions of the Tibetans. If the troops were recalled and the conference held at Darjeeling, matters would be more easily settled and peace more speedily attained. [33]

Lu Hsing Chi was unable to go to Tibet. The British Minister in Peking told the Waichoupou that until an agreement on Tibet was settled, communication between China and Tibet via India was forbidden. In spite of this ban, Lu had his own contacts and was able to give the President an informed evaluation of the balance of power in Tibet:

> That party among the Tibetans which desires to submit to China is rapidly gaining strength; secret strife between the two factions is growing very acute and before long will break out into civil war.
> The Sha-Cha has hitherto made use of the Dalai Lama to obtain for himself supreme power in Tibet; he is extremely

hostile to China and has distinct leanings towards the foreigners. Now that he is coming to the conference he will no doubt act accordingly. I now propose to send a Tibetan messenger secretly to him to persuade him to come to India and have a personal interview with me; anything requiring discussion can then be communicated by me to the Central Government for decision; if his demands are excessive there could be no difficulty in orders being issued from China, directing him to return to Tibet . . .[34]

The Cabinet in Peking replied: 'Your reports on Tibetan affairs will be submitted to Delegate Ch'en (Ivan Chen) on his arrival in Peking.' As the opening date of the Conference drew nearer, Lu became anxious, though failing to reach Lhasa, to make direct contacts. He made alternate plans which he communicated to Peking: 'I have secretly bought over certain of the Tibetan affairs retinue, partly with a view to keeping him under observation, and partly that they may, when opportunity permits, persuade him not to attempt to cast off allegiance to our country . . . Yesterday I submitted to the President by post the detailed reports which have been furnished me secretly by my Tibetan agents.'[35]

When Tibetan, Chinese and British delegations finally met in the Palace of the Maharaja of Darbhanga in Simla on October 6, 1913, the question was who could get most out of whom?

7

Conference at Simla

THE DELEGATES; THE PROCEEDINGS; THE TWO-ZONE PROPOSAL; CHINESE PRO-CRASTINATION; THE BILATERAL AGREE-MENT

THE DELEGATES

Sir A. H. McMahon was an obvious choice as chairman for the Simla Conference. His was the host country, and many years of his life had been devoted to boundary work. He was born in Simla in 1862; joined the Indian Staff Corps in 1885, the Sikhs Punjab Frontier Force two years later, and, in 1889 the Punjab Commission. From 1890 till 1914 he was in the Indian Political Department and served continuously on the frontier, on the Commission for demarcation of the Afghan-Baluchistan boundary, and as Political Agent at Gilgit, Chitral and Baluchistan. Frontier politics seem to have been a family interest. Among his papers, there is a carefully preserved pamphlet by his maternal grandfather Major Charles Head entitled *Defence of British India from Russian Invasion* (1839).

Hardinge made McMahon Foreign Secretary in 1911 and for that year he had a break from frontier affairs. He was Grand Master of Ceremonies for the last of the great Durbars, held to welcome King George and Queen Mary.

As Foreign Secretary to the Government of India McMahon was at the administrative centre of all the explorations and punitive expeditions leading to the making of the frontier line which was to bear his name. He appreciated as no-one else could have the details of the brief of the frontier required by British strategy on India's North-East Frontier prepared by the Chief of the General Staff. He dominated the Conference at Simla. At the outset Bailey and Morshead had not yet completed their journey to the Tsangpo Falls, to Migytun and Tawang; Nevill's report on Tawang was not completed; Pritchard and Waterfield were still on their journey along the Salween-Irrawaddy divide observing Chinese activity in the Nam Tamas, Deblu, Tadzu and Taron valleys; and O'Callaghan's account of the Walong promenade was still to come. When information on points of detail which could be supplied by those explorers had not arrived McMahon held up the proceedings. But the general line was clear.

Boundaries retained their fascination for him even when in retirement. He told the Royal Society of Arts in London – he was then their Chairman – that the five hundred miles which

> formed the boundary between India and Tibet, owing to our greater local knowledge and more detailed survey, supplemented by the results of special survey parties sent out to examine the less known areas, admitted of more detailed and exact definition. For great lengths of it lofty mountain ranges and watershed buried in eternal snow facilitated verbal definition and rendered demarcation on the ground (except in a few small special and more inhabited areas) either impossible or superfluous . . . No work I know of is more full of interest than boundary work, and no branch is more full of incident and adventure than demarcation.[1]

In Simla, McMahon also had the advantage of acquaintance with the Tibetan delegate Lonchen Shatra. They had met in Calcutta in March 1912 when the Tibetan had been appointed to present the Dalai Lama's thanks for British hospitality in Darjeeling and to ask for arms.[2] McMahon described the Tibetan and Chinese delegates as 'gentlemen of very courteous and polished manners and delightful to deal with. Monsieur Ivan Chen has the advantage of long diplomatic training and of experience of European capitals, but as a diplomat he has, I think, met his match in 'Lonchen Shatra, who is a remarkably shrewd and quick witted old gentleman, more than able to hold his own in discussion, and full of resource.'[3] Sir Charles Bell shared McMahon's admiration for the Tibetan. 'Lonchen Shatra had but seldom left his native land. Yet he showed a knowledge of men and a grasp of political affairs that came as a surprise to many at the Conference. His simple dignity and his charm of manner endeared him to all who met him in Simla or Delhi.'4

In domestic affairs Lonchen Shatra was a progressive. He had the courage to advocate a reduction in the vast ecclesiastical expenditure which helped to keep the country so impoverished and told Bell that he would like to see Tibetan doctors instructed in Western surgery, and the mineral wealth of the country explored. In foreign relations he was the Dalai Lama's chief assistant in his pro-Russian policy. Bell, for whom the Dalai Lama could do no wrong, commented: 'The pro-Russian attitude of the Lama and his Minister was natural enough, for they were genuinely distrustful of British designs and, in their experience, thought that this would be a good way to check them.' 5

Lonchen Shatra, while conscious of the pressures which might be exerted on him at Simla, was inclined to favour the British with whom he was not familiar as against the Chinese whose claws he knew were even at that moment digging into eastern Tibet. He stayed with Bell in Gyantse on his way to Simla and showed him Chinese letters which 'pressed the Dalai Lama and the Tibetan officials to negotiate with the Chinese officials at Chamdo'.6 He was represented in a different light to Peking by China's intelligence agent in Calcutta, Lu Hsing Chi.

> India is a very extensive country and the eyes and ears in it are very numerous; the British official(s) will hardly dare to be overbearing, and I ought to be able to find means to induce the Sha-Cha (Lonchen Shatra) to adopt a friendly attitude. If he is willing to come, I propose to place at his disposal the foreign house which I now rent. This will give him confidence; however I fear that the British will prevent him from coming, in pursuance of their policy encouraging separation between China and Tibet.7

Lonchen Shatra did not go to Calcutta. Later, in Gyantse, he showed Bell the terms he would put forward at Simla on behalf of the Dalai Lama. Bell explains that at the time the 'Dalai Lama was consulting only the Ministers, for the National Assembly took too long a time over its deliberations, and the Lama recognised the necessity for prompt decisions. The Chinese, moreover, by writing conciliatory letters had gained several of the members of the Assembly over to their side'.8 He advised Lonchen Shatra to collect all the documentation available to take to Simla. Thus, while the Chinese were delaying the opening of the conference as long as possible, the Tibetans were scouring the archives in Lhasa. The result was that the Tibetan case was brilliantly documented. McMahon reported 'tomes of delicate manuscripts bound in richly embroidered covers [including] the official history of Tibet, compiled by the fifth Dalai Lama and known as the *Golden Tree of the Index of the sole ornament of the world*, a work of great scope and colossal dimensions'. Another treasure was 'The Feast of Pleasure for the Perfected Youths' written in the time of the fifth Dalai Lama and describing early Sino-Tibetan boundaries.⁹

Ivan Chen was a man of the world, widely travelled in European countries, a diplomat who served for nine years in the Chinese Legation in London as Counsellor. When he went first to London Sir Walter Langley wrote in a Foreign Office Minute: 'His appointment is the best there could be as he is very friendly to us, speaks English very well and is most intelligent.' Thereafter, he was made Commissioner for Foreign Affairs in Shanghai and then Commissioner for the Pacification of Tibet. He remained on friendly terms with Jordan who informed Grey on one occasion:

> Mr Ivan Chen . . . told me that the Government fully realised the necessity of coming to an amicable arrangement with Great Britain on frontier questions, and that he had been specially chosen as the local agent for developing this change of policy. The Prince Regent had charged him to be friendly and conciliatory without being unduly yielding, and Prince Ch'ing had authorised him to assure me that the appointment was a friendly act intended to smooth away existing difficulties.¹⁰

At Simla, Ivan Chen was affable and skilful, but the power behind the scene was Lu Hsing Chi who had taken the precaution of bribing an official on the Lonchen's staff. Presumably Lu was an expert on Indian and Tibetan affairs, and later the author of a manuscript which Tieh-Tseng li says 'was mimeographed by the Mongolian and Tibetan Affairs Commission for official reference'.¹¹ His direct access to President and Cabinet in Peking during the Simla Conference was extremely important, and McMahon believed that it was on his advice that Chen's initialling of the Simla Convention was rescinded.

The senior British officials at Simla were Archibald Rose and Charles Bell. Rose had many years consular service in China and knew the country and its language intimately. His journey along the Himalayas in 1911 provided first-hand data for the conference. Bell was Tibetan adviser. He was born in India and in the early years of his service with the I.C.S. developed a familiarity with and respect for Tibetan culture. At the time of the Younghusband Mission to Lhasa, he was in charge of a team investigating the possibility of a road from the plains of Bengal through Bhutan to the Chumbi Valley. He was Political Officer in Sikkim from 1908 till 1918 when he retired. But he stayed in Darjeeling to collect material for his history of Tibet. He had already published – in 1905 – a Manual of Colloquial Tibetan grammar and phrase book and an English-Tibetan Dictionary which came later and remains the standard work. He was with the Dalai Lama when he fled to India in 1910. Bell believed passionately that British influence in Lhasa was in the best interests of both countries.

THE PROCEEDINGS

No time was lost in ceremonials at the opening session in the Darbhan-aga palace on October 13, 1913. Lonchen Shatra laid his claims on the table. He stressed recent Chinese excesses, asserted Tibet's independence, and indicated a frontier which included in Tibetan territory the district of Kokonor and the March country as far east as Tachienlu. Ivan Chen followed with his counterclaims to China's sovereignty over Tibet, the right to station a Resident in Lhasa with an escort of 2600 men, to guide Tibet's foreign and military affairs, and claimed a frontier reaching as far west as Giamda, within 260 miles of Lhasa. McMahon was placed in a dilemma; on the assumption that Tibet would not take part in the conference, a draft boundary had been worked out which

> foreshadowed a Chinese control far in excess of that which the Tibetans were willing to accept, whilst our existing treaties with China in regard to Tibet were based on a recognition of, and a reliance on, an extended and substantial suzerainty.[12]

In short, H.M.G. envisaged agreement with China in spheres of influence in Tibet. The Tibetans were not playing this game, and a readjustment of the British position was therefore essential. McMahon had to keep the Chinese out of the Lohit Valley. Lonchen Shatra's main concern was to keep them as far away from Lhasa as possible.

McMahon then presented a map to the Conference, which the R.G.S. had published in 1906 – "Tibet and the Surrounding Regions" – brought up to date by necessary additions East of Longitude 120° compiled from various English, French and German maps and corrections and additions Southwards from Latitude 30° and between Longitudes 93°50' and 102° compiled from recent surveys. Ivan Chen and Lonchen Shatra recorded on their copies the equivalents in their own languages of the English names, together with the course of boundaries of Tibet which they claimed. The Tibetans suspected a discrepancy between English and Chinese texts of the Chinese counterclaims, and McMahon arranged that Han, his own interpreter, should provide a correct translation.

At the second meeting on November 18, McMahon played for time since any draft he proposed had to be shown to the Russians. He urged 'some clear understanding on the limits and area of Tibet' and an examination of the claims for compensation and amnesty. Lonchen Shatra agreed but Ivan Chen refused to accept any procedure which 'did not follow the order of the claims presented by his Government – first the recognition of China's suzerainty, and then the reinstatement of the Amban at Lhasa'. He promised to refer for new instructions, whereupon McMahon reported: 'I expressed my intention, in order to save time, to commence in the meanwhile an examination of the Tibetan frontier evidence with the Lonchen Shatra.' The 'voluminous documentary evidence' produced by the Tibetan could 'be made to take as long or as short a period as circumstances demand'. McMahon described relations between the three Plenipotentiaries as 'of a very friendly character, but neither the Chinese nor Tibetan delegates appear to show any desire to meet each other more frequently than necessity compels them'.[13] Both of them complained of the 'inconvenient curiosity shown in all their doings by the members of the Japanese Consulate-General'.[14]

McMahon's warning that he would have bilateral talks with Lonchen Shatra 'elicited from the Peking Government immediate instructions to their representative to take part in these frontier discussions',[15] with the result that Ivan Chen and Lonchen Shatra read their claims in the presence of Bell and Rose at a number of informal meetings. McMahon who had received the Viceroy's proposals, dated

November 21 did not attend, believing it was wiser to hold himself 'in reserve' for the eventual debates in a full conference.

Bell and Rose tried to focus attention on the area between the two lines both claimed by Lonchen Shatra and Ivan Chen. Tibetan claims were supported by original records of each Tibetan State as far east as Tachienlu. McMahon reports:

> For some days, Mr Chen showed evident signs of panic; he protested that his Government would never consent to the production of evidence in regard to the country east of Batang or the discussion of Kokonor; he telegraphed to Paris (this is queried as a mistake for Peking in the official record) for an official copy of the *Institutes of the Manchu Dynasty*; and he stated that he relied on China's position in international law by which Chao Erh-feng's effective occupation of the country cancelled any earlier Tibetan claim.[16]

Ivan Chen had no other documents than a pamphlet written by General Fu Sung-mu and recording Chao Erh-feng's campaigns, and the published works of foreign authors, notably that of Sir Thomas Holdich.

Fu Sung-mu had been Chao Erh-feng's chief assistant, and succeeded him after his assassination. One of Fung's first acts was to submit a Memorial to the Throne proposing that Eastern Tibet should be converted into a new Chinese province to be called Hsikang (Western Kam). He had already compiled a book on the history of the Tibetan frontier, published in Chengtu in 1912. Sir Eric Teichman, a Consular Official in China at the time, made a detailed study of Fung's plans and drew valuable maps which illustrated the extent of the Chinese ambitions in Tibet.[17]

The divergence between Tibetan and Chinese claims was so great, McMahon 'felt it essential to give each of them an opportunity of growing disheartened with his own case, thus preparing them both for the acceptance of an inevitable compromise'. In due course, both Chen and Lonchen Shatra did invite McMahon: 'to suggest some definite solution of the frontier problem, which they would refer to their Governments without delay.'

THE TWO-ZONE PROPOSAL

The plan McMahon was to put forward was for the recognition of two zones, one to be known as Inner Tibet comprising Kokonor and the area between Batang and Tachienlu, but excluding Chiamdo; the other to be known as Outer Tibet and comprising the remaining portion of the country which was geographically and politically under more direct control from Lhasa. He reckoned

> this would possibly satisfy China ... ; it would prevent the absorption of Inner Tibet as a Chinese province, and so per-petuate and safeguard existing Tibetan (and indirectly British) interests there; and it would prevent the inclusion of any portion of the country within the undefined frontiers of Outer and Inner Mongolia, in which other powers have now acquired spheres of political interest; it would also tend to the creation of an effective Chinese zone between Tibet proper and the encroaching spheres of foreign influence on the North and East, a result which is generally desirable in view of the recent changes in the balance of power in Asia.[18]

Whatever happened, McMahon was determined to have a recognized British representative at Lhasa, which was 'already a centre of foreign intrigue'.

The conference, however, was adjourned on December 24, Simla being already snowbound. Lonchen Shatra left on pilgrimage to a Buddhist shrine and Ivan Chen made a motor-car tour, taking in Agra and other cities of interest. Lu Hsing Chi cabled to the Military Governor of Chengtu:

> The Conference has not yet arrived at any conclusion; the British disregard the question of our sovereign rights in Tibet and insist on first discussing the boundary between Tibet and Ssu-ch'uan. The Tibetan representative, Sha Cha has been induced to assent to this; his intention is to claim a boundary for Tibet which will include Ta Chien Lu and Kokonor. I have telegraphed in cipher to the Government and also to Commissioner Ch'en advising them to hold resolutely to that map of Fu Sung Mu's in which Chiang Ta constitutes the boundary; I do not know whether they will be able to main-tain this claim, because the Dalai Lama relies on British sup-port while the British use Sha-Cha as a puppet.
>
> Our country is at present in an enfeebled condition; our external relations are involved and difficult and our finances

embarrassed. Nevertheless Tibet is of paramount importance
to both Szechwan and Yun-nan and we must exert ourselves
to the utmost during the conference . . . . It would appear
indispensable to station a strong force in Ch'ang Tu (new
official name for Chiamdo) to check Tibetan incursions. If a
force could be secretly introduced into Po Med it would
afford the very best means of safeguarding the frontier.

I have received information that the British have already
sent out exploring parties which have penetrated deeply
into the country and carried out surveys . . . [19]

Lu Hsing Chi was right of course; Bailey and Morshead were still on
their journey to the Tsangpo Falls and Nevill on his way to Tawang.

Meanwhile, shortly after Lonchen Shatra and Ivan Chen had returned from their Christmas holidays, McMahon called a meeting at their
request on January 12, 1914. They presented their summaries of
proceedings to date and their respective claims:

Vague demands on the part of the Chinese for the inclusion
of Giamda, Jyade, Zayul, Chiamdo and Kokonor within
their territory . . . ; the Tibetans presented well-authenticated
and long-standing claims to the whole country as far east as
Tachienlu.[20]

McMahon had already received official approval for his two-zone
proposals, but it was not until February 17 that he put them forward,
by which time he could show them on a map, and simultaneously
suggest

a solution of the political issue by the recognition of autonomy for Outer Tibet, whilst reserving to China the right
to re-establish such a measure of control in Inner Tibet as
would restore and safeguard her historic position, without
in any way infringing the integrity of Tibet as a geographical
and political entity.[21]

A buffer state idea – a concept so characteristic of British policy – could
be created out of the Tibetan March country between Batang and
Tachienlu, thus safeguarding Szechuan and Yunnan; while the territory

round Kokonor, practically unadministered and inhabited only by Mongol nomads could make a second buffer state safeguarding Kansu and the new dominion. McMahon insisted that he was 'determined to prevent the absorption of any part of Tibet'.[22] In short, a Kansu corridor was intended separating Mongolia and Tibet which China might approve, and an autonomous area which conceded a considerable amount of Tibetan demands. In Britain's overall Indian policy it implied a safeguard against any indirect threat from Russia.

While Chen and the Lonchen Shatra argued the pros and cons of McMahon's proposals Chinese and Tibetan troops fought one another on the Szechuan-Tibet border. McMahon received frequent reports from Louis King, who, in August 1913, had been appointed Assistant to the Consul-General at Chengtu, with headquarters at Tachienlu 'for the special purpose of obtaining early information of Chinese movements in the Marches'. A Foreign Office Minute by Sir A. Hirtzl pointed out the

> inconvenience that might arise if, during the negotiations at Simla, the Chinese were to push forward their position on the Eastern frontier of Tibet without our having the means of knowing what they were doing, and were then in a position to force our hands at the Conference by confronting us with a *fait accompli*.[23]

Louis King's reports were to provide the basis of McMahon's insistence to both representatives that they must find a compromise. Chen and Lonchen Shatra made their comments on McMahon's proposals verbally to Rose and Bell in Delhi whither the Conference was now removed. Chen, invoking a continuous theme of Chinese frontier policy, stated that

> The territorial limits of a State in any part of the world can only be decided by the connection which has lately existed between the territory and the State which claims to have it, and not by any remote connection, and still less by any such remote connection which has been long replaced by later ones.
> The territorial limits of Tibet in the time of the Tang dynasty cannot, therefore, be admitted as evidence of any

value for her present claim to the regions of Chinghai,
Batang, Litang and Tachienlu. If one were to abide by such
hoary connection in deciding the limits of her territory, what
could be said about the connection of the same nature
which Tibet had once had, also in the time of the Tang
dynasty, with the valley of the Ganges in India and what could
be said about the subjugation of India by China in the time
of the Yuan dynasty.[24]

The theory conveniently allocated to China the territory between
Chiamdo and Giamda, which, as Chen pointed out, 'was first subjugated by Kanghi', then bestowed on a Dalai Lama and later taken
back by the Manchu Government and restored to the Province of
Szechuan. 'The Republic,' he maintained, 'has no right to alienate any
part of the territory which she has inherited from the Manchu Dynasty,
and she must maintain the extent of her territory as before.' Chen
further challenged McMahon's designations of Inner Tibet and Outer
Tibet.

> Firstly, because there have never been such designations
> known in any public record and official document, both
> Chinese and foreign; secondly because their acceptance
> would be fraught with very grave consequences to China;
> and thirdly, because the regions of Chinghai, Batang, Litang
> and such other places have nothing whatever to do with the
> question at issue. In the former, the Chinese administration
> has been long established and so it is with the latter.[25]

On the question of the autonomy of Tibet, Chen was equivocal; how
far his government were 'prepared to go will depend upon how the
whole Tibetan question is going to be discussed'.

The boundary line proposed by Chen would have legalised Chao
Erh-feng's conquests. He taunted McMahon that when Chao 'led his
army to subjugate the various independent tribes in Hsikang, the
British Government had not interfered in the matter in any way',
that the move, indeed,

> was made in response to the supplication made to China by
> the inhabitants of that place, and as Tibet is a dependency of

China, we have a perfect right to settle the matter between Hsikang and Tibet.[26]

Lonchen Shatra, on the other hand, staked his claim to Batang and Litang on 'convincing authentic documentary evidences showing the appointment of the local officers, both ecclesiastical and secular from the Tibet Government and the collection of rents and taxes, the appointment of hereditary Debas or headmen'. As for the existence of Chinese troops at Batang, Litang and Dartsedo, these were the result of 'the relation of the spiritual teacher and of the lay supporter between the Dalai Lama and the Chinese Emperor'.[27] Beyond this, the Chinese had no control over religious institutions or administration of local lands. Outside these areas which Chao Erh-feng had invaded, Lonchen Shatra said there was no Chinese control whatsoever, that the population was exclusively Tibetan.

Archibald Rose conveyed McMahon's verbal statement to Ivan Chen. He stood firmly on the red line drawn on his map as including the country 'occupied by people of Tibetan race, language, customs and religion, from the earliest recorded delimitation of Tibet in A.D. 822 without a break until the present time'.[28] Neither delegate had presented substantial new evidence, and McMahon contradicted Chen on Batang and Litang from an admission by 'that distinguished Chinese frontier authority, Fu Sung-mu', that at the time of the Anglo-Chinese Treaty,

> the Chinese had no right of interference in the administration of Batang or Litang, which were under their own Tibetan chiefs; the Chinese had commissary officers in these towns, but they exercised no administrative powers.[29]

As for Hsiang-cheng, it was even then in Tibetan hands, while in the case of Chiangta, documentary evidence exists that

> The Manchu Emperors vetoed a proposal to inaugurate an administrative district extending as far west as Chiangta.[29]

The President had assured Sir John Jordan at an interview on June 4, 1913,

> that the insertion of Chiangta in the Presidential Order of May 5th was due to a clerical error.[30]

McMahon further quoted Fu Sung-mu as admitting that in 1904, when Britain and Tibet signed their Agreement, 'there was no Chinese administration in either Inner or Outer Tibet'. Nonetheless, McMahon repeated his willingness – under certain conditions – to see the Chinese placed in the best possible position to maintain the integrity of Tibet as included within the geographical limits of China, and to consolidate a buffer state, to be called the Inner Zone of Tibet, which would safe-guard the internal interests of Kansu, Turkestan, Szechuan and Yunnan. 'Kokonor is included within the Inner Zone, as all available evidence tends to show that it is composed of a number of semi-independent districts, which are historically and actually a part of Tibet.' The line on the map between the Inner and Outer Zones was chosen on the basis of watersheds and deserts which McMahon said would afford to both sides 'the best and safest natural barrier against periodic acts of aggression'.[31]

Relying on Tibetan impatience as an excuse, McMahon warned the Chinese on March 9 that they could expect no more concessions. He brought matters to a head by calling the Conference together on March 11, and delivering a draft Agreement. Lu Hsing-Chi advised Peking not to take this Agreement too seriously, since

> the internal situation in India made it impossible . . . to force
> upon China any agreement which was distasteful to her.[32]

Turn it down categorically, he suggested, and have direct talks in the more receptive atmosphere of London or Peking. His advice was taken. Ivan Chen virtually rejected McMahon's draft on March 20, and produced new proposals on April 7.

1. The boundary between Szechuan and Tibet shall be determined by Luchiang river [Salween].

2. The territory east of Luchiang shall be under the control of China.

3. The territory west of Luchiang up to Chiangta [Giamda] shall be under the Self-Government of Tibet but it must be declared that Tibet recognises the suzerainty of China as in the case of Mongolia.

4. The whole territory of Chingai [Kokonor] shall of course remain under the full control of China.

5. The Thirty-nine Tribes shall remain under the old
system of China without establishing any magistracies.[33]

Realising that these proposals ignored his two-zone plan, McMahon
threatened to withdraw the draft agreement and map, and suspend
personal relations with Mr Chen 'until the Chinese gave evidence of a
more reasonable attitude'. Chen asked whether there was not some
concession that might be made. McMahon made what he described as

> a slight modification . . . on the map in order to meet the
> susceptibilities of the Chinese by the exclusion from Tibet of
> the Lake of Kokonor and the towns of Tachienlu and
> Atuntze.

At this point, McMahon continued, 'a sudden and complete change of
attitude now manifested itself,' and for ten hours at the Foreign Office
in Delhi, 'Chen gave his first intimations of serious negotiations. He
discussed the draft, clause by clause, debating his points with skill and
tireless persistence.' They seemed relatively small points to McMahon
who described Chen as

> Solely inspired by a desire to secure a text which would be
> palatable to the Chinese and calculated to save their position
> in the eyes of the outer world. [35]

But the same night, Chen suddenly presented five new demands, telegraphed from Peking. McMahon's hope of a tidily arranged draft was
dissolved. The following morning he simply 'removed from the table
with as much ceremony as possible' the draft Convention and waited
for reactions. 'The usually placid and inscrutable faces of my Colleagues', he wrote, 'showed for a moment the most intense astonishment and agitation'. They relaxed when he announced that the withdrawal of the Convention was not absolute until the meeting actually
terminated. The meeting was then adjourned until April 17 to allow
Chen a last opportunity to refer to his Government. Peking stood firm.
The President was prepared to accept the convention in principle,
except Article 9 relating to boundaries.

When the Conference reassembled, McMahon and Lonchen Shatra
discussed the crisis in private. McMahon explained that

it might be well to make some last concession to our Chinese colleague in order to meet the spirit of his final instructions, if we could do so without detriment to the interests of Great Britain or Tibet.[34]

A tract of country in the neighbourhood of Kokonor was excluded from Inner Tibet and included in China proper. Further, the prohibition against Tibetan representation in the Chinese National Assembly was confined to the inhabitants of Outer Tibet. These modifications were made in the Convention and the map, and McMahon and the Lonchen initialled the documents. They then considered what should happen if the Chinese still refused to initial the document. McMahon specifically mentioned that the words in Article 2 recognising the suzerainty of China – the cancellation of which had been sanctioned by H.M.G. on April 21 – would be omitted unless Chen initialled the draft before the conclusion of the meeting.

Ivan Chen was thus placed in a dilemma, which McMahon described:

> Peking, though fully informed of the conclusive nature of the meeting, had given him no indication of their willingness to accept our terms, on the other hand, he saw the possibility of losing the Chinese seat in the tripartite Conference and the danger of the conclusion of an agreement between Great Britain and Tibet alone. [35]

Chen decided to initial the draft Convention and the map, but emphasised that he felt bound 'to await definite authority from his Government before the Convention was formally signed and sealed.' On April 29, Chen announced that his Government had disavowed his action in initialling the Convention and declined to recognise the settlement. His Government, he told McMahon, was 'not anxious for a rupture of negotiations and would be quite willing to continue amicable discussions'.[36] McMahon would not reopen the negotiations. He believed that the Chinese had obtained even more than they expected, and concluded that their disavowal of Chen must be the result of 'their proverbial inability to recognise finality in any issue'. This is as good an explanation as any other, supported by a whole history of Chinese procrastination on frontier issues since 1847. But it is not the whole of the story.

In Peking, as in London, frontier policy had two faces; one involved Central Asian affairs, dominated until 1907 by Russian ambitions; the other involved British trading interests in China and was dictated by Chinese internal conditions.

No sooner had news arrived in Peking of Chen's tentative agreement to McMahon's compromise than Jordan heard from a Wai Chia-pou secretary that

> insistence upon our claims to Tibet might hamper the Chinese Government in its desire to facilitate the settlement of our claims in the Yangtse valley.[37]

Chen stayed on in Simla during the interval between initialling and ratification. Peking assumed that pressure could be more effectively exerted in Peking and London than at Simla where McMahon made no secret of his impatience, and Lonchen Shatra could repeat an impressive Tibetan argument. Besides, McMahon and his colleagues had grown up with frontier problems in India whereas Grey and Jordan were more intimately concerned with issues of trade in China and the power struggle with Russia.

CHINESE PROCRASTINATION

China made one more effort to reopen the Conference. Sun Pao-Ch'i presented Jordan with a new map showing McMahon's red and blue lines (as initialled by Chen), China's proposals in green and brown lines and a yellow line showing the boundary between Inner and Outer Tibet as proposed by Chen in the early days of the Simla Conference. Jordan wavered. He might be willing to submit some slight modification of the frontier line – in Kokonor, for instance, although this was 'exceeding his instructions'. But Sun's new proposals introduced the question of administrative control in Inner Tibet. It was true that McMahon had assured Ivan Chen that 'China would be allowed a free hand in the consolidation of her authority in Inner Tibet', but this 'assurance had been qualified by the reservation that the political and geographical entity of Tibet should nevertheless be preserved'. Sun was extremely persistent, and challenged Tibetan evidence on Batang, Litang and the Kham zone presented at Simla. The Tibetans, he complained, 'affected to think that they had rights over all places inhabited by Lamaists, but this was not so. The lamas might have ecclesiastical authority, but this did not necessarily mean that these places belonged to Tibet.'

Jordan countered: '. . . it was evident China coveted the lands raided by Chao Erh-feng and Yin Ch'ang-heng.' The only result of such demands, he warned Sun, 'would be to expedite the conclusion of the Convention by the British and Tibetan Governments.' Jordan telegraphed Grey:

> Had the Chinese proposals . . . been confined to the inclusion of Batang and Litang, and that part of the Kokonor north of the Kunlun range from longitude 86° to 97°, I should have been inclined to submit them for your favourable consideration on the clear understanding that China would accept the rest of the Convention in its present form . . . It seems to me to be important that the areas through which the northern and southern roads to Lhasa pass from Jyekundo and Chiamdo respectively should remain within autonomous Outer Tibet.[38]

The concession Jordan seriously considered submitting to London was very considerable. Sun argued that the border between Northern Tibet and China, was the Kuen Lun range, not the Altyn Tagh, which implied that the Chang Tang was Chinese territory. According to Major Robertson, the area was 'almost uninhabitable and little more than a barren waste of no present value to India, China, or Tibet, either on strategic or economic grounds, and useful only as a neutral buffer zone'.[39] Foreign travellers had been given Chinese passports through the Kokonor country for many years. The only inhabited part was conceded to China by the decision of McMahon. Sven Hedin, who crossed the Altyn Tagh in August 1896, lost most of his animals there, and for the next two months saw no human being. From Abbe Huc's journey in 1844 until the Simla Conference, every traveller emphasised the hardships and uninhabitability of the Chang Tang. The result was that the Indian Government was willing to concede the area to China. McMahon told the Viceroy 'that he might be able to obtain Tibetan consent to substitution of Kuen Lun for Altyn Tagh as northern boundary of Tibet'.[40] This would mean that there would be no tract of Inner Tibet on the north. But this proposal was not enough to persuade the Chinese to sign the Simla Convention. On June 30 they made yet another proposal of their own. They would be willing to regard the (undefined) tract to the south of the Kuen Lun range as Inner Tibet while the district of Jyade (Thirty-nine Banners) would become 'a doubtful area of Inner Tibet in which no large bodies of Chinese troops would be stationed'. McMahon rejected this as 'entirely unacceptable' and Lonchen Shatra 'categorically refused to consider it, or to sign any document which accorded fresh privileges to China without some corresponding concession to Tibet'.[41]

The Conference had already been in session for eight months. Lonchen Shatra was impatient and risking unpopularity at home. Tibetan troops were making headway in the Marches, and he assured McMahon that '. . . they would prefer to continue fighting rather than give their consent to such unjust and unreasonable demands as those now advances'.

McMahon was not only impatient; he suspected direct talks between London and Peking, which seemed always to lead to fresh Chinese demands. He insisted that no considerations put forward by China were new and that 'their reintroduction and discussion on a dual basis at the present juncture can serve no useful purpose'. The Viceroy shared his view that they only gave 'scope for interminable procrastination while offering no hope of finality',[42] and urged a return to tripartite discussions. They both believed that if China were sufficiently certain there would be a dual agreement with the Lonchen, they would sign, a view shared by Alston, the Chinese expert in the Foreign Office, who indicated:

> It seems clear to me that the actual signing by McMahon and the Tibetan will bring in the Chinese at the last moment, and I have always been of that opinion . . . If we fail to carry out our threat to sign now I fear we shall lose face with China all along the line.[43]

McMahon in a Progress Memorandum voiced this complaint:

> I was somewhat uncertain as to the exact intentions of His Majesty's Government in regard to final action; on the one hand, I had been informed that a dual signature of the Convention with Tibet would be desirable; and on the other hand, the last communication to the Chinese Government

appeared to indicate that we were not prepared to proceed to such a dual conclusion.[44]

The fact is that while McMahon and the Viceroy were prepared to *carry out* the threat implied in a dual Convention, Crewe and Jordan were only willing to *make it*. Crewe telegraphed on July 1 instructing the Viceroy that if Chen refused to sign 'the negotiations should then be terminated' by McMahon.

> Great regret should be expressed to the Tibetan delegate at the failure to arrive at a settlement, and he should be assured that in the event of China continuing an aggressive policy, Tibet may rely on receiving the diplomatic support of His Majesty's Government and any such assistance as they may find possible to give in the supply of war munitions.[45]

On July 2 Crewe telegraphed the Viceroy:

> When McMahon expresses his regret that the signature of the Convention has been rendered impossible through the action taken by China, he should add, in full conference, the statement that the settled views of His Majesty's Government with regard to boundaries and status of Tibet are represented by the Convention as initialled. You should convey privately to the Tibetan plenipotentiary the assurance which I telegraphed on the 1st instant.[46]

On July 3 Crewe sent this telegram:

> Separate signature by Tibetan and British plenipotentiaries cannot be authorised by His Majesty's Government. In event of Chinese representative declining to sign, procedure laid down in my telegrams of 1st and 2nd instant should be followed by McMahon.[47]

This third telegram did not reach McMahon in time. A Minute paper of the India Office is attached: 'This is the telegram which arrived too late'. And another Minute Paper explains: 'That the Secretary of State's Instructions of July 3 reached Sir H. McMahon "too late to affect the proceedings of the conclusive meeting" was not due to any delay on the part of this office, but primarily to the fact that no one of sufficient authority to deal with the question arrived at the F.O. on Friday last until after 1 p.m. In the circumstances, Sir H. McMahon appears to have acted most judiciously, and it is submitted that his action be approved by H.M.'s Government'.[48] It was, and duly commended.

McMahon had called the conference together on July 3 1914, delaying it till 11.15 in the evening to hear Peking's instructions to Chen. These were 'very explicit', Chen said, 'and enjoined him not to sign the Tripartite Convention'. The Lonchen then reported his instructions. Lhasa had said that 'as he had accepted the Convention, he should sign it. His Government did not consider the Convention satisfactory from their point of view, but as it had been accepted there was no alternative but to sign'.

McMahon said he was also empowered to take conclusive action and would do so in concert with his Tibetan colleague.

> By this act the document would be placed beyond the limits of discussion, and no alteration would hereafter be possible.[49]

When he announced an additional Declaration safeguarding the interests of Great Britain and Tibet Ivan Chen said his Government had instructed him to declare they

> would not recognise any treaty or similar document that might now or hereafter be signed between Great Britain and Tibet.[50]

As soon as McMahon and Lonchen Shatra had signed the document, McMahon closed the conference, but left it that if Chen was in a position to sign the Convention and would like the conference to reassemble to do so, then they would be willing to meet him once more on July 6. Nothing happened. But in Peking and in London the Wai-Chiao Pu made one more effort to re-open direct talks. Would His Majesty's Government prefer to delegate Jordan to negotiate in Peking or to negotiate with Lew Yuk Lim, China's representative in London? The door was still left open.

Jurists and historians have written on the Simla Convention at great length. When McMahon was convinced that Chen was not going to sign, he at once evolved an ingenious compromise, arguing that 'there was no time for a further reference to London'. The result was that he and Lonchen Shatra initialled the Convention, amended, since only two nations were now involved, and made a formal Declaration under which the terms would become binding on the two Governements. This tactic avoided a dual signature of the document drawn up on a tripartite basis. It gave Britain and Tibet the advantages of the Convention but precluded China.

Alastair Lamb describes the climax of the Conference as a charade, and sometimes describes McMahon as the villain of the piece and the Chinese his innocent victims, suggests that the *initialling* of the Convention was to provide for future Chinese adherence, while the *signature* on the map attached was to involve China if and when that happened. He asks: 'Could it be that McMahon had it in mind to prevent Sir John Jordan or some other employee of the Foreign Office in London, at some future date, from making any fresh concessions to the Chinese?' [51] It is just possible McMahon knew perfectly well that Jordan and Crewe were amenable to Chinese diplomacy. He was determined to finalise negotiations which had dragged on for nine months. And he had obtained almost all of the objectives that Britain's Tibetan policy required.

THE BILATERAL AGREEMENT

One substantial advantage was the right of the British Agent at Gyantse to proceed to Lhasa, and to negotiate with the Tibetan Government direct. Failure to negotiate direct had proved a great embarrassment since numerous Russian Buriats and two Japanese had had this access. Secondly, Britain obtained a most-favoured nation clause in a series of Trade Regulations which would supercede those of 1893 and 1908 to which China had also been a party. Thirdly, British firms were able to sell arms to Tibet provided they were sent through British territory. This had the effect, as McMahon intended, of strengthening Tibet in their struggle against the Chinese in the Marches.

But the most far-reaching result achieved at Simla was the delimitation of 850 miles of boundary between India and Tibet. This was arranged through talks between McMahon and Lonchen Shatra with Bell and Rose acting as Tibetan and Chinese adviser respectively. McMahon's brief was contained in the Memorandum drawn up by the

Chief of the General Staff. The objective was entirely strategic, a line of frontier intended "to meet the forward policy of China". When the conference began Bell had advised McMahon:

> The best way would be for us to show the Lonchen the frontier we want, ask him to agree to it, and hear what he has to say ... The Tawang Monastery is clearly Tibetan ... We must try to get the Tibetans to give us this up to the boundary line which we want. We will tell them that it is necessary to have a straight boundary and that we give them the area south of Tila in exchange ... We should not begin the discussion of this Tibetan-Indian frontier, until the China-Tibetan frontier is settled between Rima, Menkong, Atuntze and Sanga Chatzeng because on this will depend the easterly starting point of the Indian-Tibetan frontier, whether we can give the Tibetans the Tila area in exchange. We should also insist in getting the Tawang area south of the red line and adjoining Bhutan though this seems undoubtedly Tibetan territory, as otherwise Tibet and Assam will adjoin each other and, if Tibet should again come under Chinese control, it will be a dangerous position for us. [52]

McMahon was able to put the finishing touches to his famous red line on the map after hearing the results of an extensive survey made by Bailey and Morshead. He hoped, the Viceroy reported, 'to obviate the necessity for verbal definition of boundary line by showing frontier by line on map'. This map giving the India-Tibet frontier from the Isu Razi Pass to the Bhutan frontier was accepted by the Lonchen in February 1914 subject to confirmation by his Government and to two conditions:

> 1. The Tibetan ownership in private estates on the British side of the frontier will not be disturbed.
> 2. If the sacred places of Tso Karpo and Tsari Sarpa fall within a day's march of the British side of the frontier, they will be included in Tibetan territory and the frontier modified accordingly. [53]

Lonchen communicated these proposals to Lhasa, and Bell noted in his Diary for March 21, 1914:

Lonchen Shatra told me on the 17th instant that he had now
received orders from the Lhasa Government about Tawang.
The Lonchen said that the Dalai Lama, the Lonchens and the
Lhasa Council thinking that it would take long time to call
and consult the landed proprietors of Tawang, have therefore decided this question without consulting the landed
proprietors. The Tibetan Government have authorised the
Lonchen to surrender the Tawang land to the British
Government in consideration of the *great* kindness shown to the
Tibetans by the British Government. The Tibetan Government surrenders all the revenue that the Tibetan Government
used to receive from Tawang but requests that the income
estates of private individuals and monasteries may be given
to them as they are at present. I told the Lonchen that all
proprietory rights of private estates in Tawang will be
retained by those who at present enjoy them.[54]

The Lonchen also asked Bell for Lhasa to retain the right of appointing the Head Lama in Tawang. Bell couldn't agree to this but he
promised that the British Government would consult Lhasa when a
Head Lama was to be appointed.

The Lonchen faithfully reported the details of McMahon's proposed
boundary to his Government. He told McMahon on March 25, 1914:

As it was feared that there might be friction in future unless
the boundary between India and Tibet is clearly defined, I
submitted the map, which you sent to me in February last,
to the Tibetan Government at Lhasa for orders. I have now
received orders from Lhasa, and I accordingly agree to the
boundary as marked in red in the two copies of the map signed
by you, subject to the conditions mentioned in your letter dated
24th March and to me through Mr. Bell. I have signed and
sealed the two copies of the maps. I have kept one copy here
and return herewith the other.[55]

The map of the North-East Frontier of India on the scale of eight
miles to the inch was probably the first cartographic record of any of
these eight hundred miles of mountainous country. Much of it passed
through or bounded tribal territory which McMahon described as:

'still imperfectly known to the Tibetan Government. It is, therefore, obviously necessary to define the boundary, in any agreement relating thereto, in as great detail as possible. This has now been done in the map which the present agreement is based'. This large scale map was not produced in the full session of the Conference but a smaller scale variation was, and it was not challenged. It would seem extremely unlikely that Ivan Chen was unaware of the Indo-Tibetan talks and their outcome. The Lonchen had plenipotentiary rights to sign the Convention which therefore had validity independently of the Simla Convention. As far as available records show, Chen did not at any time complain of the bi-lateral agreement.

On any evaluation of the talks at Simla, Britain was the greatest beneficiary, and the McMahon Line the most far-reaching result. McMahon knew precisely what he wanted; negatively, the containment of China in the Assam Himalaya; positively, the extension of British-controlled territory to a strategic frontier worked out by the General Staff. This involved the addition of fifty thousand square miles of tribal or almost uninhabited country to the British Empire. Some of these tribal people had had close affinities for centuries with the Tibetans. Others were within the Tibetan ecclesiastical orbit. Jordan, who was more concerned with Britain's commercial interests in China than with strategic objectives in Tibet, privately regretted McMahon's abrupt closure of the conference, and commented: 'It looked as if the British and Tibetan Representatives knew each other's cards throughout, and as if Ivan Chen was not too loyal to his own Government.' [56] In the spring of 1914, it happened that British and Tibetan interests coincided to a considerable degree, and McMahon thereby obtained the frontier required by British strategy. The Lonchen could claim a diplomatic and a military advance in Tibet's struggle with China.

Was this all the Tibetans hoped to get from the Simla talks? Did Bell's persuasiveness explain the considerable advantages to Britain? Or did he hold out advantages which Tibetans might obtain on the eastern frontier (apart from arms and munitions)? McMahon's Outer and Inner Line would have meant the withdrawal of Chinese forces from Outer Tibet, and the theoretical surrender of claims to Batang and Litang which Ivan Chen had advanced at Simla. McMahon's buffer zone between his red and blue lines would have been to Lhasa's advantage, since it limited the advance of Chinese troops, and, if they advanced, it meant British involvement since British arms and

G

ammunitions were promised to the Tibetans. Although there was not unanimity in Lhasa, the loss of control over certain areas round Tawang and Walong seemed to be offset by safeguards for sacred places and revenue to Tibetan landlords. The Tibetans assumed that although Chen did not sign the Convention at Simla, the Chinese would agree to do so later. In the following January, Lonchen wrote to Bell.

> I have explained to the Dalai Lama and the high Tibetan officials that the signature of the Chinese Government is all that is now wanted to complete the Tripartite Convention. This coupled with the fact that the British Government have warned the Chinese against any aggression in Tibetan territory has made their minds easier and they are eagerly awaiting events. They all appreciate to its full worth the advice you have kindly given me with regard to the future of Tibet.[57]

It is easy to see the advantages which Simla conferred on Britain and Tibet. In theory, at any rate, China would seem to have forfeited such gains as her signature would have implied. The Anglo-Chinese Convention would still have operated in her favour. She could have had an Amban at Lhasa with three hundred men as a military escort. Chinese suzerainty over Tibet was explicit in the text of the Convention, while the first of the Notes which were an appendage to it reads:

> It is understood by the High Contracting Parties that Tibet forms part of Chinese Territory.[58]

Was China too unsure of her ability to exploit such theoretical gains? Did she intend signature at any time? On an analogy with her attitude to frontier issues in 1847 and 1899, she was determined to avoid commitments. Did Peking overplay its delaying tactics on the assumption that the Yangtse Valley mattered more to Britain than eight hundred miles of mountainous territory, where tribal peoples lived and where Chinese control had never been exerted? Crewe and Jordan belived that the threat of dual signature would force China's hand at the last moment. So too did the Viceroy. Ivan Chen himself believed it. He told McMahon that even if his signature were withheld

> the actual conclusion of an independent agreement between Great Britain and Tibet is likely to produce a favourable change in the attitude of Peking Government.[59]

So it was left to McMahon to force the issue at the last moment and to secure the bilateral agreement. Sir Edward Grey, who was most appreciative of McMahon's efforts and his skill in the negotiations, concluded that until agreement had been reached with the Russian Government, Britain could only act upon the initialled Convention so far as it 'does not violate the 1907 Agreement'.[60] The Russians did not make any objections either to the Simla Convention or to the bilateral agreement between Britain and Tibet. In any event, the outbreak of the First World War diverted Russian, as well as British attention, from the Himalayas.

McMahon returned to England immediately after the Conference ended. Langley wrote to Jordan:

> I saw Sir H. McMahon when he arrived in England. He was not very sympathetic about China and it is no doubt difficult to convince any one from India that there is a Chinese point of view which deserves consideration. He was certainly disappointed that he had not been allowed to sign with Tibet alone and to carry out the whole convention as it stood. I hope with you that some day, perhaps when the war is over, the Chinese will see wisdom and sign.[61]

What Happened to the McMahon Line?

ACTIVATING THE McMAHON LINE;
ASSAM AND THE SECOND WORLD
WAR; THE SIANG (DIHANG) VALLEY;
THE SIYOM VALLEY AND THE UPPER
SIANG (DIHANG); THE SUBANSIRI
VALLEY

Shortly after the Conference was ended, the Chinese planned a Mission
to Lhasa with a view to driving a wedge between Britain and Tibet.
Jordan told the Wai Chiao Pu that his Government would consider
this 'a most discourteous and unfriendly act'.[1] The mission did not
materialize, but British Intelligence soon discovered that the President
had communicated with the Dalai Lama through the Commissioner to
Chamdo, and found that Lhasa's terms for direct talks with China
were:

1. Neither party to advance beyond their present positions
   on the frontier pending the result of the negotiation.
2. The Tibetan Government to recognise both the Chamdo
   district and the Thirty-Nine Banner country as Chinese
   territory.
3. The Chinese Government to recognise the autonomy of
   Tibet.
4. The Tibetan Government to allow a Chinese Resident
   with a small bodyguard to be stationed at Lhasa.
5. No other Chinese officials nor troops to be stationed in
   Tibetan territory.[2]

Peking was under-estimating Bell's determination to follow up the
Simla Conference. His friendship with the Dalai Lama and the Lonchen
Shatra, at a time when Britain was in the throes of the First World
War, made an unusual contribution to British-Tibetan relations.

Bell envisaged Tibet as a willing satellite, whose future adminis-
trators should learn from civil and military administration in England.[3]

British engineers should go to Tibet to explore its mineral wealth and the Tibetans should be persuaded to make more money available for industrial development. They ought to be taught banking and veterinary surgery. Meanwhile, he argued, let them have arms and munitions to resist China.

McMahon was already in Cairo in November 1914, but the Dalai Lama sent him a silk scarf, a jade cup with two handles, and a letter asking for troops, '... seeing that the affairs on the Kham side are getting serious.' He reminded McMahon that he 'and his assistants, Mr Bell ... and others, whose wisdom is unequalled, continually gave good advice to my Plenipotentiary and supported him in all his rights. They worked together as if the British and the Tibetans were of the same house.'[4]

In February 1915 the Dalai Lama addressed the President of China politely enough, complaining that his Monastery guards in Ri-Wo-Che and Ngen-Da had been attacked by his troops.

> If you have no intention of fighting, please withdraw all Chinese troops and thus cause happiness to both Chinese and Tibetans.[5]

Both Britain and China were under heavy pressure at that time; Britain was at war with Germany and China had just been presented with a twenty-one point ultimatum by Japan. Yet Britain's crisis was China's opportunity to settle the Tibetan question, and on June 28, 1915, Yuan Shih Kai proposed to Jordan that Chamdo should be given to Tibet on condition that the phrase 'Tibet is a part of China' should be included in the main text of the Simla Convention.[6] Jordan at first agreed to consider minor changes but subsequently refused to reopen negotiations. The Viceroy argued it would give the impression of weakness to Peking as well as to Lhasa; it could not happen without discussions with Lhasa; a more precise definition of Chinese demands would be necessary. And 'even if satisfactory Convention were negotiated, inconvenient demands of Russia regarding Afghanistan' would have to be met before it could be operative. He was not opposed to private enquiries as to Chinese demands, but held that if at the end of the war Britain could come to terms with Russia on certain Asiatic questions 'our hands may then be more free to deal with China in regard to Tibet'. Bell argued:

If we do not help them now, there is a very real and serious danger that she may fall under the complete domination of China, and that we may be faced anew in an aggravated form with those dangers which the Simla Convention was intended to obviate.[7]

He persisted in the view that Britain and Tibet had gained many advantages from the Simla Convention, and based his policy on the assumption that it was a valid international treaty. As Political Officer in Sikkim he was within a day's march of the Natu La on the other side of which lay Tibet.

The Government of India took due note of Bell's opinions but informed him that that interest is necessarily purely academic, since the Simla Convention has not been signed by the Chinese Government or accepted by the Russian Government, and is therefore for the present invalid and proceeded in the same letter to admit:

It is true that by the secret Anglo-Tibetan declaration, which recognised the Convention as binding on Great Britain and Tibet, certain advantages under the Convention have been obtained by both parties, but no useful purpose can be gained at present by an examination of those respective advantages. The fact remains that the negotiations conducted last year in Simla broke down simply and solely because the Government of India attempted to secure for Tibet greater advantages than the Chinese Government were prepared to concede, and the fact that China has persisted in her refusal to sign the Convention can only be regarded as an indication that both the Government of India and the Tibetan Plenipotentiary, Lonchen Shatra, were unduly anxious to secure the best terms they could for Tibet.[8]

If Tibet and China succeeded in negotiating a treaty which was not objectionable from the British point of view, then, the India Government told Bell, there was no reason why this should not be embodied in a fresh convention and accepted by H.M.G. If it were objectionable then H.M.G. would repudiate it and threaten to withdraw support. And if no separate agreement were made, then '. . . things must remain for the time being in *status quo*'.[9]

Feelers were thrown out in Peking from time to time suggesting that the Chinese still wanted to reopen negotiations. Sometimes, as for instance on May 23, 1917, the Minister for Foreign Affairs asked Alston point blank whether he was in a position to take up the question.[10] But civil war broke out in Yunnan and Szechuan in the autumn of 1918 and Tibetan troops became involved. Chinese and Tibetans fought in the Marches. Internal dissensions and Japanese threats weakened the Chinese army. Tibetan troops, trained and equipped by the British, captured Chamdo, Draya, Markham, Gonjo and De-ge. As they approached Nyarong and Batang, Szechuanese officials requested Sir Eric Teichman, the British Consular Agent at Tachienlu, to mediate. It is true that the Tibetan army was stretched to its maximum, but Teichman himself observed that if the fighting had continued, 'another month or two would possibly have seen several thousand more Chinese prisoners in Tibetan hands, and the Lhasa forces in possession of all the country up to Tachienlu'.[11]

Teichman's mediation, reinforced by British refusal to supply any more arms to the Lhasa Government, had the effect of helping China. The Rongbatsu Truce, which Teichman negotiated, meant, that China remained in control of Batang, Litang, Nyarong, Kanze and the area to the east of them, while the Tibetans retained Chamdo, Draya, Markham, De-ge and the area to the west of them. Hugh Richardson makes well the point that 'Chinese writers who inveigh against British designs in Tibet, are inclined to forget the moderating influence exercised at that time'.[12]

Jordan, for his part, urged the Wai Chiao-Pu at least nine times during 1918 to begin talks on the Tibetan problem. With the expiry of the Rongbatsu Truce in October particularly in mind, he renewed his demands for a settlement in April, and in May, 1919, the Chinese Government made proposals to settle the question on the basis of a compromise frontier line. Jordan summarised them:

1. Statement that Tibet forms part of Chinese territory, now included in notes to be exchanged, to be inserted in the treaty itself.
2. Chinese Commissioners to be stationed at the trade marts.
3. Insertion of a clause in the treaty to the effect that autonomous Tibet recognised China's sovereignty.

4. A revision to the old eighteenth century line as the boundary of autonomous Tibet and the creation of an 'Inner Tibet' consisting of Derge, Nyarong, and the southern portions of the Kokoner territory.

He made these observations to Curzon:

1 and 3. These seem unobjectionable.
2. It is difficult to say whether the Chinese will insist on this or not. If they do, I submit that the presence of Chinese agents at the marts would be rendered harmless, provided we obtain as a counter-concession British representation at Lhasa itself.
4. [This proposal would mean] the transfer of Derge (now in Tibetan hands) and of the southern portion of the Kokonor territory (still in Chinese hands) to an 'Inner Tibet', the status of which remains to be defined. [13]

As compared with the Simla Conference map, they would mean 'the abandonment of a good deal of the 'Inner Tibet' of 1914 to China'. Jordan held that Batang, Litang and Tachienlu territories had 'long been integral portions of the province of Szechuan' and that the southern portion of Kokoner territory 'is now, and always has been, under the nominal control of the Chinese'. The crux of the boundary had always been the fate of Chamdo, Draya, Gonjo, and Markham which China, for the first time, since the Simla talks began, now offered to surrender to an autonomous Tibet. De-ge presented difficulties. The Tibetans had occupied it 'against our advice' and still held it. Gonjo, which the Chinese now proposed should go to autonomous Tibet, was 'a gain for the Dalai Lama'.

Jordan strongly advised discussions with the Chinese alone and then, if an agreement were made,

to present it to the Tibetans as the best we can do for them and proceed to sign it on a tripartite basis. He wanted the boundary arrangement 'to take the form of an article, and not a map', since the areas concerned were so little known and partly unexplored. [14]

Jordan believed there was at last a chance of settlement. He told Curzon:

I consider that these proposals constitute a reasonable and hopeful basis for negotiation. They are probably not China's last word; even if they are, a settlement on these lines would fully safeguard our interests and would by no means infringe Tibet's.[15]

But in the middle of the negotiations China repudiated them without explanation.

Britain was now in a dilemma; she was pledged by the Simla agreement to supply arms and munitions to Tibet 'in the event of continued aggression on the part of the Chinese'. Lhasa was naturally beginning to doubt Britain's word and her capacity to force China to the point of an agreement. Jordan tried in vain to reopen negotiations in January 1920, suggesting a conference in Lhasa. He was turned down by the Tibetans, who, at that moment, were entertaining a Chinese Mission from Kansu. Their influence, Bell wrote from Gangtok, 'was considerably augmented'. His Tibetan friends 'were almost in despair at our turning the cold shoulder to them. The Chinese Mission had done what it could to poison the minds of the Tibetan Government and people against us'.[16] He believed that personal talks with the Dalai Lama would explain Britain's position and counteract Chinese influence.

An invitation to visit the Dalai Lama arrived at a most convenient moment, and, in November 1920, Bell was busy in Lhasa making the most of his personal contacts there. His two books, *Tibet, Past and Present* and *Portrait of the Dalai Lama* provide an intimate picture of the interwoven political and religious pressures which constituted Tibetan life. He himself wanted to see Tibet within the orbit of the British Empire although he was sensitive to the view of some of his Tibetan friends who argued that one day an Indian Government might prove unable to help them against China. 'They will therefore', he wrote, 'throw in their lot with China or with any strong power that will treat them well'. Bell's argument was that Britain should safeguard India's position.

We want Tibet as a buffer to India on the north. Now there are buffers and buffers; and some of them are of very little use. But Tibet is ideal in this respect. With the large desolate area of the Northern Plains controlled by the Lhasa Government, central and southern Tibet governed by the same authority, and the Himalayan border States guided by, or in close alliance with, the British-Indian Government, Tibet forms a barrier equal, or superior, to anything that the world can show elsewhere.[17]

Bell's India-centric view of Tibet, reinforced by his personal feelings, was bound to differ from Jordan's, the latter having served many years in Peking. Jordan knew that relations with China determined the security of large investments in the Yangtse valley and a growing trade along China's eastern coast. But he also also felt that if and when the Chinese returned to Lhasa, they would 'probably make every effort . . . to insinuate themselves once more between us and the Tibetans'. He therefore wanted to give moral support to Lhasa. 'The whole history of the Chinese on Tibet and on the Tibetan border', he told Curzon, 'has been one of alternate bullying, chicanery, and intrigue'.[18]

In August 1921, the Secretary of State for Foreign Affairs invited the Chinese Government through their Minister in London, Dr Wellington Koo, to resume negotiations either in London or Peking. His Majesty's Government, the invitation outlined,

> would be prepared to make every effort to induce the Tibetan Government to accept a settlement satisfactory to China on the basis of the draft convention of 1914, modified in accordance with China's wishes as expressed in her offer of 1919.[19]

Dr Koo politely refused the offer, giving China's preoccupation with the forthcoming Pacific Conference as the reason. He was told that

> Unless the Chinese Government were willing to resume negotiations for a tripartite settlement without further delay, say within one month, we should be compelled to proceed alone. In that case we should regard ourselves as at liberty to deal with Tibet, if necessary, without again referring to China; to enter into closer relations with the Tibetans; to send an officer to Lhasa from time to time to consult the Tibetan Government; to open up increased trading intercourse between India and Tibet; and to give the Tibetans any reasonable assistance they might require in the development and protection of their country.[19]

Two years had passed since Jordan's talks on the Chinese offer of May 1919 had been so abruptly terminated. The all-clear was given to Bell, already in Lhasa, to go ahead with bilateral talks. Bell told the Dalai Lama that Tibet would now be supplied with arms and munitions 'on their giving a written assurance that such will be used solely for self-defence and the maintenance of internal order'. Limited training would be given to the Tibetan forces. A British school was founded for sons of Tibetan aristocrats. Technical aid to improve communications and assistance in the development of mineral resources were made available.

Opinion in Tibet was divided, even between leaders of the three great monasteries. The Panchen Lama was leader of the powerful pro-China faction. According to N. Dhordup, a member of the Political Officer's Staff, the pro-British faction consisted only of the Dalai Lama, Prime Minister Lonchen Shatra, four Shapes and one Chikgale.

Bell, who was in Lhasa from November 1920 till October 1921, was alarmed at the results of a Chinese Mission from Kansu. The Tibetan Government had agreed to make a settlement, 'but not without the presence and co-operation of a British representative at the negotiations and conclusion of the Treaty'.[21] They agreed that their troops on the frontier would not attack each other; that the Kansu Mission would urge on the President of the Chinese Republic both to send a Representative and to request the British Government to send a Representative also; and that the Tibetan Government would also urge the British Government to send a Representative.

A new element was introduced into this power struggle in 1922 when the Panchen Lama appealed in vain to the British Government to mediate between himself and the Dalai Lama who had insisted on a contribution to the cost of the Tibetan army. The request was refused 'on the ground that it would have constituted interference in Tibetan internal affairs'. The following year the Panchen Lama left Tashilumpo for China where he was given hospitality for the next fourteen years, until his death. Inevitably, he became the centre for intrigue and his hosts exploited him with considerable skill to counter Bell's influence in Lhasa.

Disregard for British ambitions was underlined in the appointment of a new Commander-in-Chief of the Tibetan army. Lungshar was as hostile towards India as Tsarong, whom he succeeded, had been friendly. Direct talks with China seemed now to be in Tibet's interest.

When the Nationalists took control in Nanking in 1928, the Panchen
Lama openly appealed to them to assume charge of affairs in Tibet, in
order to save it from becoming a 'second India'. Two Missions from
Chiang Kai-shek arrived in Lhasa in 1930. The Dalai Lama told a
member of the first Mission:

> The British, indeed, have a mind to draw me to their side.
> Nevertheless, I know the importance of guarding the national
> sovereignty and I have never surrendered a bit of it in spite of
> the necessity of having to deal with them, their character and
> customs being so different from ours.

And to a member of the second Mission he said:

> As from now on, the patronage relationship between the
> Central Government and Tibet is going to be faithfully
> observed and the Central Government is to show sincerity
> to make Tibet feel safe and secure; the area over which
> autonomy is to be exercised should naturally be the same
> as before. It is expected that the Central Government will
> return to Tibet those districts which originally belonged to
> it but which are now not under its control so that a perpetual
> peace and harmony will surely be the result.

and again:

> Tibet's hope for the present is only that the Central Govern-
> ment will supply it with arms. [22]

When relations between Nepal and Tibet became strained in 1930,
the Dalai Lama appealed successfully to Colonel Weir, Political
Officer in Sikkim, to visit Lhasa. In the ebb and flow of Tibeto-
British friendship, the Dalai Lama invariably chose to ask London for
assistance when in trouble.

In August 1932 Tibet was threatened on two fronts; Szechuan
chieftain Wen-hui was in arms against Tibetan troops, and the Governor
of Chinghai was proving recalcitrant. The Dalai Lama appealed to the
Government of India to intervene in Nanking. Weir returned to
Lhasa, and helped to bring about a cease-fire. During his stay, Richardson reports that

The Tibetan Government drew up proposals for discussion on the basis of the 1914 Convention. These were communicated by the Dalai Lama to the National Government and had their part in bringing about the cease-fire . . . [but the Nanking Government] was not in a mood to consider British participation in any settlement. From now on the Simla Convention was of no further interest to the Chinese Government as the basis of a settlement with Tibet, even though the British Government continued to refer to it, for some time longer, as if it still remained open to Chinese adherence.[23]

The Tibetan picture was completely transformed by the Dalai Lama's death on December 17, 1933. His policy of non-alignment was described unambiguously in his Political Testament, composed only a few months before his death.

The Government of India is near to us and has a large army. The Government of China also has a large army. We should therefore maintain firm friendship with these two; both are powerful.[24]

During the four years interregnum before a new Dalai Lama was discovered, Sino-British rivalry became the most important factor in Tibet's foreign relations. No time was lost by the Chinese in sending the high-ranking General Huang Mu-sung to lament the Dalai Lama's death and start talks aimed at winning over his successors. From Sikkim, N. Dhordup was despatched to join in the lamentations and to keep a watch on the General. Chinese and British reports differ widely, especially on the degree to which the Regent and his advisers were prepared to make concessions on Tibet's independence. According to Tien-Tseng li, Tibet was asked to observe two fundamental points: firstly that Tibet must be an integral part of the territory, and secondly she must obey the Central Government. Declarations about Tibet's political system were to give the Nanking Government the direction of the country's foreign affairs, national defence, communications and the choice of important officials. If the Regent had been willing to agree and carry out these proposals, Li ingeniously remarks, the status of Tibet would have been 'settled . . . in a constitutional sense'. He attributed their refusal to take 'such a bold step' to differences between 'conservative lamas and ambitious military men, ... fear of the consequences that might result from offending the British power or from coming more directly under Chinese authority, as well as from the loss of the advantage of sitting on the fence as a buffer state'.[25]

The Tibetan counter-proposals proved to General Huang that the Tibetans were not yet ready to become part of China, and he left Lhasa in October 1934. Describing interviews he had with Tibetans twelve years before Li's book was published, Hugh Richardson says that the Tibetans made no concessions and that

> the official Chinese report appears deliberately to ignore the frequent references by the Tibetan Government to the 1914 Convention as the basis for agreement, or to the need for associating the British Government in any settlement.[26]

One specific outcome of General Huang's visit was the Regent's agreement that the Panchen Lama could return to Lhasa. This did not materialise because the Chinese demanded that a military escort should accompany him, and the Tibetans were not prepared to risk this suspected threat to their independence. British officials seeing the escort as a thin edge of the wedge, sent a Mission to forestall it. Basil Gould, Hugh Richardson and F. Spencer Chapman spent five months in Lhasa in 1936. Their frequent talks with the Regent and other Tibetan officials undoubtedly had the effect of underpinning the pro-Indian group in Lhasa. Then the Panchen Lama's death and Japan's attack on China combined to produce a temporary halt in Sino-British rivalry at any rate, on diplomatic levels.

Meanwhile the Indian Government continued to base its policy on the assumption that the Agreement signed at Simla by McMahon and the Lonchen Shatra had settled the frontier between India and Tibet. It was not a settlement which was popular with the Tibetans, though as far as published documents show, they accepted its validity. Lonchen Shatra was criticised for the concessions he made to McMahon. In July 1915, Bell commented that Lonchen Shatra was

> said to have no voice in these intrigues of the Tibetan Government with the Chinese, [and] to be much blamed for failing in his negotiations in India and for surrendering the Tawang

tract, and for making other important concessions to the British Government in the recent Convention'.[27]

World War I diverted attention from the remote tracts of Tibetan territory bordering on those of the hill tribes of the north-eastern frontier and included the Anglo-Tibetan Agreement. The Indian Government was content to ignore the buffer territories along the whole northern frontier of Assam, between it and Tibet. Life continued as before in most of the small villages along or near the line McMahon and Lonchen had agreed was the Indo-Tibetan frontier. Shortly after the Simla Conference had ended, the Chief Commissioner prescribed 'rules for the administration of justice in the Central and Eastern Sections of the North-East Frontier' adding that

> these rules will only be enforced in the area under loose political control to the extent which may from time to time appear expedient.[28]

Expeditions along potentially strategic river valleys did bring small villages under control; between 1915 and 1918, the Dihang and the Dihong were covered by this method and a system of taxation became the immediate proof of a remote imperial presence. Sometimes there was trouble; in 1918, three men of Elapoin on the Dibang murdered a sepoy in Nizamghat. O'Callaghan visited the village in December 1920 and satisfied the Chief Commissioner that the result had 'gone far to re-establish the authority of Government after the enforced non-intervention of the last few years'[29] Again, in 1928, the Po Raja, escaping from tax-collecting Tibetans, was given sanctuary in Sadiya. He absconded, was arrested, then escaped and died. His tribe took revenge, with resulting unrest in areas south of the McMahon Line. A promenade was undertaken in the Sisseri Valley in 1934 to deal with a village in British territory where four children were killed and others injured. And again a promenade was sent up the Dibang to exact retribution for certain murders and to settle cases between tax-paying and non-tax-paying villages.[30] A more ambitious tour was made in 1936 when the Political Officer, accompanied by one British officer and 25 other ranks toured for three weeks in unadministered territory along the Dihang River. No British face had been seen north of Komsing and Pangin since 1913. In 1937 the same Political Officer, W. H. Calvert,

toured the Mishmi Hills to renew contacts with Mishmis who had had
no visitors for fifteen years. Gradually the area of control was extended
up to the difficult, mountainous miles short of the McMahon Line.

The Tawang area, to which the Chief of the General Staff had
attached so much importance in 1912 was covered by the Aka
promenade made by Captain Nevill during the Simla Conference.
He was told to study possible communications from Tawang to Odalguri, to find out about the people on the frontier, and to ascertain exactly how far Tibetan rule and influence affected the country. He wrote
a long and extremely able report, describing the chief Tibetan influence
as the Tawang Monastery, where five hundred monks lived. He
suggested that a Political Officer should be stationed at Tawang who
would supervise a subsidy to the Tawang Monastery, that police posts
should be set up at least at Dirang and Rupa, and dispensaries wherever
possible. He believed that that was the psychological moment to make
'a loose administration of the country and settlement of the affairs
with the Monastery and the Tibetans'. But nothing happened at
Tawang. Captain Nevill made a number of other expeditions, punishing raiders, and invariably recommending that posts should be built in
these strategically important hills. He made this prophecy in his final
Administration Report.

> There is no doubt that as soon as China settles down this
> Tibetan Frontier will become of great importance. China
> has still its eyes on Tibet and on Lhasa, the pro-Chinese party is
> growing in influence and should China gain control of Tibet
> the Tawang country is particularly adapted for a secret and
> easy entrance into India. Russia is also trying to establish her
> influence in Tibet, and, if successful, could safely and secretly
> send her emissaries into India by this route.[31]

But the Balipara Frontier Tract had not, as yet, played any significant
part in the calculations of Simla or Whitehall, and Captain Nevill's
reports found a convenient pigeon-hole.

ACTIVATING THE McMAHON LINE

The tribal peoples lived as they always had done along the McMahon
Line; the Tibetan tax-collectors appeared at Tawang and at one or two

points on the Upper Subansiri and Siang and as far as Walong. But it is generally true to say that 90% of what is now N.E.F.A. was as much *terra incognita* in Lhasa as it was in Delhi or Shillong, let alone Peking which was never remotely interested in the area except during the campaigns of Chao Erh-feng.

In 1935 the boundary question between India and Tibet was suddenly raised by an incident involving a remarkable botanist and traveller, F. Kingdon Ward. He was certainly more interested in collecting new botanical specimens than in the observation of a frontier, real or assumed in some almost inaccessible mountains. A Minute Paper recorded:

> In 1935 Mr Kingdon Ward penetrated into Tibet from Assam without the sanction of the Tibetan Government. He had with our assistance obtained permission to visit Tibet on several occasions in the past and was well aware that the sanction of the Lhasa authorities was required. The Tibetan Government complained to us and said it would be no use Mr Kingdon Ward applying for permission to visit Tibet in future.[32]

The Trade Agent in Lhasa elaborated the point to the Foreign Department.

> Tibetan Government allege that Kingdon Ward went far beyond Red Line even to Kongbo Pome and Poyul north of Tsangpo river. They maintain that Red Line has not been modified. They say that it will be no use Kingdon Ward applying for permission to visit Tibet in future and only passports from Tibetan Government are ever valid. Kingdon Ward has been sent back to India and Tibetan Government are willing to regard incident as closed.[33]

Sir Olaf Caroe, then Deputy Secretary in the Foreign Department, had joined the Department after an eventful career on the North-West Frontier, and was alive to the significance of seemingly small incidents along frontiers. He wrote to Hutton:

> It appears that there has been considerable misunderstand-regarding the international frontier between India and Tibet,

as determined by Sir H. McMahon in 1914 and accepted by
the Tibetan Government, the Government of India will be
glad to learn whether the Assam Government accept the letter
as a correct presentation of the position as regards the frontier
between Assam tribal areas and Tibet.[34]

The Assam Government had no copy of the Tibetan text of the 1914
Convention. Indeed, as Sir Olaf Caroe subsequently discovered

> when in 1935 the question of the location of the frontier of
> India in this region came up on a side issue for consideration,
> it was discovered that both the Assam Government and the
> Political Officer in Sikkim were ignorant of the position of the
> frontier. Williamson himself thought that in the Assam Sector,
> the international frontier ran along the foothills and was
> identical with the frontier of the administered districts of the
> province of Assam. The north-east frontier does not ordinarily
> figure very prominently in our records and it was only with con-
> siderable difficulty and almost by chance that we were able to
> unearth the true position. On the other hand, we came to
> know incidentally from a reference to the Kingdon Ward
> case that the McMahon Line, by which the delimited frontier
> in this region is known, is well known to the Tibetan Govern-
> ment and is still fully accepted by them.[35]

The Deputy Secretary, Foreign Department, did not let the matter
rest there. He wrote to Dawson:

> It is now clear that the whole of the hill country up to the
> 1914 McMahon Line is within the frontier of India and is
> therefore a tribal area under the control of the Government
> of Assam acting as Agent for the Government of Assam. I
> am to say that the Government of India would be interested to
> learn whether any measure of political control has been ex-
> tended up to that line in the course of the last twenty years,
> and in particular whether the Tibetan Government honour
> the frontier by refraining from administrative measures such
> as the collection of revenue on the Indian side of the frontier,
> more especially in the Tawang area.

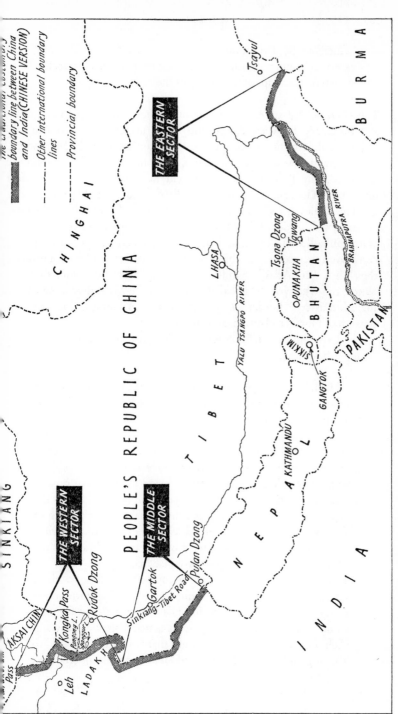

Map 16. *Traditional Customary Boundary Line between China and India (Chinese version), 1962.*

Incidentally, I am to observe that it does not appear that the external frontier of India in this sector has been correctly shown on the maps of the survey of India.[36]

The Government of Assam, ignorant of the position, did not mark any boundary between Assam and Tibet in their 1935-36 Annual Report on the frontier tribes. Ignorance and confusion on the McMahon Line in practice were partly the result of the India Office's decision not to include the Indo-Tibetan agreement in Aitchison's Treaty Series until 1936. The result was that generally dependable publications such as "The Times Atlas" still showed the frontier of India along the unadministered border of the Province of Assam. Observers said Tibetans were still collecting revenue from Tawang where the population still considered themselves as subject to the Government in Lhasa. Further, the "Shen Pao Atlas", published in Shanghai at this time, showed almost the whole of the tribal area south of the McMahon Line up to the administered border of British India in Assam together with a portion of Northern Burma, as included in China.

The Government of India now considered it necessary to make its own position clear.

H.M.G. have now agreed that the 1914 Convention with Tibet and connected agreements should be published (with the avoidance of unnecessary publicity!) and that the boundary as then laid down should be shown on maps published by the Survey of India. The Government of India however, feel that this action will hardly suffice to correct the false impressions which have already gained ground, and may present greater embarrassment in future. The position briefly is that the cartographical activities of the Chinese have set up a claim to absorb in China a very large stretch of Indian territory, while in a portion of India just west of the area claimed by the Chinese as part of Sikang province namely Tawang, the Tibetan Government over whom the Chinese claim suzerainty are collecting revenue and exercising jurisdiction many miles on the Indian side of the international frontier. China's claim does not at present actually include Tawang itself, but there can be little doubt that it will be extended to Tawang and even to Bhutan and Sikkim if no steps are taken to challenge these activities. There is moreover the danger that the exercise of jurisdiction by Tibet in the Tawang area might enable China, or other Power in a position in future to assert authority over Tibet, to claim prescriptive rights over a part of the territory recognised as within India under the 1914 Convention.[37]

Captain G. S. Lightfoot (who had taken Captain Nevill's place as Political Officer, Balipara Frontier Tract) was now sent on a Mission to observe the actual conditions on the McMahon Line itself. He was told that the Tibetan Government, 'over whom the Chinese claim suzerainty, are collecting revenues and exercising jurisdiction in the Tawang area many miles south of the international frontier'.

> The Government of India consider that some effective steps should be taken to challenge activities which may be extended to a claim on behalf of China to Tawang itself, or even Bhutan and Sikkim.

The proposal was to demand from the Tibetan Government, 'which has recently reaffirmed the McMahon Line, that collection of revenue for the latter Government in the Tawang area should be discontinued'.[38]

Sir Basil Gould was in Lhasa at the time this Note was written, and on the basis of this evidence, the Chief Secretary thought it was wise to leave for further consideration the question of replacing Tibetan by Indian officials in Tawang. One thing was clear; the people of Tawang were not aware that the Simla Agreement signed by Lonchen Shatra had placed them under Indian jurisdiction. The publication of the map would not have convinced them.

Whatever steps were taken, either actual tours or the collection of revenues, the Tibetans would have to be clearly told that there was no intention of interfering with the purely monastic collection of the Tawang Monastery. The Government of India's decision to send a small expedition to Tawang 'to explore facts' was supplemented by Gould's talks on frontier problems with the Kashag, which maintained that

1. Up to 1914 Tawang had undoubtedly been Tibetan.
2. They regarded the adjustment of the Tibet-India boundary

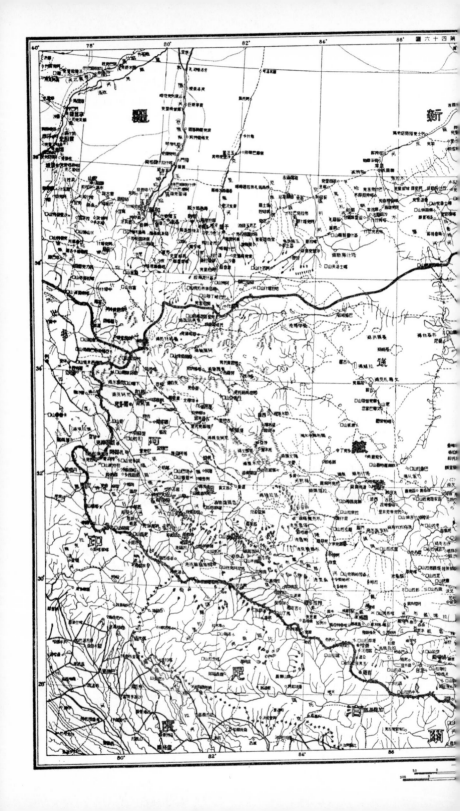

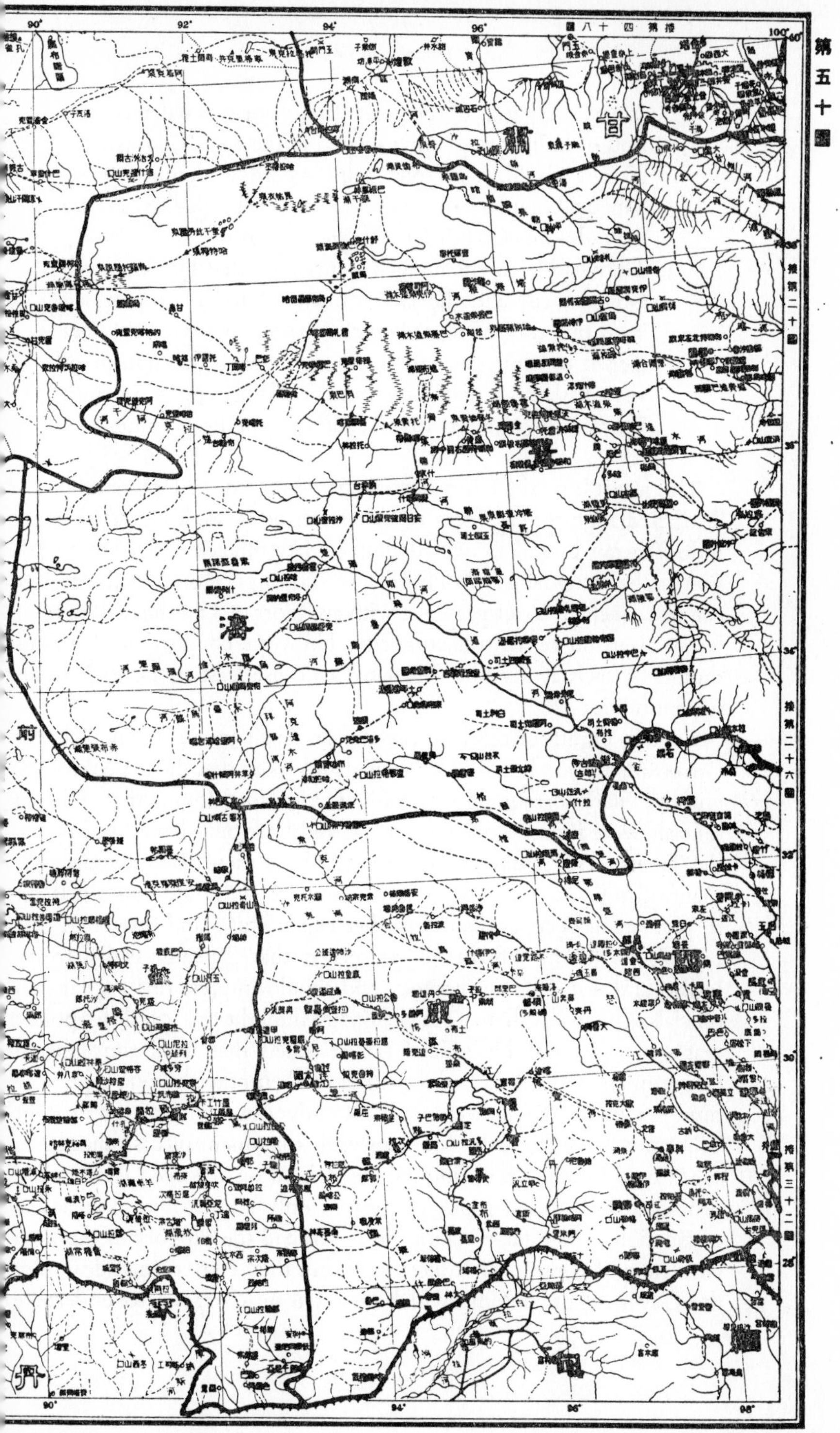

MAP 17. *The Shen Pao Atlas, 1936.*

as part and parcel of the general adjustment and determination of boundaries contemplated in the 1914 Convention. If they could, with our help, secure a definite Sino-Tibetan boundary they would of course be glad to observe the Indo-Tibetan border as defined in 1914.

3. They had been encouraged in thinking that His Majesty's Government and the Government of India sympathised with this way of regarding the matter owing to the fact that at no time since the Convention and Declaration of 1914 had the Indian Government taken steps to question Tibetan, or to assert British, authority in the Tawang area.

This is not how the Chief Secretary interpreted the Convention. He instructed Lightfoot: 'There is, of course, no possible doubt that the Indo-Tibetan boundary was definitely determined; and I am to ask you to be scrupulously careful to give no impression that the matter can be reopened. Your presence with an escort in Tawang will in itself be an assertion of British authority, but your conduct in all things should be such as may be calculated to cause least shock to Tibetan susceptibilities'.[39]

Captain Lightfoot reached Tawang on April 30, 1938. The Tibetan Government soon heard of his arrival and asked that the expedition be withdrawn. The request was refused. Lightfoot found that Tibetan officials were indeed collecting taxes, and he would have liked to see the Tibetan Government asked to withdraw them. But the Government of India were averse to 'any action which would commit them to permanent occupation and further expenditure' and suggested that Lightfoot 'should inform all concerned that Tawang is by treaty Indian and not Tibetan territory and should impress this on Tibetan officials if he meets them'. He personally thought this 'go slow' policy was equivocal and his official report stated that until the Tibetan Government had been asked to withdraw their officials India's 'prestige must inevitably be non-existent'. He advocated the withdrawal of Tibetan officials from the Monastery, that payment of cash should be substituted for the prevailing tribute in kind or in forced labour, and provided details of a *panchayat* system only compatible with actual occupation. These far-reaching proposals had the support of the then Governor of Assam, Sir Robert Reid, but they were turned down by the Government of India which persisted in its refusal to undertake permanent occupation, and would not allow Lightfoot to make a second visit.

ASSAM AND THE SECOND WORLD WAR

The Second World War served to emphasise the strategic significance of the Assam Himalayas. The boundary with Tibet had been delimited on the treaty maps in 1914, and the Tibet Government knew broadly where it was. It was not demarcated by pillars or anything else on the ground, but for much of its length it traversed the high range of the Himalayas above the snow line, where demarcation could not be undertaken in any case. Apart from the Treaty maps the external frontier of India in this sector had not been shown in detail on atlases available to the public.

In 1941, Chiang Kai-shek ordered the building of a road from southwest Szechuan across south-east Tibet into Assam via the Lohit Valley. The British Government pointed out they had certain commitments to Tibet whose permission must be obtained. Chiang Kai-shek proceeded nonetheless and sent a survey team to the Tibetan border. Tibetan troops turned it back. The British Government, now an ally of China, tried in vain to persuade Lhasa to break its neutrality. Finally, Trans-Tibet Transport took in supplies via Kalimpong or Gangtok and Lhasa and did not touch the Lohit Valley or any part of what is now N.E.F.A.

Sir Robert Reid well understood the new pattern of Asia created by the Sino-Japanese war, and how, in particular, it underlined the importance of the North-East frontier in its relations with Tibet, China, Burma and Japan. In 1941, he wrote a Note under the heading 'The future of the Present excluded, partially excluded and tribal areas of Assam':

> Beyond the administered portion of the Sadiya and Balipara Frontier Tracts (but within the McMahon Line of 1914) and outside the administered boundary of the Naga Hills and lying between that district and Burma is an immense tract of country over which we exercise, within the frontier of India though it be, only the most shadowy control. Relations with that tract were, before 1937, the concern of the Local Government subject to the control of the Central Government, but they are now specifically the concern of the latter, the

Governor being the Agent of the Governor-General. Their
ultimate fate must be bound up with that of the excluded areas,
and their great area (some 28,000 sq. miles, equal to that of the
present Totally and Partially excluded areas of the Province)
the identities of the countries with which they march and their
importance from the point of view of strategy and international politics are factors which cannot be overlooked.[40]

Reid favoured the idea (put forward by Dr Hutton to the Indian
Statutory Commission in July 1928) that an Agency and Commission
should be formed to combine the Hill Districts of Assam with the
adjacent districts of Burma. Both men believed that the creation of such
a Province would facilitate the solution of the frontier question. Dr
Hutton had earlier put down his thoughts on the potential threat of
China as an enemy.

> China at present may be a negligible quantity but should she
> ever recover from her internal disorders the question of the
> Chinese frontier is likely to become very much more important
> than it is at present and the advantages of having under one
> administration both the frontier and its bases from the ninety-
> second to the ninety-seventh degree of longitude would be
> considerable. At present the Assam Frontier Tract covers this
> section of the frontier, but the areas to the south of it including
> the Hukong Valley are administered by Burma. The proposed
> Hill Province would be triangular with its base on the frontier
> and its apex on the Bay of Bengal replacing an irregular fron-
> tier on which a narrow strip of Assam overlaps an intrusion
> from Burma.[41]

He was writing in 1941, when the future of India, Burma, Tibet
and China was unpredictable. The picture was changed again a few
months later when Pearl Harbour brought the USA into the Asian
scene. Their first aim was to get into Tibet. When the US Government
failed to get permission from the Chinese authorities to enter the
country, they found they must approach Lhasa through the Government of India. Finally, in February 1942, under heavy British and
American pressure, two U.S. army officers were allowed to enter
Lhasa. The British Government presented the facts of Tibetan independence in a Note to the U.S. which was so "firmly wedded to

Chiang Kai-shek" (the words are H. E. Richardson's) they were willing to play his game until, in 1943, he exposed his real aims by threatening to attack Tibet with American arms.

Many map publishers as well as the Chinese issued maps showing Tibet as one of her Provinces with the boundary about 100 miles south of the McMahon Line, whereby the Chinese were claiming not only the Assam Himalayas but a good deal of the Lohit-Zayul Valley. The British Government was taking no risks and decided to implement the 1914 Agreement. J. P. Mills, a member of the I.C.S. since 1913, who had served many years in Assam, was now given the task of making good the McMahon Line. He faced a variety of difficulties, one of which was the fact that the Line had not been substituted on British official maps for the boundary in its pre-Simla line along the base of the hills. Further, as he told a meeting of the Central Asian Society in 1950:

> The Tibetans issued no maps and said, in effect that they could not find the papers about the Convention. What they really meant was that if we had forgotten the boundary for over twenty-nine years we could go on forgetting about it altogether.[42]

Mills and his Assam Rifles were rarely welcomed. In Rima, which was "admittedly Tibetan territory" an official claimed as the boundary a line "a few miles downstream of the correct one", probably where O'Callaghan had once moved the boundary markers. Mills emphasised his claim by establishing a post of Assam Rifles near the frontier with supporting posts below it. In the Dirang Dzong area, he was "strenuously opposed both by Tibetan secular frontier officials and by monastic tax collectors". He informed them that they must not impose taxes on the people and established a post there too. The local people were willing to co-operate only if they were assured the post would remain. Otherwise they feared reprisals. Mills found the area troublesome to administer; he remained, however, strongly in favour of permanent occupation.

> India must hold the sub-Himalayan belt somehow, because if she had China sitting on the edge of the plains I doubt if Assam would be tenable; and she could not afford to lose Assam with its wealth of coal, oil, tea and timber.[43]

Mills' realistic work in the area was reinforced by F. P. Mainprice, Assistant Political Officer, Lohit Valley. He toured the valley in 1944 and found that four villages south of the McMahon Line frontier (a total of five houses and twenty men) were still paying revenue and doing *begar* (contract labour) for Rima. He explained to the Dzong-pon's clerk that under the terms of the Simla Convention

> our frontier ran just north of the Tho Chu and Dichu and that as this included within our frontier the four hamlets of Walong, Tinai, Dong and Kahao . . . they were subject only to the jurisdiction of Sadiya and would no more render tribute or *begar* to the Rima officials . . . To this the clerk replied that he knew nothing of treaties or the frontier and that these matters could best be discussed with his master.[44]

Mainprice selected the best site and informed the people that south of the spot was within the British frontier, and north was Tibetan. Later the Dzongpon, over a meal, asked him what was the trouble about the four villages? Mainprice's diary for February 4, 1944, records his explanation, which was that

> under the 1914 Agreement between the Governments of India and Tibet they were ours, and where the frontier ran in the Lohit Valley. He asked why no one had ever said so before, although several sahibs had visited Rima, and said he had no knowledge of the matter; nor had the Shango who had been here fifteen years . . . He said the boundary was the Chinese boundary zone at Menilkrai, which also bears an English inscription (the name of the Sappers and Miners and 1912 date). I replied that the Chinese inscription was purely *ex parte*, and that two years after the Chinese had been driven out the two parties concerned with the boundary, Indian and Tibet, had agreed amicably on their frontier, unlike China, which was still encroaching; I also emphasised the friendship between Britain, India and Tibet and the advant-ages of a fixed and agreed boundary . . . They said that no intimation of a change in the boundary had ever come from Chamdo or Lhasa, that the four villages had paid revenue to Rima at the same rates as today from time immemorial,

without any objection from Sadiya, and that we should not
have built the post walls at Walong.[45]

Mainprice insisted that Walong was a British village under the 1914
Agreement, and that if the local people made enquiries in Lhasa they
could confirm it. He saw the dangers of continued neglect and held
that it was "very necessary" to state the British case in the Upper
Lohit Valley. This, he wrote, "had been neglected and gone by default
for the last 30 years, and any failure to state it now, even though we
may not be able to make the McMahon Line frontier here fully
effective or stop revenue payments to Rima for another year or two,
would have strengthened the already forceful case the Dzongpon made
out for the *status quo*". By asserting the British position, he calculated
that the Dzongpon would be less likely to do anything to the posts at
Walong, or vent his annoyance on the local people. "We have at least
staken our claim". He concluded, "it remains to enforce it".[46]

Officials in Rima carefully observed the activities of Mainprice and
his Mission. They waited for him to leave and then examined the post
and looked at 'the Chinese boundary zone' at Menilkrai. Mainprice,
recognising the challenge, suggested that the Political Officer in
Sikkim might be alerted. Would it be advisable, he asked, for Lhasa
to be given the hint that they should inform the Dzongpon of 'the
correct position of the frontier in this area, so that they should cease all
activities south of it'?

The Mainprice Mission had demarcated the McMahon Line about
twenty miles north of Walong so that the village of Kahao was
included in British territory. Its only significance was strategic; here,
the Di Chu stream joined the Lohit. The Di Chu Valley commanded
the only possible route to the Diphu or Talok Pass into Burma. Other
Political Officers carried out missions in strategically placed valleys.

THE SIANG (DIHANG) VALLEY. After the punitive expedition against
the Abors in 1913, no Political Officer visited the area north of Kom-
sing until 1936-7. This village was well beyond the Outer Line when
Williamson was murdered there in 1911. The red line proposed by the
Chief of the General Staff in 1912 and accepted by McMahon and the
Lonchen Shatra as the boundary in 1914 crosses the Siang more than
one hundred miles to the north of Komsing. Like the Dzongpon of
Rima, the local people in Komsing had never heard of the Simla

Conference. Twenty three years later the Tibetans were still demanding tribute and labour from Abors as far south as Karko, seventy miles beyond the McMahon Line. Something had to be done to bring these Abors into the imperial family, to initiate them in the more sophisticated methods of British tax-collectors. In 1939, Mr Godfrey, Political Officer, set off to pay the village a visit when he heard that the villagers of Karko had prevented trade going up or down the Siang Valley. He was instructed:

1. To ascertain the position as regards Tibetan infiltration and oppression south of the McMahon Line.
2. To attempt to remove 'trade blocks'im posed by certain of the Abor clans in the main trade routes to Tibet and the plains on either side of the Siang Valley.
3. To settle inter-tribal disputes between the main Abor clans the Padams, Pangi, Minyong and Karko, which of recent years have become aggravated and which in the absence of an early peaceful settlement it was feared would again lead to bloodshed.[47]

Godfrey established the fact that Tibetan officials were still collecting tribute from Shimong and Karko, and that it would require a cold weather outpost to move the trade blocks.

THE SIYOM VALLEY AND THE UPPER SIANG (DIHANG). The Siyom river flows into the Siang (or Dihang) river just below Komsing. From the time it was surveyed in 1913 the Miyong and Gallon Abors remained as unaware of British authority as the Miju Mishmis. When Mr Godfrey heard that there was a territorial dispute between these two Abor groups which might develop into a tribal war, he visited the area. He toured up the right bank of the Siyom, settled the dispute, and fixed another stretch of the boundary in 1940. It was now decided that Britain's position should be consolidated 'right up to the Tibetan frontier on the McMahon Line'. Reid pointed out that 'the Tibetan Government would soon thus realise that we intend to exercise control up to the McMahon Line and no further'.[48]

THE SUBANSIRI VALLEY. Captain Nevill, Political Officer of the Western Section of the North-East Frontier Tract, advocated roads and outposts up to the McMahon Line. When he was told that this

frontier was 'worth nothing and not worth the expenses of administration', he retorted that large valleys of 'extremely rich country'
existed; that only settled conditions and roads and posts could ensure
its safety and introduce 'the benefits of civilisation . . . among a people
who at present are amongst the most miserable of any race on earth'.[48]
However, the Subansiri area was not considered sufficiently important
to warrant any special attention until 1943, when Chinese maps
included it in Chinese territory.

Christoph von Furer-Haimendorf and his wife made an extensive
tour of the Subansiri area in the season March to May 1944. He was
Special Officer, Subansiri. He had earlier served as Adviser to the
Nizam's Government for Tribes and Backward Classes and as Professor
of Anthropology in Osmania University. His instructions now were
to explore areas beyond that which was visited by the Miri Mission
thirty years before, to study the tribal peoples, to consolidate the
Government's influence among the Daflas and the Apa Tanis, and to
suggest sites for the establishment of Assam Rifles outposts. When he
approached villages the people left their houses and went into field
huts and camped there. His diary entry for March 19, 1945 reads: I
was at first at a loss to understand this extraordinary fear, but realise
now that the Miri Mission has left a legacy of deep-rooted fear of the
potential frightfulness of Government . . . it seems that after the
departure of the Miri Mission the Tali Tumir group put the blame for
their losses on the Kabak people, who had provided guides and thus
'helped the Sahibs and sepoys to get into their country'. No village
wants to risk a repetition of such a charge, and until the people are convinced of our harmlessness they shun the responsibility of taking us to
their neighbours'.[49]

The Haimendorfs had a natural, as well as a trained, gift for making
friends with tribal peoples, whose affection and loyalty responded so
warmly to a little personal interest. They studied tribal customs, and
when they met relatives of people killed by the Miri Mission they paid
the right kind of compensation in kind-cloths, brass cups, beads and
salt. The result was that these village people became friendly and
amenable. Gifts were exchanged in tribal fashion; a mithun was
sacrificed to the accompaniment of priestly incantations. As the
mithun's blood flowed into a specially prepared hole, the Haimendorfs
calculated what present they could give which was at least equal to the
sacrificial animal. They saw that this was 'an excellent means of spreading

our influence in a peaceful way, and the expense is negligible compared to the cost of touring with an escort'.[50] They visited the Sipi
Valley, going further north than any previous expedition west of the
Subansiri. They often travelled unarmed in areas not previously
explored, tactfully preparing the way for surveyors accompanied by
armed escorts.

When the Furer-Haimendorfs had completed their remarkable
journeys, a new administrative area was made of the Subansiri and
Captain F. N. Betts put in charge. His wife, like the Furer-Haimendorfs,
was a trained, if more romantic observer. Betts was instructed to
proceed 'with the greatest deliberation and caution in all his dealing
with the tribesmen and, since their only previous contacts with the
outside world had been with punitive expeditions retribution for tribal
raids on the plains, he must explain to the people that the Government's aim in entering the country was a benevolent one. He must
guide, advise and control, but he must not resort to force'.

This was the last effort to establish the McMahon Line. India's
independence came and with it their responsibility.

Independence and Challenge (1947-1959)

BARA HOTI; KHURNAK FORT; AKSAI CHIN; LOHIT VALLEY; CHINESE MAPS

Just before the transfer of power, the governments of Britain and of India informed the Tibetans that British obligations and rights under existing treaties with them would devolve upon the successor government of India. Hugh Richardson, the then British Representative in Lhasa, says that the Tibetans were assured that the British Government

> would continue to take a friendly interest in the welfare and autonomy of their country and expressed the hope that contact might be maintained by visits to Tibet from British representatives in India.[1]

It was all very diplomatic, casual and remote for London was a long way from Lhasa and so too was Delhi.

On August 15, 1947, India and Pakistan became two separate Dominions. The territories of India were defined as those

> under the sovereignty of His Majesty which, immediately before the appointed day, were included in British India except the territories which, under subsection (2) of this section are to be the territories of Pakistan.[2]

This meant that the two new Dominions inherited the frontiers which the British Government had acquired by treaty, agreement and occupation.

In Lhasa, the government saw that this new situation might mean an opportunity for them to extend their own areas of jurisdiction. On

H

October 16, 1947, having merely acknowledged the note from London and Delhi, the Tibetan Bureau telegraphed to the Indian government asking for the return of territories on the boundaries of India and Tibet

> ... such as Sayul and Walong and in direction of Pemakoe, Lonag, Lopa, Mon, Bhutan, Sikkim, Darjeeling and others on this side of river Ganges, and Lowo, Ladakh etc. up to boundary of Yarkhim.[3]

These claims were not treated very seriously by Delhi where the government was already overwhelmed by events in Kashmir. Richardson, by this time *India's* representative in Lhasa, was not deeply concerned about them, and informed Delhi that they were

> perhaps, an attempt to test the Indian attitude to border regions where their British predecessors had, by a series of agreements, established the frontier of India; but it was also ... the counterpart of the message conveyed to the Chinese Government by the goodwill mission in 1946, in which they asked, in equally wide terms, for the return of all Tibetan territories still in Chinese hands.[4]

When, years later, Chou En-lai recalled these claims, Nehru told him:

> It will be seen that the areas claimed by Tibet had not been defined. If they were to be taken literally, the Tibetan boundary would come down to the line of the river Ganges. The Government of India could not possibly have entertained such a fantastic claim. If they had the faintest idea that this telegram would be made the basis of a subsequent claim to large areas of Indian territory, they would of course have immediately and unequivocally rejected the claim.[5]

But in 1947, Nehru was not thinking of boundaries. Nor were they reckoned in the calculations of his strategic advisers. So Delhi merely replied to Tibet in these terms:

> The Government of India would be glad to have an assurance that it is the intention of the Tibetan Government to

continue relations on the existing basis until new agreements are reached on matters that either party may wish to take up. This is the procedure adopted by all other countries with which India has inherited treaty relations from His Majesty's Government.[6]

The Tibetan Government considered this letter for several months, and then, they 'eventually announced their acceptance of the continuation of the former relationship with the new Indian Government'.[7]

Chiang Kai-shek also wanted to know where his country stood vis-a-vis the new Government in Delhi. His ambassador asked for a clarification of Indian policy on November 7, 1947.

> Whether after the transfer of power the Government of India have replaced the fromer Government of India in assuming the treaty rights and obligations hitherto existing between British India and Tibet and whether the Government of Pakistan are also assuming part of such treaty rights and obligations. In the latter case, the Charge d'Affaires would very much appreciate it if he could be informed as to (i) what rights and obligations are now assumed by the Government of India, (ii) what rights and obligations are now assumed by the Government of Pakistan and (iii) how such rights and obligations are divided between and shared by the two Governments.[8]

The contents of this Note were not made known until 1963 and the answer has yet to be published. At the time the request was probably considered as a mere formality.

India's policy towards Tibet was a smooth continuation of Britain's. Almost the only outward sign that the Indian Empire had come to an end was the saffron, white and green flag with Asoka's wheel of righteousness in the centre which took the place of the red, white and blue of the Union Jack.

The Chinese communists, then struggling for power with Chiang Kai-shek, assumed that Nehru would adopt and pursue the British lines of policy. The Chinese newspaper *Jen Min Jih Pao* commented: 'The retaining of Mr Richardson's service demonstrated the collaboration of Nehru's reactionary Government with British imperialism.' [9] Chiang Kai-shek was highly suspicious when a Tibetan delegation visited Delhi in 1948. His ambassador informed K.P.S. Menon (formerly Ambassador in Nanking, Foreign Secretary) that he hoped 'Indian dealings with the Tibetan Mission would not be in any way detrimental to the sovereignty and territorial integrity of China'. Menon replied that 'there was no such intention on the part of the Indian Government'.[10]

The Mission visited Washington and London, and arrived in Nanking in April 1949 where they were described as a delegation to the National Assembly. Communist armies were then sweeping across China, and no follow-up was made by Chiang Kai-shek. Meanwhile Tibetan officials, as anti-communist as Chiang Kai-shek, took what seemed to them to be a sensible precaution against communist infiltration. They dismissed everyone associated with Chiang Kai-shek's Government, took over the radio station and forbade communication with China. The K.M.T. angrily retorted that all their officials in Tibet had been carefully screened, and protested that no proper approach had been made to the Central Government. This implied that Tibet was a part of China. Indeed, *China Handbook* (1935–1946) placed Tibet with Mongolia as 'Special Territories'.

In the last days of the K.M.T. Chiang Kai-shek still treated Tibet as a part of China. In 1948, he proposed to Delhi that the 1908 Tibetan Trade Regulations should be revised. Nehru, recognising that this was in effect a trap to obtain India's admission that the Simla Agreement was not a valid document, replied that India recognised only the validity of that Agreement which superceded the 1908 Regulations.

This was Chiang Kai-shek's last approach to India. On January 4, 1949, Peking surrendered to the communists and on October 1 that year, Mao Tse-tung proclaimed the Chinese People's Republic. He made no specific reference to Tibet, but declared that his Republic would wage 'the war of liberation to the very end' and 'liberate all the territory of China'. To the Indian Communist Party which had congratulated him, he replied:

> I firmly believe that relying on the brave Communist Party of India and the unity and struggle of all Indian patriots, India will certainly not remain long under yoke of imperialism and its collaborators. Like free China, a free India will

one day emerge in the Socialist and People's Democratic family; that day will end the imperialist reactionary era in the history of mankind.[11]

As early as January 1, 1950, the 'liberation of Tibet' was officially announced as one of the 'main tasks of the People's Liberation Army' and was repeated as such in the following months by Mao Tse-tung and by Chu Teh and General Liu Po-chen, his Commander of the Second Field Army and Chairman of the South-West China Military Affairs Commission.

Nehru was convinced that China and India must remain on good terms and genuinely thought that the Chinese would clarify their relations with Tibet by peaceful means. He told a press conference in March 1950 that he did not want to interfere in Tibet and Krishna Menon, his High Commissioner in London, told journalists that talks were going on 'in the hope of moderating Chinese action in Tibet' The Indian Government, he said,

> fully recognised the validity of Chinese claims but wished simply to advise against precipitate action. He believed that China would listen when asked not to take a strictly legalistic view on India's recognition of Chinese suzerainty over Tibet.[12]

The Ministry of External Affairs rebuffed, but did not contradict, him. Richardson and his Tibetan friends, felt that Nehru was disregarding

> the obligation, which he had inherited under the Simla declaration of 1914, not to accord Chinese suzerainty over Tibet, of any sort whatsoever, until the Chinese acknowledged Tibetan autonomy in the strict terms of the 1914 Convention.[13]

Nehru certainly assumed that Tibet would inevitably fall under Chinese rule, but his belief was that in an Asia, freed from Western imperialism, China and India would move hand in hand towards an enlightened Asianism. It was a romantic aspiration which overlooked both the rigidity and the ruthless expediency of communism. His

Ambassador in Peking, K. M. Panikkar, largely agreed with him. He
was also immensely impressed by the new China and flattered by their
skilfully arranged hospitality. In his prolific writings he had always
based Indian strategy on the Indian Ocean, not on the Himalayas. He
underestimated the persistence and determination of Chinese official
views about Tibet. The point is well illustrated by Nehru's statement
in August 1950 that Panikkar had informally told the Chinese Government how desirable it was to settle the Tibetan regime peacefully. He
seemed satisfied by Peking's evasive reply that, while it regarded Tibet
as an integral part of China, it had no intention of forcing the issue, and
was willing to negotiate with Tibetan spokesmen for a settlement.

Did Panikkar not know, or did he deliberately overlook preparations
for the invasion of Tibet? Did he not hear broadcasts from Sining and
Peking in May 1950 saying that Tibet was to be liberated, and that
Tibetans could expect no help from the U.S.A. or the United Kingdom? During this period Panikkar frequently saw Chou En-lai, but
seems not to have raised the question of frontiers. He preferred to
philosophise on Sino-Indian friendship.

> I knew, like everyone else, that with a communist China
> cordial and intimate relations were out of the question, but
> I was fairly optimistic about working out an area of co-oper-
> ation by eliminating causes of misunderstanding, rivalry, etc.
> The only area where our interests overlapped was in Tibet,
> and knowing the importance that every Chinese Government,
> including the Kuomintang, had attached to exclusive Chinese
> authority over that area I had, even before I started for
> Peking, come to the conclusion that the British policy
> (which we were supposed to have inherited) of looking upon
> Tibet as an area in which we had special political interest
> could not be maintained. The Prime Minister had also in
> general agreed with this view.[14]

Panikkar claims that Indian pressure modified China's policy. Chou
En-lai assured him that while the liberation of Tibet was a 'sacred duty'
they wanted to achieve it by negotiations and not military action. Yet
at that time – August 22, 1950 – the military build-up must have been
well under way, and Chou En-lai on the first anniversary, confirmed
his Government's determination 'to liberate the people of Tibet and

stand on guard at the Chinese frontiers'. A week later, Chinese troops moved into East Tibet and by the end of October a full-scale military campaign had begun.

Chinese troops claim to have entered Tibet by 3 routes. First from Szechuan and Sikang, where Tibetans had been 'softened up' earlier in the year. Second, through Chamdo, and third, from the north-west where troops from Sinkiang entered the Ari district through the Aksai Chin using an ancient track between Sinkiang and Tibet.* (This is generally assumed to have been the same route the Dzungars took in 1716 when they captured Lhasa in a surprise attack.)

The Indian Government's protest against military action was promptly delivered.

> The Government of India can only express their deep regret that in spite of friendly disinterested advice repeatedly tendered by them the Chinese Government should have decided to seek the solution of the problems of their relations with Tibet by force instead of by the slower and more enduring method of peaceful approach.[15]

Peking replied:

> Tibet is an integral part of Chinese territory. The problem of Tibet is entirely the domestic problem of China. The Chinese People's Liberation Army must enter Tibet, liberate the Tibetan people and defend the frontiers of China.[16]

The last paragraph of this Note suggested that India's attitude had 'been affected by foreign influences hostile to China in Tibet'. Delhi

---

* A Note given by the Ministry of Foreign Affairs of China to the Embassy of India in China, December 26, 1959, (White Paper III, p. 67) stated:
This area [Aksai Chin] is the only traffic artery linking Sinkiang and western Tibet, because to its northeast lies the great Gobi of Sinkiang through which direct traffic with Tibet is practically impossible. . . . In the latter half of 1950, it was through this area that the Chinese Government despatched the first units of the Chinese People's Liberation Army to enter Tibet.

immediately and angrily repudiated this. As for 'unwarranted interference in Chinese affairs', Delhi described the communiqué as

> well-meant advice by a friendly Government which has a
> natural interest in the solution of problems concerning its
> neighbours by peaceful methods.[17]

Nehru persisted in basing his policy on the notion that friendship
with China was desirable and a reasonable expectation. Left-wing
opinion in India did not share his optimism, and socialist leaders
believed that this was the moment when China's bluff should be called
and her expansionist objectives exposed. This view was shared by
Tibetophils in India as well as in the West. Hugh Richardson strongly
condemned the U.K. and India which,

> far from supporting the Tibetan appeal to the United Nations,
> took a leading part in obstructing it . . . It must be recorded
> with shame that the United Kingdom delegate, pleading
> ignorance of the exact course of events and uncertainty
> about the legal position of Tibet, proposed that the matter be
> deferred. That was supported by the delegate of India, the
> country most closely affected, and uniquely, bound to Tibet
> by treaty obligations, who expressed certainty that the
> differences could be settled by peaceful means which would
> safeguard Tibetan autonomy. Both the Soviet and Chinese
> Nationalist delegates opposed discussion on the ground that
> Tibet was an integral part of China.[18]

The debate in the U.N. was adjourned and the subject was not again
discussed for nine years.

With the wisdom of hindsight, this criticism of the Indian leadership
is more general today than it was in 1950, and certainly more freely
expressed. At the time Nehru not only believed that China would sooner
or later rule Tibet and help the Tibetan people to emerge from a long
stagnation, but he gave top priority to the crisis in Korea. His active
and timely intervention undoubtedly played a major part in preventing
the escalation of that war. He told Parliament that the Korean problem
could 'only be solved in co-operation with the Chinese, or, if you like,
with their acquiescence'. (This linking of China with Korea was
described by Walter Lippmann as a 'recognition of the deeper and

lasting reality of the matter, which is that the Chinese interest in Korea is greater than that of any other foreign Power'.[19])

Nonetheless, Chinese methods in Tibet were a shock to Nehru. He was alive to the possible repercussions of China's control of Tibet. He told Parliament on December 8 that the McMahon Line of the Simla Convention was the definitive frontier of India and that no-one would be allowed to cross it. India believed that Tibet should remain autonomous but would not guarantee autonomy. He was sharply challenged by M.P.s of widely differing denominations. Professor N. G. Ranga, a congress leader from Andhra, and later one of the founders of the Swatantra Party, held that Chinese views of sovereignty implied

> expansion of their own control, political, economic and social, over other people. It was not impossible for the same China which had sent troops like an avalanchic sweep into Korea to pour into India too under the same pressure of ideological and imperialistic urges.

Acharya J. B. Kripalani, formerly an enthusiastic supporter of Gandhi, warned that People's China might one day send an army of 'liberation' to Kathmandu, in which case India would go to war. M. R. Masani, a Swatantra leader, asserted that,

> by attacking Tibet and deceiving the Indian Government, [the Chinese] have cut Asia into two, Communist and non-Communist Asia.

Dr S. P. Mukherjee, who retired from Nehru's Cabinet in 1950, was uncompromising about the Chinese frontier claims.

> It is a fact that the boundary between India and Tibet is yet to be definitely defined. The Prime Minister said the other day that we stand by the McMahon Line but the maps of China which are in circulation even now, include portions of Assam, Ladakh and Leh and territories in which India is vitally interested. The reply which China has sent to India on the question of Tibet definitely indicates that China will do everything necessary for the purpose of keeping intact which it considers to be China's border, and when it refers to the Chinese border it includes Tibet as well and the undefined

boundary of Tibet so far as it touches India's border. Similarly with regard to Nepal . . .²⁰

Nehru repeatedly stated his unwillingness to issue ultimata which could have no other certain effect than to extend the cold war to India. He saw Asia in a 'tremendous ferment of change' and peace in the whole Asian continent as dependent on India's relations with China. He continued to abide by the expectation of Chinese goodwill. It may be argued that his trust in China, and his demonstrable preference for Chou En-lai among Asian leaders exceeded the necessities of Sino-India friendship, and that he overlooked the fact that communist goodwill is guided by expediency, not by any personal choice or calculation. But how else could he have acted? His father once said of him: 'He trusts everybody, for he thinks others are like himself . . . People will take undue advantage of him. He will be duped and deceived often.' ²¹

The Sino-Tibetan Agreement on Measures for the Peaceful Liberation of Tibet signed in Peking on May 23, 1951, sealed China's complete control. Article 1 declared that 'the Tibetan people shall unite and drive out imperialist aggressive forces from Tibet; the Tibetan people shall return to the big family of the Motherland – the People's Republic of China'. Article 8 laid down the reorganisation of the Tibetan army and its integration in the People's Liberation Army. Article 14 gave Peking 'the centralised handling of all external affairs of the area of Tibet' and Article 15 set up a Military and Administrative Committee and a Military Area HQ in Tibet. In plain language Tibet had become a military area of China. Chinese troops could now be stationed on the borders of India, Burma, Pakistan, the U.S.S.R. and Afghanistan. Their Commander in Chief, General Chu Teh called the seventeen-point Agreement 'a victory for the unity of the Chinese people and a great failure for the imperialistic, aggressive influences which tried to interfere with Tibet's peaceful liberation'.²²

There was astonishingly little reaction in India to this vital change in the balance of power in Asia. The Korean war still absorbed the minds of the Indian leaders, who were playing a prominent part in bringing about a cease-fire. A revolution in Nepal, the Kashmir issue, internal difficulties in Telangana – all those diverted attention from Tibet. 'The Government of India,' one writer comments, 'was considerably relieved when the Tibetan problem was settled mutually between

Tibet and China.' *The Statesman* (Calcutta), without criticising the terms or the method of achieving the Agreement, observed:

> Indian statesmen would be neither human nor politic if they failed to consider the latent dangers, were Tibet subsequently absorbed in a more drastic manner. Even as things are a Communist Power might prove an uneasy neighbour.[23]

It was left to the *Manchester Guardian*, in an editorial, to evaluate the strategic significance of the Sino–Tibetan Agreement of 1951.

> The impassability of the Himalayas has been exaggerated, though no army could force them unless it had air supremacy. The immediate danger to India is that China may build air bases near the Himalayas, from which it might threaten the Ganges valley, and second that, by political infiltration, the Communists may work revolutionary havoc all along the frontier ... But Assam is the chief problem. India may have only a limited time to put the province into better order before the pressure comes from China ... There is another reason why the trouble in the North-East should impel India to settle with Karachi, and that is, that Assam cannot be defended except in conjunction with East Pakistan.[24]

American journalists were more alerted to the strategic consequences of China's occupation of Tibet than those of any other country. Though many reports proved later to be exaggerated the *New York Times* frequently carried articles consistent with their high level of reporting. In August 1951 it forecast:

> Within one month the Chinese communists will control all passes through the Himalayas from Tibet into India and Nepal. The communist strategy ... appears to include the disposition of small but effective forces at vital points along the entire Indian–Tibetan frontier, with check points at all important passes. ... Thus, in effect, the Iron Curtain can be extended to the Himalayas if the Chinese communists so wish.[25]

The Chinese, meantime, had not stood still in Tibet. By September 1952, they had built a new road running through Southern Sinkiang which, *The Times* correspondent, writing from Srinagar, pointed out would 'ultimately open up Lhasa for mechanised traffic from Russia'. Editorially, the same paper realistically wrote that 'Although present relations between China and India are good, the long and for the most part imperfectly demarcated frontier between them keeps both countries alert',[26] and gave the first hint that Indian strategists were building airstrips in Ladakh.

Nehru's aim was to stabilise relations between the two countries. 'As between the Chinese Government and us,' he told the Council of State,

> there are no territorial questions. The questions relate to trade, posts and telegraphic arrangements and such matters. Obviously, we have no desire to claim any position in Tibet which may not be in keeping with the full sovereignty of China.[27]

He took the initiative in Sino-Indian talks which began in Peking in December 1953 and led to the Sino-Indian Agreement in April 1954. Officials on both sides were at their most conciliatory. India's representatives refrained from raising such potentially explosive topics as frontiers. They believed that in formulating the five principles of co-existence – the Panch Shila – they had set the pattern for peace in Asia.

China, which was to prove, in the main, the beneficiary of this 1954 Agreement, also won immediate advantages. Tibet was referred to as the Tibet Region of China, 'a recognition,' as Nehru claimed, 'of the existing situation there.' [28] The main parts of the Agreement concerned trade and communications. It was extremely convenient for the Chinese negotiatiors that Nehru was anxious to shed what he regarded as the cumbersome inheritance of British imperialism. He was also realistic enough to see that treaties and trade regulations meant nothing in practice without Chinese goodwill. He was therefore

> pleased to withdraw completely within six months the military escort now stationed at Yatung and Gyantse in the Tibet Region of China; at a reasonable price the postal, telegraph and public telephone services together with their equipment operated by the Government of India in the Tibet region of China; the twelve rest houses of the Government of India in the Tibet region of China.[29]

He also relinquished buildings in the compound walls of trade agencies at Yatung and Gyantse. Specified areas were laid down where both countries might trade and places of pilgrimage noted.

The boundary question arose only indirectly during discussions on Article 4. Chinese officials introduced a draft stating that the Chinese Government 'agrees to open a number of mountain passes'. T. N. Kaul, extremely familiar with the Chinese mind, at once objected on the ground that this was a way of claiming ownership over what were in effect border passes. The Chinese then withdrew their draft, making a virtue of their action by describing it as a concession. Finally, it was laid down that pilgrims and traders could travel through the following passes and routes: (i) Shipki La; (ii) Mana pass; (iii) Niti pass; (iv) Kungri Bingri pass; (v) Darma pass and (vi) Lipu Laku pass. The customary route leading to Tashigong along the valley of the Shangatsangpu (Indus) valley was also proclaimed open for travellers.

Looking back, it seems extraordinary that Indian representatives did not raise the frontier issue as such; the Panch Shila Agreement was a moral, if not a lasting victory for the Indian idea of peaceful relations. It was surely naive of the Indians to settle for pious phrase-making, and to assume that Chou En-lai meant what he said when he told them the Agreement settled all problems. This would have been an opportunity to raise the issue of the McMahon Line, which Nehru had already described in the Lok Sabha as India's boundary. A settlement might have been reached on the Aksai Chin and the McMahon Line in 1954. Neither China nor India had formally claimed the Aksai Chin, and Indian officials tied their own hands at the beginning of the Conference by agreeing to the Chinese proposal that frontiers should not be discussed.

India wanted this Agreement to stand for twenty years; China agreed only to eight, with an extension if either party requested it six months prior to the expiry and the request was agreed by the other party. Indian newspapers and politicians praised it, claiming the great superiority of Indian diplomacy over that of Curzon's days and self-righteously setting the achievement against American efforts at the time to drag India into their strategic network against China. There were only a few tears shed for 'poor Tibet'. The frontier issue was largely overlooked. The *Amrita Bazar Patrika* was one of the few papers which saw the implications of Nehru's trust in China's goodwill.

'From the very start [Nehru] had ruled out any discussion of the India-China frontier, and in the resulting agreement he succeeded in getting a tacit approval of the McMahon Line.'[30]

The *National Herald*, usually considered as reflecting Nehru, wrote categorically:

> The frontier, as Prime Minister Nehru had occasion to remind the House of the People a few weeks ago, remains fixed and cannot be altered. From Sikkim and Bhutan to the northeast extremity of Assam, the frontier follows the McMahon Line laid down at Simla in 1913 and in the north and northwest, to the northernmost part of Ladakh, the frontier though undefined, has followed too clear a customary line to be considered changeable.[31]

The *Times of India* assumed that silence on the border question was

> welcome, inasmuch as it is an acknowledgement of the validity of the existing boundary line ... In any case, the Indian Government will stand by the McMahon Line and will not allow anyone to cross that boundary.[32]

In short, journalists were lulled into an acceptance of Indian skill in obtaining a Panch Shila agreement with China. Had they read the history of Sino-British talks on boundary problems, they might have understood that a unilateral statement by Nehru was no more likely to be accepted by communist China than British unilateral statements had been accepted in 1847 and 1899.

A few cautious remarks appeared. *Pioneer*, for instance, wrote that

> Nothing has been secured to rule out further penetration of Chinese communists into regions bordering on China. India has yet to wake to the reality on her north-eastern frontiers and to events which are likely to follow.[33]

In the Lok Sabha and occasionally in the press, Chinese maps were again discussed. Dr Mukerjee, who raised the issue in the Lok Sabha in 1950, pointed out that they were still in circulation in October 1954.

That month Nehru visited Peking. He mentioned the Chinese maps showing the whole of N.E.F.A. in China. Chou En-lai replied that they were reproductions of old pre-liberation maps. Nehru gracefully said that he could well understand how the 'many and heavy pre-occupations' of the Chinese Government led to the postponement of more up-to-date cartography. Nehru's idea of inter-Asian solidarity was so much uppermost in his mind, he was prepared to go to great lengths to avoid any unpleasant feelings. Yet China had already given some warning of her frontier policy in Burma where Chinese troops had infiltrated into the Wa States. Nehru dissuaded U Nu from raising the issue, and himself discussed it privately with Chou En-lai.[34]

The Chinese leader continued to give the impression that no potential hostility towards India existed on the subject of frontiers. At Bandung, where Nehru's Panch Shila diplomacy had opened the door for China's entry into the Afro-Asian world, Chou En-lai spoke to the Political Committee.

> We have common borders with eight countries. With some of these countries we have not yet finally fixed our border line and we are ready to do this with neighbouring countries. But before doing so, we are willing to maintain the present situation by acknowledging that those parts of our border are parts which are undetermined. We are ready to restrain our Government and our people from crossing even one step across our border. If such things should happen, we would like to admit our mistake. As to the determination of common borders which we are going to undertake with our neighbouring countries, we shall use only peaceful means and we shall not permit any other kind of methods. In any case we shall not change [the existing border].[35]

The Bandung Conference was a fanfare for Chou En-lai who gave an open invitation to all delegates to visit Peking. Many of them accepted. But there were already cracks in the surface of Sino-Indian relations. They were papered over mainly because Nehru maintained his idealistic view of China, and his belief that at all costs the two countries should stand together in the face of America's military presence in Asia and the encirclement policies of S.E.A.T.O. which she initiated. Nehru and Chou En-lai avoided open references to border disputes, but there was tension enough between the two. In the summer of 1954, the Chinese complained that over thirty Indian troops armed with rifles had crossed over the Niti Pass (one of the six mentioned in the Sino-Indian Agreement). India denied it, a party of Border Security forces had been encamped in the Hoti Plain, south-east of the Niti Pass, but none had crossed north of the pass. On the other hand, an Indian Note said Tibetans had tried to cross into the Hoti Plain.

In September 1956, Delhi presented a *Note verbale* to the Chinese chargé d'affaires in Delhi, protesting that ten Chinese soldiers had taken up positions on the Indian side of the Shipki Pass. Both sides accused the other of failing to honour the pledges of non-aggression expressed in the 1954 Agreement.

While Chinese and Indian troops behaved like enemies on the remote Niti and Shipki Passes, students, politicians, trade unionists, teachers, journalists and many VIPs were lavishly entertained in China, and Chinese acrobats and dancers, and opera singers, all keen ambassadors, visited India. Slogans of 'Hindi-Chini bhai-bhai' were heard everywhere while Chou En-lai was excessively garlanded in India and Nehru extravagantly greeted by well-drilled millions in China. Nehru, at the height of his influence in international affairs, looked on these frontier disputes as stemming from Chinese frustration, her isolation, her exclusion from the United Nations. In his efforts to extend the area of peace they seemed trivial compared with the activities of S.E.A.T.O. and the American Seventh Fleet in the China Seas.

India's foreign policy was almost exclusively the product of Nehru's own ideas. He and Chou En-lai could surely determine peace in Asia.

What mattered most to the peace of Asia and the world, he said at a banquet given to Chou En-lai, was how India and China behaved towards each other and on the degree of co-operation they could show in mutual relations.

In October 1956, when he and Chou En-lai were travelling back to Delhi across the Punjab from the Bhakra-Nangal dam, they talked about recent Sino-Burmese discussions on the McMahon Line from the Diphu Pass to the Izu Razi Pass. That evening he wrote the following record for his personal and confidential use:

> Premier Chou referred to the McMahon Line and again said that he had never heard of this before though of course the then Chinese Government had dealt with this matter and

not accepted that line. He had gone into the matter in connection with the border dispute with Burma. Although he
thought that this line, established by British imperialists was
not fair, nevertheless, because it was an accomplished fact
and because of the friendly relations which existed between
China and the countries concerned, namely India and
Burma, the Chinese Government were of the opinion that
they should give recognition to the McMahon Line. They
had, however, not consulted the Tibetan authorities about
it yet. They proposed to do so.[36]

Some years later Nehru regretted not asking Chou to initial this
account of their conversation. At the time his trust was such that he
acted as mediator between Chou and the Dalai Lama – then on an
extended sojourn in India – whom he persuaded to return to Tibet.
Nehru was assured that Tibetan autonomy would be respected and
that reforms would not be imposed on the country. The following
February, when the Dalai Lama was back in Lhasa, Mao Tse-tung
announced the postponement of far-reaching reforms for at least
five years. This, plus the token withdrawal of Chinese troops and
political cadres from Tibet, were regarded by Nehru as concessions he
had won for the Dalai Lama. The explanation, however, was to be
found in the genuine resistance by the Khampas to Chinese control.
    Clouds on the Sino-Indian horizon grew larger as the dispute over
grazing grounds on the Niti Pass remained unsettled and on the Shipki
Pass a Chinese patrol refused to vacate disputed territory. The public was
unaware of these events. But the issue of Chinese maps was raised
several times in the Indian Parliament. Nehru still described the border
problems as 'small matters' which could be settled without much
difficulty. At the end of 1957 he told the Rajya Sabha that India did not
share the Western obsession that hostility must be assumed between
communists and their neighbours. He gave Russia, China and India as
an example.

    I can say with complete honesty that I am convinced that
    there is not the remotest chance, or if I put it more strongly,
    not the remotest chance of a remote chance of India being
    afraid of Russia or China, of India coming into any kind of
    military conflict with Russia and China . . . India is so situated

geographically that it would not be easy to attack her . . .
Any person who wants to attack India will have to face enor-
mous difficulties . . . apart from the Himalayas, apart from the
seas, the Indian people are not a people to be played with by
any aggressor whoever he may be. But the real geographical
advantage to India is that India is not in the way of Great
Power conflicts.[37]

Not even reports from his Military Intelligence disturbed Nehru's
belief in possible co-existence. He watched, with apparent unconcern,
the increase of activity in potentially strategic areas which his Minister
of Defence initiated. The road from Gangtok to the Natu La in Sikkim
was completed. Expeditions in Ladakh increased. Indian patrols spread
out over the desolate areas of the Aksai Chin.

In the summer of 1957, the Head Lama of Ladakh, Kushak Bakula,
visited Tibet and noticed extensive road building between Tibet and
Sinkiang. Shortly afterwards, the Chinese announced the completion
of the road between Sinkiang and Tibet without giving precise details,
though subsequently they marked them on their maps. As soon as
weather conditions permitted Indian patrols were sent to the Aksai
Chin and found that the road crossed Indian territory. At that point no
Chinese posts existed to the west of it. One Indian patrol was captured
by Chinese frontier guards and another was prevented from carrying
out their instructions. Chinese troops, in fact, already controlled the
newly-levelled jeep-able road across the Aksai Chin. Given goodwill
between India and China, there was every reason why jeeps might
travel along tracks where only occasionally mules had plodded for
centuries. But India's suspicions were aroused at last. Nehru, so determined to maintain good relations with China, remained silent. Questions in the Lok Sabha were barracked. The issue of the Chinese maps
was bedevilled by politicians who regarded it as primarily another stick
with which to beat the Prime Minister and his Minister of Defence.

It is possible that Nehru intended raising these matters in Lhasa,
where he proposed meeting Chou En-lai in April or May 1958. But
the visit was first of all postponed and then the Chinese asked Nehru to
postpone it indefinitely. Tension was already building up in Tibet
which was to lead to the Khampa rebellion. And behind the façade of
'Hindi Chini bhai-bhai', mutual irritation crept into the correspondence
between Chou En-lai and Nehru.

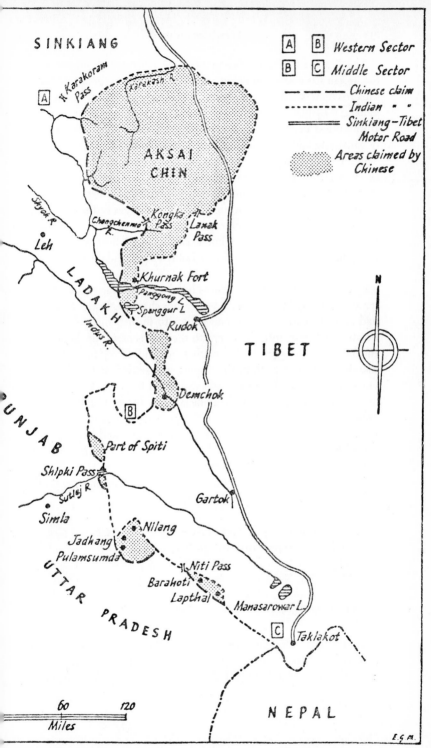

MAP 18. *The Present Boundary Dispute: Western and Middle Sectors.*

The Chinese Foreign Office in July 1958 then formally complained to the Indian Counsellor in Peking that Kalimpong was used as a centre of subversive activities 'by Tibetan reactionaries, by Americans, by the Chiang Kai-shek clique and local special agents' smuggling weapons and ammunition 'in preparation for armed revolt' and with 'the hideous object of damaging China–India friendship'.[38] The Indian reply was equivocal, denying some charges, saying that others had been investigated and steps taken to remove the border friction. From that time onwards, the tones of the official, but at the time secret, correspondence between the two Governments developed through a series of charges and countercharges to a bitter crescendo until fighting broke out. The principal points at issue were Bara Hoti, which the Chinese call Wu Je, Khurnak, a fort on the Pangong Lake, the Aksai Chin, the Lohit Valley, and the Chinese maps.

BARA HOTI. Here was a trans-Himalayan grazing ground, where herdsmen moved their goats as the seasons changed. Both Governments had agreed in 1956 not to send troops to disturb this peaceful scene. For the first year both sides kept to their agreement. In the next year, Indian officials suggested that neither side should try to exercise jurisdiction over the area until the dispute was settled. If Chinese officials entered Barahoti, Indian officials would do likewise. Chinese officials arrived on June 29, 1958. Indian officials, sent by the U.P. Government, arrived on July 8. They left on September 9 and were immediately followed by a Chinese party carrying small arms and later by 25 fully armed soldiers. A complaint by the Indian Government was left unanswered when, in December 1958, the Chinese were accused of bringing about, 'a change in the existing situation during the pendency of talks between the two Governments.'

KHURNAK FORT. In July 1958, a *Note verbale* to the Chinese Counsellor in Delhi, complained that troops had visited this fort to which no claim had ever been made that it 'formed part of the Tibet Region of China'. The Note added that India was planning 'a reconnaissance party to the area with clear instructions that the party will remain within the Indian side of the frontier'.[39]

AKSAI CHIN. This vital arena, where Chinese troops claim to have crossed into Tibet in 1950–51, surveyed it in 1954–55 and then built the road between March 1956 and October 1957, was first officially disputed in October 1958. Historical evidence was presented which supported India's claims to the area. Later, when Chinese troops arrested a party of Indian officers and men, they held them for two months. The Indian Ambassador in Peking commented:

> It is now clear that the Chinese Government also claims this area as their territory. The question whether the particular area is in Indian or Chinese territory is a matter in dispute which has to be dealt with separately.[40]

Yet all that seems to have happened is an exchange of increasingly hostile correspondence.

LOHIT VALLEY. In October 1957 and in September 1958, Chinese troops crossed into the Lohit Frontier Division of the North-East Frontier Agency. India's complaint, not formally made until January 1959, pointed out that as the frontier in this area was 'well recognised and clearly demarcated', the Chinese parties 'which were engaged on survey work crossed into Indian territory by mistake'.[41]

CHINESE MAPS

This issue really came to a head in July 1958 when issue No. 95 of *China Pictorial* carried a map marking the borders by a thick brown line to include 'as Chinese territory' (i) four of the five Divisions of India's N.E.F.A.; (ii) some areas in the north of Uttar Pradesh; (iii) large areas in eastern Ladakh which were part of Jammu and Kashmir. The entire Tashigong area of eastern Bhutan and a considerable slice of territory in north-east Bhutan were also included in Chinese territory. This was too much for the Ministry of External Affairs which acidly retorted that four years earlier they had accepted that there had been no time to change maps, but since 'the present Government of the People's Republic of China has now been in office for so many years and new maps are being repeatedly printed and published in China, the Government of India would suggest that necessary corrections in the Chinese maps should not be delayed further'.[42]

Chou En-lai's Memorandum given to the Counsellor of India in November 1958 recalled that in 1954, when Nehru was in Peking, he (Chou En-lai) had explained that the offending maps were 'drawn on

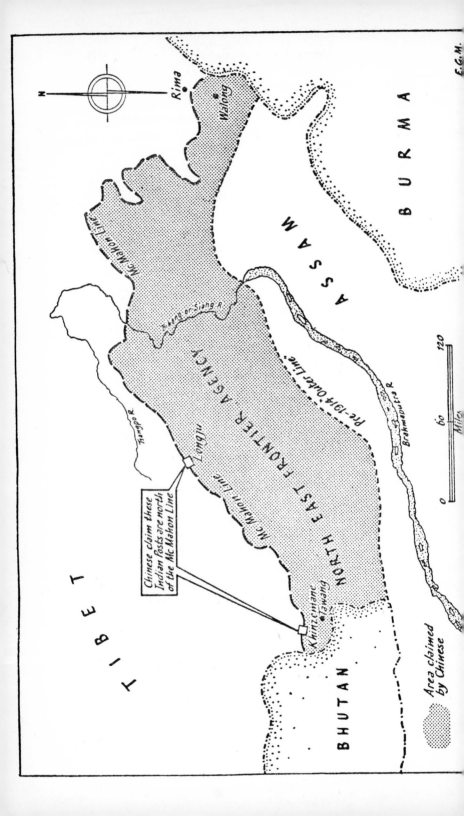

TIBET

Rima

Walong

N

Mc Mahon Line

Tsangpo R.

Dihang or Siang R.

BURMA

ASSAM

Longju

Pre-1914 'Outer' Line

NORTH EAST FRONTIER AGENCY

Mc Mahon Line

Brahmaputra R.

Chinese claim these
Indian posts are north
of the Mc Mahon Line

Khinzemane
Tawang
Bhareng

BHUTAN

Area claimed
by Chinese

0   60   120
         Miles

E.G.M.

the basis of maps published in China before the liberation . . .', that the reason why the boundary was drawn according to these old maps was 'that the Chinese Government has not yet undertaken a survey of China's boundary, nor consulted with the countries concerned, and that it will not make changes in the boundary on its own'. But by 1958 the situations had changed, and Chou's concluding paragraph stated that

> The Chinese Government believes that with the lapse of time, and after consultations with the various neighbouring countries and a survey of the border regions, a new way of drawing the boundary of China will be decided on in accordance with the results of the consultations and the survey.[43]

Nehru now began to query China's position, to express embarrassment on the continued misrepresentation of her borders. In short, controversy between the two Prime Ministers had begun in earnest, and the language of peaceful co-existence was soon replaced by that of the cold war. For the first time Chou En-lai stated the Chinese position.

> First of all, I wish to point out that the Sino-Indian boundary has never been formally delimitated. Historically no treaty or agreement on the Sino-Indian boundary has ever been concluded between the Chinese Central Government and the Indian Government. So far as the actual situation is concerned there are certain differences between the two sides over the border question. . . . It is true that the border question was not raised in 1954 when negotiations were being held between the Chinese and Indian sides for the Agreement on Trade and Intercourse between the Tibet region of China and India. This was because conditions were not yet ripe for its settlement and the Chinese side, on its part, had had no time to study the question.[44]

In other words, Nehru's assumption proved unwarranted that China's willingness to omit the frontier from the Sino-Indian talks in 1954 implied a recognition of Indian views on the subject. His romantic attitude towards China had undermined his sense of history. China can always wait.

This same letter outlined China's views on the McMahon Line. By calling Tibet 'a region of China', Chou En-lai maintained that the agreements signed at Simla by Lonchen Shatra were not legal, were never recognised by the Chinese central Government, and were hotly contested at the time by Tibetans and Chinese. An independent India and Burma could not take the same line as British imperialists; the Chinese hoped their attitude would be more realistic, prudent and carefully considered. Chou continued:

> Precisely because the boundary between the two countries is not yet formally delimitated and some differences exist, it is unavoidable that there should be discrepancies between the boundary line drawn on the respective maps of the two sides. On the maps currently published in our country, the Chinese boundaries are drawn in the way consistently followed in Chinese maps for the past several decades, if not longer. We do not hold that every portion of the boundary line is drawn on sufficient grounds. But it would be inappropriate for us to make changes without having made surveys and without having consulted the countries concerned. Furthermore, there would be difficulties in making such changes, because they would give rise to confusion among our people and bring censure on our government. As a matter of fact, our people have also expressed surprise at the way the Sino-Indian boundary, particularly the western section, is drawn on maps published in India.[45]

Chou En-lai then proposed that in order to avoid incidents,

> so far as possible before the boundary is formally delimitated, that ... as a provisional measure, the two sides temporarily maintain the *status quo*, that is to say, each side keep for the time being to the border areas at present under its jurisdiction and not go beyond them.[46]

In effect, this meant that China remained in control of the Aksai Chin while India continued to administer the North-East Frontier Agency which the Chinese maps claimed as Chinese territory, and which was bounded by the McMahon Line. In his reply two months later, Nehru did not refer to this proposal but referred to the treaties of 1842 and

1847 between Ladakh Region of the State of Jammu and Kashmir with the Emperor of China and the agreements signed with McMahon in 1914. There was, Nehru argued, 'sufficient authority based on geography, traditions as well as treaties' for the boundary which India claimed.

The inescapable fact was that sectors of Indian public opinion, and many officials especially in the Indian Ministry of Defence, no longer considered it safe to count on China's goodwill. Krishna Menon, Minister of Defence since March 1957, had a long record of fierce hostility towards Pakistan; he now was convinced that China was also a threat to India. Mr. George, his biographer says that he had not shared his Prime Minister's views on China in the first years of freedom.* Unhappily we can have no endorsement of this statement by Nehru himself. Nehru assumed 'that there was no possibility of any clash between India and China',[47] and was greatly encouraged by Panikkar. 'Menon questioned the assumption then, but had no evidence to put forward in support of his suspicions.'[48] Aksai Chin gave him that evidence, and although he did not carry the whole cabinet with him for a variety of financial, personal and ideological reasons, 'he launched a crash programme of road-building, mountain warfare training and armament manufacture.'

For the first time in her history, India was building up defences in remote areas where geography gave China a permanent strategic advantage. General Thimayya, one of many Generals to quarrel with Krishna Menon, wrote:

> Whereas in the case of Pakistan I have considered the possibility of a total war, I am afraid I cannot do so in regard to China. I cannot even as a soldier envisage India taking on China in an open conflict on its own. China's present strength in man-power, equipment and aircraft exceeds our resources a hundredfold with the full support of the U.S.S.R. and we could never hope to match China in the foreseeable future. It

* In *India and World Politics. Krishna Menon's View of the World* Michael Brecher has recorded 17 hours of taped interviews, including one on China. These reveal the afterthoughts of a politician, wisdom after the event, explanations which do not wholly excuse ignorance or miscalculation, the intermingling of loyalty and ambition which leave the Nehru-Krishna Menon relationship an enigma.

must be left to the politicians and diplomats to ensure our security.[49]

In the event, China struck first in Tibet. In March 1959, after a period of strained relations with the Dalai Lama, shells were fired into the Norbu Lingka near his palace. He was persuaded to leave his country and, after making an extraordinary escape, he was given political asylum in India.

The reaction in India was explosive; the Dalai Lama was revered and popular and was given a great welcome. Nehru underestimated events in Lhasa which he described as more 'a clash of wills than a clash of arms'. The depth of feeling in the Lok Sabha and in the press came as a surprise to him. Since 1953 he had withheld from press and parliament most information passed on to him from his Military Intelligence, always believing that he was more likely to restrain China through personal contacts with Chou En-lai than by public agitation. It was only under the heaviest parliamentary pressure that he reacted to Chinese propaganda which described his help to the Dalai Lama as 'interference', and the rebellion in Tibet as having been master-minded in Kalimpong by Tibetan traitors, Indian expansionists, American reactionaries and the Kuomintang in Formosa. He confessed to being 'greatly distressed at the tone of the comments and the charges made against India by responsible people in China. They have used the anguage of cold war regardless of truth and propriety.' [50]

China's Ambassador in Delhi complained that his country was being slandered and insulted by 'groups of ruffians', that Indian help to the Dalai Lama, 'no matter what the subjective intentions might be, undoubtedly played an objective role of encouraging the Tibetan rebels'; that China's 'main attention and policy of struggle are directed to the east, to the west Pacific region, to the vicious and aggressive American imperialism, and not to India or any other country in the south-east Asia and south Asia'. The Ambassador's declaration is almost touching.

> China will not be so foolish as to antagonise the United States in the east and again to antagonise India in the west. . . . You will ultimately see whether relations between the Tibet region of India and China are friendly or hostile by watching three, five, ten, twenty, a hundred years. We cannot have two centres of attention, nor can we take friend for foe. . . .

Friends! It seems to us that you too cannot have two fronts.
Is it not so? If it is, here then lies the meeting point of our two
sides. Will you please think it over? [51]

India's Foreign Secretary deplored such language and described
Chinese mis-statements as 'wholly out of keeping with diplomatic
usage and the courtesies due to friendly countries'. A polite concluding
remark to the Foreign Secretary's reply said that India would 'not
discard or vary any of their own policies under any pressure from
outside'.[52]

The rebellion in Tibet was, in effect, the end of the road of Sino-
Indian friendship. In the summer months of 1959, incidents sparked
off flames till the whole frontier was alight. The Migyitun area was
the first point of conflict. Peking accused Indian troops of occupying
this area and of 'unscrupulous collusion with the traitorous Tibetan
rebel bandits'. The Indian Government denied these allegations,
claimed to have scrupulously observed the traditional border between
India and the Tibet region of China along the entire Indo-Chinese
frontier.

The Chinese Foreign Office informed the Indian Counsellor that
'a group of Indian armed troops intruded into Chinese territory south
of Migyitun and suddenly opened fire on Chinese frontier guards'.[53]

The following day, the Indian Ambassador complained that in 'a
number of instances . . . Chinese troops have violated the international
frontier and trespassed into Indian territory. . . . On the 25th August a
strong Chinese detachment crossed into Indian territory south of
Migyitun on the N.E.F.A. border and fired without notice on an
Indian picket'.[54]

Again in August, India had charged that 'armed Chinese patrol
strength approximately two hundred committed violation of our
border at Khinzemane . . .'.[55]

A similar incident occurred at Spanggur in the Pangong Tso area
and at Khurnak Fort to its east. A Chinese detachment of some two
dozen soldiers was found by Indian police engaged on reconnaissance
within Indian territory. The Chinese replied that six Indian soldiers
had intruded into Chinese territory in the Pangong Tso area. These
probing and counter-probing incidents were not in themselves of great
importance but they were pointers to the breakdown of Sino-Indian
relations. Added to propaganda on India's relations with Sikkim and

Bhutan, their cumulative effect was to inflame Indian public opinion.
It was unprepared, since Nehru had taken personal responsibility for
foreign policy and Chinese violations of India's territory were scarcely
known outside the Ministry of Defence and Military Intelligence.
When, at last, on August 28, 1959, the Prime Minister told the Lok
Sabha what had happened, he was faced with a volley of questions
from all parties. Until now, both Ladakh and N.E.F.A. were hardly
known, even to the majority of M.P.s and to most journalists. Nehru
had to explain that the McMahon Line did not extend to Ladakh! He
himself was so indifferent about the Aksai Chin, that he described it at
one time or another as treeless, grassless, uninhabited, frightfully cold,
so remote that if 'he sent a party of explorers with exploring kit' it
would take them about a month to get there. Perhaps the most
significant part of this Debate was Nehru's specific statement on the
McMahon Line and on Ladakh. He repeated complaints made privately
to Chou En-lai about Chinese maps:

> ... colouring half of the North-Eastern Frontier Agency,
> one-third of Assam and one-third of Bhutan as if they belong
> to China. That is really an affront.[56]

He continued:

> But having accepted broadly the McMahon Line, I am pre-
> pared to discuss any interpretation of the McMahon Line;
> minor interpretation here and there – that is a different matter
> – not these big chunks but the minor interpretation whether
> this hill is there or this little bit is on that side or on this side,
> on the facts, on the maps, on the evidence available. That I am
> prepared to discuss with the Chinese Government. I am pre-
> pared to have any kind of conciliatory, mediatory process to
> consider this ... But the broad McMahon Line has to be
> accepted, and so far as we are concerned, it is there and we
> accept it.[57]

He realised that the position of Ladakh was different. The actual
boundary of Ladakh with Tibet

was not very carefully defined. It was defined to some extent
by British officers who went there. But I rather doubt if they
did any careful survey . . . As people do not live there, by and
large, it does not make any difference. It did not make any
difference. At that time nobody cared about it.[58]

He then said that India was prepared to discuss this problem with
China on the basis of treaties, existing maps, usage, geography, etc.
He presented a White Paper to the Lok Sabha on September 7, which
contained Notes, Memoranda and letters exchanged between the two
Governments between April 1954 and August 1959.

Chou En-lai did not reply to Nehru's detailed letter of March 22
1959, until September 8. He then roamed over the history of Sino-
Indian relations; how Britain, 'using India as its base, conducted
extensive territorial expansion into China's Tibet region, and even the
Sinkiang region'; how India now seemed to be following in Britain's
footsteps. Pending 'an over-all settlement of the boundary question . . .
as a provisional measure, the two sides should maintain the long-
existing *status quo* of the border, and not seek to change it by unilateral
action, even less by force'. He then set out to prove that the Sino-
Indian boundary had 'never been formally delimited', which was, in
fact, the exact opposite to Nehru's contention that most parts of the
Sino-Indian boundary had the sanction of specific agreements between
Britain and China. *Hsinhua*, a week later, followed up the Note.

> Incontrovertible facts were given today by the Vice-President
> of the Political Science and Law Association, Wu Teh-feng,
> exposing the illegality of the so-called McMahon Line. He also
> expressed resolute opposition to the unilateral claims of the
> Indian Government on the Sino-Indian boundary question.[59]

The crux of Wu's argument was that the Chinese representative

> did not sign the Simla Treaty, and no Chinese Central
> Government has ever recognised the Treaty itself, or the
> boundary lines on the map attached to the Treaty.[60]

He gave a highly coloured account of McMahons's strenuous efforts
to persuade Ivan Chen to sign. Having failed, the Treaty still remained

to the present day, simply a draft, and had no legal force whatever.
The ingenious notion was put forward that since

> Tibet was part of China, its representative ... could only
> participate in the Conference by accompanying the repre-
> sentative of the Central Government in the capacity of the
> representative of the local Government concerned, and he
> could never cut himself off from the representative of the
> Central Government, and himself sign a valid Treaty with
> Britain.[61]

The theme was entirely contrary to known facts. Wu also produced
an argument about the Agreement signed by Lonchen Shatra and
McMahon. It was only mentioned in general terms, whereas 'a
delineation treaty should clearly show where the boundary begins ...
and ends, and then this boundary line is marked on attached maps'.[62]
Lonchen Shatra's *The Collection of information and materials relating to
the Simla Conference* 'admitted that Tibet had taken the poisonous notes
as "good medicine" and had swallowed them "under special circumstances".' [63]

Child’s propaganda barrage had begun. In Lhasa, simultaneously,
two former high-ranking officials of the Tibetan Government were
quoted as saying that 'the area south of the so-called McMahon Line
had always come under the jurisdiction of China's Tibet Region'.[64]
Gashu Chuji-Nima and Rompa Tutan-Kinching, Kalloons in the
Kashag between 1943 and 1949 said it had issued passports to British
citizens wanting to collect plants in the Mon-Tawang area, which
showed that it was under Tibetan control. After Indian independence,
Gasha Chuji-Nima said, the Kashag had been told by the Indian
Government that it wished to occupy certain areas. Representatives
of the three great monasteries and members of the Kashag replied to
Nehru,

> once again refusing to recognise the secret exchange of Notes
> on the boundary, expressing determination that not an inch
> of land would be ceded and asking India to return the
> other territories of the Tibet region already occupied by
> India.[65]

Chuji-Nima also revealed that officials and people in Tawang between 1947 and 1949 had urgently informed the Kashag

> that Indian troops had occupied territory . . . that residents also protested to the invading Indian troops, telling them 'we are Tibetans, we are not governed by the Indians'.[66]

Chinese cartographers joined the campaign. Ouyang Ying 'with forty years experience in cartography' maintained that maps of the Sino-Indian boundary line east of Bhutan had 'always kept strictly to traditional custom' and quoted The New Atlas of China (1907), the Shen Pao Atlas of China and others which were to figure later in talks between officials.

Tseng Shih-Ying, co-editor of the "Shen Pao Atlas", said British imperialism had not dared to draw the McMahon Line openly on its maps while it still ruled India. Other cartographers quoted selected maps published in Britain between 1917 and 1943, German, Russian and American maps to support their case that the McMahon Line had never been defined. They conveniently overlooked the last "Imperial Atlas of China" (1908) which put the frontier much closer to the McMahon Line than to China's present claim. Similarly, their cartographers did not quote the fact that of the dozens of Chinese atlases which rejected the McMahon Line, only two of them supported their claims to Ladakh, – the "Russian World Atlas" (1954) and "Shen Pao Atlas" in 1933.

The battle over the maps was a prelude to battle on the ground. On October 20, 1959 nine Indian soldiers on patrol near the Kongka Pass in Ladakh were killed and ten taken prisoner. Indian public opinion was roused and even those politicians who had been Gandhi's most devoted followers now called for revenge. Nehru cautioned a meeting of Congress workers in Meerut three days after the clash:

> Our border question with China is a question which has caused us and continues to cause a lot of anxiety. I do not say that there will be war with China (on this issue) . . . we have to act with restraint and responsibility . . . There are some people in our country who indulge in brave talk and demand "attack China". These people say this quite smugly because they do not have to go themselves to these areas.[62]

Later that day he told a vast public meeting that India and China had been friends for two thousand years. The sudden war fever reflected in newspapers and in parliament distressed him.

> Even supposing that near this border there was some difference of opinion over a patch of territory, then is this the way of dealing with it as the Chinese have done, to send their armies and try to take it by force, raining bullets on our patrol and killing our people? . . . We should not allow ourselves to be swept away by anger, that is the way of the inexperienced. India's voice has been raised firmly in the world in the defence of peace. We have therefore to endure that in dealing with problems relating to our own country we do not set a different example.[63]

It was almost too late. Blood had been shed and India's mood was revengeful.

All Reason Spent

The Prime Minister was loudly abused and urged to take revenge for the lives of these Indian soldiers killed at the Kongka Pass. Six days after the incident he was in the unusual position of having to justify himself at a Conference of Provincial Governors, *The Hindu's* Delhi correspondent described him as giving the impression of

> standing alone against the rising tide of national resentment against China . . . Observers have noted that in the present conflict with China, the resentment against the Chinese is taking the form of a personal attack on Mr Nehru.[1]

He told a large audience in New Delhi that he refused to consider any abandonment of non-alignment.

> It is the surest sign of weakness to ask others to save us from external danger . . . the only result of a policy of seeking military alliances with others for defending India would be to jeopardise our freedom and shatter completely our place in the world.[2]

Far more than the normal battery of questions was fired at him four days later at his press conference. He deprecated anti-Chinese demonstrations all over India and he still insisted that it was firm policy 'so far as is possible to settle matters peacefully . . . just as it is also a firm policy to fight if necessary'.[3] Parodying a famous slogan, he described his own basic strategy as 'Trust in conciliatory policies and keep your powder dry'. The flavour of his rhetoric was turning under the pressure of public opinion.

Nehru's hopes of peaceful co-existence with China faded even as the spell of his own personality waned. He remained outwardly calm and

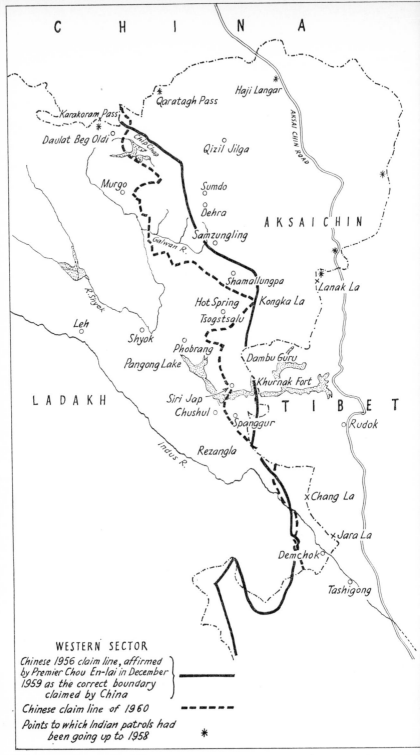

C H I N A

Qaratagh Pass

Haji Langar

Karakoram Pass

Daulat Beg Oldi

Chip Chap

Qizil Jilga

AKSAI CHIN ROAD

Murgo

Sumdo

Dehra

AKSAICHIN

Galwan R.

Samzungling

R. Shyok

Shamallungpa

Lanak La

Hot Spring

Kongka La

Tsogstsalu

Leh

Shyok

Phobrang

Dambu Guru

Pangong Lake

Khurnak Fort

Siri Jap

Chushul

LADAKH

Spanggur

TIBET

Rudok

Rezangla

Indus R.

Chang La

Jara La

Demchok

Tashigong

WESTERN SECTOR

Chinese 1956 claim line, affirmed
by Premier Chou En-lai in December
1959 as the correct boundary
claimed by China

Chinese claim line of 1960

Points to which Indian patrols had
been going up to 1958

MAP 20. *The Chinese Claim Lines of 1956 and 1960 in the Western Sector.*

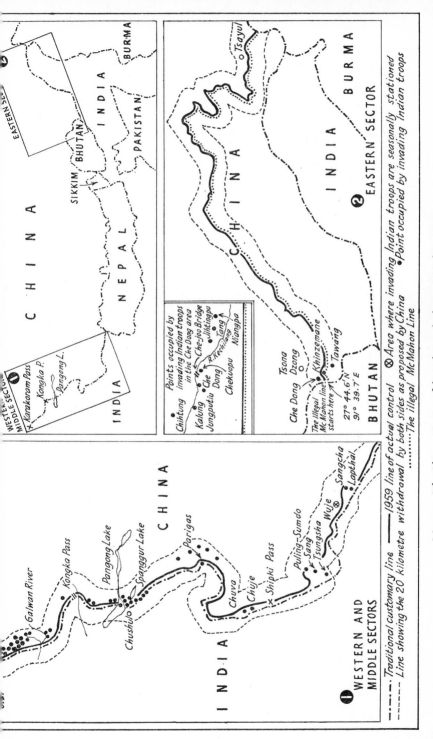

MAP 21. The Chinese Version of the Indian and Chinese Boundaries, 1962.

WESTERN AND MIDDLE SECTORS

⊗ Area where invading Indian troops are seasonally stationed
● Point occupied by invading Indian troops

Points occupied by invading Indian troops in the Che Dong area

The illegal McMahon line starts here
27° 44.6'N
9° 39.7'E

① WESTERN AND MIDDLE SECTORS

② EASTERN SECTOR

–·–·– Traditional customary line
——— 1959 line of actual control
– – – Line showing the 20 kilometre withdrawal by both sides as proposed by China
·········· The illegal McMahon Line

balanced, though he was profoundly dismayed by the setback to his policy of Panch Shila. He recalled the wisdom of a Foreign Minister who told him sometime in 1949–50: 'For Heaven's sake, don't fall into the error of treating this revolutionary China as you or we treated the Soviet Union after its revolution. We took a wrong step then which pursued us for years afterwards. It is still pursuing us.' [4]

In the Lok Sabha he was criticised with unprecedented vehemence. He sadly retorted: If this House thinks that the way our Government has carried on this particular work is not satisfactory, then it is open to this House to choose more competent men on whom it has faith. But if in the balance this House feels that this Prime Minister has got to face this challenge, then hold to him and help him, and do not come in his way. [5] He faced at last the possibility of war with China, but it would, he urged, be 'a tragedy of the deepest kind – a tragedy for us, a tragedy for China and a tragedy for Asia and the world. Therefore, let us not think lightly of it. Let us not take steps which will automatically push us in that direction'. [6]

A worsening of the crisis was not yet inevitable. Nehru suggested to Chou En-lai, in his letter of September 26, that Chinese forces should be withdrawn from posts 'opened in recent months at Spanggur, Mandal and one or two other places in eastern Ladakh . . . also . . . from Longju.[7] Chou En-lai sent no formal reply until November 7, but Chinese official views were in the meantime informally indicated to Ajoy Ghosh, the General Secretary of the C.P.I., in an interview with Mao Tse-tung.

> Mr Mao Tse-tung in his characteristically poetic language told me that the stream of India–China friendship could never dry up but would keep flowing strong and serene . . . I may state that in the course of our talks, Mao Tse-tung returned more than once to the theme that the border disputes were a temporary phenomenon, an episode, in the long, long years unmarked by any conflicts. Whether it was Mao, Liu Shao-chi or Chou En-lai, all were enormously keen that the border dispute be settled through friendly negotiations as quickly as possible. The Chinese leaders were quite confident that such a settlement would be brought about. They said that they were quite conscious of the fact that Premier Nehru and the Indian Government were also anxious for a settlement. It was

this mutual desire to end the dispute amicably that would, they (Chinese) were convinced, find fruition in establishing a firm frontier of abiding amity, between both the mighty Asian countries.[8]

A second indication was given to Dr A. V. Baliga, the President of the Indo-Soviet Cultural Association, and of the Indo-Chinese Friendship Association. During a ten-day visit to China he had twice met Chou En-lai. He told newspapermen in Hong Kong that he 'had received the impression from Premier Chou that Communist China was prepared to exchange the recognition of the McMahon Line for territory in Ladakh'.[9]

This suggestion was implicitly made in Chou En-lai's reply to Nehru on November 7.

> The Chinese Government proposes that the armed forces of China and India each withdraw twenty kilometres at once from the so-called McMahon Line in the east, and from the line up to which each side exercises actual control in the west, and that the two sides undertake to refrain from again sending their armed personnel to be stationed in and patrol the zones from which they have evacuated their armed forces, but still maintain civil administrative personnel and unarmed police there for the performance of administrative duties and maintenance of order. This proposal is in effect an extension of the Indian Government's proposal contained in its note dated September 10 that neither side should send its armed personnel to Longju, to the entire border between China and India, and moreover a proposal to separate the troops of the two sides by as great a distance as forty kilometres.[10]

Nehru answered immediately and categorically that 'the Government of India had not posted any army personnel anywhere at or near the international border. . . . It was only after the recent unfortunate incidents that we asked our Army to take over responsibility for the protection of our border'.[11] He challenged Chou En-lai's contention that China had been in occupation of the area shown in their maps, and held that as the facts concerning the status quo were themselves disputed, any agreement about its observance would be 'meaningless'. He made an alternative proposal about Ladakh.

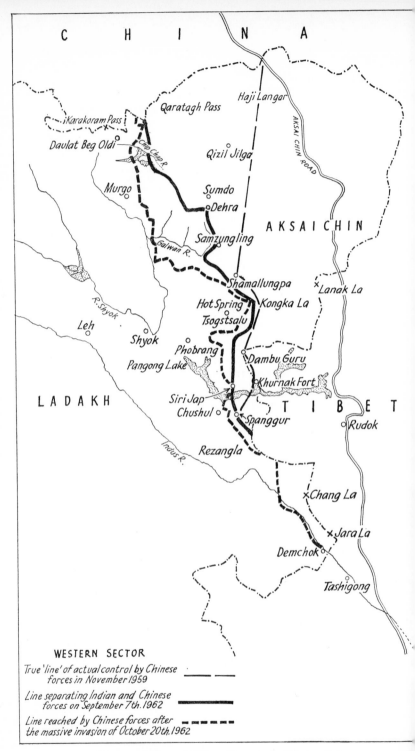

C H I N A

Karakoram Pass

Qaratagh Pass

Haji Langar

Daulat Beg Oldi

Chip Chap R.

Qizil Jilga

AKSAI CHIN ROAD

Murgo

Sumdo
Dehra

Galwan R.

Samzungling

AKSAI CHIN

Shamallungpa

Lanak La

Hot Spring
Tsogstsalu

Kongka La

R. Shyok

Leh

Shyok

Phobrang

Pangong Lake

Dambu Guru

Khurnak Fort

Siri Jap
Chushul

Spanggur

Rudok

LADAKH

T I B E T

Indus R.

Rezangla

Chang La

Jara La

Demchok

Tashigong

WESTERN SECTOR

True 'line' of actual control by Chinese
forces in November 1959

Line separating Indian and Chinese
forces on September 7th. 1962

Line reached by Chinese forces after
the massive invasion of October 20th. 1962

MAP 22. Indian and Chinese Forces in the Western Sector.

The Government of India should withdraw all personnel to the west of the line which the Chinese Government have shown as the international boundary in their 1956 maps which, so far as we are aware are their latest maps. Similarly, the Chinese Government should withdraw their personnel to the east of the international boundary which has been described by the Government of India in their earlier notes and correspondence and shown in their official maps. Since the two lines are separated by long distances, there should not be the slightest risk of border clashes between the two forces on either side. The area is almost entirely uninhabited. It is thus not necessary to maintain administrative personnel in this area bounded by the two lines on the east and the west.[12]

The Times, in an editorial article aptly pointed out that this 'would mean the evacuation of some thousands of square mile of Ladakh, in which the Chinese have asserted their claims with troops. India would have to quit only a fifty square mile strip in the south-east corner of the disputed area which contains one checkpost'.[13] An American commentary on the other hand, observed that 'acceptance of this proposal would have seriously jeopardised Indian defence positions in the east and would have at the same time made a gift to the Chinese of the vital Aksai Chin area'.[14]

It is probable that Krushchev, despite his having incurred Chinese reprimands for his neutrality, had some influence in Chou En-lai's abrupt invitation to Nehru on December 17 to meet him nine days later in Rangoon or Peking. Along with the invitation came another proposal for tranquilising the border – that patrolling 'should apply to the entire Sino-Indian border, and no different measure should be adopted in the sector of the border between China and India's Ladakh'.[15]

But, apart from the difficulties of arranging a meeting at such short notice, Nehru no longer saw the usefulness in a meeting when the area of disagreement was so wide. He answered:

Your present letter once again reiterates claims to extensive areas which by history, by custom or agreement have long been integral parts of India. I am particularly sorry to find that you have based your claim on recent intrusion by Chinese personnel into parts of Indian territory. It is these intrusions

which have brought about the present situation and created
apprehensions.[16]

The letter was dated New Delhi, December 21. China's reply, on
December 26, was accompanied by a five thousand word long Note. It
was obviously in the Chinese Ministry of Foreign Affairs at the time when
Chou En-lai's earlier letter was sent and reflects the dual line of Peking.
At the same time, Nehru's sharp refusal did not put reason to the test.
Chou En-lai's Note had evidently been prepared as a brief for his
proposed meeting with Nehru. China's case had never before been
put so completely. It was their reply to the frequent Notes from India
as well as to the Note on the Historical Background of the Himalayan
Frontier of India attached to White Paper No. 2 of the Ministry of
External Affairs.

Had Nehru responded to Chou's invitation to go to Rangoon or
Peking at less than a fortnight's notice, might some basis of agreement
have been found? It was made at the time when non-communist
groups were converging on Delhi and has in a number of aspects the
appearance of a try-on. But Nehru's policy was excessively personal.
Until Indian public opinion had been inflamed by the loss of lives at the
Kongka Pass, he could almost certainly have obtained sanction for
any policy he cared to formulate. But by this time he no longer had
any personal trust in Chou's bona fides, and for the first time public
opinion was giving him a lead. We may assume that Chou En-lai's
Note of December 26 was intended as the basis of his talks had he met
Nehru. Nehru's blunt reply therefore did not alter the facts of Chinese
claims, but personal confrontation might have postponed the deteriora-
tion in Sino-Indian relations which sharply increased from now
onwards.

Nehru based his case on history, Chou on facts of the moment. 'The
entire length of the border,' Nehru said, 'has been either defined by
treaty or recognised by custom or by both and until now the Chinese
Government have not protested against the exercise of jurisdiction
by the Government of India up to the customary border.'[17] Chou
replied: 'The reason for the present existence of certain disputes over
the Sino-Indian boundary is that the two countries have never formally
delimited this boundary and that there is a divergence of views between the two countries regarding the boundary.'[18] Where agreements
– the McMahon Line is an excellent example – made by British

diplomats were quoted, Chou challenged Nehru's willingness to benefit from British imperialism. He used the argument of an undefined boundary in neighbouring countries to encourage bilateral agreements. The permanent factor of geography gave China a strategic trump card. Even the 1954 Sino-Indian Agreement which Nehru assumed was an implicit agreement on the boundary was now thrown back at him. Chang Han-fu, the Chinese pointed out, 'in his talk with the Indian representative, Ambassador Mr N. Raghavan, on April 23, 1954, clearly stated that the Chinese did not wish, in those negotiations, to touch on the boundary question. And Ambassador N. Raghavan agreed forthwith. The Chinese Government therefore maintains that there is no ground to say that this sector of the boundary has been delimited and that there is no need to conduct negotiations for its delimitation.' [19] For Chou En-lai the negotiations dealt only with 'outstanding questions between the two countries' which were 'ripe for settlement'.

'Has the Sino-Indian Boundary been formally delimited?' was the title of Question No. 1. This was the summary of its 'incontestable conclusion'.

> The entire Sino-Indian boundary, whether in its western, middle or eastern sector, has not been delimited. The 1842 Treaty, on which the Indian Government bases itself, did not define any boundary line for the western sector of the Sino-Indian border; and moreover, China's Sinkiang region, which is most concerned with this sector of the boundary, was no party to this Treaty. The 1954 Agreement, on which the Indian Government bases itself, did not involve the middle or any other sector of the Sino-Indian boundary. The 1914 Convention, on which the Indian Government bases itself, is itself void of legal validity, and the Sino-Indian boundary was never discussed at the 1914 Conference. That the Sino-Indian boundary is yet to be delimited has been recognised by the Indian and British Governments over a long period of time, and is borne out by indisputable evidences. In order to achieve a reasonable settlement of the Sino-Indian boundary dispute satisfactory to both sides, there is no other way except the holding of friendly negotiations. [20]

Question No. 2 asked 'What is the Traditional Customary Sino-Indian Boundary Line?' And whereas the absence of delimitation was given as justification of the Chinese case in Question 1, a customary line was given to support it in Question 2. The most controversial area was the thirty-three thousand square kilometres in the western sector which was said to have 'always belonged to China', the major part 'under the jurisdiction of Hotien County of the Sinkiang Uighur Autonomous Region of China, while the minor part under that of Rudok *Dzong* of the Tibetan Autonomous Region of China'.[21] In evidence it was claimed that the names Aksai Chin and Karakash were in the Uighur language and meant 'the desert of white stones' and 'the river of the black jade'.

> This area is the only traffic artery linking Sinkiang and western Tibet, because to its north east lies the great Gobi of Sinkiang through which direct traffic with Tibet is practically impossible. Therefore, since the middle of the eighteenth century, the Government of the Ching Dynasty of China had established Karens (check-posts) to exercise jurisdiction over and patrol this area. In the decades from the founding of the Republic of China till the liberation of China, there were troops constantly guarding this area. After the liberation of Sinkiang in 1949, the Chinese People's Liberation Army took over the guarding of the frontier in this area from Kuomintang troops. In the latter half of 1950, it was through this area that the Chinese Government dispatched the first units of the Chinese People's Liberation Army to enter Tibet. In the nine years since then, the Chinese troops stationed in the Ari district have regularly and frequently brought up indispensable supplies from Sinkiang through this area. From March 1956 to October 1957, the Chinese Government built along the customary route a motor-road from Yeycheng of Sinkiang to Gartok of Tibet of a total length of one thousand two hundred kilometres, of which a section of the one hundred and eighty kilometres runs through this area, and over three thousand civilian workers took part in its construction.[22]

After references to Nehru's comments in parliament that as far as he knew 'this area was neither inhabited by any people nor were there any outposts during British rule', China's Note continued:

The Indian Government says that it has been sending regular patrols to this area, and that this is one way India exercises its jurisdiction. According to data available to the Chinese Government, however, armed Indian personnel intruded only three times into this area to carry out reconnaissance, namely in September 1958, July 1959 and October 1959, and on each occasion they were promptly detained and then sent out of China by Chinese frontier guards. Apart from these three intrusions they have never been to this area. It is precisely for this reason that the Indian Government has been so unaware of the long-term activities of the Chinese personnel in this area that it declares that it was in 1957 that Chinese personnel first entered this area.[23]

The Chinese also used the 'traditional customary' argument to support their case in the middle sector.

The maps published by the two sides also show that it is China, not India, which has abided by the traditional customary line. The delineations of this sector of the boundary on past Chinese maps, though leaving a few very small pieces of Chinese territory outside of the Chinese boundary, on the whole reflected the correct traditional customary line. On the other hand, no boundary line was drawn for this sector on official Indian maps even as late as 1950, and only the words 'Boundary Undefined' were marked.[24]

On the eastern sector, the Chinese made far wider claims than in any earlier correspondence.

The area between the so-called McMahon Line and the boundary line at the southern foot of the Himalayas as shown on Chinese maps has always belonged to China, and was until recently still under Chinese jurisdiction. This is proved by a mass of facts.[25]

The Note challenged the exchange of 'secret letters on March 24, 1914, between the British representative of the then Tibet local authorities'. But if they were secret and unknown to the Chinese, how could the

Chinese Government, whether K.M.T. or Communist, make the many protests they claimed to have made? Chou En-lai now put on record what were his real intentions in 1954. Nehru had referred to his meeting with the Chinese Prime Minister and his assumption that China stood by the McMahon Line. In fact, Chou En-lai explained, a statement of his that it was illegal and had never been recognised by China could 'by no means be interpreted as recognition of this line by the Chinese Government'.[26] In the ten years since liberation, Chinese military and administrative personnel had been 'under orders not to go beyond the areas which have always been under Chinese jurisdiction, and even not to cross the so-called McMahon Line in the eastern sector'.[27] The Note then suggested that the armed forces of the two sides along the border respectively withdraw twenty kilometres or some other distance considered appropriate and in the meantime to stop patrolling along the whole border.

This Chinese Note was not answered until February 5, 1960. Nehru once again deplored the emphasis Peking placed on the 'entire boundary never having been delimited'. Nevertheless, although he stated that negotiation on the basis suggested by China was out of the question, he thought it might be helpful to arrange a meeting between the two Prime Ministers and invited Chou En-lai to visit Delhi some time in March. He would be treated as 'an honoured guest'. They met in April.

Chou En-lai was the least garlanded V.I.P. who visited Delhi that spring. Public opinion was suspicious.

The Jana Sangh, the P.S.P., and the Swatantra Party combined to urge Nehru 'not to arrange any public reception or functions in honour of the visitor'. Predictably, Nehru answered that 'it would be extraordinary, improper and not in keeping with India's cultural traditions, for us not to abide by those rules and conventions and refrain from giving every courtesy to a distinguished guest'.[28]

Six days of private talks between the two Prime Ministers, who had once pledged eternal friendship, ended in deadlock. On the eve of his departure for Kathmandu, Chou En-lai gave a two-and-a-half hours press conference [Text in Appendix 15]. He maintained that he had tried unsuccessfully to gain India's support for the following points as the basis of further negotiations:

> 1. There exist disputes with regard to the boundary between the two sides.

2. There exists between the two countries a line of actual control up to which each side exercises administrative jurisdiction.

3. In determining the boundary between the two countries, certain geographical principles, such as watersheds, river valleys and mountain passes, should be equally applicable to all the sectors of the boundary.

4. A settlement of the boundary question between the two countries should take into account the national feelings of the two peoples towards the Himalayas and the Karakorum Mountains.

5. Pending a settlement of the boundary question between the two countries through discussions, both sides should keep to the line of actual control and should not put forward territorial claims as pre-conditions, but individual adjustments may be made.

6. In order to ensure tranquility on the border so as to facilitate the discussions, both sides should continue to refrain from patrolling along all sectors of the boundary.[29]

Chou En-lai made it clear that 'the only possible approach to a settlement would involve India's tacitly or formally recognising Chinese rights in the Aksai Chin area in Ladakh in exchange for reciprocal forbearance by Peking from any assertion of her claims for territory below the McMahon Line in the east'.[30] Nehru, with equal emphasis, said the day following that Chou En-lai had once again tried to link acceptance of actual position (i.e. the McMahon Line) to India's recognition of the fact of Chinese occupation of Ladakh. He was uncompromisingly against barter in such matters.

When Nehru suggested that officials of the two countries should meet immediately to discuss their respective claims, Chou En-lai said that most of the data was in Peking. Indian officials had assumed the excessive luggage of their Chinese counterparts had brought with them was their evidence. It contained, it seems, lavish presents to celebrate Chou's anticipated victory.

Nehru did not easily convince the Lok Sabha that he had stood firm. He was attacked for interviews Chou En-lai had had with his Ministers, notably Krishna Menon. He explained that they were held at his suggestion, since he was anxious that Chou En-lai should find out by experience just how bitter Indian opinion had become. Little enthusiasm was shown for the decision of the two Prime Ministers that their officials 'should meet and examine, check and study all historical documents, records, accounts, maps and other material relevant to the boundary question, on which each side relied in support of its stand, and draw up a report for submission to the two Governments'.[31]

The first session in Peking agreed, with difficulty, that the agenda pattern should contain these items: (i) Location and Terrain features of the boundary; (ii) Treaties and Agreements; Tradition and Custom; both these were to be dealt with separately for the entire length of the boundary; (iii) Administration and Jurisdiction; and (iv) Miscellaneous, treating each sector separately.

The boundary was divided into western, middle and eastern sectors. The boundary west of the Karakorum Pass was not considered by the Chinese as coming within the terms of reference, and they subsequently made a separate agreement with Pakistan. The Indian officials suggested a fourth sector to include the boundaries of Bhutan and Sikkim with Tibet, but this was turned down by the Chinese for similar reasons.

The question of alignment immediately raised problems. It was only at the fifth meeting on June 27, 1960, that an authoritative map showing the whole alignment claimed by the Chinese Government was made available. The Indian side stressed the watershed principle, describing it as 'a valid and legitimate one in determining boundaries' and by no means only a British concept. In the case of agreements just signed with Nepal and Burma, the Chinese had themselves accepted validity of the watershed principle in determining customary boundary alignments. In the Middle Sector both sides had referred to the watershed and were clear where it lay. In the cases where the Chinese departed from the watershed principle, they 'curiously enough' were such as 'to include Indian territory in Tibet, and in no case the other way round'.

The divergence between the Chinese claim and the traditional customary boundary along the watershed was greatest in the Eastern Sector, where the Chinese claimed over thirty thousand square miles and the traditional and customary line along the southern foothills of the Himalayas. The alignment swooped down to the foothills, while both to the east and west of this sector it lay along the main watershed range. The Chinese officials had an explanation: geographical features were related to the formation of a customary line, 'but they are not the decisive factors'. People who live in high mountains, do not necessarily find them a barrier, particularly when rivers or passes cut across the ridges. Nor can mountain ridges limit 'a country's administrative jurisdiction. To drive this point home, suffice it to mention the fact of people of China's Tibetan nationality having spread to so many places on the southern side of the Himalayas and the administrative juris-diction of the Tibet region of China having extended to these places'. In the course of time, the Chinese argued, administration and the activities of a people change and, 'therefore the formation of a tradition-al customary line must also be through a process of change and could not have been predestined or mechanically determined by a certain geographical feature.'[32] This was particularly so in the Sino-Indian boundary with its complicated terrain, and if translated into specific terms, it means that the Chinese were claiming that the Monbas, the Daflas, the Miris, etc. all tribal peoples along the mountain ranges, were Tibetans, and therefore, for political purposes, Chinese. Which is nonsense. In earlier chapters the story is told of how the peoples in question came to be a part of the Indian Empire by punitive expedition, occupation, and ultimately by the agreement of March 1914 signed by Lonchen Shatra and McMahon.

The establishment of and the settlement of the borders in 1914 of the North-East Frontier Agency were the means to contain China. That the country remained undeveloped and the McMahon Line unimple-mented for some years did not change the basic fact that it came under British jurisdiction. Indian reluctance to accept this fact, which was intelligible enough, played into Chinese hands, Alastair Lamb, pungently concludes his well-documented book, *The Simla Conference and the McMahon Line*:

> Why Mr Nehru, while declaring himself committed to a policy of friendship of peaceful coexistence, with Communist China, should have adhered with such tenacity to those symbols, at least in Chinese eyes, of British Imperialism, the Simla Convention and the McMahon Line notes, is one of the mysteries of the twentieth century. If this book does no more than suggest that there is indeed a mystery requiring solution, then it will have achieved its purpose.[33]

Indian officials, in presenting their case, chose to avoid the challenge of having inherited the frontiers made by British imperialism. They would have been less vulnerable had they chosen to emphasise the fact subsequently made by Sir Olaf Caroe, Secretary to the Government of India 1939–1945.

> There is no treaty authority of any kind for the line claimed by the Chinese in the plains of Assam. That line merely re- presents the limit of regular administration by the province – now state – of Assam . . . It is true that over many periods the Dalai Lama, not the Chinese Government, had exercised authority in certain small regions south of where the McMahon Line now runs and north of the forest region, and notably in Tawang, where there is a famous Buddhist monas- tery. But Tibetan authority had never been extended to the forest tribes such as the Mishmis, Abors and Daphas. And there has never been any Chinese jurisdiction of any sort in this regions. As for Tibet, by the 1914 Convention, she agreed to the McMahon Line.[34]

While the Chinese argued against the watershed principle in the section covered by the McMahon Line insofar as it conflicted with their ambition to impose their own rule in N.E.F.A. they acted on it in the case of Burma, wherein the Sino-Burmese agreement of October 1, 1960, followed almost exactly the line from the Diphu Pass to the Izu Razi Pass drawn on the map of the Simla Conference. At the tri- junction of India, Burma and China, the Chinese had tried to take the line five miles south of the watershed which would have given them the Diphu Pass with access to the plains of Assam. The Burmese were anxious to avoid controversy and although the map attached to the agreement took the frontier down to the Diphu Pass, they stated that this would be open to modification if and when India and China came to an agreement which would result in placing the point elsewhere. A new map would then have to be drawn. China's anxiety to effect the treaty with Burma is used by some writers as evidence of Chinese moderation, and by others of Chinese subtlety in bringing pressure to bear on India.

The Indian officials legitimately made this deduction:

> This [the Sino-Burma] agreement proves that the traditional boundary lay along the Himalayan watershed and that it was

precise long before the recent treaties of formal delimitation. If there was for northern Burma such a precise traditional boundary along the watershed as has now been confirmed, it could not possibly be suggested that the traditional boundary for the Eastern Sector of India did not run along the same watershed but much to the south along the foothills; and if it is now accepted, as it must be, that the 'McMahon Line' adhered to the traditional boundary of northern Burma, it could not be something else in the Indo-Tibetan sector.[35]

Similarly, in the case of the middle sector. In the Sino-Indian Agreement of 1954, six passes were agreed upon (Art. IV) as routes by which traders and pilgrims of both countries might use. Recognition of the watershed principle was herein implicit.

Wherever the Indian and Chinese alignments coincided, as they did for the main part in this middle sector, it was along the watershed line. Where the alignments diverged, 'it was because the Chinese line arbitrarily swung westwards or southwards away from the watershed line, and always towards India and never towards Tibet.'[36]

In the western sector, east of the Karakorum Pass, the alignment claimed by China lay along the lower ranges, but every river on the map provided to the Indian side cut across them. At some point, Indian officials pointed out, 'the boundary claimed by China zig-zagged from range to range. The claim of the Chinese side, that the different ranges along which their alignment ran, were linked by spurs, was unsubstantiated.'[37] The range dividing the main systems, which was the major watershed in this region, lay east of the Chinese alignment. It was along this range, the Indians held, that 'the traditional and customary boundary lay, and it was along that range that the Indian alignment was shown . . . The main watershed in any region was that range which divided the greater part of the volume of the waters of two river systems; and it was the Kuen Lun range which divided the greater part of the volume of waters of the two big river systems in that area'.[38]

For their part, the Chinese challenged the Indians to explain why they stood by the watershed principle so tenaciously in the eastern sector, when in the case of India's boundaries with Nepal, Sikkim and Bhutan, the boundary followed the foothills of the Himalayas.

But the severest stumbling block was the Chinese assertion that there was, in the matter of settling frontiers, no actual frontier, at any time agreed upon, from which to proceed. 'Up to now, no boundary, treaty or agreement delimiting the entire boundary has ever been concluded between China and India, nor has there been any treaty or agreement delimiting a certain sector of the boundary concluded between them; and none of the treaties and agreements concluded between the two countries in the past contain terms pertaining to the defining of the Sino-Indian boundary. This is a well-known fact. Nobody on earth can cite a treaty concerning the delimitation of the Sino-Indian boundary.'[39] They were even able to quote Nehru to support the point; he had told the Lok Sabha, before the Kongka Pass had put an end to reasonable speculation,

> The actual boundary of Ladakh with Tibet was not very carefully defined. It was defined to some extent by British officers who went there. But I rather doubt if they did any careful survey. They marked the line. It has been marked all along in our maps.[40]

Wide divergencies of opinion, interpretation and of evidence marked every section of the Official Report. The description of the boundary line provided by India differed from that of the Chinese; each side sought clarification of the other's data. Separate reports were presented on Basis in Tradition and Custom; Treaties and Agreements. Indian documentation was meticulously detailed and impressive evidence presented from European as well as their own scholars. The Chinese officials were fighting a case based on an ideology rather than precise evidence. Aksai Chin, previously almost unknown to the great majority of Chinese and Indians, emerged as the most controversial issue.

Both sides referred to 10th Century Ladakhi Chronicles and gave their own interpretation of treaties, notes and agreements in 1684, 1842, 1847, 1852 and 1899. Chinese officials queried the existence of the 1684 treaty at their seventeenth meeting. Indian records show that this treaty laid down that 'the boundaries fixed in the beginning when Skyid-Lda-ngeemagon gave a kingdom to each of his three sons shall still be maintained'.[41] The division was defined at the time. Admittance of this division implied the validity of agreements on the Ladakh-Tibet frontier, and this would have upset China's case. Indian officials quoted the treaty of 1842 as evidence that a boundary line between Ladakh and

'ibet existed. It was in the form of an exchange of documents embody-
ıg undertakings given by each side to the other. The Kashmir and
adakh authorities promised those of Tibet and China: 'We shall
ᵉmain in possession of the limits of the boundaries of Ladakh and
ırrounding dependencies, in accordance with the old custom, and
ıere shall be no transgression and no interference beyond the old,
stablished frontiers. We shall remain within our own limits and
oundaries.'⁴² Chinese officials challenged India's interpretation, hold-
ıg that this was 'clearly an agreement of mutual non-aggression . . .
 is quite obvious that it was not at all a treaty for defining the boundary,
ut a guarantee of respect by each side for the other's territory'.⁴³
Vith an acrimony which they frequently injected into the discussions,
ıey added: 'Even if the boundary between Ladakh and Tibet was
ctually confirmed at that time, how could India assert that this line
vas the boundary line now claimed by it and not the traditional
ıstomary line maintained by the Chinese side? On the contrary, in
ıe maps published by Indian officials during that period, the delinea-
on of the boundary between Ladakh and Tibet was in the main
ɔnsistent with that shown in Chinese maps.'⁴⁴

The controversy over the 1847 agreement illustrated the pattern of
ıbtle noncommitment on China's part and arrogant assumption on
ıat of Britain. The Chinese Imperial Commissioner at Canton wrote
▸ the British Government in 1847: 'Respecting the frontiers, I beg to
mark that the borders of these territories have been sufficiently and
stinctly fixed so that it will be best to adhere to this ancient arrange-
ent and it will prove far more convenient to abstain from any
lditional measures for fixing them.'⁴⁵ Chinese officials now dis-
genuously explained:

> The proposal for delimiting the boundary between Ladakh
> and Tibet was made by the British at a time precisely
> after the Opium War of British aggression against China.
> Just as the Viceroy stated in his memorial to the Chinese
> Emperor, the British intention to delimit the boundary was
> "highly suspect". At that time the Chinese Government,
> fearing that Britain would take this opportunity to invade and
> occupy Chinese territory, rejected the proposal of Britain.
> The old borders between Ladakh and Tibet mentioned by the
> Viceroy of the Kwangtung and Kwangsi Province also could

only mean the traditional customary line maintained by
China. At that time India did not put forward the alignment
it now claims, how could the then Chinese Government proceed to confirm it? [46]

Indian officials stated that in 1852 'an agreement was reached between the local Ladakhi and Tibetan officials of the area, Thanedar
Bastira of Ladak and Kalon Rinzin of Rudok, confirming the existing
boundaries, as there had been a local dispute'. It reads: 'The boundary
between Ladakh and Tibet will remain the same as before.' [47] The
Chinese replied: 'As a matter of fact, however, this agreement only
referred to the maintenance of the old boundary by the two sides of
Ladakh and Tibet, and provided that Ladakhis should pay 'annual
tribute' to Tibet, but made no provision whatever about the boundary
between Tibet and Ladakh. Of course, one cannot assert on the basis
of this agreement that the boundary between Tibet and Ladakh was
confirmed at that time.' [48]

As to the Aksai Chin, the most controversial single issue, both sides
quoted a British proposal of 1899 to suit their own strategic ends. At
that time, Russian intervention in the Punjab was a distinct threat and
Sir Claude MacDonald proposed a frontier giving maximum encouragement to China's advance. In 1960 India's main strategic
objective was the containment of China and the Soviet Union, at any
rate temporarily, shared this objective.

A change of government in London contributed to the abandonment of the 1899 proposal. But Peking passed on the proposal to the
Governor of Sinkiang who reported in favour of the boundary as
outlined, and nothing more happened. Five years later, the Government of India recommended that as China 'had shown no grounds for
dissenting from the two proposals contained in Sir C. Macdonald's
Note of the 14th March 1899, we should henceforth assume Chinese
concurrence and act accordingly'. The recommendation was not
accepted in London where the Foreign Office 'considered it inadvisable
to make any communication on the subject of the boundary unless the
Government of India were able to exercise effective control up to the
frontier claimed'. [49]

In the disparity of the Indian and Chinese interpretations of the
Note lay the core of the problem. The essence of the Indian claim was
this:

In 1899 the British did not propose to delimit the boundary between Ladakh and Kashmir on the one hand and Tibet on the other. As there had been some discussion regarding the status and rights of the ruler of Hunza, the British Government gave a description of the northern boundary of Kashmir with Sinkiang. It was stated explicitly in that context that the northern boundary ran along the Kuen Lun range to a point east of 80° Longitude, where it met the eastern boundary of Ladakh. This made it clear beyond doubt that the whole of the Aksai Chin area lay in Indian territory. The Government of China did not object to this definition of this boundary. If nothing came of the 1899 proposals, it was not because the Chinese Government declined to recognise the boundary according to the traditional alignment shown on Indian maps, but because even then they did not seem to consider necessary any formal definition of what was a well-known and well-recognised boundary in this area.[50]

And the Chinese counterclaim was thus:

Britain at that time did not describe the northern boundary of Kashmir for China, as the Indian side asserts but put forward a specific proposal for the delimitation of the boundary. The British side clearly stated in its note that if this delineation of the boundary was accepted, that part of the territory on this side of the line should be henceforth considered as Chinese territory; the British side also asked China for consideration of an answer to their note. It can thus be seen that this is nothing but a proposal for delimiting the boundary. It is also inconceivable to hold that the territory of another country can be annexed by a unilateral proposal.

It may be remembered in passing that the proposal of British at that time also admitted that the entire area around the source of the Karakash River should not remain within Chinese territory, an area far to the south of the alignment claimed by the Indian side. Now, the Indian side cannot but recognise the fact that the proposal put forward by Britain to delimit the boundary was not accepted by the Chinese Government. This shows that the contention of the Indian side in the past

that China did not oppose the British proposal of 1899 about
the delineation of the boundary is not true. The Indian side,
however, came out with a strange explanation that the Chinese
Government did not accept the line proposed by Britain
because China would rather accept a boundary line which
proved more unfavourable to itself, that is, the boundary line
now claimed by India. Anyone with the slightest bit of common sense cannot of course believe such an assertion.[51]

Indian officials asserted that the Macdonald-Macartney letter 'made
clear beyond doubt that the whole of the Aksai Chin lay in India
territory' and various Indian writers have quoted this rather blan
announcement without reservation. But several disinterested historia
have challenged it. Professor Robert A. Huttenback writes that th
Indians,

> emphasised that part of the sixth paragraph which described
> the frontier east of Kizil Jilga as running south-east along the
> Lak Tsung range. Here the letter strongly implied a change
> from former British concepts by stating that this spur of the
> Kunlun had "hitherto been shown on our maps as the
> Eastern boundary of Ladakh. This is a little east of 80° East
> Longitude". The Indian delegates duly pointed this out, but in
> referring to the letter in detail, they altered its provisions
> considerably. Instead of saying that it was the spur running
> south from the Kunlun range which former British maps
> had shown as the *eastern* boundary of Ladakh – a situation
> which the proposals in the letter did not essentially change –
> they said it was the Kunlun range itself which the British had
> described as being the *northern* frontier of Ladakh.[52]

A Dutch diplomat, Willem F. van Eekelen, makes a similar challenge

> The proposal has often been misquoted to show that the
> frontier was intended to run along the Kuenlun mountains
> but, in fact, it did not follow this range at all. The proposed
> alignment conceded the headwaters of the Karakash to China
> and then ran generally south-east, following the Lok hung
> range "until that meets a spur running south from the Kuenlun

range which has hitherto been shown on our maps as the eastern boundary of Ladakh". In his explanation Macdonald stated
that it was unnecessary to mark out the alignment since this
natural frontier was the crest of a range of mighty mountains.[53]

The Macdonald proposals, which would have given China more than
half her present claims to Aksai Chin, much of the 1957 Aksai Chin road
and a part of that built in 1959–60, were not followed up at the time.
A modification was put forward by Ardagh, and also rejected, and only
once again did Aksai Chin feature prominently in British policy
making. In September 1912 the real possibility of Russian occupation
of Kashgaria which 'would bring Russia within one hundred and fifty
miles of Srinagar and three hundred miles of Simla' and Hunza Nagar
possibly under Russian control prompted Lord Hardinge to telegraph
a line of action to the Secretary of State for India, lest the need arise:

> The first essential is to demand as a preliminary to negotia-
> tions, recognition of a boundary line which will place Tagh-
> dumbash, Raskam, Shahidula and Aksai Chin outside Russian
> and within our territory. A line similar to that proposed by
> Sir John Ardagh in 1897 . . . will attain this object . . . A good
> line would be one commencing from Baiyik Peak running
> eastwards to Chang Pass, leaving Taghdumbash and Dehda
> on British side, thence along crest of range through Sargon
> Pass and crossing Yarkand River to crest of Kuen Lun Range,
> north of Raskam, and along crest of that range through . . .
> Kukahang and Dozakh and Yargi and Kilik Passes, to Sanju
> or Grim Pass, thence crossing Karakash River along Kuenlun
> watershed to Tibetan frontier, including Aksai Chin plain in
> our territory.[54]

This is the line which seems to have been adopted and was inherited
by India when power was transferred in 1947. It had no particular
significance until China's occupation of Tibet in 1950 when Chinese
troops passed over the track which later became a jeep-able road.

Indian and Chinese officials both presented cases under administration and jurisdiction to prove their respective ownership of Aksai
Chin. Indian officials leant heavily on records made by British travellers
in the 19th Century. The Chinese replied that these could only have

been made 'after the British invaded Ladakh and cannot constitute a
tradition in history'.[55] But when it suited their case, they themselves
used the data produced by British travellers. Deasy, for instance, who
had 'several times . . . requested the local government of Sinkiang to
let him go from Yutien to Ladakh by way of Aksai Chin, but was not
given permission'. Indian officials produced Kashmir state records
showing Aksai Chin and Lingzi Tang as part of the ilaqa (sub-district) of
Tanktse in Ladakh tehsil (district). Revenue records with regular
assessments and settlements were made from time to time 'and revenue
collected from all inhabited places up to the boundary'. In uninhabited
places 'control was exercised through the levy of duty on flocks and
pastures, maintenance of caravan routes and rest houses and supervision
and control over trading parties'.[56] Chinese officials stated categorically:
'The region east of the traditional customary line from the Karakorum
Pass to the Kongka Pass has always belonged to Hotien of China's
Sinkiang throughout history. Since Sinkiang was formally made a
component part of the Ching Empire in 1759, this region has been
even more conclusively a part of China's territory.'[58] They produced
one document as evidence, a petition from the Governor of Sinkiang
to the Chinese Central Government on August 30, 1927, suggesting
that 'a Sheh-Chih-Chu be set up at Shahidulla'. In the following
March the Ministry of Finance and the Ministry of the Interior informed the Governor that they approved the suggestion. But no
evidence was produced to show that the post of country head assistant
for border defence was ever set up at Shahidulla. Indian officials noted
that the main proposal for a post at Shahidula contradicted a number of
Chinese statements that they had had effective jurisdiction in the area
since 1759.

It is extraordinary that Indians had remained so ignorant of Aksai
Chin until they discovered the Chinese road across it. They now
produced extracts from the Great Trigonometrical Survey describing
the area in the 1860–1880 period when new trade routes were being
considered. They stated that in the area right up to the traditional
boundary in the north and east 'the exercise of jurisdiction by the
Governments of Kashmir and India had, indeed, continued right down
to the present times. During the years 1911–1949, Indian official survey
parties and patrols constantly visited these areas up to the traditional
alignment . . . In 1951 an expedition went from Leh to Lingzi Tang
and Aksai Chin. In 1952 an army reconnaissance party went up to

Lanak La via Tanktse, Tsogatsalu, Hot Spring and the Kongka Pass. In August 1954 and August 1956 patrol parties repeated this tour to Lanak La'.[58] Reconnaissance parties in 1957, 1958 visited up the Qara Tagh Pass, they visited Haji Langar by two ways via the Aksai Chin. 'Other places near the Pangong Lake and in the Chang Chenmo valley were also under constant patrol until the recent unlawful Chinese occupation.'[59] Chinese officials quoted surveys made by two expeditions in 1891 and 1892 which conducted surveys of the boundary between Sinkiang and Ladakh. They were instructed 'to go to the south-west and north-west borders for inspection and survey'.[60] The Indians pointed out that Aksai Chin was on Sinkiang's southern border and that the report of the surveys did not mention this area. Other inconsistencies of place names threw doubts on the validity of the Chinese case. Chinese officials had no answer and, in part, admitted the confusion.

Their next evidence concerned a survey made jointly with Soviet experts in 1940–41, of which they produced a topographical map of 1/200,000 scale. Indian officials challenged the authenticity of the map, and believed that it was a blow-up of a small scale map. Fisher, Rose and Huttenback analysed the photostat. 'There seems to be ample justification,' they commented, 'for the suspicion that this was just one more instance of Chinese officials busily manufacturing evidence . . . The border talks were being conducted in Peking at that point, so there could not have been any difficulties involved in producing the map . . . Moreover, if it had been prepared by a Chinese survey team in 1941, why was it that there is so much divergence among the various Chinese maps published after that? There appears to be only one possible answer here – and it scarcely enhances the reputation of the Chinese Communist Government.'[61]

And, while admitting the extraordinary complexity of the terrain, they concluded that 'the most striking contrast in the two reports is the basic differences in their approach. The Indian government was both thorough and careful in presenting its case . . . On the other hand the Chinese Government showed no interest in the substance of the talks, as their astonishingly careless presentation amply demonstrated. The maze of internal inconsistencies, quotations out of context, and even blatant and easily discernible falsehoods – easily discernible, that is. Those *with access to the materials cited* make it obvious that China had paid little or no attention to the preparation of their case'.[62]

The Middle sector proved less troublesome than the others. The watershed was known and accepted. Where the Chinese alignment departed from it, the points of divergence from the Indian alignment always conveniently swung to the south and west so as to include Indian territory in Tibet. The Chinese argued that, 'as in the Western sector, the Indian side cannot advance any treaty basis whatever which could prove that the middle sector of the boundary has been formally delimited'. The Chinese divergence from the watershed concerned four areas: Spiti (the Chinese called it Chuva and Chuje); Shipki Pass; the Nilang-Jadhang area (Sang and Tsungsha); and Barahoti (Wu-je) Sangchamalla and Lapthal.

SPITI: Indian officials quoted documents ranging from the seventh century when Spiti was ruled by a Hindu dynasty to the first Sikh War in 1846 when the Maharajah ceded the district to the East India Company. Subsequently, many British travellers visited Spiti and their reports were published in such journals as those of the Asiatic Society and the Royal Geographical Society.

SHIPKI: Indian evidence was mainly based on reports from European travellers who testified to Shipki as being the 'frontier of Hindustan'.

NILANG-JADHANG AND BARAHOTI: Nilang-Jadhang is very close to the source of the Ganges at Gangotri and of religious significance to India. Indians quoted a copper-plate inscription of 1667 to show that this territory, originally in Bushahr (now in Himachal Pradesh) belonged to India. It was transferred to the Tehri state in that year and remained until 1949 when it became part of Uttar Pradesh. As for Barahoti, China had never laid claims to this area until 1959.

SANGCHAMALLA AND LAPTHAL: this was an area which like many in the Middle Sector held a special religious significance for Indians. Chinese officials made the sweeping statement: 'The areas to the east and north of the traditional customary line in the middle sector maintained by the Chinese side such as Chuva Chuje, the area west of Shipki Pass, Sang, Tsungha, Pulingsumdo, Wu-je, Sangcha and Lapthal are all traditional Chinese territories.' Extremely scant evidence was given.

CHUVA CHUJE: a document by the Fifth Dalai Lama in 1665, and its renewal by the Seventh Dalai Lama in 1737, had 'clearly stipulated that Chuva Chuje was a Gzhigkha under the jurisdiction of the Ashigong Gyupa Tsatsang'. 'The Chuva Chuje area has always been Chinese territory and for centuries it was under the administration of the Tshigong Gyupa Tsatsang of the Ari district of China's Tibet.' 'It was in 1958 that Chuva and Chuje were occupied by India, and the administrative jurisdiction which had long been exercised by China's Tibet there could not but be broken off. . . At the end of 1958, the responsible official in Tasigong reported to his superiors about the advancing of Indian troops, stating that the Indian troops entered China's Chuva Chuje area in April of that year.' [63] This directly contradicted a wall map which China published in November 1953, showing this territory within India. Evidence about the Shipki Pass was almost as flimsy: 'The pastures on the eastern bank of the river have always belonged to Shipki Village of Tsaparang Dzong in China's Tibet region.' In 1934, the British representative in Lhasa asked: 'Is the British Government allowed to construct a road in the sector of Tibetan territory from the Hupsang to Shipki in the Ari district measuring six miles long?' The local Tibetan representative answered: 'Since it is Tibetan territory, it is not allowed for the British Government to build a road.' The next evidence quoted was that in 1954 Indian personnel 'once came to Shipki Pass where they carved without permission on a stone surface the following inscription: *Hindustan-Tibet*, in an attempt to move the boundary forward from the Hupsang Khud to Shipki Pass . . . Since 1957 Indian armed personnel further entered the Chinese territory east of the Hupsang Khud, setting up permanent strongholds in this area and putting it under their control . . . Only since then China has been obliged to cease exercising its jurisdiction over the area west of Shipki Pass'.

SANG, TSUNGSHA AND PULING-SUMDO were said by the Chinese to 'have always been a part of the district under the jurisdiction of Tsaparang Dzong of the Tibet region of China'. The evidence is that 'the Tsaparang Dzong government collected taxes, exacted corvee and conducted census in this area . . . as early as 1693 . . . Although Britain began its encroachment around 1919, the Tsaparang Dzong government, until recently, still maintained certain administration in these places'.[64] Then the same argument, that 'in 1952 Indian troops pushed forward and occupied Sang and Tsungsha and prevented the local inhabitants from rendering corvee and paying taxes to the local authorities of China . . . As for Puling-Sumdo, the Chinese side has time and again pointed out that this place is one of the ten markets for trade designated by the Chinese side as stipulated in the 1954 Agreement. It can be seen, therefore, that the fact that this market is under China's jurisdiction has long been recognised and accepted by the Indian Government'.

WU-JE, SANGCHA AND LAPTHAL: the same formula was used. 'Wu-je, Sangcha and Lapthal had always been under the jurisdiction of the Daba Dzong of China's Tibet Region.' [65] Land-deeds sanctioned by P'olha in 1729 and the Seventh Dalai Lama in 1737 said these areas were within the jurisdiction of Daba Dzong. 'It was not until 1954 that Indian troops began to enter Wu-je and prevented Chinese personnel from exercising their normal administrative power there . . . As for the occupation of Sangcha and Lapthal by Indian troops, it took place even later.' [66]

The six-hundred page *Report of the Chinese and Indian Officials* was presented to Parliament on February 14, 1961. China did not publish it until April, 1962. It was an extraordinary compilation of historical and geographical data which needed a great deal of specialised knowledge to make any responsible evaluation. Indian documentation was meticulously prepared, carefully documented and evidence impressively compiled. The Chinese taunt that much of Indian documentation was obtained from British sources was clearly absurd. The areas involved in the boundary dispute had been under British rule, much of it actually explored, surveyed and then administered from Delhi and London. The motives were indubitably imperialist, but the reporting of British officials was ably done and knowledge of vast, remote areas, largely unknown in Peking was made available for future historians in the officials' report. The taunt of British imperialism was used by Chinese officials to obscure the inadequacy of their own documentation. Indian officials would have strengthened their case by admitting their sources were often to be found in official and unofficial data in British and Indian records, while, at the same time, demonstrating the undeniable fact that the advance of Chinese imperialism was an important motivating force in the formulation of British policy. The zigzag of British interests in the boundary areas was determined by the calculated strategic needs of the moment. The containment of Russia stimulated interest in the Karakorum. The containment of China equally led to exploration and the McMahon Line. But the strategist and the politician did not always time their propaganda precisely.

The Hindu reflected a general reaction in its summing up after the Report had been published in Delhi: 'the irresistible conclusion that will be drawn from any reader of the officials' report . . . is that the prospect of a settlement either in the immediate or even the distant future is indeed very, very dim . . . Neither the present Chinese temper nor the atmosphere in India lends encouragement to the prospect of another round of talks at Prime Ministers' level in the foreseeable future.'[67] Leaders of public opinion in the press and in and out of parliament were far more impressed by the casual change of boundary on Chinese maps. In Peking, on June 27, 1960, for example, the Chinese suddenly produced a new map which added two thousand square miles of Ladakh to their territory. When challenged, the Chinese Foreign Minister Chen Yi, to the astonishment of Indian officials, stated the boundary was the same as on their earlier map published in 1956. It was demonstrably untrue.

The Report of the Officials was never followed up. Throughout 1961 many Notes were exchanged between the two Governments. They concerned border issues and incidents, violations of territorial air space, alleged treatment of Chinese nationals in India, the Chinese trade agency in Kalimpong. They became increasingly acrimonious in tone. In the Lok Sabha M.P.s, now more informed, challenged the basis of Nehru's policy. The two Prime Ministers never met again.

It is very doubtful whether Nehru, already a sick man, could have pushed through another round of negotiations. He was bitterly criticised for allowing a meeting between R. K. Nehru, Secretary General to the External Affairs Ministry, and Chinese officials on his way back via Peking from Mongolia. 'Talking to them', he felt compelled to tell the Rajya Sabha,

> did not mean that he was offering anything to them or that he was showing any weakness . . . We should always look upon this not as a present evil but as a continuing evil, a continuous conflict which might govern generations, because as far as I can see – I want to be quite frank to the House – whatever the results of this immediate issue might be, there

are basic issues which will always create tension – by always
I mean in the foreseeable future – between India and China,
and we have to prepare for it, prepare a great deal for meeting that situation, meanwhile hold that situation and hold it
the way we can.[68]

All reason seemed spent. The Fifth White Paper presented to the Lok
Sabha on November 28, 1961, was mainly a series of charges and
counter-charges, of two countries sparring for military positions. He
read out one paragraph which illustrates the whole document.

> Reports received in August-September 1961 show that the
> Chinese forces have spread even beyond the 1956 Chinese
> claim line in Ladakh to establish the following new posts, and
> that they have constructed roads to link these posts with rear
> bases.
> Post at E.78.12. No.35.19: this is the location of the post.
> Post at Nyagzu.
> Post at Dambuguru.
> These fresh instances of violation of Indian territory by the
> Chinese establish conclusively that the Chinese are guilty of
> further aggression against India and their protestations to
> the contrary are only a cloak to cover up these renewed incur-
> sions and aggressive activities.[69]

In this same debate, Nehru reported action taken by his own Ministry
of Defence.

> We have built an important military post right near the
> Karakorum Pass, which is a very important route of entry.
> Although now it is not used very much, it used to be a very
> important route from India to Sinkiang and Central Asia.
> We have built a very important post there at a place called
> Daulatbeg Oldi which is about ten miles from the Karakorum
> Pass ... at about nearly seventeen thousand feet altitude.
> The Chinese post which they have built up is to the east of
> this, ten to twelve miles to the east of this ...
> It is not an easy matter to conduct a warfare in these regions,
> but it has to be done, and, therefore, we have to prepare for

it, if necessary, and the base of that preparation is this system of roads that are being built rapidly, not only there, but over a large part of the border.[70]

Until December 2, 1961, Nehru still had a chance to initiate talks with Peking or to call their bluff if they did not mean negotiations. This was the deadline on which either India or China could request an extension of the 1954 trade agreement. India had wanted it to last for twenty years. China had insisted on eight years, with the proviso that it would lapse on June 2, 1962, unless either side asked for an extension. Peking did not overlook this opportunity. On December 4 Nehru received a Note suggesting discussion of the terms of a new treaty.[71] The Indian reply recalled their strict adherence to Panch Shila and summed up China's flagrant violations of the 1954 agreement, the curtailment of facilities for traders and pilgrims, the attempts – 'at first insidiously and later on openly' – to make claims on Indian territory, and finally their 'aggressive military activity'. In view of this record, the Indian Note said, 'the first essential for the starting of such negotiations is the reversal of these aggressive policies . . . and the restoration of climate which assures the strict observance of the Five Principles both in letter and spirit'.[72] It was a gift to Peking's propaganda machine. China had suggested discussions ostensibly to make a new agreement. Delhi had replied in characteristically moralising phrases. Whether or not Peking would have reconsidered the 1954 Agreement is incalculable. The fact is that India did not put her to the test.

On March 3, 1962, Peking carefully disowned any connection between the Sino-Indian boundary and the 1954 agreement, and emphatically accused India of repeatedly violating the Five Principles.

Despite the increasing bitterness of the exchanges Nehru made a further effort to create a climate in which negotiations might still take place. One month before the 1954 agreement lapsed, his Ministry of Foreign Affairs wrote to the Embassy of China in India:

The Prime Minister of India stated in Parliament on 2nd. May 1962, "India does not want, and dislikes very much, a war with China. But that is not within India's control . . ." The Government of India would urge the Chinese Government to give serious consideration to the offer made in the Indian Prime Minister's letter dated 16th November 1959 to Premier

Chou En-lai which *inter alia* proposed as an interim measure that, in the Ladakh region, the Government of India should withdraw their personnel to the west of the line shown in the 1956 Chinese map and the Government of China should withdraw their personnel to the east of the international boundary shown in Indian official maps ... The Government of India are prepared, in the interest of a peaceful settlement, to permit, pending negotiations and settlement of the boundary question, the continued use of the Aksai Chin road for Chinese civilian traffic.[73]

It was a perfectly reasonable proposal, but the timing was ill-judged. Why had he not taken the diplomatic initiative five months earlier? Peking's reply on June 2, 1962, refused to take Nehru's proposals seriously. It asked: 'Why should China need to ask India's permission for using its own road on its own territory? What an absurdity!' And why, if India were serious, did it not suggest that China and India should 'withdraw all their personnel from the area between the so-called McMahon Line and the section of the Sino-Indian boundary as shown on Chinese maps?' [74]

The following day, the Sino-Indian agreement lapsed.* As the snows melted in Ladakh, patrolling increased. Indian forces had regularly patrolled the Galwan valley, the lower reaches of which were

---

* Correspondence between the two governments on the lapsed agreement continued with rising choler and wretched pettiness on both sides until, on October 24, 1963, Peking finally slammed the door. A Note on that day, said:

It was entirely out of a desire to improve the Sino-Indian relations that the Chinese Government took the initiative in making this proposal. ...

The Indian Government, however, proceeding from its set anti-China policy, adopted an extraordinarily rigid attitude and totally unreasonable position on this question. It took the friendly proposal ... for a sign of weakness on the part of China, thinking that China was asking India for a favour; therefore it vainly tried to take the opportunity to blackmail and swindle China on this question. It deliberately linked the question together with the Sino-Indian question in a far-fetched way and absurdly insisted on China's unconditional acceptance of India's unilateral claims on the boundary question as a precondition to the negotiation of the proposed agreement; and in this way it unreasonably rejected the friendly proposal of the Chinese Government. ...

twenty-eight miles beyond the Chinese claim line in a 1956 map described by Chou En-lai as correctly showing the boundary alignment in this sector of the border. Peking now accused Delhi of intruding its troops into Sinkiang 'six kilometres inside the Chinese territory in the Galwan valley area and attempting to establish there a new base for aggression'.[75] Chinese and Indian patrols began a cat-and-mouse war game and on July 10 Indian and Chinese troops came within a hundred yards of each other in the Galwan valley. The Chinese withdrew a short distance and a clash was avoided. But on July 20 two Indian patrols came under Chinese fire on the Chipchap river and near the Panggong Lake. Protests were lodged the same day in Peking and Delhi, each accusing the other side of firing the same shot. But yet another effort was made by India to forestall an irraparable collision. On July 26 an Indian Note to Peking said:

> The Government of India are prepared, as soon as the current tensions have eased and the appropriate climate is created, to enter into further discussions on the India-China boundary question on the basis of the report of the officials as contemplated during the meeting of Prime Minister Chou En-lai with the Prime Minister of India in 1960.[76]

Paragraph 3 of the Note lamented the tension as being 'a result of the recent establishment of a number of Chinese military posts ... in Indian territory in the Ladakh region'. Peking took up this point: 'The fact is that the Chinese side has never crossed its national border which has always been under China's control, and that the tension was created solely by the Indian side advancing into Chinese territory, establishing new posts and making provocations.'[77] Peking concluded by approving the suggestion for talks, but added that she could not consider India's proposal for a one-sided withdrawal. Neither could she agree to any

In view of the fact that the 1954 Sino-Indian agreement ceased to be in force long ago and all the hackneyed arguments of the Indian side have long been duly refuted, the Chinese Government does not prepare to continue the exchange of notes with the Indian Government on this question, as that would be devoid of any practical meaning. Therefore, if the Indian Government should further haggle over this question by sending in another note, the Chinese Government will ignore it.
White Paper X, February, 1964, pp. 52/53.

K

precondition for discussions. India replied that she would be glad to receive a Chinese representative to discuss essential preliminary measures. Peking again proposed the withdrawal of twenty kilometres on both sides of the line of actual control along the entire border and proposed discussions should start on October 15.

During this period a misleading lull enabled Nehru to hold back members of parliament who believed that he might surrender. While it is true that he seemed to have lost the initiative, he was in no mood for surrender. 'We would prefer to be reduced to dust than submit to dishonour of any kind,' he told the Lok Sabha.[78] But he did not hold that the idea of talks should be discarded altogether, and he made a distinction between talks and negotiations. He continued to hope that talks would create an atmosphere in which some way back might be found from what was the brink of open conflict. From a position of relative weakness, militarily, he probed the possibilities of peace with all manner of righteousness, while Chou En-lai, with fewer philosophical inhibitions, merely talked until the Chinese army was ready for an extensive campaign.

Talking and Fighting
(September 1962–May 1964)

ADVANCE AND ESCALATION; THE FIRST
CHINESE OFFENSIVE – OCTOBER 1962; THE
SECOND CHINESE OFFENSIVE – NOVEMBER
1962; THE COLOMBO CONFERENCE –
DECEMBER 1962; NO COMPROMISE

ADVANCE AND ESCALATION

Throughout the summer of 1962, acrimonious Notes were exchanged by the Indian and Chinese foreign ministries, while their defence ministries continued to set up military outposts in Ladakh and N.E.F.A. *The People's Daily* accused India of 'nibbling away' at Chinese territory. The Indian press in increasingly militant tones sharply deplored China's destruction of the 'climate of confidence'. As Chinese troops spread along the frontier, political leaders on both sides took up positions from which it became more and more difficult to retreat. The culmination of Indian bitterness was reached when China and Pakistan discussed their border from the Kilik Pass to the Karakorum Pass. An Indian Note lodged 'an emphatic protest' against 'any arrangements, provisional or otherwise, between the Governments of China and Pakistan regarding territory which constitutes an inalienable part of the Indian Union', and warned Pakistan 'of the grave consequences of their action'. Pakistan was not unduly concerned; it had administered these areas since 1947.

The turning point was reached in the Galwan valley in July, and in N.E.F.A. in September. Dhola, or Che Dong as the Chinese call it, was the most strategically sensitive spot where India had built a military

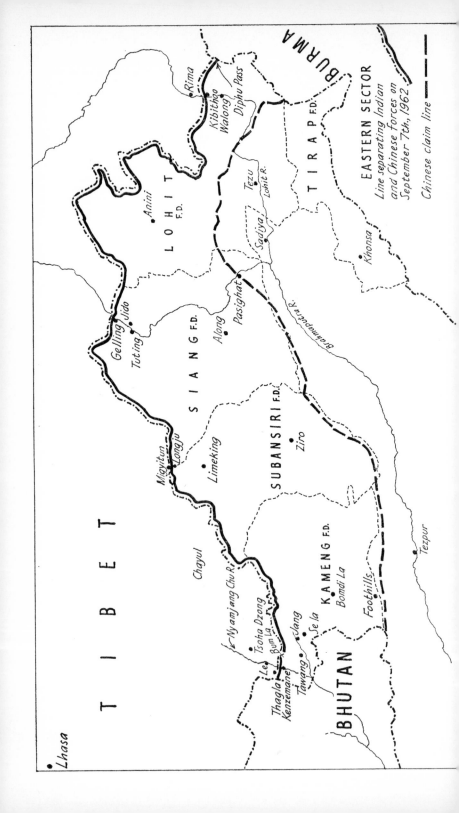

EASTERN SECTOR
Line separating Indian
and Chinese forces on
September 7th, 1962

Chinese claim line

BURMA

TIBET

BHUTAN

TIRAP F.D.

LOHIT F.D.

SIANG F.D.

SUBANSIRI F.D.

KAMENG F.D.

Lhasa

Rima

Kibithoo
Walong
Diphu Pass

Tzu

Lohit R.

Sadiya

Khonsa

Anini

Gelling
Tuting
Jido

Along

Pasighat

Brahmaputra R.

Migyitun
Longju

Limeking

Ziro

Tezpur

Chayul

Nyamjang Chu R.

Tsona Dzong
Bum La

Lap

Kenzemane
Thagla

Tawang

Jang
Se la

Bomdi La

Foothills

KAMENG F.D.

post in June 1962 considering it to be in Indian territory. China fiercely contested this point.

Dhola was nearly sixty miles west of Tawang, in that wedge of territory which the Chief of the General Staff judged essential for the defence of India's northern frontier in 1912.

On September 8, Chinese troops infiltrated south of the Thag La. They were variably reported as numbering 300, 800 and 1200. On September 20, Chinese guns went into action against an Indian auxiliary outpost two miles east of Dhola. Two Indian Generals have since publicly expressed their views of their unpreparedness to meet this situation. General Thimayya explained:

> In this area, we also had strong-points acting as bases to and from which we were developing a communication system. Along the main axis of advance, that is from the foothills to Tawang, we had developed a jeep road via Bomdila, dividing Dzong and Se La, and we were beginning to establish a series of defensive posts to maintain and protect our line of communications. But, even so, we had the greatest difficulty in maintaining our forward posts which had to depend mainly on airdrops and helicopters. All the other forward posts eastwards, along the McMahon Line, had no road communications. In some cases, they were connected by goat/mule tracks, but chiefly maintained by helicopters and supply drops; so, it was not possible to make any kind of defensive stand.[1]

General Kaul, reconstructing the background to the events of September 12, writes:

> Lt-Gen. Umrao Singh informed Lt-Gen. Sen that the task of clearing the Chinese south of Thag La ridge was beyond the capability of their troops. Our build-up in the Dhola area compared adversely to that of the Chinese. Our ability to reinforce due to lack of troops and roads was limited. Our troops were on restricted scale of rations, and had no reserves. Clothing was scanty for the extreme cold. We were short of ammunition and there was hardly any defence stores available. We did not have adequate fire support.
>
> Lt-Gen. Umrao Singh told Eastern Command that an attempt to clear the Chinese south of Thag La Ridge would

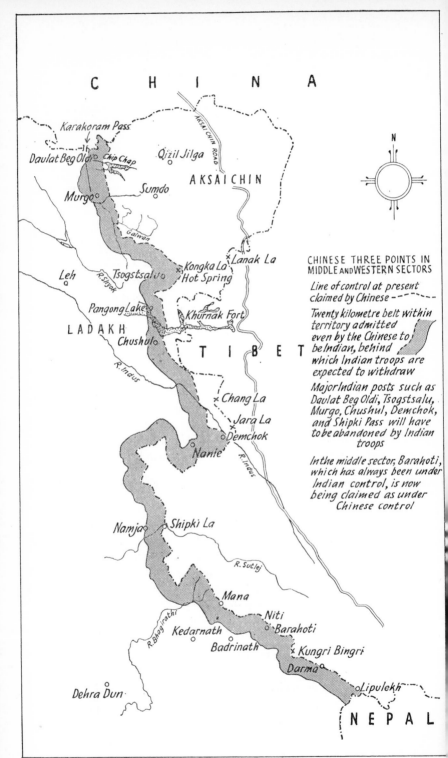

N

CHINESE THREE POINTS IN
MIDDLE and WESTERN SECTORS

Line of control at present
claimed by Chinese - - - - -

Twenty kilometre belt within
territory admitted
even by the Chinese to
be Indian, behind
which Indian troops are
expected to withdraw

Major Indian posts such as
Daulat Beg Oldi, Tsogstsalu,
Murgo, Chushul, Demchok,
and Shipki Pass will have
to be abandoned by Indian
troops

In the middle sector, Barahoti,
which has always been under
Indian control, is now
being claimed as under
Chinese control

MAP 24. *Chinese Three Points in the Western and Middle Sectors.*

amount to rashness. To produce even a semblance of the resources required for this purpose, he would have to completely uncover Tawang and also withdraw troops from Nagaland. He pointed out that Tawang was our vital ground and its fall into the Chinese hands would have more disastrous consequences than the fall of Dhola. This is actually what happened later.[2]

The Defence Ministry in Delhi decided that 'as a matter of policy there was no alternative but to evict the Chinese from the Dhola area'. The Army Chief pointed out the consequences of such a step. Defence Minister Krishna Menon was at the United Nations at the time, but on his return said that Government policy was to make an impact on the Chinese in N.E.F.A. before they settled down for the winter. It sounded well, but General Kaul, who had earlier been Menon's right hand in introducing politics into army affairs, asked some four years later: 'Was this "tough posture" an attempt on Menon's part to appear in line with his oft-repeated claims in the past, made publicly from time to time, that India was capable of defending herself against aggression from any quarter; or was it a typical political statement with a double meaning to appease public opinion? Or, could it have been just bravado?'[3] Unquestionably politicians – and Menon was, above all else, a politician – talked far too glibly about Indian military preparedness. While they invariably believed their troops would be aimed against Pakistan, both Nehru and Menon, according to General Kaul, believed as late as October 2, 1962, that they had 'good reasons to believe that the Chinese would not take any strong action against us'. All official statements played down increasing incidents in the Dhola area. Opposition leaders accused the Government of trying to keep 430 million Indians in ignorance of the facts.

THE FIRST CHINESE OFFENSIVE—OCTOBER 1962

On October 10 the Chinese used heavy mortar and medium machine guns against the Indian positions and escalation of the war was irretrievable. Yet when Nehru flew to Ceylon on October 12 he remarked almost casually that the Indian army had been ordered to clear the Chinese from the area which they were occupying south of the McMahon Line.

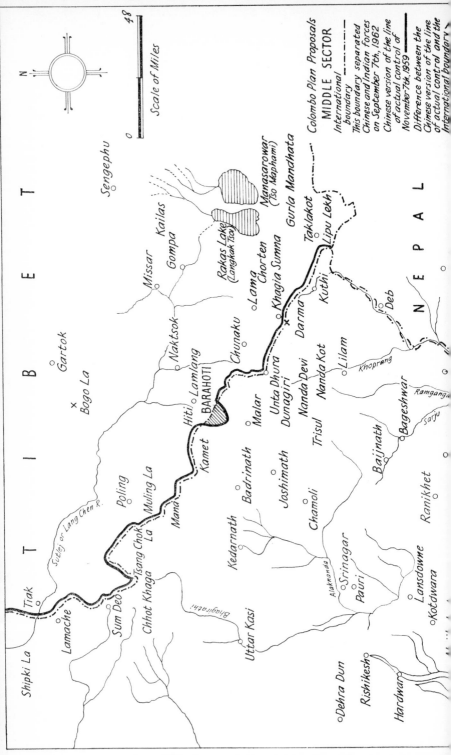

MAP 25. *Middle Sector: Colombo Conference Proposals.*

A massive attack began on October 20. The Chinese claim that India had opened the offensive was obviously nonsense. The border posts of Khinzemane and Dhola fell almost immediately and other posts fell after little resistance; Lumpu, near Khinzemane, the last hold on Thag La ridge; Longju and others to the south-west; Bum La whose fall exposed Tawang; and Kibitoo, whose fall exposed Walong, guarding the Lohit valley. When Jang, to the east of Tawang and directly to the north of Se La collapsed, the Indian defences in the Kameng area were virtually destroyed. The Chinese were in a position to dominate N.E.F.A.

Simultaneously, Chinese troops launched attacks on Indian military outposts in the northern sector of Ladakh. It was in this sector, at the Kongka Pass in October 1959, that Indian lives were first lost. Following that incident, India had built a number of military outposts in the Chip Chap valley – at Daulet Beg Oldi, near the Karakorum Pass, and in the Pangong Lake area. They were extremely difficult to supply, and in some cases they were behind the Chinese Line. In this Himalayan game of cat-and-mouse, China was in such a vastly superior strategic position and had made plans so far ahead that when her troops launched the attack in October 1962, one outpost fell after another.

Every outpost had fallen inside 48 hours and Nehru broadcast to the nation that India must unite to face 'the greatest menace that has come to us since independence'. In two days all posts within the Chinese claim line as shown on her maps of 1960 had been taken. India had had no co-ordinated plan in either of the two sectors and little experience of the logistical problems involved in either of them.

China's next move was diplomatic and skilful. On October 24 their news agency broadcast a three-point cease-fire offer which Chou En-lai proposed to Nehru:

1. Pending a peaceful settlement, the Chinese Government hopes that the Indian Government agree that both parties respect the line of actual control between the two sides along the entire Sino-Indian border, and the armed forces of each side withdraw twenty kilometres from this line and disengage.

2. Provided that the Indian Government agrees to the above proposal, the Chinese Government is willing, through consultation between the two parties, to withdraw its frontier

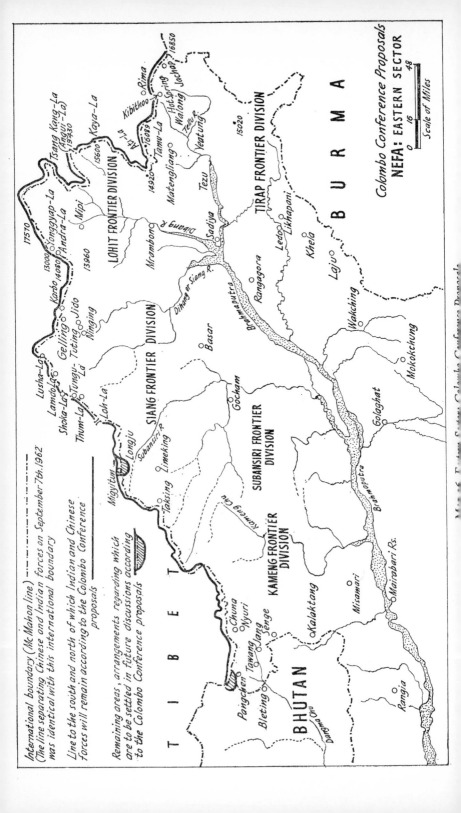

Colombo Conference Proposals
NEFA: EASTERN SECTOR

0   16   48
Scale of Miles

International boundary (McMahon line) — — — — —
(The line separating Chinese and Indian forces on September 7th 1962
was identical with this international boundary

Line to the south and north of which Indian and Chinese
forces will remain according to the Colombo Conference
proposals

Remaining areas, arrangements regarding which
are to be settled in future discussions according
to the Colombo Conference proposals

T I B E T

BHUTAN

B U R M A

LOHIT FRONTIER DIVISION

SIANG FRONTIER DIVISION

SUBANSIRI FRONTIER DIVISION

KAMENG FRONTIER DIVISION

TIRAP FRONTIER DIVISION

Tsang Kang-La
19430
Yongyap-La
Andra-La
Korbo 14080
13000
Lusha-La
17510
Lambo-La
Shoka-La
Gelling
Tungu-Tuting-Jido
Thum-La
Ningjing
13960
15600 Kaya-La
Mipi
Loh-La
Ati-La
16000
Kibithoo
Rima
14920
Tamu-La
Hot Spring
Walong Jachap 16850
Matengliang
Yeatung
Telur R.
Mrombong
Sadiya
Tezu
15020
Dihang or Siang R.
Basar
Gocham
Dibang R.
Brahmaputra
Rangagora
Ledo
Likhapani
Khela
Laju
Walching
Mokokchung
Golaghat
Migyitun
Longju
Taksing
Limeking
Subansiri R.
Kameng Chu
Pangchen
Bleting
Tawang
Jang
Senge
Chuna
Nyuri
Kalaktang
Misamari
Mairabari Rs.
Darma Chu
Rangia
Brahmaputra

Map 16 Eastern Sector: Colombo Conference Proposals

guards in the eastern sector of the border to the north of the line of actual control; at the same time, both China and India undertake not to cross the line of actual control, i.e. the traditional customary line, in the middle and western sectors of the border.

3. In order to seek a friendly settlement of the Sino-Indian boundary question, talks should be held once again by the Prime Ministers of China and India.[4]

On the same day, Chou En-lai circularised these very reasonably phrased proposals to the Heads of State of the Afro-Asian bloc. Few among their leaders recognised how tendentious was the accompanying statement, charging India with the occupation of 'more than 90,000 square kilometres of Chinese territory in the eastern sector, with provoking the border clashes in 1959, and with claiming large tracts of Chinese territory – all since she became independent. Chou En-lai contrasted India's behaviour with that of China which 'had always stood for a peaceful settlement of the Sino-Indian boundary question through negotiations', and made this provocative charge:

> Especially shocking to China is the fact that the Indian Government after rejecting China's peaceful proposal, on October 12 ordered the Indian forces to "free" Chinese frontiers of Chinese troops. Then on October 20, Indian forces started a massive offensive in both the eastern and western sections of the Sino-Indian border. In these serious circumstances, the Chinese frontier guards had no choice but to strike back in self-defence.[5]

Nehru made reply, two days later,

> There is no sense or meaning in the Chinese offer to withdraw twenty kilometres from what they call 'line of actual control', What is this 'line of actual control'? Is this the line they have created by aggression since the beginning of September? Advancing forty or sixty kilometres by blatant military aggression and offering to withdraw twenty kilometres provided both sides do this is a deceptive device which can fool nobody. If the Chinese professions of peace and peace-

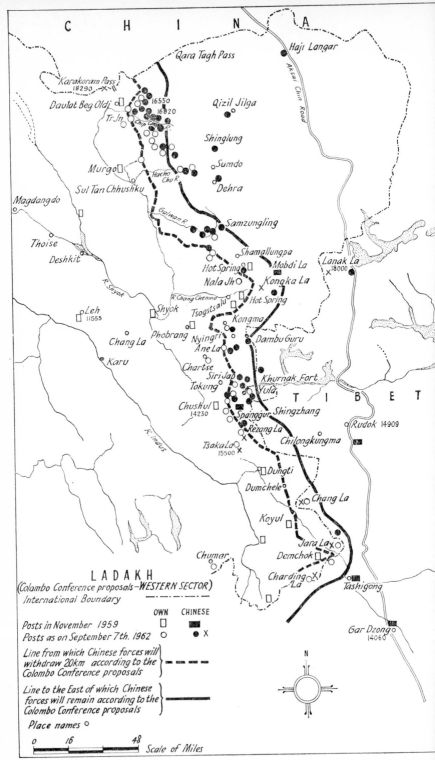

MAP 27. *Western Sector: Colombo Conference Proposals.*

ful settlement of differences are really genuine, let them go
back at least to the position where they were all along the
boundary prior to 8th September 1962.[6]

The date is crucial. Chou En-lai replied on November 4 that by the
'line of actual control' he meant the line which existed on November
7, 1959, when he had made a similar proposal.

> To put it concretely, in the eastern sector it coincides in the
> main with the so-called McMahon Line, and in the western
> and middle sectors it coincides in the main with the traditional
> customary line which has consistently been pointed out by
> China.[7]

This was an implicit recognition of the McMahon Line in N.E.F.A.
China had already accepted it from the Diphu Pass to the Izu Razi
Pass in a treaty then under discussion with Burma. Equally implicit
was China's demand for the Aksai Chin in the western sector. It would
have meant the official abandonment by India of all the military checkposts set up in Ladakh between 1959 and 1962 which had in any case
already been wiped out.

Nehru rejected the three-point proposal on November 14. In the
Western sector, he said: the line of November 7, 1959

> not only includes all the Chinese posts established in the three
> years since 1959, but also includes all the Indian posts in the
> territory till 20th October 1962, and extends even further
> westwards, thus taking in an additional 5000 to 6000 square
> miles since their 7th November 1959 position. . . . [In the
> Middle sector] the suggestion that the 'line of actual control'
> whether on 7th November 1959 or now, coincides only 'in the
> main' with the traditional and customary boundary is
> absolutely without foundation. The Chinese have never had
> any authority south of the main Himalayan watershed ridge,
> which is the traditional boundary in this sector . . . [And in
> the Eastern sector, the proposed withdrawal] would leave
> Chinese forces in command of the passes leading into India
> while Indian forces would be twenty kilometres to the south,
> leaving the entire Indian frontier defenceless and at the mercy
> of any fresh invasion.[8]

China, by insisting that the entire length of the frontier was un-delimited, was proposing to exclude any past treaties or agreements from consideration. Further, on November 7, 1959, evidence of administration and of past treaties had not yet been presented by India. It was given in great detail when Chinese and Indian officials met in 1960. Their report was published by India in February 1961 and by China in April 1962.

India would have been very much at the mercy of China had she agreed to the three-point proposal. Nevertheless, the Soviet Union, involved at the time in the Cuban crisis, urged Nehru to accept them. *Pravda* described them as 'constructive' and a settlement based on them as 'a new blow against the forces of imperialism and colonialism, against the intrigues of the aggressive circles of the United States who have just undertaken a most dangerous adventure aimed not only against Cuba and the Socialist States but also against all peace-loving peoples'. *Pravda* repeated Peking's propaganda line that the 'notorious McMahon Line, which was never recognised by China, was foisted on the Chinese and Indian peoples'.[9]

The United States Ambassador in India, J. K. Galbraith, chose this moment to announce that his government 'recognised the McMahon Line as the accepted international border . . . sanctioned by modern usage'.[10] When the Cuba crisis was over, Kosygin put Soviet policy in a more diplomatic framework; he urged a cease-fire 'on a reasonable basis. All the more so as there are no basic contradictions between India and China, no disagreements that could not be solved in round-table talks'.[11] Did he calculate that American support for India might extend the area of the conflict? Or that India might be edged out of non-alignment? One Indian journalist, Dr Shelvankar of *The Hindu*, welcomed it as an indication that Russia 'has moved back a little from its earlier pro-Chinese stand'.[12]

Public opinion in India demanded a tough line. The Indian President had declared a state of national emergency on October 26. Nehru was now under considerable pressure to accept the Chinese challenge and to find a successor to Krishna Menon who had had so large a share of the responsibility for India's military debacle. The country was put on a war footing. Indian troops were moved from the West Pakistan border to the plains of Assam. All parties condemned Chinese aggression, and the final touch to national unity was given when the Communist Party of India adopted a resolution reaffirming its belief that the

McMahon Line was the border and pledging 'its support to the government's efforts . . . to defend the country'. When Parliament was called, communist M.P.s denounced China, praised Nehru and urged the Chinese press and radio to stop calling him 'an agent of U.S. imperialism and expansionism'.[13]

Chinese propaganda projected Nehru as a fascist monster, as a man who dreamed of a great Indian empire long before Indian independence, as an enemy who wanted to see China a weak country, and as the stooge of the United States. The editorial department of *Renmin Ribao* produced an article 'More on Nehru's Philosophy in the light of the Sino-Indian Question' which became the brief for the communist press of the world. Chinese researchers had gone to extraordinary lengths to find quotations which could be distorted to show Nehru's associations with the western world, the Indian bourgeoisie and landlords. The Indian communist leader, S. A. Dange, was described as a 'self-styled "Marxist-Leninist" trailing behind Nehru'. This propaganda offensive ended characteristically: 'May the Himalaya and the Karakorum mountains bear witness to the great friendship between the peoples of China and India'.[14]

THE SECOND CHINESE OFFENSIVE—NOVEMBER 1962

Heedless of the strategic realities, Indian leaders talked grandly about facing the challenge. It came on November 15, the day after the three-point proposal had been rejected when Chinese troops attacked on a 500-mile front in N.E.F.A. from Walong to Se-La. Walong fell after twenty four hours of fighting. Instead of meeting Indian troops in difficult terrain on the Se-La, the Chinese crossed the Palit range by means of a yak track and surprised them in the rear. Another column by-passed Se-La from the east and cut off the road between Se-La and Bomdi La, cutting off the Indians concentrated in the north for the defence of Se-La. Bomdi La was left undefended and fell in a few hours.

India was no more equipped to meet the attack in Ladakh. Chinese artillery shelled Indian positions around Chusul, the main Indian base. And when Indian troops had been forced to retreat in both sectors, Peking suddenly announced that from 00.00 hours on November 22 their frontier guards (they never called them troops) would cease fire along the entire Sino-Indian border. As from December 1 they would withdraw to positions twenty kilometres behind the line of actual control which existed on November 7, 1959. In short, they had taken by force what they had proposed after their first attack on October 20. India had turned down the proposals for reasons we have already analysed. North of the line China would set up checkpoints with civil police assigned to each one and the Indians would be informed of their location. Peking reserved the right to strike back in self-defence in three circumstances:

1. if the Indians 'should continue their attack after the Chinese frontier guards have ceased fire and when they are withdrawing;
2. if after Chinese withdrawal, Indians advanced to the line of control in the eastern sector and/or refused to withdraw but remained on the line of actual control in the middle and western sectors, and
3. if, after withdrawal, the Indian troops should cross the line of actual control and recover their positions prior to September 8th 1962.

The Chinese announcement categorically forbade the Indians to cross again

the illegal McMahon Line and reoccupy the Kechilang River area north of the Line in the eastern sector, reoccupy Wuje in the middle sector, and restore their forty-three strongpoints for aggression in the Chip Chap River valley, the Galwan river valley, the Pangong Lake area and the Demchok area or set up more strongpoints for aggression on Chinese territory in the western sector.[15]

Peking was not making proposals to a defeated India, but stating explicitly how she meant to exploit her victory. Kingsley Martin, in Delhi at the time described India's dilemma: 'Whatever the justice of the claims and counterclaims, the particular subtlety of the Chinese move lay in the fact that it presented India with a cruel choice – to negotiate from a point of weakness, or dare refuse and thus provoke further unequal war. The Indians who thought that Assam was to be cut off . . . are left to watch the voluntary withdrawal of the Chinese . . . They must feel some humiliation, they will not like to admit their immense relief, they will continue to say that they will fight to regain all their territory in Ladakh, though they know that this is not militarily feasible; they will continue to recruit soldiers and to regroup and strengthen their armies and to build bigger and stronger frontier posts, and to expect in the future renewed Chinese attacks. All this they will do and it will be of no harm but in fact, many of their reactions will look like meaningless gestures once the Chinese have actually withdrawn from the passes supposed to be impregnable, which they so quickly won and so bloodlessly restored.'[16]

The unilateral declaration of a cease-fire was a military victory for China, not only because it underlined her superiority in arms, communications, strategy, logistics and planning, but because it showed how deep were the political divisions in the Indian command. The training of their troops, Defence Minister Y. B. Chavan was to admit later, 'did not have orientation towards operations vis-a-vis the particular terrain in which the troops had to operate . . . [they] . . . did not have a slant for a war being launched by China . . . [they . . . had no requisite knowledge of the Chinese tactics, and ways of war, their weapons, equipment and capabilities'.[17] This was a fundamental cause of India's inability to meet China's invasion. But there were other basic factors; the organisation and establishment, equipment and logistics for mountain warfare compared unfavourable with those of China; military intelligence was extraordinarily inadequate; basic equipment of engineer units was deficient; most of the wireless sets and signal equipment were old and too heavy for operating in mountainous terrain; winter clothing was too elaborate and seldom available. By contrast, rivalry between different arms of the defence forces and a disastrous confusion of what was militarily feasible and politically desirable corrupted the strength in the Indian leadership.

Communications were far more developed by Chinese than Indians, with roads much nearer the Chinese forward posts giving them greater mobility and regroupement facilities. Chinese soldiers were toughened, acclimatised and well led.

The Indian deficiencies were clearly exposed to Peking in November 1962. Undoubtedly, Chinese troops could have pushed forward into the plains of Assam if this had been their intention. True, Nehru's appeal for military assistance in this war of forty-eight hours had immediate response from London and Washington, with hope even of adding Moscow to the list. But the Chinese were far too shrewd to risk involvement of the big powers, especially when it meant stretched communications at the beginning of winter. They had far more to gain from a drawn-out peace than an uncertain war.

Chou En-lai's letter of November 15 to Afro-Asian leaders was the first move in an astute political campaign. Beneath the overt propaganda it was an impressive statement of China's case, which few people had enough knowledge to dispute, let alone to follow. Tracing boundary questions to their roots in imperialist policy, he held that the Five Principles of Peaceful Coexistence and the Ten Principles adopted at the Bandung Conference should be the basis of settlement among newly independent powers. Recent boundary agreements with Burma and Nepal were cited as evidence of China's friendly spirit and genuineness in solving boundary questions by peaceful means. Only India had resisted such magnanimity. 'While it was occupying large tracts of Chinese territory,' Chou En-lai said, 'India suddenly made a unilateral alteration of the Sino-Indian traditional customary line in its official map published in 1954. It presented in its entirety the version of the Sino-Indian boundary insidiously contrived by British imperialism and tried to impose this version on China as the delimited boundary between China and India'.[18]

This highly-coloured story of Sino-Indian relations since the occupation of Tibet was not taken seriously by Afro-Asian leaders. At the same time they were not uncritical of Indian policy and as Nehru played for time, resisting the wildest pressure of public opinion to take a tough line with China, six African and Asian Governments considered whether they might make some contribution towards a peaceful settlement.

The Chinese slowly withdrew their troops as announced in the cease-fire proposals. Twice Nehru asked for a clarification of the alignment of the line of actual control. Chou En-lai proposed that officials from both sides should meet to discuss the problems implicit in a twenty kilometres withdrawal of the armed forces, the establishment of checkpoints by each party on its own side of the line of actual control and the return of captured personnel.[19] Nehru answered specific points by a statement of general principles:

1. We should create a proper atmosphere for peaceful settlement of our differences.
2. We should settle our differences in a friendly way through peaceful talks and discussions. If we fail, we can consider

what other agreed peaceful method of settling our differences should be adopted.

3. There should be no attempt to force any unilateral demand on either side on account of the advances gained in recent clashes.

4. The necessary preliminaries for talks and discussions suggested should be consistent with the decency, dignity and self-respect of both sides.

5. The implementation of these proposed arrangements will not in any way prejudice either side's position in regards to the correct boundary alignment.[20]

Once more, Nehru was expressing himself in high moral tones from what was a position of no real strength. Chou En-lai's position was militarily very strong, and by his rapid withdrawal had headed off western or Soviet military intervention which alone could have threatened that strength.

THE COLOMBO CONFERENCE—DECEMBER 1962

The Ceylonese Government took the initiative in calling a conference which met in Colombo from December 10–12. The non-aligned countries Burma, Cambodia, Ceylon, Ghana, Indonesia and the U.A.R. were represented in this attempt to find some compromise proposals which might bring Delhi and Peking to the conference table. Chou En-lai sent a felicitous telegram to the opening session. At the same time both he and Nehru showed their diplomatic hands. Chou En-lai's took the form of a sharply worded Memorandum demanding a 'clear and definite reply' to three questions:

Does the Indian Government agree, or does it not agree to a ceasefire? Does the Indian Government agree, or does it not agree, that the armed forces of the two sides should disengage and withdraw twenty kilometres each from the November 7, 1959, line of actual control? Does the Indian Government agree, or does it not agree, that officials of the two sides should meet and discuss matters relating to the twenty kilometre withdrawal of the armed forces of each party from the line of actual control of November 7, 1959, to form a demilitarised zone? [21]

Nehru's speech in the Lok Sabha on the opening day of the Colombo
Conference was an implicit reply to Chou's three questions which he
describes as being 'couched in a peremptory and dictatorial tone . . .
replete with factual distortions'. First, India would do nothing to
impede the implementation of the cease-fire declaration. Second,
'that negotiations . . . would be possible only on the basis of undoing
the further aggression committed by the Government of China on
Indian territory since 8th September 1962'. Third, 'India does not agree
to the so-called line of actual control of 7th November 1959 which
is not in accordance with the facts.' [22] The Indian position was as rigid
as the Chinese, but the Chinese had the advantage of being in occupation of disputed areas. Nehru did suggest that if parliament approved
he would be willing to refer the dispute to the International Court of
Justice, but he had added a nullifying proviso that this could only
happen when aggression was abandoned.

Meanwhile, the six representatives in Colombo unanimously agreed
on certain proposals which Mrs Bandanaraike presented first, to the
Chinese government and then to the Indian. After certain clarifications
the Indian Parliament agreed to support the Colombo proposals in
toto [see Appendix 16 for text of Proposals along with these
clarifications.]. The opposition in the Lok Sabha argued against them;
they were against any talks with China. Nehru was denounced for
going 'on bended knees' to China and the Colombo powers were
described as 'the cowering satellites of imperialist China'. But Nehru
argued convincingly that the proposals were more favourable than the
cease-fire and approximated to Indian demands. In fact, they were a
realistic compromise. In the western sector, the line of actual control
was taken as that of November 7, 1959, as defined on Chinese maps.
Chinese troops would withdraw their troops twenty kilometres from
this line. Indians would be kept on and up to this line. In the demilitarised zone of twenty kilometres created by China's withdrawal
civilian posts could be kept by both sides, their location, number and
composition to be decided in direct talks between Indian and Chinese
officials. This meant, in effect, that the Indian defence-posts overrun
by China could not function, but they had already proved practically
indefensible. In the eastern sector, Indian forces could move right up to
the south of the line of actual control, i.e. the McMahon Line, except
for the Thagla Ridge and Longju area. Similarly, the Chinese could
move right up to the north of the McMahon Line except for these two

areas, arrangements for which would be settled directly between Peking and Delhi. In the middle sector, the pre-September *status quo* should be maintained and neither side should do anything to disturb it. The proposals further implied a no-man's land of twenty kilometres in Ladakh.[23] All in all, this represented a workable compromise between the Indian and Chinese demands.

India's acceptance of the proposals was followed the same day by a Chinese announcement that they would accept them 'as a preliminary basis' for negotiations between Indian and Chinese officials. But they also insisted on two points of interpretation: one, that the stipulation regarding Indian troops keeping their existing military position should not apply only to the western sector, but to the entire border; and second, that China would not set up civilian posts in the twenty kilometre zone on her side of the actual line of control providing neither Indian troops or civilians re-entered the area. It was evident that Peking would favour direct talks with Indian officials from this point onwards. Delhi, mindful of just such talks in 1960, preferred the participation of a third party, and certainly Mrs Bandanaraike and her colleagues were close to finding an acceptable formula.

China announced the withdrawal of her frontier guards along the entire border and the number and location of civilian check posts within the twenty kilometre line vacated for the purpose of countering saboteurs and maintaining local order. 'In response to the peace appeal of the Colombo Conference', Peking informed Delhi, the Chinese were vacating four controversial areas and not establishing civilian checkpoints when the military had withdrawn. They were Che Dong (Dhola) and Longju in the eastern sector; Wuje (Barahoti) in the middle sector; and, 'the area in the western sector where India once established forty-three military strong points and where China had set up additional frontier posts in order to resist Indian invasion'. Peking described these proposals as 'yet another important effort made by China along the road of conciliation . . . and also represents a great regard for the honour and self-respect of India'.[24]

This sensible line was shortlived. The Colombo Conference powers continued their search for a formula, but new charges and counter-charges followed monotonously. India accused China of 'continuing to establish strong points of aggression while talking of peace and friendship,' and China accused India of using Sikkim as a base for intrusions into Chinese territory.

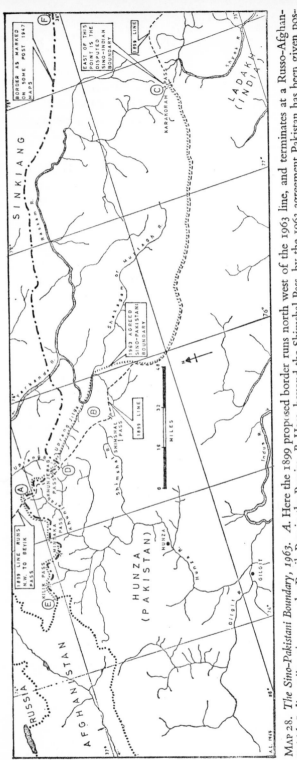

MAP 28. *The Sino-Pakistani Boundary, 1963.* *A.* Here the 1899 proposed border runs north west of the 1963 line, and terminates at a Russo-Afghan-British Indian trijunction near the Beyik Pass in the Pamirs. *B.* Here, beyond the Shinshal Pass, by the 1963 agreement Pakistan has been given possession to the north of the main Karakoram watershed. *C.* The Karakoram Pass marks the eastern end of the boundary agreed upon in 1963 and the beginning of the disputed Sino-Indian boundary in Ladakh. *D.–E.* The alignment here agreed upon in 1963 coincides with that shown on most modern maps. It follows the watershed between streams flowing into the Indus and those flowing into the Taklamakan Desert of Sinkiang. *D.–F.* This line, shown as the boundary on many modern maps, represents a theoretical British border including the Mir of Hunza's claims over the Raskam Valley. The British, in fact, never administered north of the main watershed, and in 1927 the Indian Government abandoned this boundary, even in theory. However, the 1927 decision did not find its way on to the maps, which explains why critics of the Sino-Pakistani Boundary Agreement of March 1963 have been able to find cartographic support for their claim that Pakistan has surrendered much territory to China. In fact, the 1963 [...] lies [...] represented the state of affairs obtaining since the end of the 19th century.

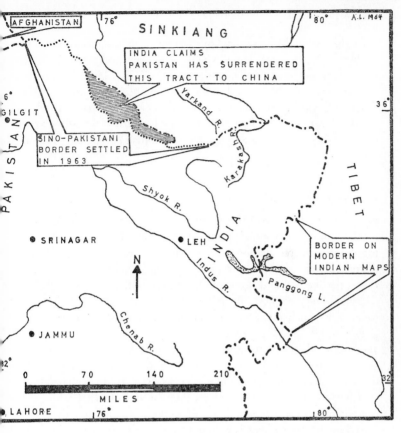

MAP 29. *The Border Region between China and India and Kashmir.*

MAPS 28, 29, and 30 and the caption for Map 28 are printed with acknowledgement to Alastair Lamb. They appeared in an article, *The Sino-Pakistani Boundary Agreement of 2 March 1963* in the *Australian Outlook*. Volume 18. No. 3, December 1964.

At this point, Moscow lent the weight of its support to Colombo proposals in a personal letter which Krushchev addressed to Nasser, Nkrumah, Sukarno, Bandanaraike and Ne Win, asking them to help in every way possible to settle the conflict by peaceful means.[25] And at this point, too, agreement was reached between China and Pakistan on the location and alignment of the boundary actually existing between them. This was a severe blow to Indian composure, such as it was.

NO COMPROMISE

Nevertheless, the two Prime Ministers continued to exchange letters on the Colombo proposals. India argued that China must first accept them without reservations, after which acceptance officials could discuss their implementation on the ground. Nehru reminded Chou En-lai that he had said he was willing to refer the dispute to an international body. Chou En-lai retorted that questions involving sovereignty, such as the Sino-Indian boundary question, 'can be settled only through direct negotiations between the two parties concerned, and absolutely not through any form of arbitration. The Chinese Government has never agreed to refer the Sino-Indian boundary dispute to arbitration, nor will it ever do so . . . If,' he concluded, 'the Indian Government, owing to its internal and external political requirements, is not prepared to hold negotiations for the time being the Chinese Government is willing to wait with patience.'[26] He hinted that the Chinese and Indian peoples and the peoples of the whole world would deplore any action India might take 'under outside influence' to provoke fresh conflicts on the Sino-Indian border. But on April 20, 1963, Peking peremptorily announced: 'It is entirely meaningless for Indian Notes to repeat over and over again the hackneyed phrases which were thoroughly refuted long ago. If in future India continues to make such unreasonable haggling, the Chinese Government will not reply any more.'[27]

In the course of an irate correspondence between the two sides the reasonable line achieved with so much diplomacy by the six non-aligned powers had drifted out of reach. Both countries gave the impression of using the proposals as part of their own struggle to win over non-aligned nations to their side in the broader field of struggle for the leadership of the Afro-Asian world – in which respect Chou En-lai's astuteness lent flexible appearance to Chinese propaganda as contrasted with Nehru's rigidity which was, in part, imposed on him by pressure in parliament and in the press. For example, Chou En-lai, in addressing a banquet in Peking in honour of Ali Sabry, Chairman of the U.A.R. Executive Council, said, with some effect:

> I can tell you that although India is not yet prepared to return to the conference table, provided it does not renew its military provocation and armed intrusion, the existing state of cease-fire and disengagement will continue. We are firmly opposed to any foreign interference in the Sino-Indian boundary dispute, for any such interference will only undermine Asian-African solidarity and thus put additional obstacles in the way of seeking a peaceful settlement of this dispute.[28]

When Ali Sabry passed through Delhi on his way back from Peking to Cairo, he found Nehru still insisting that India would only negotiate with China on the basis of an unreserved acceptance of the Colombo proposals. As Sabry and Mrs Bandanaraike continued their mediatory efforts, however, Nehru grew less unbending and, as his health worsened, so increasingly he dwelt on the tragedy of bequeathing to India unresolved frustrations with her neighbours China and Pakistan. When Mrs Bandanaraike set off on a new round of visits to Peking and Delhi in February 1964, she found both Prime Ministers nearer compromise. Chou was reported to have offered to withdraw Chinese posts in Ladakh, and India to have offered to accept an arrangement whereby neither side would maintain posts of any kind in the twenty kilometre zone on the Chinese side of the line of actual control.

In April, Nehru told the Lok Sabha of his commitment to Mrs Bandanaraike,[29] and he was quite explicit in the matter to the Central Committee of the Congress party in Bombay.[11] While still adhering to the Colombo proposals as a proper basis for negotiations with China, India *was* prepared to negotiate on the basis of neither side maintaining posts in the proposed demilitarised zone in Ladakh.

But Nehru died in May. His Government did not follow-up his talks. The posts remain to this day.

Undecided Frontiers: The Eternal Triangle

CHINA AND PAKISTAN; INDIA AND
PAKISTAN; ON THE PERIPHERY; PRIME
MINISTER SHASTRI; A POSSIBLE
SOLUTION

In this complex story of Himalayan frontiers, the most important unresolved question is whether China intended to reach agreement with India or only to isolate her with a view to domination at a later date. Whereas Nehru had always thought of China as a fellow Asian victim of western imperialism and a potential comrade-in-arms, the Chinese clearly regarded Nehru's India as a potential outpost of the West and Nehru himself as a British stooge. 'Even before the attainment of independence by India,' Dr S. Gopal who, as Head of the Historical Division of the Ministry of External Affairs worked intimately with Nehru, writes, 'Nehru had been thinking in terms of India and China, both victims of imperialism, working together as free nations with a sense of shared interest'[1] and he reminds us that Nehru once wrote to his sister from prison:

> During this year that is passing one thing has pleased me – the greater contacts between the people of India and the people of China. The contacts are not always as they should be, but even so, they are all to the good. The future of which I dream is inextricably interwoven with close friendship and something almost approaching union with China. [2]

Nor, Dr Gopal adds, 'was this intensity of desire for association with China dulled by the civil war in that country.'[3]

Was it within the scope of Chinese tradition or of communist ideology to reciprocate Nehru's attachment? The Middle Kingdom was and Mao believes that it still is the one and only centre of civilisation. The perimeter has widened; the Asian neighbours who used to pay tribute to the Emperor have their modern equivalent in obeisance from the Afro-Asian world and Albania. Communist or Kuomintang,

China must restore her greatness and regain any territory that she considers was once hers. Communist China has been far more ambitious than Yuan Shikkai or Chiang Kai-shek in this respect.

Thus there has always been an element of insincerity in Chou En-lai's assurances to India, though the word insincerity has a moral implication to which no Marxist could, by definition, subscribe. If Chou En-lai had not been one of the world's most subtle diplomatists and communist foreign policy a carefully calculated opportunism he would have said not only that he wanted negligible revisions of frontiers, but that he needed the Aksai Chin as a short cut to Tibet, and that though willing to negotiate on the N.E.F.A. frontier he would not accept the McMahon Line without re-negotiation because it was the handwork of British imperialism.

Nehru did not lack astute diplomacy. He was a bold and sagacious politician, though he had a blind spot where Pakistan was concerned. He was an idealist and, in his romanticized policy towards China, whatever government was in power, he was the victim of his own trustfulness. Like other idealists when they learn that they have been duped and taken advantage of, and that their goodwill has been exploited, Nehru was bitterly aggrieved by China's change of face. By the time the truth had lodged, Indian public opinion and parliament were almost hysterically hostile towards China, and Nehru was perhaps less amenable to the notion of a compromise than a more realistic and therefore less disillusioned man might have been.

Nehru, with his background and sense of responsibility could have had no alternative to a policy of peaceful co-existence with China. Certainly world opinion would have been relentlessly outraged, and rightly so, if from 1949 he had spent money, which he sorely needed for developing India's numerous resources on making the Himalayas, the greatest natural fortress in the world, into an armed frontier against a weak, and apparently, friendly revolutionary state. Nehru is in no way open to criticism because he did not plot a radar screen across the Himalayas. But he is open to criticism for failing to initiate serious frontier discussions at a much earlier stage when he, though not the Indian public, had evidence of the Chinese challenge, first in their maps and later on the ground. It is at least arguable that in 1950 when he condoned the Chinese occupation of Tibet, in 1954 when Indian and Chinese officials signed an Agreement on Trade and Intercourse, and in 1961 when notice was due for its cancellation or replacement, Nehru might have struck mutually advantageous bargains with Chou En-lai.

Had he been willing to discuss a new trade agreement, it might have constituted a step towards a wider area of negotiation. It is at least possible that a solution could have been arrived at whereby China got what she wanted in terms of frontier adjustment without a war. In the event she won the war and humiliated India.

Would India, in fact, have been poorer, or more vulnerable, if the equivalent of the McMahon Line were now a demarcated boundary or the Aksai Chin redrawn to give China the line she now holds by dint of military action? It seems certain that in the last months of his life Nehru was thinking along these lines, and that, sick and disillusioned as he was, he might have persuaded his embittered colleagues to accept his point of view. We shall never know.

What is certain is that the triangle which geographical proximity and national rivalry made eternal have now brought Communist Russia and a supposedly non-aligned India into the same camp against China.

On the basis of communist theory and Chinese practice, the long-term objectives of China might be summed up as consolidation of the Chinese revolution; neutral, controllable or friendly powers on her periphery; leadership of the Afro-Asian world; and a political and military strategy with which to undermine Western imperialism and Soviet revisionism. Her emergence as a nuclear power strengthens her military position, as well as her bargaining power.

In the early days of the Chinese revolution, foreign policy ran parallel with that of the Soviet Union. Treaties with surrounding countries were considered as part of the imperialist past. In 1949 Peking announced that it would either 'recognise, abrogate, revise or re-negotiate' treaties made with foreign powers. In April 1955 at Bandung the sophisticated Chou En-lai, who outshone and surpassed Nehru, said that with some countries on her border the boundaries were not yet finally fixed. Before fixing them, he told an unsuspecting audience:

> We are willing to maintain the present situation by acknow-ledging that those parts of our border are parts which are undetermined ... As to the determination of common borders which we are going to undertake with our neigh-bouring countries, we shall use only peaceful means and we shall not permit any other kinds of method. In no case shall we change this.[4]

Burma came first on the list, and at her request. In 1951 the Chinese Embassy in Rangoon displayed a map showing Chinese frontiers extending right across Burma, taking in a large part of the Kachin states down to a point about 50 miles north of Myitkyina. When the then Burmese Ambassador asked for an explanation in Peking, he was told that the Chinese Government 'had had no time to draw up a new map and had reproduced the old one'.[5]

Chen Shu-peng of the Institute of Geography, Academica Sinica, drew a map, sold cheaply in Peking, showing the Irrawaddy flowing through south-west China, the Shan states east of the Salween and the northern parts of the Kachin states all included in China. Peking explained, when complaints were made, that the publication was an oversight. Subsequently, clashes occurred between Chinese and Burmese troops in the Wa areas. The incident was not publicised, and the Prime Minister believed a settlement could be made by personal contacts with Chou En-lai. Finally, in January 1960, after a great deal of bargaining, in which the Burmese knew precisely what they wanted and what concessions they were willing to make, an agreement was signed by General Ne Win and Chou En-lai. After field work by Joint Survey teams, a treaty was signed with great fanfare in Peking, and boundary pillars subsequently set up along the agreed frontier between the two countries. It was, in fact, almost identical with the McMahon Line, though no one drew attention to the fact. The Chinese were not slow to suggest that 'what has happened between China and Burma can take place between China and other countries'.[6] In any speculation as to what might have been, it seems legitimate to wonder whether India's failure to reopen talks when the 1954 Agreement had only six months to go closed the door to a negotiated settlement in which both sides might have been ready to make concessions.

China made boundary agreements with all her other neighbours. A Treaty of Peace and Friendship was signed in Katmandu in April 1960 and was followed by increased trade and economic aid, spent primarily on building a road from the capital of Nepal to the Chinese frontier. King Mahendra signed a Boundary Treaty with Lu Shao-chi, the then Head of State, in October 1961. Afghanistan signed a Treaty of Friendship and mutual non-aggression in 1960 and a Boundary Treaty was signed three years later in Peking.

CHINA AND PAKISTAN

At the Bandung Conference, Chou En-lai made his first contacts with Pakistan's Prime Minister, who assured him his country had no fear that China would permit aggression against her. The result was a mutual understanding and an exchange of visits. Mohammed Ali's successor, Prime Minister Suhrawardhy, spent twelve days in China in 1956 and later in the same year Chou En-lai made a goodwill tour of Pakistan. Yet in 1959, when the shooting incident at Longju revealed the dangers to India of a Chinese invasion, President Ayub Khan made a bid for joint defense of the Indian sub-continent. After the idea had been turned down by Prime Minister Nehru, Ayub Khan told a meeting in Dacca early in 1960:

> The crux of the whole matter was that the armies of both countries were continuing to face each other when they could have been released to defend their respective territories.[8]

And a few days later he said at Chittagong:

> The need to have a joint defense originated from the basic fact that India and Pakistan lived in the same region which had to be defended after an understanding between the people of the two countries.[8]

In July 1960, a decisive year in the history of Indian relations with Pakistan as well as with China, Ayub Khan formulated his policy in *Foreign Affairs*.

> As a student of war and strategy, I can see quite clearly the inexorable push of the north in the direction of the warm waters of the Indian Ocean. This push is bound to increase if India and Pakistan go on squabbling with each other. If, on the other hand, we resolve our problems and disengage our armed forces from facing inwards, as they do today, and face them outwards, I feel we shall have a good chance of preventing a recurrence of the history of the past, which was that whenever this sub-continent was divided – and often it was divided – someone or the other invited an outsider to step in.[9]

These statements were vague and may have implied that there could be no joint defence without a Kashmir settlement. In other words, it was not, as some writers have interpreted it, an unconditional offer. But India's unwillingness to discuss a joint defence policy with Pakistan was unquestionably a factor in the development of relations between China and Pakistan. Ayub Khan first publicly discussed the 300 mile-long, undefined border between Sinkiang and that part of Kashmir under the control of Pakistan at a news conference on October 23, 1959. A Chinese map, he said, showed certain areas of Pakistan as part of China, and he wished to see a peaceful outcome to this situation. His first step, after private discussion, was to send a formal Note to Peking on March 28, 1961. When the Chinese replied, nearly a year later, they suggested a provisional agreement pending the settlement of the Kashmir dispute. To this Pakistan agreed, and on October 12, 1962, talks began in Peking. Agreement in principle was achieved at the end of 1962 and on February 22, 1963, a joint committee announced complete agreement on the location and alignment of the boundary. The text of the border agreement was released in Karachi on March 2, 1963 [Appendix 19]. It came into force with immediate effect and provided for a joint demarcation commission to conduct a survey of the boundary area on the ground, to fix boundary markers at jointly-agreed points to facilitate the delineation of the boundary line on jointly-prepared maps. Chou En-lai, in an interview with the Associated Press of Pakistan, rather blandly spoke of China's generous treatment of her neighbours Burma, Nepal, Pakistan, Afghanistan and Mongolia.

> Since the boundary questions left over by history are settled through friendly negotiations, and since China is bigger than these neighbouring countries and the border areas are mostly sparsely populated, China always made more concessions than the opposite party in the process of mutual accommodation in order to seek a settlement of the question.[10]

The Sino-Pakistan Treaty alignment followed the main Karakorum watershed, except for the Sokh Bulaq pocket which Pakistan claimed. The area in dispute from the overlapping borders shown on Pakistan's and China's maps was, according to *The Times* about 3400 square miles. 'The compromise border now agreed upon leaves about two-thirds of it (2050 square miles) on China's side; but while Pakistan has

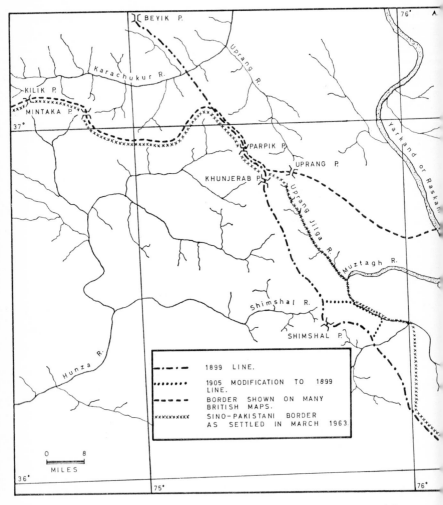

MAP 30. *The Sino-Pakistani Boundary Agreement of March 2, 1963, and the 1899 Line.*

given up only claims on maps, China will be withdrawing her frontier forces and administration from about 750 square miles.' [11]

The settlement of the Sino-Pakistani boundary was a triumph for commonsense which was naturally exploited fully in Peking and in Karachi. The Indian Government had opposed it as soon as it was mentioned in May 1962. Its unhappily rigid outlook on Kashmir was reflected in a Note delivered to the Embassy of China.

> In lodging an emphatic protest with the Government of the People's Republic of China for this interference with the sovereignty of India over the State of Jammu and Kashmir, Government of India solemnly warns the Government of China that any change, provisional or otherwise, in the status of the State of Jammu and Kashmir brought about by third parties which seeks to submit certain parts of Indian territory to foreign jurisdiction will not be binding on the Government of India and that the Government of India firmly repudiate any agreements provisional or otherwise regarding her own territories arrived at between third parties who have no legal or constitutional *locus standi* of any kind. [12]

Peking challenged as 'totally untenable' the assumptions that 'Kashmir is under Indian sovereignty, that there is no common boundary between China and Pakistan, and that therefore China has no right to conduct boundary negotiations with Pakistan'. 'Why is it,' their reply continued 'that the Indian Government cannot negotiate and settle its boundary question with the Chinese Government . . . ? One who tries to make use of Sino-Pakistan negotiations to whip up anti-Chinese sentiments will only be lifting a rock to crush his own toes in the end . . . Would it not be better to make some earnest effort towards a peaceful settlement of the Sino-Indian boundary question rather than wasting its strength in such fruitless quarrel?' [13] Notes, increasingly acrimonious in tone, passed between Peking and Delhi. The boundary Treaty was a diplomatic reverse for India. Pakistan had earned Peking's open support for her Kashmir policy. In 1963, trade and barter agreements helped Pakistan's economy, and, in spite of Washington's disapproval, an air service was opened between Dacca, Canton and Shanghai. Increased communication by air was followed by the construction of modern highways on both sides of the Sino-Pakistan

L

border. Where camels were the only transport since Marco Polo passed that way, jeepable roads were now built from Kashgar up to the Karakorum Mountains. On Pakistan's side, the Indus Valley highway provides an all-weather road to Gilgit and beyond, in Hunza a jeep track crosses over dangerous slopes and wooden bridges across high precipices up to the Chinese border. This all-weather road between China and Kashmir can carry goods or provide one more invasion route into India. It was the second potential use of the track which caused India to protest when the Sino-Pakistan border was finally demarcated on the ground in mid-1965. Peking's reply to Delhi's protest said: 'Unwilling to settle its own boundary question with China, India has made desperate attempts to prevent others from settling boundary questions with China'.[14] And in this sparring match, so far mainly confined to belligerent correspondence, Delhi had retorted that the boundary agreement was legally invalid and politically mischievous. It was 'an integral part of the growing . . . collaboration and collusion between the Chinese and Pakistan Governments against India'.[15] Pakistan has administered the area since 1948. legalistically but unrealistically, Delhi argued that Pakistan was a neighbour of China only by virtue of aggression in Jammu and Kashmir and 'what the so-called Sino-Pakistan boundary has done is to share between them the fruits of aggression at the expense of India'.[16]

Nothing could alter the facts of geography and China and Pakistan appreciated how much they could gain from developing their commercial, strategic and political interests. An agreement, signed on October 21, 1967, though the text was kept secret, arranged for the opening of a Sinkiang-Gilgit link road. Already, by May 1968, the Chinese had completed their road north of the 15,000 ft Mintaka Pass. On the Kashmir side a fair weather road between Gilgit and Pasu was improved and Pakistan also started on a new jeepable road from Pasu to Mintaka Pass. Thus Sinkiang was linked with Kashmir on the Pakistan side of the cease-fire line. In time a direct overland route between Rawalpindi and China will be open during the summer season. India has protested to China and to Pakistan, firstly on the grounds that the agreement seeks to interfere with Indian sovereignty in Kashmir and secondly that it should have been kept secret. Meanwhile the two countries exchange many cultural troupes, a barter agreement was signed in May 1968 for the exchange of goods worth Rs. 110 million, China supplied substantial amounts as interest-free loans for the setting up of heavy industries and exports from Pakistan to China which were valued at Rs. 160 million in 1964 reached the Rs. 220 million mark in 1967.

INDIA AND PAKISTAN

Indo-Pakistani relations were undoubtedly worsened by Pakistan's relations with China. In the Rann of Kutch affair in June 1965, large-scale fighting was avoided. In Indian minds, it was related to Ayub Khan's dealings with Peking. 'Many Indians', Alastair Lamb reports, 'including Cabinet Ministers, were convinced that somehow the Chinese had got at the Government of President Ayub Khan much as Americans are convinced that the Chinese lurk as *éminences grises* behind the Government of Ho Chi-minh in North Vietnam. . . . In this atmosphere Lal Bahadur Shastri deserves much credit in having been able to convince his own followers of the wisdom of a cease-fire.' [17] But another crisis was already developing in Kashmir, where Pakistani guerillas infiltrated across the cease-fire line. When they were joined by regular units, it was clear that Pakistan meant war. India's immediate reaction, on September 6, 1965, was to occupy two Pakistani outposts near Kargil, thus securing the vital route to the Ladakh-Chinese border and preventing any Sino-Pakistani link-up near the Karakorum Pass. Now was the real test of Sino-Pakistani co-operation. Chen Yi, in Pakistan at the time, supported her 'just action' against Indian 'armed aggression', while Chou En-lai, speaking at a North Korean Embassy reception in Peking, attributed blame to 'United States imperialism and its partners'. He pledged China's firm support for Pakistan's 'just struggle against aggression' and the Kashmir people's 'struggle for freedom and the right of national self-determination' and sternly warned Delhi 'that it must bear full responsibility for all consequences arising from its extended aggression'.[18] General Lo Jui-ching, Chinese Chief of Staff, without mentioning the Soviet Union or the United Nations by name, poured contempt on those who impertinently tried to end the war. He solemnly prophesied that the 'Krushchev revisionists would be swept like dust from the stage of history by the mighty broom of the revolutionary people'.[19]

The Chinese were now openly backing Pakistan's cause. They went far beyond verbal support by creating a diversion on the Sikkim border. Note after Note accused India of intrusions over the border, especially at Nathu La. The threat of escalation was virtually realised on September 16 when Yang Kung-su, deputy director of the Foreign Ministry Asian affairs department, summoned J. S. Mehta and handed him an ultimatum. It demanded that India should dismantle all its military installations on the Chinese side of the China-Sikkim border or the boundary itself within three days of the delivery of the Note. It also demanded that India should halt all intrusions along both boundaries, return kidnapped border inhabitants and seized livestock, and promise to refrain from further harrassing raids across the boundary. 'Otherwise the Indian Government must bear full responsibility for all the grave consequences arising therefrom'. This diversion was generally considered to be part of the assistance which Bhutto's extremely pro-Chinese policy had achieved. Clearly, China must have decided at some point that Pakistan played a sufficiently important part in their scale of strategic values to make this minimum contribution worth while.

The world-wide reaction to China's ultimatum, was of a violence they could not afford to ignore. The U.S. Government made it very clear that if China took advantage of the Indo-Pakistan war, Mao Tse-tung could expect instant retaliation. The Soviet Union faced a complex dilemma: if Moscow joined with Washington in trying to end the war, China, as well as Afro-Asian communists would condemn her as betraying communism; if she took no action, then the U.S.A. would extend her influence in the Indian sub-continent; if her weight were thrown on India's side, Pakistan might become a satellite of China. Thus, as two *Herald Tribune* correspondents concluded:

> For wholly different reasons, the two nuclear giants have only limited room for public manoeuvre in their common aim of preventing China from profiting from the Indo-Pakistan war.[20]

The line of Chinese propaganda was predictable. 'If there are people who are adding fuel to the flame of Indo-Pakistan dispute,' the *People's Daily* fulminated, 'they are precisely the Soviet leaders in addition to the U.S. imperialists'.[21]

The weekend of September 18–20 was the most tense since the Cuban crisis. As Indians and Pakistanis fought their reckless war, the Security Council sat in session in New York and U Thant made abortive efforts to bring President Ayub Khan and Prime Minister Shastri to the conference table. In the Lok Sabha on September 17

Prime Minister Shastri had said that India agreed to investigate jointly with China the forward posts which China accused her of building. The Chinese had several times asked for, and the Indians refused this joint inspection of alleged 'aggressive installations'. Announcing their decision, Shastri added:

> "We do hope that China will not take advantage of the present situation and attack India. But if they do we will fight for our freedom. The might of China will not deter us from defending our integrity."

These were brave words which happily were not to be put to the test.

Tension suddenly eased and for two reasons. The first was the intervention of the Soviet Prime Minister, Mr Kosygin, who invited Shastri and Ayub Khan to hold talks on Soviet soil. The second was the extension of China's ultimatum for 3 days, made, it is generally believed, at the urgent request of Ayub Khan. China's face was saved by Shastri's agreement to the joint investigation of the borders. The ultimatum expired on September 22 without incident. It is possible that China was not prepared to risk war a for Pakistan's benefit.

In this 17 day war both sides had unnecessarily squandered the lives of men who were sometimes members of the same family. Chinese intervention had demonstrated to the world her extraordinary combination of strategic withdrawal and propaganda bravado. The United Nations emerged as an effective arbitrator and the Soviet Union succeeded in the unaccustomed role of a mediator by bringing Ayub Khan and Shastri to the conference table at Tashkent. The tangible result was the withdrawal of armed personnel from territories occupied or otherwise penetrated during the September war. But the 'Taskhent spirit' engendered by the conference began to evaporate almost as soon as Lal Bahadur Shastri's sudden death robbed India of a leader whose patience and judgment had promised a happier chapter in Indo-Pakistan relations. Optimism proved shortlived. Once more India's attention was diverted from constructive thinking about her neighbour.

ON THE PERIPHERY

China and India are both neighbours of Nepal and vie with one another for supremacy. In the early days after the defeat of the Ranas in 1951, India was in a strong position to develop trade, cultural relations, and, above all, communications on which all of them depend. In May 1967 the first trans-Himalayan highway capable of two-lane traffic for its 67 mile length was completed with Chinese money and know-how and Nepalese engineers. It stretches from Kodari, at the head of the Kuti Pass which provides easy access to Kathmandu, and, beyond, to India. The East-West highway, in the south of Nepal, is built by Indians and Russians with British aid.

Bhutan is also a neighbour of India and China. It is now linked to India by a Treaty of 1949 which says that Bhutan agrees 'to be guided' by India in her external affairs while India accepts responsibility for Bhutan's communications and defence. At the same time, India undertakes 'to exercise no interference in the internal administration of Bhutan'.[22] In practice this means that Indian technical and financial aid has been provided for 400 miles of roads, while she is entirely responsible for the country's Second Plan. Not all Bhutanese welcome this virtual dependence on India. The winds of change are blowing in Thimpu. The King wants his country to become a member of the United Nations – it is already one of the Colombo Plan countries. Some members of his government want diplomatic relations with countries other than India. A small group staged a rebellion in 1966 which was unsuccessful. Its leaders are now in Nepal. In short, there exists a potential 'fifth column' in Bhutan which Delhi cannot afford to ignore and which Peking might find amenable to its propaganda. The Tibet-Bhutan boundary is recognised in the north where the traditional boundary follows the crest of the Himalayas. But China claims 300 square miles of north-eastern Bhutan and a considerable area to the north of Punakha, the former Bhutanese capital.

India's ties with Sikkim are closer than those with Bhutan. The Anglo-Chinese Convention of 1890 recognised the British protectorate over Sikkim and settled its boundary with Tibet.* This boundary which communist China has not challenged, follows the crest of the Himalayan range separating the waters flowing into the Tista river in Sikkim and its affluents from those which flow into the Tibetan Mochu and northward into the other rivers of Tibet. In 1947, India inherited British responsibilities in Sikkim, and in 1950 made a new treaty with the Maharajah, Sir Tashi Namgyal. This gave India the responsibility for Sikkim's external affairs (political, economic and

* See Appendix 2.

financial). His successor, the Chogyul, has not hidden his desire for greater freedom from India, and in May 1967, for the first time publicly, he suggested a review of the 1950 treaty, though he clearly recognised that the defence of India is the defence of Sikkim.

The government in Delhi has not always shown tact in its dealings with the young and intelligent Chogyul whose family comes from Tibet with which he also has religious ties. His Third Year Plan is almost entirely underwritten by India. Vast sums are being spent on roads reaching up to the Tibetan frontier. He obtained one concession in February 1967 when India agreed that in future the Indo-Sikkimese boundary will be treated as an international line, and all maps published in India will incorporate the change. But in Sikkim, to a greater degree than in the less politically advanced Bhutan, there exists an anti-Indian feeling, usually anti-feudal, which could provide a fertile soil for Peking's active propaganda.

A recently published book on the history of Sino-Indian relations makes the valid point that whereas 'Curzon saw the Himalayan regions of Kashmir, Nepal, Sikkim, Bhutan and Assam Himalaya as an inner defence line for India protected by a Tibetan buffer region, Communist China today views Himalaya as its outer line of defence, necessary for the protection of Tibet. Peking, which sees the Himalayan states as irredentist regions to be regained as soon as possible, also assigns to them an offensive role. They can be future bases for the subversion of India'.[23]

Meanwhile the need for a mutually acceptable solution to the problem of Kashmir remains the indispensable necessity for India and Pakistan, not only in terms of their internal economies and social progress but because the existence of the dispute maintains the instability of the region, and gives an opportunity to the U.S.S.R., the U.S.A. and China to interfere or to take an interest in the affairs of India and Pakistan in support of their global policy.

India is, in effect, faced with the dilemma of a strategical extravaganza which might provoke Chinese action, or a positive gesture of re-opening talks to which China might find it in her own interests to respond. Fortification of the Himalayan frontiers might enrich the American arms industry to the extent of £500 million – a low estimate – but it would be no guarantee of peace, it would provoke China, it would postpone for generations the social changes which alone can make India a nation without poverty.

Indian dependence on U.S. and Soviet aid, and to a far less extent on British aid, is at least a makeshift policy adopted at a moment of near panic when it was assumed that China threatened Assam and, beyond, West Bengal. It has been suggested by a shrewd diplomat who served at the Netherlands Embassy in New Delhi from 1957 to 1960, that if China's cease-fire proposals had been made 48 hours earlier, Nehru would not have made appeals for aid to the United States.[24] It might be argued that the immediate response to Nehru's appeal was a contributory factor in China's sudden withdrawal, that China saw the unwisdom of bringing the United States, and possibly the Soviet Union into active opposition on her frontiers. But this is not the only interpretation of Chinese action. What advantage could she expect from moving southwards to the Brahmaputra, extending her supply lines at the beginning of winter? She had already destroyed the image of India as a great Asian power by exposing her strategic shortcomings. Further advance would have meant challenging America, the U.K. and possibly the Soviet Union. She had everything to gain and nothing to lose by sudden cease-fire and withdrawal.

The Chinese invasion raised the broader problems of what was her immediate objective and there was, inevitably, a great deal of speculation as to what were her ultimate aims. Nehru's evaluation was drastically changed by the events of 1962. In an article 'Changing India' in *Foreign Affairs*, he made this admission:

> ... despite our friendliness, China's behaviour towards us has shown such utter disregard of the ordinary canons of international behaviour that it has shaken severely our confidence in her good faith. We cannot, on the available evidence, look upon her as other than a country with profoundly inimical intentions toward our independence and institutions. The Himalayan barrier has proved to be vulnerable. If it is breached, the way to the Indian plains and the ocean beyond would be exposed; and the threat to India would then likewise, be a threat to the other countries of South and Southeast Asia. India's determination to resist aggression and retain her territorial integrity is, therefore, a vital factor in the safeguarding of peace and stability throughout this whole area.[25]

The underlying assumption of Chinese expansionism to which Nehru now subscribed was shared by many Indian officials, parliamentarians and writers who used it to reinforce their appeal for massive foreign aid. Any assessment of Chinese objectives is to a considerable degree speculative, but their 'cartographical aggression' as it has been called, is a valid starting point. When Nehru first complained of maps which included Ladakh and N.E.F.A. in China, Chou En-lai said they were old maps which they had had no time to change. Nehru accepted this explanation at face value for some years. More significant is the map published in 1952 for internal consumption. This was the frontispiece to Liu Pei-hua's *Brief History of Modern China* and it was repeated when the second issue of the book appeared in 1954. Apparently it was not known in India until 1962, at which point Peking denied official responsibility.

On March 8, 1963, a *People's Daily* editorial gave some indication of Chinese territorial objectives. They were based, as Francis Watson points out, on what appertained in 1840 'when the frontiers of the Manchu Empire were still at their greatest extent' before the period of what are generally called 'the unequal treaties', with the Western powers and those of Aigun, Tientsin, Peking and Ili with Czarist Russia. They include areas which were neither controlled nor administered by the Chinese Empire. Mongolia and Tibet are 'namelessly absorbed . . . A southern frontier for China is indicated, taking in the claim-line subsequently advanced against India'.[26] But too much must not be read into this particular map which embraces Burma, Nepal, Sikkim and Bhutan, Assam, Thailand, Malaya and Singapore, and the Soviet maritime territories and the 'Great North-East' beyond the Amur River. Apart from the fact that it was officially repudiated, new boundaries were given official sanction in treaties with Burma, Nepal, Afghanistan and Pakistan, and in the course of discussions on the Colombo proposals, Chou En-lai agreed to further concessions.

The Colombo proposals, if implemented, would have provided a no-mans land of 20 kilometres in Ladakh and in N.E.F.A. True, they mplied the loss to India of an area which she could not hold militarily, and which had no particular significance within the framework of Indian economy or administration. In the latest map produced by China – in 1964 – she incorporated the advanced 1960 claim-line which, in turn, was an extension of the 1956 claim-line. West of the Karakorum the boundary shown was that laid down by the Sino-

Pakistan Agreement. Indian continues to incorporate this area in her own maps, though Pakistan has administered it since 1947. Does India seriously believe that she can march up to these mountains and remove Sino-Pakistan pillars as British officials once removed Chinese pillars on the Karakorum or in the Lohit valley? China's latest map, in effect, registers her military gains in 1962. Peking is taking unilateral action without any agreement with India in much the same way as the British acted in 1847 and 1899. This implies that she is no longer interested in the machinery of the Colombo proposals, though she has not repudiated their terms.

PRIME MINISTER SHASTRI

After Nehru's death, Shastri seemed edging towards the re-opening of talks with China. Jayaprakash Narayan, as in the long drawn-out issue of Kashmir, came forward with constructive proposals. In August 1964, he suggested the lease of Aksai Chin to China as a possible solution to end the deadlock, and that the proposal should come from the Colombo powers. He maintained that China was not very much interested in N.E.F.A., that her claim to this territory was purely a bargain counter to its claim to Aksai Chin. But Jayaprakash Narayan's idea was not realistic, since it implied India's ability to dispose of the Aksai Chin. He held that 'geographical and other evidence supported India's claim to Aksai Chin'. But China had made it abundantly clear that she was not prepared to go by the evidences India was able to produce.

Shastri again spoke in friendly terms when, on July 6, 1965, during a visit to Hyderabad, he said: 'We are always prepared for a settlement with China with honour and dignity.' Radhakrishnan spoke out with his customary rationality: 'Peace with honour with China and Pakistan would enable India to divert more funds from defence to development.' Such remarks were observed in Peking, where, according to an East European diplomat, the machinery of the Colombo powers was no longer regarded as potentially a form of mediation. The same source (according to K. V. Narain, *The Hindu* correspondent in Tokyo) 'also said China was fully aware that the improvement of Sino-Indian relations was essential for itself and for the peace of Asia and that notwithstanding its public proclamations, it also realised that Asian peace depended on only three countries, namely, India, China and Japan'.[27]

The Hindu's editorial comments on Shastri's speech were realistic:

The position today is that the Chinese occupy 12,000 sq. miles of Ladakh presumably to safeguard the Aksai Chin highway into Tibet. They have built a network of roads and fortifications in the area south and west of the road and they hold passes through the mountain ranges that separate Kashmir from Tibet. Though there are three major highways leading from China into Tibet, the Aksai Chin road from Sinkiang is the best all-weather route and is linked with the railway in Sinkiang. The Aksai Chin is the gateway to Lhasa, the capital of Tibet. Thus, if India is to settle with China, it must be prepared to abandon its right to the occupied Ladakhi territory including the Aksai Chin highway. In return it might get a guarantee of the McMahon Line in the east, though it is doubtful if, along the northern border, the Chinese will withdraw from some of the Himalayan passes which they now hold. It should also be pointed out that the great change in our military deployment in the Himalayas (where we were only holding the foothills before the invasion) was that we moved up into the high ranges which we had previously supposed formed a natural barrier against invasion. Since the whole northern border is some 2500 miles long, our forces have to be doubled in strength.

While military alliances of the Dulles type have fallen into disrepute, it should be possible to work pragmatically with other nations to maintain a balance of power which will not permit Chinese domination of Asia or Africa. And while the United Nations should still take precedence over every other diplomatic forum, it is still not a substitute for the defence preparedness of the nation states that co-exist in the world today. India has to face the facts of a new world political strategy that has unmistakeably come into being.[28]

A POSSIBLE SOLUTION

The pattern of Asia was enormously changed a few months after this editorial was written. China's potential dominance of south-east Asia was undermined by the defeat of communists in Indonesia, and a gradual return to more friendly relations with India. Secondly, war between India and Pakistan was ended by the intervention of Western powers and the Soviet Union. For a short time, India and Pakistan were brought together round the conference table in Tashkent, largely because Kosygin, Shastri and Ayub Khan were willing to speak the same diplomatic language. In the middle of this conference, Jayaprakash Narayan again spoke out boldly on the Sino-Indian border dispute. Why, he asked, should a third party mediation not produce results in this case, as Harold Wilson had done in the Rann of Kutch dispute and Kosygin in Tashkent? Both sides, he rightly observed, could produce the evidence of maps and treaties to prove their case. Attempts to dislodge the Chinese from Indian territory they occupied in 1962 might now spell disaster. Chinese aggression was not so much of a military nature as ideological and the best solution to this 'ideological aggression' could be found in the Sarvodaya movement, which stood for meeting the challenge posed by poverty and maldistribution of land in that country.

How far Sarvodaya can meet the challenge to India on her home front or on her borders may be open to doubt. But it is certain that no solution can be found by an impoverished India, combining a vast expenditure on defence, on arms and planes, which, if used on any effective scale, would only make her a satellite of the U.S.A., and, in terms of a questionable non-alignment, also dependent on the U.S.S.R. Nehru's personal diplomacy did not succeed; his early trust in China was exploited, and he failed to take advantage of India's usefulness to China before her revolution was consolidated. His moral generalisations made no appeal and did not constitute any threat. By the time the meetings of Indian and Chinese officials had revealed China's policy, incidents on the border had already created a war psychosis in India. Chinese invasion and withdrawal left a stunned and humiliated India, yet Nehru was still the only leader who could have made the sensible compromises implicit in the Colombo proposals. They remain today the most hopeful solution to the Sino-Indian border dispute though the time has passed when its machinery was practicable.

Clearly, any settlement of the Sino-Indian border involves compromise. In the first place, the five hundred and fifty pages of documentation produced by the Chinese and Indian officials provides a basis for discussion. But it can be argued that there has been too much discussion already on maps and documents and historical records. The innumerable discrepancies on maps might lead the most naïve student of cartography to the view that 'the devil can quote maps to serve his own purpose' – but of course political agreement must preceed it. A joint survey on the ground is called form.

The fact that China accepted the Red Line of the 1914 Simla Tri-partite maps in her discussions with Burma, suggests that this might be a starting point in the case of India. Both sides have more knowledge of the terrain than either had when McMahon drew the map, and Chinese and Tibetans initialled it. (China did not, of course, proceed to a signature.) The Red Line, after detailed surveys, could be open to minor local adjustments, one way or the other, to fit geographical or ethnic factors on the ground. It could be argued that this way India would get all she really requires, a defensible frontier both in Ladakh and in N.E.F.A. China would get admission that the road across Aksai Chin, which she built unknown to India, is within her territory. A settlement of this kind could be based on the Red Line and the Macartney-Macdonald Line of 1899, accepted by Sinkiang officials but not endorsed by Nanking. These two lines could re-enforce one another and correct one another.

India today seems to be the victim of three traumas: Kashmir, the Aksai Chin, and poverty. To try to resolve the first two by vast military expenditure can only divert her funds and energies from the struggle against poverty. India cannot afford to play Russia's war game with China, nor her own war game with Pakistan. China, what-ever the ruling power, will continue to make the same demands that Peking is making today, since her national interests must remain the same and the geographical background is permanent. She, too, cannot risk two enemies on her frontier nor a series of Vietnams round her periphery. India is, in fact, faced with the alternatives of the Himalayas as one vast radar screen or the initiation of an active foreign policy to re-open talks with Pakistan and China. To settle for the present stale-mate is to condone a militarily active frontier across Asia.

References

Chapter One

INDIA AND CHINA IN ASIA

1. Havell, E. B., *The Himalayas in Indian Art*, p. 2. John Murray, 1924.
2. Needham, Dr Joseph, *Science and Civilisation in China* Volume 1 *Introductory Orientations*, p. 194. Cambridge University Press, 1954.
3. Bagchi, P. C., *India and China*. A thousand years of cultural relations, revised and enlarged edition, p. 82. Hind Kitabs, Bombay, 1950.
4. Ibid., Preface to 1st Edition, p. 1.
5. Curzon, Marquis of Kedleston, *The Romanes Lecture 1907*, p. 7. Clarendon Press, 1907.
6. Holdich, Sir Thomas, *Political Frontiers and Boundary Making*, pp. 280–1, Macmillan, 1956.
7. Nehru, Jawaharlal, *The Discovery of India*, p. 191. Meridian, London, 1956.
8. Ibid., p. 192.
9. 7th I.N.C. 1891, pp. 31–2.
10. Home Correspondence, Volume 129, 1892. This subject is treated in detail on pp. 276–95 in *The Making of Burma* by Dorothy Woodman, Cresset Press, 1960.
11. Ibid.
12. 11th I.N.C. 1895, p. 29.
13. 19th I.N.C. 1904, p. 24.
14. I.N.C. 1920–1923, pp. 70, 75–6.
15. Nag, Dr Kalidas (Ed), *Tagore in China*, p. 62.
16. Prasad, Bimla, *The Origins of Indian Foreign Policy*, p. 264 (the complete text of the report which Nehru submitted to the A.I.C.C., pp. 262–80).
17. Ibid., pp. 272–3.
18. Ibid., p. 280.
19. I.N.C. 1936, Nehru's Presidential Speech, p. 33.
20. Ibid., p. 15.
21. Nehru, Jawaharlal, *Essay: Indian Problems* (record of a meeting in London held under the auspices of Indian Conciliation Group, 4 February 1936).
22. Nehru, Jawaharlal, *Eighteen Months in India 1936–1937*, pp. 174–5.
23. Tan, Professor Yun-shan, *Cultural Interchange between India and China*, p. 2. Calcutta, 1934.
24. Nag, Dr Kalidas (Ed.), *Tagore in China*, p. 60.
25. 51st I.N.C., pp. 3–4.
26. Nehru, Jawaharlal, *China, Spain and the War*, p. 18.
27. Prasad, Bimla, Op. cit. pp. 171–2.

28. Ibid., pp. 181–2.

29. Prasad, Bimla, *The Origins of Indian Foreign Policy*, p. 204.

30. Ibid., p. 205.

31. Radhakrishnan, Dr Sarvapalli, *India and China*. Lectures delivered in China, May 1944. Hind Kitabs.

32. Ibid.

33. Prasad, Bimla, Op. cit., p. 310.

Chapter Two

THE FRONTIER THAT WAS ASSUMED

1. Fisher, Rose and Huttenback, *Himalayan Battleground,* p. 21 note, Pall Mall Press, 1963.

2. Desideri (edited by Filippi), *An Account of Tibet*, p. 81, Routledge, 1937.

3. Li, Tieh-Tseng, *The Historical Status of Tibet*, p. 53, Columbia University, New York, 1956.

4. Davis, Sir John, *China during the War and since the Peace* Volume 1, p. 149. London, 1852.

5. Moorcroft, William, Moorcroft's voluminous correspondence in the India Office Library was edited by H. H. Wilson, but the letters describing frontiers, and many political letters were not included in the edited selection.

6. Moorcroft Papers, I.O.L. MSS. Eur. D.263.

7. Moorcroft Papers, I.O.L. MSS. Eur. D.260.

8. Moorcroft Papers, I.O.L. MSS. Eur. D.260. *Letter to J. Adam*, May 12, 1821.

9. Moorcroft Papers, Folio 31. G.28, p. 141. *Letter to* Metcalfe, August 15, 1821.

10. Moorcroft Papers, Folio 34. G. 28.

11. Moorcroft Papers, I.O.L. MSS. Eur. D.263. Letter to Swinton, April 1822.

12. Moorcroft Papers, I.O.L. MSS. Eur. D.256. Letter to Metcalfe, November 30, 1820.

13. Ibid.

14. Ibid.

15. Moorcroft Papers, I.O.L. MSS. Eur. D.245.

16. Ibid.

17. Moorcroft Papers, I.O.L. MSS. Eur. D.261.

18. Ibid.

19. Moorcroft Papers, I.O.L. MSS. Eur. C.42.

20. Moorcroft and Trebeck, *Travels in the Himalayan Provinces of Hindustan etc, Volume 1, pp. 358–9.* Edited by H. H. Wilson. London, 1841.

21. Lloyd and Gerard, *Narrative of a journey from Caunpoor to the Boorendo Pass in the Himalayan mountains.* 2 Volumes, Madden, 1840. Volume 2, pp. 91–2.

22. Ibid., Volume 2, p. 150. Camp Shipke, August 5, 1921.

23. Ibid., Volume 2, pp. 156–7. Camp Nako, August 8, 1821.

24. Ibid., Volume 2, p. 206. Camp Soongnum, August 18, 1821.

25. Ibid., Volume 2, p. 250. Camp Manes, September 5, 1821.

26. Journal of Capt. A. Gerard, 1818.

27. Ibid.

28. Gutzlaff, Dr, R.G.S.J., Volume 20, 1851. Lecture to R. G. S., February, 1849.

29. E.S.L., Volume 79, No. 76. August 4, 1841.

30. Ibid., August 22, 1841.

31. Fisher, Rose, and Huttenback, *Himalayan Battleground*. Appendix, pp. 155–76.

32. Panikkar, K. M., *The Founding of the Kashmir State*, Allen & Unwin 2nd. im. 1953. pp. 88–9.

33. Panikkar, K. M., Treaty of Lahore 1846. pp. 161–4.

34. Cunningham, Alexander., *Ladakh, Physical, Statistical and Historical,* p. 3. London, 1854.

35. E.S.L.F.I., Volume 106. No. 33. July 23, 1846.

36. Ibid., August 14, 1846.

37. Ibid., Volume 114. No. 36. July 16, 1847.

38. S.L.F.B.I., Volume 32. Hardinge to E.I.C. Directors, July 28, 1847.

39. E.S.L.F.I., Volume 110. No. 38. Keying to Davis, January 13, 1847.

40. Ibid., Davis to Keying, January 21, 1847.

41. Ibid., Keying to Davis, January 30, 1847.

42. S.L.F.B.I., Volume 32. Hardinge to E.I.C. Directors, July 28, 1847.

43. Cunningham, Alexander, *Ladakh*, p. 261.

44. Ibid., p. 355.

45. R.G.S.J., Volume 19, Part 1, pp. 25–9. 1849.

46. E.S.L.F.I., Volume 120. No. 44. December 1, 1848.

Chapter Three

WHERE THREE EMPIRES MET

1. Montgomerie, T. G., *Report on the Trans-Himalayan Explorations.* In connection with Great Trigonometrical Survey of India. During 1865–1867.

2. Montgomerie, T. G., R.G.S.J., Volume 36, 1866. *On the Geographical Position of Yarkand and Other Places in Central Asia.*

3. Hayward, G. W., R.G.S.J., Volume 40, 1870, page 49. *Journey from Leh to Yarkand and Kashgar.*

4. Ibid., p. 51.

5. Shaw, Robert, Proceedings of the R.G.S., Volume 20. *Visits to High Tartary, Yarkand and Kashgar.*

6. Ibid.

7. Ibid.

8. Shaw, Robert, Letters from India Volume 5. *Routes between British India and Yarkand.* September 1869.

9. Ibid., *Russian Advances in Asia.* October, 1869.

10. Forsyth, Sir T. D., *Report of a Mission to Yarkand,* p. 3, 1873.

11. Ibid., p. 59.

12. Ibid., p. 35.

13. Punjab Foreign Proceedings, Reports of February 20 and April 29, 1874.

14. Military Department. Nos. 1608–9. May 1891. Intelligence Reconnaisance.

15. Foreign Department. Secret F. Pros. 160–9. Noted signed L. December 30, 1892.

16. Dunmore, The Earl of, *The Pamirs*. A narrative of a year's expedition on horseback and on foot through Kashmir, Western Tibet, Chinese Tartary and Russian Central Asia. Volume 1, pp. 228–9. John Murray, 1893.

17. Memorandum by Lord Lansdowne, File, S.F. Oct. 1889, Nos 182–97.

18. Schlagintweit, H. A. and R., *Scientific Mission to India and High Asia* in 4 Volumes. Trubner, 1866–7.

19. Ibid., Volume 1, p. 50.

20. Hayward, G. W., R.G.S.J., Volume 40, 1870, pp. 38–39. *Journey from Leh to Yarkand and Kashgar.*

21. Drew, Frederick, *The Jummoo and Kashmir Territories*; A Geographical Account, p. 496. Stanford, 1875.

22. Johnson, W. H., R.G.S.J., Volume 37, 1867. *Report on Journey to Ilchi, the Capital of Khotan in Chinese Territory.*

23. Godwin-Austen, H. H., R.G.S.J., Volume 37, 1867, p. 347. *Notes on the Pangong Lake District of Ladakh* from a Journal made during a survey in 1863.

24. Ibid., p. 355.

25. Wellby, M. S., *Through Unknown Tibet*, p. 47. Lippincott, 1898.

26. Ibid., p. 49.

27. Malcolm, Lt., Letter in R.G.S.J., February 1897.

28. Carey, A. D., Proceedings of the R.G.S., Volume 9, 1887. *A Journey round Chinese Turkestan and along the Northern frontier of Tibet.*

29. Ibid.

30. Ibid.

31. Bower, Hamilton, *A Journey across Tibet*, p. 1. London, 1894.

32. Deasy, H. H. P., R.G.S.J., Volume 16, 1900, p. 142. *Journeys in Central Asia.*

33. Ibid.

34. Ibid., p. 149.

35. Rawling, C. G., *The Great Plateau*, p. 38. London, 1905.

36. Hedin, Sven, *Southern Tibet,* Volume 4, Chapter III.

37. Cayley, Dr H., L.F.I. Volume 7, 1870. *Karakorum and Chang-tang*. Report dated June 21, 1870.

38. Report of the Great Trigonometrical Survey of India, 1866, p. 6.

39. P.C.I.D., Volume 91, 1867. Surveyor-General's Report, January 25, 1861.

40. P.C.I.D., Walker to Bayley, January 3, 1867.

41. Ibid., January 24, 1867.

42. Deasy, H. H. P., R.G.S.J., Volume 16. *Journeys in Central Asia.*

43. CR. Page 77.

44. Macartney, G., Kashgar Diary. F.O. 11/1255.

45. Clarke, E. H. S., Foreign Department, Secret F. Proceedings January, 1898. Nos 160–9.

46. Lyall, S. C., Note, dated July 15, 1898. Home Correspondence. Volume 178. Register 2072.

47. F.O. 17/1356, Elgin to Hamilton. No. 198 of October 27, 1898.

48. P.S.M. Nos. A 131–95. MacDonald to the Tsung-li Yamen. Peking March 14, 1899. For text see Appendix 7.

49. Ibid.

50. P.S.F., File 2426, (Pts 4, 5 and 6) 1912. Dane to Ritchie, July 4, 1907.

51. P.S.F., Par. 12. *Note on the History of the Boundary of Kashmir between Ladakh and Kashgaria.*

52. F.D., 535/15 Enclosure in No. 208. Kashgar. September 12, 1912.

53. Hudson, G. F., St Antony's Papers No. 14, *Far Eastern Affairs* No. 3. *The Aksai Chin*, p. 17.

54. Trinkler, Dr Emil, Himalayan Journal, Volumes 3 and 4, 1931–32, April 1931. *Notes on the Westernmost Plateau of Tibet.*

Chapter Four

WEST OF THE KARAKORUM: TRIANGULAR DIPLOMACY

1. Alder, G. J., *British India's Northern Frontier, 1865–1895*, p. 135. Longman's, 1963.

2. Wollaston, A. N., P.S.M. A.18. *Memorandum on Chitral including Frontier State of Gilgit and Yassin.* Oct. 8, 1878. Instructions to Capt. Biddulph on becoming Special Officer at Gilgit.

3. Lord Lytton, P.S.L.E.F.I. Volume 21, No. 49. February 28, 1879.

4. Younghusband, Sir F., *Routes from Russian Territory in Central Asia towards Afghanistan and India.* Section 1. The Pamir line of advance by W. R. Robertson 1893.

5. P.S.L., G.I., p. 357.

6. Knight, E. F., *Where Three Empires Meet,* Preface, p. 8. Longmans, Green, 1896.

7. Bayley, S. C. A. 83, P.S.M. *Note on the complication with Hunza,* July 1892. Par 10.

8. Ibid.

9. Ibid., par. 11.

10. Ibid.

11. Ibid., par. 15.

12. Ibid., par. 12.

13. Ibid., par. 16.

14. Correspondence in regard to the Pamir Frontier. No. 3 Cunningham to Neel. October 30, 1890.

15. Younghusband, Sir F. E., Foreign Dept. Secret F. Proceedings, March 1891, par. 16. Proceedings of Capt. F. E. Younghusband since his deputation in 1890 to Chinese Turkestan.

16. Correspondence in regard to the Pamir Frontier. October 1891 Encl. in No. 1 Lansdowne to Cross July 14, 1890.

17. Ibid.

18. Ibid., Encl. 1 in No. 4. Lansdowne to Cross, March 11, 1891.

19. P.S.H.C., Volume 126, p. 107. India Office to F.O. November 27, 1891.

20. Knight, E. F., Op. cit., p. 382.

21. Younghusband, Sir F. E., Correspondence in regard to the Pamir Frontier. Younghusband to Gov. of India, November 18, 1891.

22. Ibid.

23. P.S.C.H., Volume 128, Encl. with 22. Salisbury to Walsingham.

24. Alder, G. J., *British India's Northern Frontier* op. cit., footnote, p. 242.

25. Foreign Dept., Secret F. Proceedings October 1893. *Boundary between Kashmir and Chinese Turkestan.* Macartney to Resident in Kashmir July 23, 1893.

26. Parliamentary Papers, Volume 109, CMD 7643, 1895. *Agreement between the Governments of Great Britain and Russia with regard to the spheres of influence of the two countries in the region of the Pamirs, March 11, 1895.*

27. P.S.M., A. 160. *Frontier between Hunza and the Chinese Dominions.* Telegram to Viceroy, August 16, 1895.

28. P.S.M., India Letter No. 186, September 25, 1895.

29. P.S.M., Letter from F.O., June, 1896.

30. Ardagh, Sir John, Ardagh Papers, PRO. /0/40/14. Also FO/17/1328. *The Northern Frontier of India from the Pamirs to Tibet.* January 1, 1897. See Appendix 5.

31. F.O.17/1361. Director of Military Intelligence to F.O. Kashgar, July 18, 1898.

32. Ibid., Viceroy to F.O. Kashgar, July 20, 1898.

33. I.O.L. P.S.M., A.160 op. cit. Letter to F.O. December 1, 1898.

34. Ibid.

35. Ibid., Appendix op. cit.

36. F.O. 17/1373, No. 81. Macdonald to Bax-Ironside, Peking, April 7, 1899.

37. Lamb, Alastair, *The China-India Border*, pp. 168–76. Op. cit.

38. F.O. 405/85, No. 101 Bax-Ironside to Salisbury, Peking, April 18, 1899.

39. F.O./405/85, Enclosure in No. 251. Gov. of India to Hamilton, May 1, 1899.

40. Curzon Papers, India Office Library. Eur. MSS. D/510/1 Curzon to Hamilton. May 10, 1899.

41. Ibid.

42. F.O. 405/85, No. 472. Bax-Ironside to Salisbury. June 23, 1899.

43. Curzon Papers, Op. cit. Eur. MSS. D/5L 031. Curzon to Hamilton.

44. Ibid.

45. I.O.L. P.S.M., Gov. of India's Secret Letter No. 70. March 24, 1904. Quoted in A.170. Pt. 2. par. 7.

46. Ibid., par. 8.

47. I.O.L. P.S.M., A. 170 par. 8. Broderick's telegram. August 9, 1904.

48. I.O.L. P.S.M., A. 170 par. 11. Gov. of India's letter 371/05. Terms of proposed settlement.

49. I.O.L. P.S.M., A. 170 par 14. Jordan to Grey. No. 471, November 13, 1906.

50. I.O.L. P.S.M., A. 170 par. 16. Note by Macartney, August 13, 1911.

51. Rose, Archibald, A. 170. par 17 (summary); full text in P.S.D.B. D.174. *Report on the Chinese Frontiers of India*, October 3, 1911.

52. F.O.535/15., Memorandum respecting the situation in the countries bordering on the North-Eastern Frontier of India. Enclosure in No. 177 Gov. of India to Crewe. July 27, 1912.

53. Ibid.

54. Ibid.

55. F.O.535/15. Enclosure in No. 208. Gov. of India to Crewe. Kashgar, September 12, 1912.

56. *The Times*, March 6, 1963.

Chapter Five

CHINA AND BRITAIN ON THE FRONTIER OF INDIA: BRITAIN UNCHALLENGED

1. Elwin, Verrier, *India's North-East Frontier in the Nineteenth Century*, Introduction, pp. XV–XVI, Oxford University Press, 1959.

2. Holdich, T. H., *Tibet the Mysterious*, p. 336, op. cit.

3. Dalton, E. T., *Ethnology of Bengal*, p. 28, 1872.

4. Ibid., p. 36.

5. Wilcox, R., Asiatic Researches, 1832. Volume XVII. *Memoir of a Survey of Assam and the* Neighbouring countries, executed in 1825–1828.

6. Elwin, Verrier, op. cit.

7. Griffith, Dr William, J.A.S.B., 1837.

8. Rowlatt, E. W., J.A.S.B. Volume XIV, 1845. *Report of an Expedition into the Mishmee Hills to the north-east of Sudyah.*

9. Butler, John, *A Sketch of Assam*, 1847.

10. Elwin, Verrier, *India's North-East Frontier*, Introduction, p. xxviii. Op. cit.

11. Ibid., p. xxxi.

12. Shuckburgh, J. E., P.S.M. B.180. 1910. *North-Eastern Frontier of India.*

13. Ibid.

14. *Military Report on Assam* 1908.

15. Mackenzie, A., *History of the Relations of the Government with the Hill tribes of the North-Eastern Frontier of Bengal*, p. 43.

16. Dalton, E. T., *Ethnology of Bengal*, p. 34. Op. cit.

17. Elwin, Verrier, Quoted in *India's North-Eastern Frontier*, p. 168. Op. cit.

18. Mackenzie, op. cit., pp. 21–4.

19. Ibid.

20. Schuckburgh, J. E., P.S.M. B.180, 1910. *North-Eastern Frontier of India.*

21. Ibid.

22. Ibid.

23. Lamb, Alastair, Chatham House Essays, 2. *The China-India Border*, p. 127 Oxford University Press, 1964.

24. Needham, J. F., R.G.S. Supplementary Papers, ii 1889. *Journey along the Lohit Brahmaputra.*

25. Bailey, S. C., P.S.M. B.68. Note on Abor Expedition (Secret Letter from India No. 182 of October 3, 1894).

26. Report of Chief Commissioner, 231, Foreign Dept. Assam Secretariat, April 17, 1900.

27. Reid, Sir Robert, History of the frontier areas bordering Assam, pp. 207–8.

28. King, Louis, Pol. & Secret Dept. 1913. Volume 108, File 5062. Minute Paper, Register 379, King to Alston November 5, 1913.

29. FO/535/15, Encl. 2 of No. 320. *Memorandum respecting Chao Erh-Feng's effective administration in Eastern Tibet.*

30. Richardson, H. E., *Tibet and its History*, p. 98. Oxford University Press, 1962.

31. Ibid., p. 99.

32. Li Tieh-Tseng, *The Historical Status of Tibet*, p. 67. Op. cit.

33. Bell, Sir Charles, Bell Papers, I.O.L. Eur. MSS. F. 80.

34. Schuckburgh, J. E., P.S.M. B.177. *Chinese 'Forward' Policy on The North-Eastern Frontier of India.* November 2, 1910.

35. Bell, Sir Charles, Bell to Gov. of India in the Foreign Dept. August 26, 1910. Encl. 3 in Secret Despatch 182, dated December 22, 1910 from India to Secretary of State.

36. Ibid.

37. Ibid.

38. Ibid.

39. Ibid.

40. Foreign Dept. 1910 External Files, No. 182, December 22, 1910. *Hardinge to Crewe.*

41. Ibid.

42. Ibid.

43. Bailey, F. M., Pol. & Secret Dept. 1910. Volume 16 File 1918. Pts. 5, 6 and 7.

44. Ibid.

45. Schuckburgh, J. E., P.S.M. B.189. *Chinese Activity on the Mishmi Border.* September 9, 1912 par. 1.

46. Ibid., par. 3.

47. Ibid., par. 4.

48. Ibid., par. 5.

49. Ibid., Appendix to B. 189 op. cit. par. 2.

50. Ibid., par. 3.

51. Ibid., par. 6.

52. Ibid., par. 9.

53. Political and Secret Files 1918, Part 2, Annexure E. Notes by Mr Dundas on (i) the North-East Frontier and (ii) political results of the Mishmi Mission.

54. Ibid.

55. Stansfield, Major C., *The Road to Rima.* Shillong, 1914.

56. O'Callaghan, T. P. M., P.S.R. 1913 File 732. Volume 28 Reg. 4745. Reid to India. May 6, 1914.

57. Reid, Sir Robert, *History of the Frontier Areas,* op. cit. quoting Eastern Bengal and Assam Secretariat, Political, A., p. 220.

58. Hirtzl, Sir Arthur, Political and Secret Files, Volume 13, 1910.

59. Viceroy to Secretary of State, June 29, 1911., *Operations against Abors,* Cd. 5961, 1911.

60. Ibid.

61. Montague, the Hon. E. S., *Hansard.* Nov. 7, 1911. Cols 1457, 1458.

62. General Staff, India. 1913., Official Account of the Abor Expedition, 1911–1912. Quoted by Reid, p. 231.

63. Reid, Sir Robert, *History of the Frontier,* op. cit., p. 238.

64. Ibid., p. 242.

65. E.S.L.F.I., No. 235 of 1847. Enclosing Jenkins to Bushby No. 73, Gauhati, August 19, 1847.

66. Lamb, Alastair, *The China-India Border,* op. cit. p. 121.

67. O'Connor, W. F. Capt., Report on Tibet. August 24, 1903.

68. See Appendix 9.

69. Nevill, G. A. Capt., Military Report, India General Staff. Also see P.S.D. 1913. File 732. Volume 28. Register 3461.

Chapter Six

NORTH-EAST FRONTIER: PRELUDE TO SIMLA

1. Lamb, Alastair, *The McMahon Line,* Volume 2, p. 279 and p. 385.

2. Wolpert, S. A., Morley and India 1906–10, p. 93. C.U.P., 1967.

3. P.S.F. 1910, No. 1918, Pt. 1. F.O. to I.O. No. 41263/11. October 26, 1911.

4. F.O. 371/1065. No. 1773-E-B. McMahon to Bower, September 25, 1911.

5. Ibid.

6. F.O. 371/1065. No. 35166. Clarke to Weir, August 15, 1911.

7. P.S.F. 1910, No. 1918. Pt. 2, Hirtzel to Ritchie April 26, 1912.

8. F.O. 371/1065. No. 39762. Encl. in No. 1. Hardinge to Crewe, September 21, 1911.

9. Ibid.

10. F.O. 371/1065.

11. P.S.F. 1910. This includes all these reports No. 1918 Pt. 2. W. J. Reid to Government of India, July 7, 1912.

12. F.O. 371/1326, No. 24384. Jordan to Grey. Encl. 5 in No. 1 April 21, 1912. Note by Military Attache on the route laid down for the Chinese Survey Party despatched to survey the Anglo-Tibetan Border from the Dihang to the Salween.

13. P.S.F. 1910, No. 1918 Pt. 2. W. J. Reid to Government of India. July 7, 1912. See Appendix 9 for text.

14. Journal of the Royal Society of Arts. February 23, 1912. Volume LX.

15. P.S.F. 1910, No. 1918 Pt. 2. Annexure E. Notes by Mr Dundas. Political Results of the Mishmi Mission.

16. P.S.F. 1910, No. 1918. Pt. 2. Secretary of State to Viceroy. Nov. 8, 1911. Register 1493.

17. F.O./535/15, Gov. of India to Crewe, Memorandum signed J.D.G. Sept. 1, 1912.

18. F.O./535/15, No. 29. Extract from Note of Conversation between the Marquess of Crewe and M. Sazonof at Crewe Hall, September 29, 1912.

19. F.O. 371/1609, No. 4477, Crewe to Grey, January 22, 1913.

20. F.O. 371/1329, No. 51749. I.O. to F.O. December 3, 1912.

21. F.O. 371/1909, 1052. Gov. of India to Crewe. Encl. in No. 1. January 4, 1913.

22. F.O. 371/1909, 1162. Grey to Jordan, January 11, 1913.

23. F.O. 371/1610, 20247. Encl. 1 in No. 1 India to Crewe. April 30, 1913.

24. F.O. 371/1611, 27455. Jordan to Grey, May 29, 1913.

25. Ibid.

26. F.O. 371/1612, 33233. Alston to Grey, July 2, 1913.

27. F.O. 371/1612, 34848. Encl. in No. 1. India to Crewe, June 27, 1913.

28. F.O. 371/1612, 36258. Alston to Grey, August 5, 1913.

29. F.O. 371/1612, 36932. Alston to Grey. August 10, 1913.

30. F.O. 371/1612, From Viceroy, July 18, 1913.

31. Bell, Sir Charles, *Tibet Past and Present*, p. 152.

32. P.S.F. 1913, Volume 69. Register 7. 2350. Lu Hsing Chi to Peking, May 13, 1913.

33. P.S.F. 1913, Register 2572. Dalai Lama to Lu Hsing Chi June 4, 1913.

34. P.S.F. 1913, Register 3096. Lu Hsing Chi to President and Cabinet. June 23, 1913.

35. P.S.F. 1913, Register 4272. Lu Hsing Chi to Peking. September 4, 1913.

Chapter Seven

CONFERENCE AT SIMLA

1. J.R.S.A., No. 4330, November 15, 1935. Sir A. McMahon *International Boundaries*.

2. FO/371/1326, No. 14134, File 149. April 3, 1912. Note on Conversation between McMahon and Lonchen Shatra at F.O. Calcutta, on February 28, 1912.

3. P.S.F. 1913, Pt. III. Register 5014, Sir A. McMahon, Progress Memorandum October 6–November 20, 1913.

4. Bell, Sir Charles, *Tibet Past and Present*, p. 158. Clarendon Press, 1924.

5. Ibid., p. 64

6. Ibid., p. 152.

7. Pol. and Secret Dept., Volume 69. 1913. Register 3096. Lu Hsing Chi to President and Cabinet. June 23, 1913.

8. Bell, Sir Charles, Op. Cit. pp. 152–4.

9. P.S.F. 1913, Loc. Cit. Progress Memorandum, November 21–December 24, 1913.

10. Jordan to Grey. F.O. 371/1329.

11. Li, Tieh-Tseng, *The Historical Status of Tibet,* p. 249, note 232. op. cit.

12. P.S.F. 1913, Memorandum regarding progress of negotiations, October 6–November 20, 1913.

13. P.S.F. 1913, Progress Memorandum, October 6–November 20.

14. P.S.F. 1913, Progress Memorandum, October 6–November 20.

15. P.S.F. 1913, Progress Memorandum, November 21–December 24.

16. Ibid.

17. Teichman, Sir Eric, *Travels of a Consular Officer in Eastern Tibet,* Map 3. C.U.P., 1922.

18. P.S.F. 1913, Progress Memorandum November 21–December 24, 1913.

19. Pol. and Secret Dept. 1913, No. 2350, Volume 69. Register 537. December 29, 1913. Lu Hsing Chi to Military Governor, Chengtu.

20. FO 371/1931, Progress Memorandum December 25, 1913–April 30, 1914.

21. Ibid.

22. Ibid.

23. F.O. 371/1931. Minute by Sir A. Hirtzl.

24. P.S.F. 1913, File 464 Pt. IV Register 1215. Verbal statement by Ivan Chen; communicated March 7, 1914, handed to Tibetan Plenipotentiary, March 8, 1914.

25. Ibid.

26. Ibid.

27. P.S.F. 1913, Verbal statement by Lonchen Shatra, communicated March 5, 1914. Handed to Ivan Chen, March 7, 1914.

28. P.S.F. 1913, Verbal statement by Sir H. McMahon, communicated by Rose to Chen, March 9, 1914.

29. Ibid.

30. F.O. 371/1931.

31. Ibid.

32. F.O. 371/1612, Lu Hsing Chi to Peking.

33. Progress Memorandum, December 25, 1913 to April 30, 1914.

34. Ibid.

35. F.O. 371/1931, Ibid.

36. Ibid.

37. Ibid.

38. Ibid.

39. F.O. 535/17. Jordan to Grey, April 30, 1914.

40. F.O. 371/1930, No. 28677. Viceroy to Secretary of State, June 23, 1914.

41. P.S.F. 1913, File 464 Pts. 5 and 6 Register 2565. McMahon to Viceroy, June 30, 1914.

42. Ibid.

43. F.O. 371/1931 No. 30064/14, Alston, India Telegram, July 2, 1914.

44. Progress Memorandum, May 1 – July 8, 1914.

45. F.O. 371/1931. Encl. No. 1 in No. 30192. Crewe to India, July 1, 1914.

46. F.O. 371/1931. Encl. No. 1 in No. 30487. Crewe to India, July 2, 1914.

47. F.O. 371/1931. Encl. No. 1. in No. 30825. Crewe to India, July 3, 1914.

48. P.S.F. 1913. Pts. 5 and 6. File 464. Register 2593.

49. Progress Memorandum, May 1 – July 8, 1914.
50. Ibid.
51. Lamb, Alastair, *The McMahon Line* Volume 2, p. 520 (note), Routledge & Kegan Paul, 1966
52. Bell Papers I.O.L. Eur Mss F. 80.
53. Ibid.
54. Ibid.
55. Ibid.
56. Jordan Papers, F.O. 350/12. Jordan to Langley, June 28, 1914.
57. Bell Papers, I.O.L. Eur Mss. F. 80.
58. P.S.F. 1913. File 464, Pts. 5 and 6.
59. Ibid.
60. F.O. 371/1610, No. 16537. F.O. to I.O. April 30, 1913.
61. Jordan Papers, F.O. 350/12. Langley to Jordan, November 18, 1914.

Chapter Eight

WHAT HAPPENED TO THE MCMAHON LINE?

1. P.S.M. 1913, File 464, Pts. 5 and 6. Register 2891. Wai-Chiao Pu to Jordan. July 6, 1914.
2. P.S.M. 1913, File 5062, Pt. 3 Jordan to Chinese Minister, Foreign Affairs, September 19.
3. Bell, Sir Charles, *Tibet Past and Present*, 1924. Op. cit., pp. 245–57.
4. Dalai Lama to McMahon, November 21, 1914.
5. P.S.M. 1913, File 5062, Pt. 3. Dalai Lama to President of China. Encl. in Bell to India.
6. F.O. 228/2588, Jordan to Gov. of India, Tel. 179.
7. F.O. 535/18, Bell to India. Sikkim, August 6, 1915.
8. F.O. 535/18, India to Bell. Simla, September 3, 1915.
9. Ibid.
10. F.O. 535/20, Alston to Balfour, June 2, 1917.
11. Teichman, Sir E., *Travels of a Consular Officer in Eastern Tibet*, 1922.
12. Richardson, H. E., *Tibet and its History*, op. cit., p. 120.
13. F.O. 228/2962, No. 253. Jordan to Curzon, June 1, 1919.
14. Ibid.
15. F.O. 535/22, No. 82499. Jordan to Curzon, May 31, 1919.
16. Bell, Sir Charles, *Tibet Past and Present*, op. cit., p. 176.
17. Ibid., pp. 244–6.
18. F.O. 228/2962, No. 253. Jordan to Curzon, Peking, June 1, 1919.
19. F.O. 228/2962, Memorandum to Chinese Minister. August 26, 1921.
20. F.O. 228/2962, No. 824. Wellesley to Alston. Foreign Office, August 26, 1921.
21. F.O. 535/26, Report of Lhasa Mission, 1920–1921.

22. Li Tsieng-Li, *The Historical Status of Tibet,* op. cit. pp. 151–5.

23. Richardson, H. E., *Tibet and its History*, op. cit. 156.

24. Bell, Sir Charles, *Portrait of the Dalai Lama*, 1946, p. 379.

25. Richardson, H. E., *Tibet and its History*, p. 143 and Li Tsieng-li, pp. 168–172.

26. Ibid.

27. Bell, Sir Charles, Bell Papers. I.O.L., op. cit. Eur. MSS. F.80.

28. Reid, Sir R., *History of the Frontier Areas*, op. cit. p. 249.

29. Ibid., p. 254.

30. Ibid., p. 259.

31. Ibid., pp. 292–3.

32. P.Z. 3176/1937, Minute Paper. Pol. Dept.

33. P.Z. 3176/1937, Trade Agent, Lhasa to Foreign Dept. Delhi, November, 1935.

34. D.O. D 5300–X/35, Caroe to Hutton. Pol. and Secret Collection, No. 36, File 23, Delhi, November 28, 1935.

35. P.Z. 2785/36, Caroe to Walton. Pol. and Secret Collection; For. and Pol. Dept., April 9, 1936.

36. D.O. F 493–X/35, Caroe to Dawson. Pol. (External) Dept. Collections, No. 36, File 23. For. and Pol. Dept. February 6, 1936.

37. P.Z. 6153/36, F 493–X 35, Gov. of India to India Office, FO 371. Simla, August 17, 1936.

38. Reid, Sir R., *History of the Frontier Areas*, op. cit., p. 295.

39. Ibid., p. 296.

40. Ibid.

41. Reid Papers, I.O.L.

42. Mills, J. P., *Problems of the Assam-Tibet Frontier* J.R.C.A.S., 1950.

43. Ibid.

44. Mainprice, F. P., Mainprice Diary, R.G.S. Library.

45. Ibid.

46. Ibid.

47. Reid, Sir Robert, *History of the Frontier Areas Bordering on Assam*, op. cit., p. 261.

48. Ibid., p. 262.

49. von Furer-Haimendorf, C., *Tour Diaries 1944/45 of the Speical Officer.* Shillong. 1947. RGS Library.

50. Ibid.

Chapter Nine

INDEPENDENCE AND CHALLENGE (1947–1951)

1. Richardson, H. E., *Tibet and its History*. O.U.P. 162. p. 173.

2. Menon, V. P., *The Transfer of Power in India*, Longmans, Green & Co., 1957. Appendix XI. p. 516.

3. White Paper II, Nehru to Chou En-lai, September 28, 1959, p. 39.
4. Richardson, H. E., op. cit., p. 174.
5. White Paper II, Nehru to Chou En-lai, September 28, 1959, p. 39.
6. Ibid.
7. Richardson, H. E., op. cit. p. 174.
8. *The Chinese Threat*, Ministry of Information, New Delhi, 1963. (Appendix VI.)
9. *Jen Min Jih Pao*, August 1947.
10. Li, Tieh-Tseng, *The Historical Status of Tibet*. King's Crown Press. Columbia University. 1956, p. 198.
11. *The Communist* – Bombay, January 1950.
12. *New York Times*, August 16, 1950.
13. Richardson, H. E., op. cit., p. 179.
14. Panikkar, K. M., *In Two Chinas*. Memoirs of a diplomat. Allen & Unwin, 1955. p. 102.
15. *India News Bulletin*, November 14, 1950. Gov. of India to Foreign Minister of China. October 26, 1950.
16. *India News Bulletin*, People's Republic of China to Gov. of India. October 30, 1950.
17. *India News Bulletin*, Gov. of India to Foreign Minister of China. October 31, 1950.
18. Richardson, H. E., op. cit., p. 186.
19. Lok Sabha Debates, December 1950.
20. Lok Sabha Debates, December 1950.
21. Seton, Marie, *Panditji*: A Portrait of Jawaharlal Nehru. Dobson, 1967, p. 363.
22. *Hsinhua News Agency*, May 1951.
23. *The Statesman* (Calcutta), May 29, 1951.
24. *Manchester Guardian*, June 9, 1951.
25. *New York Times*, August 28, 1951.
26. *The Times*, September 24, 1952.
27. Nehru to Council of State, September 23, 1953.
28. Lok Sabha Debate, May 15, 1954.
29. *The Sino-Indian Agreement of Tibet,* signed April 29, 1954.
30. *Amrita Bazar Patrika*, June 7, 1954.
31. *National Herald*, May 1, 1954.
32. *Times of India*, May 1, 1954.
33. *Pioneer*, May 1, 1954.
34. Woodman, Dorothy, *The Making of Burma*, 1962, p. 527.
35. Report of Bandung Conference.
36. White Paper I, Nehru to Chou En-lai. December 14, 1958, p. 49.
37. *The Hindu*, December 14, 1967.
38. White Paper I, Ministry of External Affairs, India, p. 60. China to India, July 10,1958.
39. Ibid., India to China, July 2, 1958, p. 22.
40. Ibid., India to China, November 8, 1959, p. 29.
41. Ibid., India to China, January 17, 1959, p. 33.

42. Ibid., India to China, August 21, 1958, p. 46.
43. Ibid., Memo by Foreign Office of China to India. November 3, 1958, p. 47.
44. Ibid., Chou En-lai to Nehru. January 23, 1959, p. 52.
45. Ibid., p. 53-4.
46. Ibid., p. 54.
47. George, T. J. S., *Krishna Menon*. Jonathan Cape, 1964, p. 221.
48. Ibid., p. 221.
49. *Seminar*, July 1962.
50. Lok Sabha Debates, March 30, 1959.
51. White Paper I, Chinese Ambassador to Foreign Secretary, May 16, 1959, p. 76.
52. White Paper I, Foreign Secretary to Chinese Ambassador, May 23, 1959, p. 78.
53. Lok Sabha Debates, September 4, 1959.
54. Ibid.
55. Ibid.
56. Ibid.
57. Ibid.
58. Ibid.
59. *Hsinhua News Agency,* September 16, 1969.
60. Ibid.
61. Ibid.
62. Meeting of Congress workers, Meerut. October 24, 1959.
63. *Indian Express*, October 26, 1959.

Chapter Ten

ALL REASON SPENT

1. *The Hindu*, October 29, 1959.
2. Ibid., November 2, 1959.
3. Ibid.
4. Nehru at a Press Conference, New Delhi, November 5, 1959.
5. Lok Sabha Debate, Nehru's speech printed in India-China Relations. Ministry of Information. November 27, 1959.
6. Ibid.
7. White Paper II, Nehru to Chou En-lai, September 26, 1959, p. 45.
8. *The New Age*, October 1959. Quoted in *The Hindu*, October 3, 1959.
9. *New York Times*, November 13, 1959.
10. White Paper III, Chou En-lai to Nehru, November 7, 1959, p. 46.
11. Ibid., Nehru to Chou En-lai, November 16, 1959, p. 48.
12. Ibid., p. 50.
13. *The Times*, November 23, 1959.
14. Fisher, Rose and Huttenback, *Himalayan Battleground*, 1963, p. 89.

15. White Paper III, Chou En-lai to Nehru, December 17, 1959, p. 53.

16. Ibid., Nehru to Chou En-lai, December 21, 1959. p. 58.

17. White Paper II, Nehru to Chou En-lai, September 26, 1959, p. 35.

18. White Paper III, Chou En-lai to Nehru, December 17, 1959. p. 54.

19. White Paper III, Note given by the Ministry of Foreign Affairs of China to the Embassy of India in China, December 26, 1959, p. 63.

20. Ibid., p. 66.

21. Ibid., pp. 66–7.

22. Ibid., p. 67.

23. Ibid., pp. 67–8.

24. Ibid., p. 70.

25. Ibid., p. 70.

26. Ibid., p. 75.

27. Ibid., p. 75.

28. *The Hindu*, April 7, 1960.

29. Ibid., April 26, 1960.

30. Ibid.

31. Lok Sabha Debates, April 29, 1960.

32. Officials' Report, M.E.A. Gov. of India, 1961. Chinese Report, p. 3–4.

33. Lamb, Alastair, *The Simla Conference and the McMahon Line,* op. cit. Volume 2, p. 590.

34. Caroe, Sir Olaf, *Indian Case for McMahon Line,* The Guardian, February 13, 1960.

35. Official's Report, Indian Report, p. 283.

36. Ibid., p. 236.

37. Ibid., p. 37.

38. Ibid., p. 38.

39. Officials' Report, Chinese Report, p. 7.

40. Lok Sabha Debate, *Prime Minister on Sino-Indian Relations,* September 4, 1959.

41. Francke, A. H., *Antiquities of Indian Tibet,* Archeological Survey of India, Volume II, pp. 116–117.

42. Officials' Report, Indian Report, p. 53.

43. Officials' Report, Chinese Report, p. 15.

44. Ibid., Op. cit. p. 15.

45. E.S.L., Davis to Hardinge, August 12, 1847, Volume 114.

46. Officials' Report, Chinese Report, pp. 15–16.

47. Ibid., Indian Report, p. 54.

48. Ibid., Chinese Report, p. 15.

49. F.O. 17

50. Ibid., Indian Report, p. 55.

51. Ibid., Chinese Report, pp. 16–17.

52. Huttenback, Robert A., *A Historical Note on the Sino-Indian Dispute over the Aksai Chin.* The China Quarterly, No. 18, April/June 1964, p. 204.

53. van Eekelen, W. F., *Indian Foreign Policy and the Border Dispute with China.* Martinus Nijhoff, 1964, p. 162.

54. F.O. Confidential Print, *Affairs of Tibet and Mongolia,* 1912.

55. Officials' Report, Chinese Report.
56. Ibid., Indian Report, p. 137.
57. Ibid., Chinese Report, p. 75.
58. Ibid., Indian Report, p. 143.
59. Ibid.
60. Officials' Report, Chinese Report, p. 80.
61. Fisher, Rose and Huttenback, Op. cit., pp. 124–5.
62. Ibid., p. 126.
63. Officials' Report, Chinese Report,p. 84.
64. Ibid., p. 86.
65. Ibid., p. 88.
66. Ibid., p. 90.
67. *The Hindu*, February 15, 1961.
68. Rajya Sabha Debate, August 23, 1961.
69. Lok Sabha Debate, November 28, 1961.
70. Ibid.
71. White Paper VI, M.F.A. to Embassy of India in China. December 3, 1961, p. 188.
72. Ibid., M.E.A. to Embassy of China in India, December 15, 1961, pp. 189–90.
73. Ibid., M.E.A. to Embassy of China in India, May 14, 1962, p. 43.
74. White Paper VI, M.F.A. to Embassy of India in China, June 2, 1962, pp. 56–8.
75. Ibid., July 8, 1962.
76. White Paper VII, Delhi to Peking, July 26, 1962, p. 4.
77. Ibid., Peking to Delhi, August 4, 1962, p. 17.
78. Lok Sabha Debate, August 14, 1962.

Chapter Eleven

TALKING AND FIGHTING—SEPTEMBER 1962–MAY 1964

1. Thimayya, General K. S., *Chinese Aggression and After*, International Studies. Volume V, July/October, 1963.
2. Kaul, General B. M., *The Untold Story*, p. 357.
3. Ibid., p. 363.
4. White Paper VIII, Chou En-lai to Nehru, October 24, 1962, p. 1. Note accompanying letter, p. 3.
5. *Hsinhua News Agency*, October 24, 1962.
6. Ibid., Annexure to letter from Nehru to Chou En-lai, October 27, 1962, p. 6.
7. Ibid., Chou En-lai to Nehru, November 4, 1962, p. 8.
8. Ibid., Annexure to Nehru's letter to Chou En-lai, November 14, 1962, pp. 14–16.
9. *Pravda*, Editorial, October 25, 1962.

10. *The Hindu*, October 28, 1962.
11. *The Times*, 'Russian attitude changed', Monitor, November 7, 1962.
12. *The Hindu*, Kosygin's speech analysed by K. S. Shelvankar, November 8, 1962.
13. Ministry of External Affairs Publicity Division, *Indian Communists condemn Chinese aggression* with texts of resolution of the CPI. December 11, 1962.
14. *Renmin Ribao*, October 27, 1962.
15. White Paper VIII, Statement given by Chinese Government, November 21, 1962, p. 19.
16. *New Statesman*, November 30, 1962.
17. Bhargava, G. S., The Battle of N.E.F.A. Appendix ii, p. 175. Allied Publishers Private Ltd., 1964.
18. *The Sino–Indian Question*. Premier Chou En-lai's letter of November 15, 1962.
19. *White Paper VIII*, Memorandum by M.F.A. to Embassy of India in China. November 26, 1962, pp. 21–3. Chou En-lai to Nehru, November 28, 1962. p. 24.
20. Ibid., Nehru to Chou En-lai December 1, 1962. pp. 28–9.
21. Ibid., Memorandum by M.F.A. to Embassy of India in China, December, 8, 1962, pp. 34–5.
22. Lok Sabha Debate, December 10, 1962. Text of reply: Delhi to Peking, December 19, 1962.
23. White Paper IX, See Appendix, 'Letter from Mrs Bandanaraike and enclosures, pp. 184–7.
24. Ibid., Chou En-lai to Nehru, April 20, 1963, pp. 10–13
25. *The Hindu*, January 31, 1963.
26. White Paper IX, Chou En-lai to Nehru, April 20, 1963, p. 13.
27. Ibid., Peking to Embassy of India in China, April 20, 1953, p. 39.
28. *Hsinhua News Agency*.
29. Lok Sabha Debate, April 13, 1964.
30. A.I.C.C. Session, Bombay, May 17, 1964.

Chapter Twelve

UNDECIDED FRONTIERS: THE ETERNAL TRIANGLE

1. Gopal, Dr S., *India, China and the Soviet Union*. Australian Journal of Politics and History. August 1966. Volume XII, No. 2.
2. Hutheesing, Krishna, *Nehru's Letters to his Sister*, Faber & Faber, 1963, p. 95.
3. Gopal, Dr S., Op. cit.
4. Kahin, Prof. G. M., Report of Bandung Conference, p. 60.
5. UN u, Burmese Parliamentary Debates, March 9, 1952.
6. *People's Daily*, Peking, February 1, 1960.
7. *Dawn*, Karachi, January 22, 1960.

8. *Dawn*, Karachi, January 25, 1960.

9. Khan, President Ayub, Foreign Affairs (U.S.A.), July, 1960.

10. *Dawn*, Interview with Associated Press, April 11, 1963.

11. *The Times*, March 4, 1963.

12. White Paper VI, M.E.A. Delhi to Chinese Embassy, May 10, 1962, p. 96.

13. Ibid., M.F.A. Peking to Indian Embassy in Peking, May 31, 1962, p. 99.

14. *The Times*, June 21, 1965.

15. *The Times*, June 21, 1965.

16. Ibid.

17. Lamb, Dr Alastair, *Crisis in Kashmir*, Routledge & Kegan Paul, 1967, pp. 118–9.

18. *The Times*, September 10, 1965.

19. *People's Daily*, September 18, 1965.

20. *New York Herald Tribune, A Warning to China* by Rowland Evans and Robert Novak, September 18, 1965.

21. *People's Daily*, September 18, 1965.

22. Lok Sabha Debate, September 21, 1965.

23. Rowland, John, *A History of Sino-Indian Relations*: Hostile Coexistence D. van Nostrand, 1967, pp. 74–5.

24. van Eekelen, W. F., *Indian Foreign Policy and the Border Dispute with China*, Njjhoff, 1964.

25. *Foreign Affairs (U.S.A.)*, April 1863, pp. 453–65.

26. Watson, Francis, *The Frontiers of China*, op. cit. p. 28.

27. *The Hindu*, August 7, 1965.

28. Ibid.

Bibliography

Primary Sources

The documentation for this book has been studied in the India Office Library; the Public Records Office and the Library of the Royal Geographical Society in London and in the National Archives in New Delhi.

The main series consulted in the India Office Library were: Collections to India Political Despatches; Secret Letters and Enclosures from India and Madras; Political and Secret Letters received from India; Political and Secret Despatches to India; Enclosures to Secret Letters from India; India Foreign and Political Secret Proceedings; Political and Secret Department Library and Political and Secret Department Memoranda. (Much of the material included in the last two categories is contained in the record volumes above.)

Political and Secret Memoranda

The following Political and Secret Memoranda were particularly valuable:

A 18	1878	A. N. Wollaston	Chitral, Gilgit, Yassin, Part 1.
	1881	A. N. Wollaston	Ibid. Part 2.
A 79	1888	Departmental Note	India Frontier Policy, with remarks by Sir W. Lockhart on the Hindu Kush Passes.
A 82	1891	S. C. Bayley	The Pamir question and the N.E. Frontier of Afghanistan.
A 86 A	1892	S. C. Bayley	The Russian expedition to the Pamirs of 1892.
A 87	1892	S. C. Bayley	Alichur Pamir; Chinese and Afghan territorial claims.
A 95	1895	F. E. Younghusband	Northern Frontier of India; Roads and Passes.
A 135	1898	R. P. Cobbold	Report on his journeys on the Pamirs and in Chinese Turkistan.
B 68	1894	S. C. Bayley	Note on Abor Expedition.
B 177	1910	J. E. Shuckburgh	Chinese 'Forward Policy on The North-East Frontier of India'.
B 189	1912	J. E. S. (Shuckburgh)	Chinese Activity on the Mishmi Border.
B 324	1919	J. E. S. (Shuckburgh)	Tibet.
C 14	1876	T. D. Forsyth	Mission to Yarkand.
C 15	1876	A. W. Moore	Mission to Yarkand with notes by others.

M

C 19   1877   China and Kashgar.
C 101   1899   E. F. H. McSwiney   Summary of information obtained
                                          during a recent journey through
                                          Central Asia and Chinese Turkestan.

Private Papers in India Office Library

Curzon Papers.   Eur. MSS. F.111.
Bell Papers.   Eur. MSS. F.80.
Elgin Papers.   Eur. MSS. F.84.
Moorcroft Papers.   Eur. MSS. 5 263: D.256, D.260, D.245, D.261.
                        Eur. MSS. C.42: G.28.
Lansdowne Papers.   Eur. MSS. D.558.

Public Record Office

Documentary Series: F.O. 17 (China); F.O. 65 (Russia) and F.O. 371 (General);
    F.O. 535, Foreign Office Confidential Print series.
Private Papers.
Ardagh Papers – The correspondence of Sir John Ardagh: PRO/30/40.
Jordan-Langley correspondence: F.O. 350/12.

Indian Official Publications

Notes, Memoranda and letters exchanged between the Governments of India
and China. Published by Ministry of External Affairs, New Delhi, in 14 parts
covering 1954 to April 1968. No. 2 (September–November 1959 contains
a 'Note on the historical background of the Himalayan Frontier of India'.
Report of the Officials of the Governments of India and the People's Republic of
    China on the Boundary Question. Ministry of External Affairs, New Delhi,
    1962.
Also, printed separately, Concluding Chapter of the Report of the Indian
    Officials on the Boundary Question, 1962.
Parliament of India: Debates in the Lok Sabha and in the Rajya Sabha. *The
    Chinese Threat.* Ministry of Information and Broadcasting, January 1963.

Chinese Official Publications

The Sino-Indian Boundary Question. Foreign Languages Press, Peking, 1962.
Peking Review (Published weekly in English, French, Spanish, Japanese and
    German).
Mao Tse-tung: *Problems of War and Strategy.* Foreign Languages Press, Peking,
    1954.

Pakistan Official Publications

Ayub Khan, Field Marshal Mohammed, *Speeches and Statements.* Volumes
    I–VIII (1959–65).

Pakistan Perspective. Pakistan Embassy, Washington, 1964.
  The Pakistan-American Alliance: Stresses and Strains. Foreign Affairs. New York, 1964.
  The Crisis over Kashmir, 1965.
Bhutto, Zulfiqar Ali, *Speeches before the Security Council in 1964*. Ministry of Foreign Affairs, Karachi, 1965.
  The Quest for Peace. Selection of Speeches and writings, 1964–5. Pakistan Institute of International Affairs.
Department of Films and Publications Karachi, *Pakistan-China Boundary Agreement*. August, 1963.
  India Sets the Subcontinent Ablaze. September, 1965.
  Tashkent Declaration in Perspective. February, 1966.
Gauhar, Altaf, *The Tashkent Declaration and after*. Pakistan Publications Karachi, 1966.

Unofficial Pakistan Publications

Choudhry, G. W. and Hasan, Parvez, *Pakistan's External Relations*. Pakistan Institute of International Affairs. Karachi, 1958.
Isphani, M. A. H., *Pakistan Foreign Policy Yesterday and Today*, 1947–64. Thinker's Forum. Karachi, 1964.
Sherwani, Latif Ahmed and others, *Foreign Policy of Pakistan – An Analysis*. Allies Books Corporation, Karachi, 1964.
Sherwani, Latif Ahmed, *India, China and Pakistan*. Council of Pakistan Studies Karachi.
Siddiqi, Aslam, *A Path for Pakistan*. History of Pakistan with special emphasis on current affairs.

International Publications

The Question of Tibet and the Rule of Law. International Commission of Jurists, Geneva, 1959.
Tibet and the Chinese People's Republic. A Report to the International Commission of Jurists by its Legal Enquiry Committee on Tibet. International Commission of Jurists, Geneva 1960.
United Nations General Assembly, 5th Session, Official Records Genera Committee 73rd meeting. U.N. Publications, New York.

Books Published in India Since 1947

Bagchi, P. C., *India and Central Asia* National Council of Education, Bengal. Calcutta, 1955.
Bains, J. S., *India's International disputes*. A legal study. Asia Publishing House, 1962.
Bhargava, G. S., *The Battle of N.E.F.A.* The undeclared war. Allied Publishers Private Limited, 1964.
Chakravarti, P.C., *India-China Relations*. Firma K. L. Mukhopadhyay, Calcutta, 1961.

Chaliha, Parag., *The Outlook on N.E.F.A.* Asam Sahitya Sabha. Calcutta, 1958.
Dutta, Parul., *The Tangsas of the Namchik and Tirap Valleys.* North-East Frontier Agency, Shillong, 1959.
Elwin, Verrier, *A Philosophy for N.E.F.A.* (foreword by the Prime Minister of India). North-East Frontier Agency, Shillong, 1957.
Gajendragadkar, Dr P. B., *Kashmir-Retrospect and Prospect Patel Memorial Lecture.* University of Bombay, 1967.
Ghose, Kalobaran, *Chinese Invasion of India.* Mrs Banachhaya Ghose, Calcutta, 1963.
Gupta, Sisir, *Kashmir.* A study in India-Pakistan Relations. Asia Publishing House. Under auspices of the Indian Council of World Affairs, 1966.
Jain, Girilal, *India meets China in Nepal,* Asia Publishing House, 1958.
    Panchshee la and After. Asia Publishing House, 1959.
Kaul, B. M. General, *The Untold Story.* Allied Publishers Private Limited, 1967.
Nargolkar, Kusum, *In the Wake of the Chinese Thrust* (Foreword by Y. B. Chavan). Popular Prakashan, Bombay, 1965.
Rao, G. Narayana, *The India-China Border – a Reappraisal.* Asia Publishing House, 1967.
Sanghvi, Ramesh, *India's Northern Frontier and China.* Contemporary Publishers. Bombay, 1962.
Sen, Chanakya, *Tibet Disappears.* A documentary history of Tibet's international status, the great rebellion and its aftermath. Asia Publishing House, 1960.
Shukla, B. K., *The Daflas of the Subansiri Region.* North-East Frontier Agency, Shillong, 1959.
Varma, S. P., *Struggle for the Himalayas.* University Publishers, Jullundur, Ambala, Delhi, 1965.

A SHORT GENERAL LIST

The following books are indispensable for a study of the present relationt between India, China and the Soviet Union,

Alder, G. J., *British India's Northern Frontier* 1865–95. Published for the Royal Commonwealth Society by Longmans, 1963.
Elwin, Verrier, *A Philosophy for N.E.F.A.* Shillong, 1959.
    India's North-East Frontier in the Nineteenth Century. O.U.P., 1959.
Fisher, M. W., and J. B. Bondurant, *Indian views of Sino-Indian Relations.* Indian Press Digests. Monograph series, No. 1, University of California, 1956.
Fisher, M. W., L. E. Rose, and R. A. Huttenback, *Himalayan Battleground.* Pall Mall, London, 1963.
Hudson, G. F., *The Aksai Chin.* St Antony's Papers, No. 14. Far Eastern Affairs, 1963.
Watson, Francis, *The Frontiers of China.* Chatto & Windus, 1966.

A GENERAL LIST

Aitchison, Sir Charles, *A Collection of Treaties, Engagements and Sanads relating to India and neighbouring countries*. Volume 14. Gov. of India, 1929–33.

Anon., *The Boundary Question between China and Tibet*. Peking, 1940.

Bagchi, P. C., *India and China. A Thousand Years of Cultural Relations*. Hind Kitab, Bombay, 1950.

Bailey, F. M., *No Passport for Tibet*. 1957.
    China-Tibet-Assam. 1945.

Bains, J. S., *India's International Disputes. A legal study*. Asia Publishing House, 1962.

Barber, Noel, *The flight of the Dalai Lama*. Hodder & Stoughton, 1960.

Bell, Sir Charles, *Tibet; Past and Present*. Clarendon Press, 1924.
    Portrait of the Dalai Lama. Collins, 1942.

Boggs, S. W., *International Boundaries*. Columbia University Press, 1940.

Brecher, Michael, *Nehru; A Political Biography*. O.U.P., 1959.
    India and World Politics. O.U.P., 1968.

Buchan, Alastair (ed.), *China and the Peace of Asia*. Chatto & Windus, 1965.

Burrard, S. G., and H. H. Hayden, *A Sketch of the Geography and Geology of the Himalaya Mountains and Tibet*. Government of India, Delhi, 1933–4.

Cammann, S., *Trade through the Himalayas*. Princeton, 1951.

Candler, Edmund, *The Unveiling of Lhasa*. Thomas Nelson, 1905.

Chapman, F. S., *Lhasa; The Holy City*. 1940.

Crocker, W. R., *Nehru. A Contemporary's Estimate*. Allen & Unwin, 1966.

Cunningham, Sir A., *Ladakh, Physical, Statistical and Historical*. London, 1854.

Curzon, G. N., *Frontiers*. Romanes Lecture. Oxford, 1907.

Das, C. C., *Narrative of a Journey to Lhasa*. Calcutta, 1885.

Deasy, H. H. P., *In Tibet and Chinese Turkestan*.

Drew, Frederick, *The Jummoo and Kashmir Territories*. Edward Stanford, 1875.

Durrand, Algernon G. A., *The Making of a Frontier*. John Murray, 1900.

Filippi, F. de Desideri, *An account of Tibet*. Broadway Travellers, 1937.

Fitzgerald, C. P., *The Chinese view of their place in the world*. O.U.P., 1964.

Fleming, Peter, *Bayonets to Lhasa*. Hart-Davis, 1961.

Francke, A. H., *History of Western Tibet*. S. W. Partridge, 1907.

Fraser, James Baillie, *Journal of a tour through part of the Snowy range of the Himala Mountains and to the Sources of the Rivers Jumma and Ganges*. Rodwell and Martin, 1820.

Fuchs, W., *Der Jesuiten-Atlas der Kanghsi-Zeit*. Text and maps in 2 volumes. Peking, 1943.

Furer-Haimendorf, C. von, *Himalayan Barbary*. 1955.

Gould, Sir Basil, *The Jewel in the Lotus*. Chatto & Windus, 1957.

Hamilton, W., *A Geographical, Statistical and Historical description of Hindoostan*. London, 1820.

Harris, Richard, *Independence and after; Revolution in Underdeveloped Countries*. O.U.P., 1962.

Hedin, Sven, *Southern Tibet*. Lithographic Institute Swedish Army, 1916–22.

Jackson, W. A. D., *The Russo-Chinese Borderlands*. van Nostrand, Princeton, 1961.

Kahin, George McT., *The Asian-African Conference, Bandung 1955*. Cornell University Press, 1956.

Kennon, Major R. L., *Sport and Life in the Further Himalayas*. Blackwood & Sons, 1910.

Khan, Ayub, Field Marshal, *Friends not Masters* – A political autobiography. O.U.P., 1967.

Lama, Dalai, *My Land and my People*. Weidenfeld & Nicolson, 1962.

Lamb, Alastair, *The China–India Border*. The origins of the disputed boundaries O.U.P., 1964.

   The McMahon Line. A study in the relations between India, China and Tibet, 1904 to 1914. Volume 1: *Morley, Minto and Non-interference in Tibet*. Volume 2: *Hardinge, McMahon and the Simla Conference*. Routledge & Kegan Paul, 1966.

   Britain and Chinese Central Asia. The Road to Lhasa 1767–1905. Routledge & Kegan Paul, 1960.

Lattimore, Owen, *Studies in Frontier History*. Collected Papers 1928–58. O.U.P., 1962.

Li, Tieh-tsing, *Tibet. Today and Yesterday*. Revised with Introduction. Bookman Associates, New York, 1960. *The Historical Status of Tibet*, 1956.

Luard, Evan, *Britain and China*. Chatto & Windus, 1965.

Mackenzie, (Sir) Alexander, *History of Relations with the Hill Tribes of the N.E. Frontier of Bengal*. Calcutta, 1884.

Markham, Sir Clements R., *Memoir on the Indian Surveys*. Secretary of State for India in Council, 1878.

Mason, Kenneth, *Abode of Snow*. A History of Himalayan Exploration and Mountaineering. Hart-Davis, 1955.

Mehra, P. L. Prof. *The Younghusband Expedition; an Interpretation*. Asia Publishing House, 1969.

Menon, K. P. S., *Delhi-Chungking, a travel diary*. O.U.P., 1947.

Moorcroft, William, and Trebeck, *Travels in the Himalayan Provinces, etc*. John Murray, 1841.

Moraes, Frank, *The Revolt in Tibet*. Macmillan, 1960.

Nehru, Jawaharlal, *Spain and the war*. Kitabistan, 1940.

   Independence and after. A collection of speeches. 1946–9. John Day, New York, 1950.

   Jawaharlal Nehru's speeches, 1949–53 (Volume 1), 1953–57 (Volume 2). Publications Division, Delhi.

   The Discovery of India. Meridian, London, 1956.

   A Bunch of Old Letters. Asia Publishing House, 1958.

Panikkar, K. M., *The Founding of the Kashmir State*. A Biography of Maharajah Gulab Singh (1792–1858). Allen & Unwin, 1953.

   In Two Chinas. Memoirs of a Diplomat. Allen & Unwin, 1955.

   India and China. A study of cultural relations. Asia Publishing House, 1957.

Patterson, G. N., *Peking versus Delhi*. Faber, 1963.

Petech, Luciano, *China and Tibet in the Early eighteenth Century*. History of the

Establishment of Chinese Protectorate in Tibet. T'oung Pao Monograph 1. *A Study on the Chronicles of Ladakh.* Calcutta, 1931.

Brill, Leiden, 1950.

Radhakrishnan Sarvepalli, *India and China.* Lectures delivered in China, 1944. Hind Kitab, 1944.

Reid, Sir Robert, *History of the Frontier Areas bordering on Assam from 1883-1841.* Assam Gov. Press, Shillong, 1942.

Richardson, H. E., *Tibet and its History.* O.U.P., 1962.

Schlagintweit, H. A., and R. de, *Results of a Scientific Mission to India and High Asia.* Leipzig, 1861-6.

Schomberg, Col. R. C. F., *Unknown Karakorum.* M. Hopkinson, 1936.

Shakespear, C. W., *History of Upper Assam, Upper Burma and North East Frontier.* London, 1914.

Shen, T. L., and S. C. Liu, *Tibet and the Tibetans.* Stanford, 1953.

Snellgrove, David, *Buddhist Himalaya.* Cassirer, Oxford, 1957.

Stamp, Sir Dudley, *India, Pakistan, Ceylon and Burma.* Methuen.

Stephens, Ian, *Horned Moon.* Chatto & Windus, 1953.

Teichman, Sir Eric, *Travels of a Consular Officer in East Tibet.* Cambridge University Press, 1922.

Van Eekelen, W. F., *Indian Foreign Policy and the Border Dispute with China.* Martinu Nijhoff. The Hague, 1964.

Vigne, G. T., *Travels in Kashmir, Ladak, Iskardo and the countries adjoining the mountain-course of the Indus and the Himalaya north of the Punjab.* 2 Volumes. Colburn, 1842.

Ward, Barbara, *India and the West.* Hamilton, 1961.

Ward, F. Kingdon, *Assam Adventure.* 1941.

Wellby, M. S., *Through Unknown Tibet.* J. B. Lippincott, 1898.

Wessels, Cornelius J. (S.J.), *Early Jesuit Travellers in Central Asia, 1607-1721.* Martinus Nijhoff, 1924.

Williams, L. F. Rushbrook, *The State of Pakistan.* Faber & Faber, 1966.

Wolpert, Stanley, *Morley and India 1906-1910.* University of California Press, 1967.

Woodman, Dorothy, *The Making of Burma.* Cresset Press, 1962.

Wu, Aitchen K., *China and the Soviet Union.* A study of Sino-Soviet relations. John Day, 1950.

Younghusband, Sir F. E., *India and Tibet.* Murray, London, 1910. *The Heart of a Continent.* Murray, London, 1896.

SELECTED PERIODICALS PUBLISHED IN:

Australia

Australian Journal of Politics and History.

Australian Outlook.

The Australian Year Book of International Law.

China
New World Review.
The Peking Review.

India
Asian Survey.
India Quarterly.
International Studies.
United Asia.

Hong Kong
Far Eastern Economic Review.

Pakistan
Pakistan Journal of International Affairs.

United Kingdom
Asian Review.
China Quarterly.
Economist.
International Affairs.
Journal of the Royal Central Asian Society.
Journal of the Royal Geographical Society.
New Statesman.
The World Today.

United States
Far Eastern Survey.
Foreign Affairs.
Pacific Affairs.

Appendixes

APPENDIX I

(Moorcroft Papers, I.O.L. Eur. MSS. Folio 31. G. 28. p. 141)

COPY of an ENGAGEMENT given by William Moorcroft, Superintendent of the Hon'ble Company's Stud to the Raja and Kaloon and other Chiefs and Elders of LADAKH for establishing commercial intercourse with British merchants and for their passage through the country of LADAKH to Chinese and Oosbuk TURKISTAN

I, William Moorcroft, deputed on the part of the British Merchants of Calcutta to establish a commercial intercourse with the North-Western Parts of Asia, having arrived at LEH, the capital of LADAKH, have had various interviews with the Raja and authorities of that country and have been treated with attention and civility by them.

Having signified a desire that British Merchants should have as free, commercial communications with this country as Traders from other places, the AUTHORITIES of LADAKH have entered into a written engagement that such communications should be established. And for their satisfaction, I hereby promise that any caravan destined for Turkestan by the way of YARKAND shall be accompanied by no more than fifteen or twenty soldiers for its protection.

And also that any caravan intended to proceed to the same countries by other roads shall have along with it for safeguard no more than fifty soldiers including non-commissioned officers.

The usual DUTY on Merchandise entering LEH is thirteen Rupees Mahmood Shahee or seventy Munwattus each Munwattu being one and a half the Yamboo* of China.

To mark a friendly preference to British Merchants the Authorities of LADAKH have agreed that the DUTY on the above weight of seventy Munwattus of their Merchandise shall be ten Mahmood Shahee Rupees. And on the part of the British Merchants of Calcutta I engage that the DUTY according to this rate upon such merchandise of theirs as shall enter LEH shall be duly paid by the Person or Persons having charge of it to the Officers of the Customs at that place. And as far as I have it in my power, I also promise that friendship shall always be maintained between British Merchants and the Rulers of LADAKH and that such of the former as shall enter this country shall abide by the above terms as being the sole conditions by which an intercourse should be maintained.

* The Yamboo weighs 166–7 Fur-Rupees.

And further that no injury shall happen to the country of LADAKH from the Commercial Engagement now made.

And that British Caravans shall not go from LEH to GURDOKH until one shall come from GURDOKH to LEH.

And having now received from the Authorities of LADAKH their before mentioned agreement in writing duly sealed and executed in the manner with them customary, on the part of the Merchants by whom I am deputed and myself I engage that as long as they shall act in conformity with it, the above articles shall not be acceded from.

DATED at LEH this fourth day of MAY in the year of Christ one thousand eight hundred and twenty one.

Sealed and signed in the presence of George Trebeck.

WILLIAM MOORCROFT.

APPENDIX 2

Peace Treaty between the Ruler of Jammu, the Emperor of China and the Lama Guru of Lhasa (1842). [This Treaty was signed in September, A.D. 1842. The Parties to the Treaty were on the one hand, Shri Khalsaji and Shri Maharaj Sahib Bahadur Raja Gulab Singh, and on the other hand the Emperor of China and the Lama Guru of Lhasa. By this Treaty the traditional boundary between Ladakh and Tibet was reaffirmed.]

As on this auspicious day, the 2nd of Assuj, Sambat 1899 (16th or 17th September A.D. 1842), we, the officers of the Lhassa (Government), Kalon of Sokan and Bakshi Shajpuh, Commander of the Forces and two officers on behalf of the most resplendent Sri Khalsaji Sahib, the asylum of the world, King Sher Singhji and Sri Maharaj Sahib Raja-i-Rajagan Raja Sahib Bahadur Raja Gulab Singhji, *i.e.,* the Muktar-ud-Daula Diwan Hari Chand and the asylum of vizirs, Vizir Ratnun, in a meeting called together for the promotion of peace and unity, and by profession and vows of friendship, unity and sincerity of heart and by taking oaths like those of Kunjak Sahib, have arranged and agreed that relations of peace, friendship and unity between Sri Khalsaji and Sri Maharaj Sahib Bahadur Raja Gulab Singhji, and the Emperor of China and the Lama Guru of Lhassa will henceforward remain firmly established for ever; and we declare in the presence of the Kunjak Sahib that on no account whatsoever will there be any deviation, difference or departure (from this agreement). We shall neither at present nor in future have anything to do or interfere at all with the boundaries of Ladakh and its surroundings as fixed from ancient times and will allow the annual export of wool, shawls and tea by way of Ladakh according to the old established custom.

Should any of the opponents of Sri Sarkar Khalsaji and Sri Raja Sahib Bahadur at any time enter our territories, we shall not pay any heed to his words or allow him to remain in our country.

We shall offer no hindrance to traders of Ladakh who visit our territories. We shall not even to the extent of a hair's breadth act in contravention of the terms that we have agreed to above regarding firm friendship, unity, the fixed boundaries of Ladakh and the keeping open of the route for wool, shawls and tea. We call Kunjak Sahib, Kairi, Lassi, Zhoh Mahan, and Khushal Choh as witnesses to this treaty.

The treaty was concluded on the 2nd of the month of Assuj, Sambat 1899 (16th or 17th September A.D. 1842).

APPENDIX 2a

(The Founding of the Kashmir State by K. M. Panikkar pp. 111–5)

The text of the Treaty of Amritsar is as follows:

TREATY BETWEEN THE BRITISH GOVERNMENT on the one part and MAHARAJAH GULAB SINGH OF JAMMU on the other concluded on the part of the BRITISH GOVERNMENT by FREDERICK CURRIE, Esquire, and BREVET-MAJOR HENRY MONTGOMERY LAWRENCE, acting under the orders of the RIGHT HONOURABLE SIR HENRY HARDINGE, G.C.B., one of HER BRITANNIC MAJESTY'S MOST HONOURABLE PRIVY COUNCIL, GOVERNOR-GENERAL of the possessions of the EAST INDIA COMPANY, to direct and control all their affairs in the EAST INDIES and by MAHARAJAH GULAB SINGH in person – 1846.

ARTICLE 1

The British Government transfers and makes over for ever in independent possession to Maharajah Gulab Singh and the heirs male of his body all the hilly or mountainous country with its dependencies situated to the eastward of the River Indus and the westward of the River Ravi including Chamba and excluding Lahul, being part of the territories ceded to the British Government by the Lahore State according to the provisions of Article IV. of the Treaty of Lahore, dated 9th March, 1846.

ARTICLE 2

The eastern boundary of the tract transferred by the foregoing article to Maharajah Gulab Singh shall be laid down by the Commissioners appointed by the British Government and Maharajah Gulab Singh respectively for that purpose and shall be defined in a separate engagement after survey.

ARTICLE 3

In consideration of the transfer made to him and his heirs by the provisions of the foregoing article Maharajah Gulab Singh will pay to the British Government the sum of seventy-five Lakhs of Rupees (Nanukshahee), fifty lakhs to be paid on ratification of this Treaty and twenty-five lakhs on or before the 1st October of the current year, A.D. 1846.

ARTICLE 4

The limits of the territories of Maharajah Gulab Singh shall not be at any time changed without concurrence of the British Government.

ARTICLE 5

Maharajah Gulab Singh will refer to the arbitration of the British Government any disputes or questions that may arise between himself and the Government of Lahore or any other neighbouring State, and will abide by the decision of the British Government.

ARTICLE 6
Maharajah Gulab Singh engages for himself and heirs to join, with the whole of his Military Forces, the British troops, when employed within the hills or in the territories adjoining his possessions.

ARTICLE 7
Maharajah Gulab Singh engages never to take or retain in his service any British subject nor the subject of any European or American State without the consent of the British Government.

ARTICLE 8
Maharajah Gulab Singh engages to respect in regard to the territory transferred to him, the provisions of Articles V., VI., and VII., of the separate Engagement between the British Government and the Lahore Durbar, dated 11th March, 1946.*

ARTICLE 9
The British Government will give its aid to Maharajah Gulab Singh in protecting his territories from external enemies.

ARTICLE 10
Maharajah Gulab Singh acknowledges the supremacy of the British Government and will in token of such supremacy present annually to the British Government one horse, twelve shawl goats† of approved breed (six male and six female) and three pairs of Cashmere shawls.

This Treaty of ten articles has been this day settled by Frederick Currie, Esquire, and Brevet-Major Henry Montgomery Lawrence, acting under directions of The Right Honourable Sir Henry Hardinge, G.C.B., Governor-General, on the part of the British Government and by Maharajah Gulab Singh in person, and the said Treaty has been this day ratified by the seal of The Right Honourable Sir Henry Hardinge, G.C.B., Governor-General.

(Done at Amritsar the sixteenth day of March, in the year of our Lord one thousand eight hundred and forty-six, corresponding with the seventeenth day of Rubee-ul-Awal 1262 Jijree).

(*Signed*) H. HARDINGE (Seal).

(*Signed*) F. CURRIE.
(*Signed*) H. M. LAWRENCE.

By Order of the Right Honourable the Governor-General of India.

(*Signed*) F. CURRIE,
Secretary to the Government of India, with the Governor-General.

* Referring to jagirdars, arrears of revenue and the property in the forts that are to be transferred.

† On the 13th March, 1884, it was arranged by mutual consent that in future the Maharajah should present, instead of 12 goats, 10 lbs. of pashm in its natural state as brought to Kashmir from Leh, 4 lbs. of picked and assorted black wool, 4 lbs. grey wool, 4 lbs. white wool, and 1 lb. of each of the three best qualities of white yarn.

APPENDIX 3

Enclosures to Secret Letters from India Volume 110. No. 39 of 8 June 1847

A few remarks on the Maha Raja Gulab Singh's Boundary with China by Mr Vans Agnew.

1. The only doubtful points on this boundary according to present information are its two extremities.

2. It is the ancient boundary of Ladakh and Chanthan and Yarkand and by the Chinese is well known and undisputed.

3. It runs entirely through almost desolate tracks. A deviation of many miles would not to an appreciable amount cause territorial advantage or disadvantage.

4. The right to roads and passes is nowhere dubious except near DEMCHOK one of the termini.

5. The exact point where the boundary of PITI, LADAKH and CHANTHAN meet does not, I believe, at present exist.

6. As rivers are lost in a desert, the three boundaries become undefined in the uninhabitable mountains, south of a line drawn from the Southern extremity of the CHIMMARERI LAKE to the Monastery of RANDLA.

7. The Chinese, I believe, touch the PITI (British) frontier on the PACA river near AKEHE. Thence they follow the crest of inaccessible ridges round the end of the valley of HANDLA and run down on the river near a village called DEMCHOK.

8. Here then may possibly be a doubt. This place has been claimed for Maha Raja GULAB SINGH and may be so by the Chinese. It *may* interfere with intercourse between RADOKH and GARO by the valley of the Indus.

9. But here, or a little higher the boundary crosses the river Indus and, ascending the opposite mountains, runs along the ridge, so that the pass to RADOKH as the HANDLA road via CHIHRA is in the hands of the Chinese.

10. The boundary continues along the top of the ridge so as just to leave to LADAKH the little rivulet running by RAHNANG and leading up to the pass called the 'TSAKA LA' as also the 'CHUSHOOL' rivulet running down the other side into the LAKE PANKUNG.

11. Thence the boundary runs along the 'PANKUNG' and then the ridge forming the Eastern Boundary of the river 'DARGULEH' till it falls int the 'SHAYUH'.

12. Therefore the ridge bounding the valley of the 'SHAYUH' in the east is the boundary up to the KARAKORUM Mountains.

13. And thence they run westwards from the boundary between YARKAND and NOBRA of LADAKH, the states of 'LITTLE THIBET' and the independant tribes further west:

14. When the KARAKORUM ceases to be the Maha Raja GULAB SINGH's boundary, it will be when the independent tribes – say NAGUERRE or HOONZ, interposes between Little Tibet and that chain.

15. It is of course highly advisable that all boundaries be defined but on reference to the map, and, after comprehending the grand natural characteristics of the boundary above detailed, the absence of all grounds for variance, the undisputed right of LADAKH to the roads up the SHAYUK and the Indus to certain fixed points and that of the Chinese beyond them, while there is absolutely nothing else to acquire nearer, than YARKAND, RADOKH and GARO.

I conceive that, as safe and unmistakeable a boundary could be traced by the Commissioners on paper at their first meeting, as if they were to travel along its whole length.

16. There remains, however, I admit, the termini. I would suggest that the Officer in charge of, or on boundary duty near PITI, fix the one and the Commissioner to lay down the Maha Raja GULAB SINGH's boundary on N.W. determine the other.

· · · · · · · · ·

19. The appointment of a Commission by the Chinese Govt. with a view to fix this and perhaps other boundaries with China, and to open lines of traffic is in every point of view desirable.

20. The question is whether this Commission would be more likely to yield reasonable terms, if received at the Head Quarters of Government and in communication with the highest authorities, than amidst the discomforts of an arduous journey and, in the total absence of all that pomp and ceremonial to which this nation is so much addicted.

21. In fact, unless the Chinese officials who may come on this duty, turn out much more patriotic than their countrymen are reported, a hint that any frivolous delays or excuses would make such a journey necessary, might, I think, have no small effect in making the Commission manageable.

22. Whether any other boundary except that of Maha Raja GULAB SINGH is required with China or not I know nothing.

· · · · · · · · ·

44. I was also informed that there is another road from YARKAND East of the SHAYUB River to RADOKH, but it was prohibited by the Chinese Government.

· · · · · · · · ·

65. The consequence of opening another route to Shawl wool and the Turkistan trade will be the final ruin of Cashmere even supposing the former amount of trade in tea to continue.

66. Maha Raja GULAB SINGH will not or cannot see this. It rests with the British and Chinese Governments to decide the fate of Cashmere.

R. A. VANS AGNEW

May 13th, 1847

APPENDIX 4

(Secret Letters from Bengal and India, Volume 32)

Lord Hardinge's letter to the Director of the East India Company explaining the background of the Boundary Commission of 1847 (No. 48GG)

Foreign Department
Secret
Simla. The *28th July, 1847*

Answered October 2
To,
The Honorable
The Secret Committee
of the Honorable
the Court of Directors.

Hon'ble Sirs,
I have the honor to report for your information, that in a few days a mission will depart from Simla for the purpose of laying down the Boundary between the Territories of Maha Raja Goolab Sing and the Emperor of China.

2. I have endeavoured through His Excellency Sir John Davis to induce the Chinese authorities to depute on their side a mission to their Thibetan frontier for the purpose of co-operating with our Commissioners. His Excellency has used his best exertions to overcome the repugnance felt by them to take this step, and the tenor of the last advices on this subject from Hong Kong was favourable and gives me some reason to hope that Boundary Commissioners have been by this time appointed by the Emperor.

3. I am happy to inform you that I have lately received intelligence from Bushehir that some Chinese Chiefs are expected at Gartope, and that supplies are now being laid in for them; but, as it is not improbable that these Chiefs may have been sent as much for the purpose of preventing our Commissioners from crossing the Boundary, as for defining it, I am not too sanguine respecting this information.

4. The British mission will consist of Captain A. Cunningham, Lieutenant H. Strachey, and Dr. T. Thomson. These Officers have been selected by me, not only on the ground of their general qualifications of energy temper and prudence, but more especially on account of their scientific attainments, for which they are favorably known to the Indian community – Captain Cunningham was a member of the Commission which was sent last year to define the boundary between the new British possessions on the Hills and Maharaja Golab Sing's Territory. Lieut. Strachey has lately returned from an adventurous tour to the Manasorawar Lake, and Dr. T. Thomson is understood to possess manifold acquirements in several departments of natural History.

5. It was to countervail the disappointment, which would be felt if no mission were sent from China, that I wished the British Commissioners to be

possessed of such attainments as would qualify them to increase our knowledge of the new and interesting countries which they will have to visit during the period of their absence.

6. I have taken every care to see that they are provided with Barometers, Sextants, Thermometers, an Altitude and Azimuth Circle, Magnetic and other philosophical instruments; and as two of the Officers are already practised observers, I am confident that these valuable means will not be thrown away upon them. They have held frequent discussions with my Secretary Mr. Elliot on all the chief objects of interest in the Ethnography natural History, Geography, Religion and Literature of these Countries; so that I am led to hope that their deputation will at least be attended with some results which will be interesting and satisfactory to the scientific world.

7. The Commissioners have also been plentifully provided with medicines and vaccine matter, in the hope that the advantages of our medical skill may be widely diffused among the people with whom they will be brought in contact.

8. It will be one of the chief duties of the mission to make particular inquiries respecting the lines of trade, and to improve our commercial position by communicating with traders on the subject of the advantages to be obtained by intercourse with a country where no duties of any kind are levied (the transit duties even in the Hill States having been lately abolished) and by taking measures to procure the abolition of that article of the late Treaty in 1842 between Maharaja Golab Sing and the Chinese Government under which it is stipulated that no Shawlwool shall be exported from Garoo and the adjacent Countries into our protected Province of Busshehir, but be taken exclusively to Ladak. This convention has been found to operate very injuriously on the interests of the Kunawur traders, and is not at all favorably looked upon by the Chinese themselves.

9. The Hon'ble Mr. Erskine, our Political Agent in the Hill States, informs me that about two years ago an intimation was conveyed to the Raja of Busshehir by the Garpon stationed at Garoo, that if the Raja could procure a letter from the Political Agent to the address of the Chief of Lassa intimating the wish of the British Government that the clause in the Treaty above alluded to, granting to Maharajah Golab Sing a monopoly in the Shawlwool trade, should be set aside, an order would be issued to the Frontier authorities to abstain from all interference with the Kunawar traders bringing Shawlwool across the border.

10. Abuses also are said to impede the trade of this Frontier through Ladak The Kunawur Traders who previous to the conquest of Ladak by the Seiks, used to proceed through that country to Yarkund on commercial speculations, how of late years been altogether prohibited by the Agents of the Maharaja from passing the Ladak Northern frontier.

11. The Kunawur Exports to Yarkund consisted of Indigo, English cotton piece goods, Chintzes, opium, tobacco, sugar, groceries, ginger, hardware, and a variety of sundries, and from Yarkund were received in exchange tea, churrus, cheenee, carpets, puttoo, gold coins, horses, coarse broadcloth, dried fruits, and some other articles.

12. The Busshehir and Lahoul merchants have expressed to the Politica Agent their earnest desire to have the road to Yarkund opened to them again,

and have stated that every facility was afforded to the traders from India by the Chinese when they were formerly able to reach Yarkund all these obstructions the deputation of our Commissioners will be calculated to remove, as the Maharaja is, if not from affection, at least from self-interest, so well disposed towards the British Government, that he is not likely to risk our dissatisfaction by persisting in a course against which they have reason to remonstrate, while it is not attended with any freat advantages to himself.

13. I have no doubt that our trade on the Northern Frontier may be somewhat increased to the profit of those concerned and to the comfort and advantage of the neighbouring countries, although the population is scanty, and the communication very difficult. The Commissioners will be instructed to obtain the most accurate information of the population of the Country through which they pass, and their means by barter of carrying on trade and to what probable extent, in yearly value. My Secretary Mr. Elliot has under my orders placed himself in communication with Mr. George Lushington, Commissioner of Kumam, with a view to improve our commercial relations with the Bhohjas on the Frontier. I have authorised Mr. Lushington to expend a small sum on account of Government in purchasing goods for the Bhotya Market, in order to ascertain what the chief wants if the people are, and to what investments the attention of our subjects may be most advantageously directed. It seems to me strange, not withstanding even the Mountain-barrier of the Himalaya assuming the passage to be equally difficult on both sides, that Russian goods, burdened with all the additional expense of a tedious as well as dangerous land carriage, should be able to complete successfully with those of British manufacture in countries adjoining our own Empire; and I trust that this mission will be able to develope some means whereby our own subjects may share, more than they have hitherto done, in a trade which is found essential to the wants of the inhabitants of 'high Asia'.

14. As the Province of Ladak, and especially the Capital Leh, is comparatively so well known to European Geographers it is my wish that, if possible the Commissioners should winter beyond the Karakorum range. If they can obtain the permission of the Chinese Commissioners to proceed to Yarkund, or even to Khoten, nothing could be more satisfactory. In the event of their not being able to pass the Karakorum to the North, Rohdokh on the borders of the great desert (where all is at present unknown) would be their best resting place, and it is to be hoped that the Chinese Commissioners may not object to their going there. It is possible that friendly intercourse may subdue the prejudices they entertain, and pave the way to a more intimate relationship with the British Government. When they see that we are not actuated by any spirit of Political aggression, but solely by a desire to participate in and extend the blessings of commerce, they may begin to feel more gratified than alarmed at the extension of our influence to the farthest Land Boundary of their Empire, and at our meeting them on the West, as well as the East, with proffers of fellowship and good will.

15. As the greater part of the Boundary between Ladak and Chinese Tartary is laid down by nature, the Chibra Hills, the Pangkung Lake, and the Karakorum Mountains forming the line of direction, and as scarcely any portion,

except the two Termini, can admit of dispute, the business with the Chinese Commissioners will most probably be soon adjusted; and when every thing has been accomplished and the border, or (if nothing can be accomplished on the border from the absence of a Chinese Mission) as soon as the weather permets, it is my wish that, before returning to the British Dominions, the Commissioners should individually use their best endeavours to increase the bounds of our Geographical knowledge in those remote regions. It is desirable that Captain Cunningham should follow the course of the Indus, and extend his observations on both sides of the Indus, until he reaches Gilghit – to which place Mr. Vans-Agnew has lately been sent by the Resident at Lahore. From Gilghit Captn. Cunningham should proceed to the Dardu country, which, in furtherance of certain antiquarian researches, he has an eager desire to visit and should thence return through the Huxana country to the Punjab. It is desirable that Lieut. Strachey should follow up his researches in Ngari, and should penetrate through Chanthan and Goordokh to Manasorawar, and as much farther Eastward as he can go even to Lassa following the course of the Sanpu, and so return through Darjeling, or Bhotan, to the British Provinces – Dr. Thomson may more fitly employ himself in ascertaining the mineral resources along and within the British frontier – on no account is the period of their absence to exceed two years, and on no account are they to cross the Bolor Tagh Mountains to the Westward, so as to bring themselves into collision with the bigoted and jealous Mahometans of Independent Turkistan.

16. With this exception, they may be left to their own discretion as to the best mode of meeting my wishes in prosecuting their several journeys of discovery; as I am persuaded that in whatever circumstances they are placed and whatever difficulties and privations they may have to undergo, they will maintain unimpaired the credit and dignity of the British character.

I have the honour to be
with the greatest Respect
Hon'ble Sirs
Your most faithful
humble Servant.

Simla,
The 28 July,
1847.

APPENDIX 5

(Ardagh Papers P.R.O./30/40 and F.O./17/1328)

The Northern Frontier of India from the Pamirs to Tibet

The collapse of China in the late China-Japan war showed the futility of our trusting to that Power as a possible ally, and there is every reason to believe that she will be equally useless as a buffer between Russia and the Northern Frontier of India.

The war was followed by a serious Mahomedan rebellion in the provinces of Kansu which has been dragging on ever since, and has lately received an additional stimulus by the adhesion of the Kolao Secret Society, the most powerful and ubiquitous organization of its kind in China.

China maintains her hold on Kashgaria by one single line of communication, namely the road between Kashgar and Peking which passes through the disaffected Mahomedan district of Kansu, and is some 3,500 miles in length.

Though this alone is sufficient to demonstrate the precarious nature of China's sovereignty in Kashgaria, it may be added that in July last Mr. Macartney reported that the stability of Chinese rule in Kashgaria had been much shaken and that riots were taking place, not so much due to the inhabitants as to the unruly Chinese soldiers quartered there.

The general history of Russian expansion in Central Asia, the eagerness with which she has advanced her borders towards India over such inhospitable regions as the Pamirs, the comparative fertility and natural wealth of Kashgaria as well as the political activity displayed by the Russian representative in Kashgar lead one to suppose that an eventual Russian occupation is far from improbable. In this connection too it is worthy of remark that Russia has not demarcated her frontier with Kashgaria further south than the Uzbel Pass between the latitudes of Kashgar and Yarkand thus leaving herself untrammelled in the natural process of expansion from the Pamirs eastward.

The rumours current during the summer of 1896 of an impending Russian advance into Kashgaria appear to have been unfounded. Mr. Macartney confirming this view, is of opinion that the Russians have made no preparations for intervening, as the time is not yet ripe, and as a Russian demonstration, unless it were immediately followed up by annexation, would only serve to strengthen the hands of the Chinese by intimidating the rebels.

If then the eventual annexation of Kashgaria by Russia is to be expected, we may be sure that Russia, as in the past will endeavour to push her boundary as far south as she can, for political reasons, even if no real military advantage is sought. It is evident therefore that sooner or later we shall have to conclude a definite agreement regarding the Northern Frontier of India.

We have been accustomed to regard the great mountain ranges to the north of Chitral, Hunza, and Ladak as the natural frontier of India; and in a general sense they form an acceptable defensive boundary, easy to define, difficult to pass, and fairly dividing the peoples on either side. But the physical conditions of these mountains, their great extent, high altitude, general inaccessability, and sparse population, render it impossible to watch the actual watershed; and the measures requisite for security, and for information as to the movements of an enemy, cannot be adequately carried out unless we can circulate freely at the foot of the glacis formed by the northern slope, along these longitudinal valleys which Nature has provided on the northern side at a comparatively short distance from the crest – a configuration which, it may be observed, does not present itself on the southern slope of the range.

For military purposes therefore, a frontier following the highest water-sheds is defective, and we should aim at keeping our enemy from any possibility of establishing himself on the glacis, occupying these longitudinal valleys, and there preparing to surprise the passes. We should therefore seek a boundary which shall leave all these longitudinal valleys in our possession or at least under our influence.

The application of this principle to the further demarcation of the northern frontier of India leads to the following results. The Hindu-Kush, the Mustagh Range, and the Karakorum Range, form the principal line of water-parting between the basin of the Indus on the south, and the basins of the Oxus and the Yarkand rivers on the north.

On this range are situated, inter alia, the Kilik, Mintaka, Khunjerab, Shimshal, Mustagh, and Karakorum passes: access to which we desire to debar to a possible enemy, by retaining within our territory the approaches to them on the northern side, and the lateral communications between these approaches.

This object is to be obtained by drawing our line of frontier so as to include the basins of the Danga Bash river and its affluents above Dehda, at the junction of the Ili Su and Karatchukar, called by Captain Younghusband Kurghan-i-Ujadbai; of the Yarkand river above the point where it breaks through the range of mountains marked by the Sargon and Ilbis Birkar Passes, at about latitude 37° north and longitude 75°.50' east on Mr Curzon's map, published by the Royal Geographical society; and of the Karakash river above at a point between Shahidullah and the Sanju or Grim Passes. Those three basins would afford a fully adequate sphere of influence beyond the main crests.

During the disturbances in Kashgaria Shahidullah was occupied by Kashmir.

At the time of Sir Douglas Forsyth's mission to Yarkand in 1873 the frontier post of Kashgaria was situated at Shahidullah. When Captain Younghusband visited that place in 1889 the fort had long been abandoned and he granted money to a Kirghiz chief to rebuild it and keep it in repair, as a protection to the trade route from Leh to Yarkand. He forestalled Captain Grombtchevsky, whom he met on the Yarkand River.

In 1890 the Chinese pulled down the Shahidullah fort, and built another near the Sujet Pass, where, in 1892, Lord Dunmore saw a notice board to the effect that 'anyone crossing the Chinese frontier without reporting himself at this fort will be imprisoned'.

In 1874, Dr Bellew found an abandoned Chinese outpost at Kirghiz Tam near Shiragh Saldi. In 1889 Captain Younghusband likewise found Shiragh Saldi outside the recognized Chinese Frontier.

We are therefore justified in claiming up to the crests of the Kuen-Lun Range.

We now represent on our maps the Yarkand River as a boundary – the Tagh-dumbash Pamir is claimed by China, at least as far as Bayik. It is therefore clear that the three basins described above may encroach upon Chinese territory to a certain extent which may be difficult to define, and our solicitude should be to obtain from China an agreement that any part of those basins which may eventually be found to lie outside our frontier, shall not be ceded to any country but Great Britain. If China were strong enough to maintain possession, and to act the part of a buffer state, this assurance would not be needed; but in view of her decadence, and of the prospect of Kashgar, Yarkand and Khotan falling before long into the hands of Russia, it will be well to take timely precaution to prevent her from becoming so close a neighbour to the mountain rampart of India as she has lately become on the Chitral Frontier.

The present value of this very sparsely inhabited country is insignificant, but its importance as a security to the Indian Frontier is considerable.

The same principles and arguments may have to be applied at a future period to the Upper Basins of the Indus, the Sutlej and even the Brahmaputra, in the event of a prospective absorption of Tibet by Russia. At the present moment however, we are only concerned in the definition of a frontier between British India and Kashgar, Yarkand and Khotan.

Dealing first with the main portion of the line, marked on our maps as following the Yarkand River, we find that Captain Younghusband in 1889 pointed out that this stream would form a bad boundary, as it is fordable, and the road along the valley frequently crosses from one side to another. This objection is well founded. If we are to keep this valley which contains mines of iron and copper, hot springs, and possibly petroleum and gold; and which, formerly cultivated, has within late years become depopulated in consequence of Kanjuti raids – now at an end in consequence of our occupation of Hunza: we should include the northern slope of its basin up to the crests of the Kuen Lun Mountains. It is not likely that China in her present state would offer much objection, or indeed that her influence extends to the south of the Kuen Lun. This then is the line which it would be preferable to claim. But, if it be found that there should arise inseparable objections to the Kuen Lun Line, and that we cannot adopt the line of the river, there is yet a third alternative which will still give us a glacis in front of the Mustagh – viz: the mountain crest commencing at the summit marked 14680, near the Kurbu Pass, passing by the Uruk Pass to the summit marked 8815, crossing the mouth of the Mustagh or Uprang river, and following the line of waterparting between that river and the Yarkand River, to which it would descend at a point near the ruins of Kugart Auza and mount on the northern side at some point between the Sokh-buluk and Sujet Passes, following the latter range eastward across the Karakash, and onwards to the point where the frontier makes its great bend southward.

This second line as defined by river basins would comprise within our territory the basin of the Mustagh River from its junction with the Yarkand river or Raskarn Daria, the basin of the Upper Yarkand River above the ruins of Kugart Auza, and the basin of the Karakash above latitude 36° north.

At the western extremity of both this line and the Kuan Lun Line we have to deal with Chinese claims to the Taghdumbash Pamir. The Chinese have their furthest post up the valley at Chadir Tash or Bayik, where the road from the Bayik Pass meets the Karatchukar river. Above that point the nomad Kirghiz pay taxes to both China and Hunza, and we may claim on behalf of Hunza the basin of the Karatchukar above some point between the Bayik Chinese post, and Mintaka Aksai, the boundary to the north of the river being one of the spurs descending from the Fovalo Shveikovski Peak. This would cover the debouches from the Tagerman-su, Mikhman-Guli, Kuturuk, Wakh-jir, Kilik, Mintaka and Karchenai Passes. It is therefore of much importance to secure the possession of Mintaka Aksai.

On the eastern side of the Tagdumbash Pamir, the debouches of the Khunjerab and Kurbu passes can be secured by the possession of Mazar Sultan Sayid Hassen. A parallel of latitude south of the Bayik post is the simplest mode of laying down a boundary here so as to include Mazar Sayid Hassan. From thence the boundary should mount to the waterparting near the Zeplep Pass, and thence join the Kuen Lun, the Yarkand River or the Uruk lines, already described.

Under the circumstances of China quoted at the commencement of this paper, the settlement of this frontier question appears now to be urgent. If we delay, we shall have Russia to deal with instead of China, and she will assuredly claim up to the very farthest extent of the pretensions of her predecessors in title – at least to the very summits of the Mustagh and the Himalayas.

I venture therefore to recommend that the matter should now be brought to the notice of the Government of India, if the proposal meets with approval at the Foreign and India Offices.

When the Government of India has studied the question, and pronounced an opinion as to the line which would be most advantageous, the matter will, on our part, be ripe for further action. But, as it may happen that, at that moment, other considerations may render it unadvisable to communicate with China, it may be well to the point out that there are other steps, short of actual delimitation of international agreement, which would tend greatly to strengthen our position, while awaiting a favourable opportunity for arriving at a definite settlement.

The Governor-General's Agents and Officers adjacent to the frontier may arrange to procure the recognition of our supremacy and protection by the chiefs of the local tribes; and to assert it by acts of sovereignty, annually exercised within the limits decided upon; and in this manner acquire a title by prescription.

(Sd) J. C. ARDAGH, Major General
D. M. I.

1st. January, 1897.

No. 170 of 1897, Government of India, Foreign Department, Secret, (Frontier)

To
THE RIGHT HON'BLE LORD GEORGE F. HAMILTON,
Her Majesty's Secretary of State for India.

FORT WILLIAM, *the 23rd December 1897.*
MY LORD,
            Your Lordship's Secret despatch No. 5, dated the 12th February 1897, transmitted for our consideration a letter from the Foreign Office, enclosing a memorandum by the Director of Military Intelligence on the northern frontier of India, contiguous to the Chinese dominions. We understand that Her Majesty's Government remain of opinion that it would not be politic to bring before the Chinese Government the question of the settlement of their boundaries with Kashmir, Hunza and Afghanistan. The matter for examination is therefore whether it is advisable to take any other steps in the direction of consolidating the boundaries of India in the region under notice.

    2. Sir John Ardagh considers a frontier following the highests watersheds defective for military purposes, and suggests that we should aim at keeping our enemy from any possibility of establishing himself on the glacis, occupying the longitudinal valleys, and there preparing to surprise the passes; he proposes that, if it is unadvisable to communicate with China on the subject, our frontier officers might arrange to procure the recognition of our supremacy and protection by the chiefs of the local tribes, and to assert it by acts of sovereignty, annually exercised within the limits decided upon, and in this manner acquire a title by prescription. He thinks it unlikely that China, in her present state, would offer much objection. Our experience leads to an opposite conclusion.

    3. The Chinese have, on more than one occasion, evinced a determination to assert their territorial rights in the direction of the Indian frontier. Your Lordship will remember the pertinacity with which they insisted on what they consider their suzerain rights over Hunza, as demonstrated by the 'tribute' of gold which Hunza still pays to Kashgar. They have erected boundary pillars on the Karakoram. In October last year the Taotai of Kashgar, purporting to act under instructions from the Governor of the New Dominion, made a verbal representation to Mr. Macartney to the effect that, in a certain copy of a Johnston's Atlas, Aksai Chin had been marked as within British territory, while the tract belonged entirely to China. Still more recently, in replying to an application for a passport for one of the officers of the Gilgit Agency to cross the Kilik to shoot, the Taotai evinced his interest in China's rights to the Taghdumbash up to the very borders of Hunza, by conceding the request subject to the condition that the British officer should not stay more than ten days in Chinese territory. Again, during the month of October 1897, a report reached

us from our Political Agent at Gilgit that the Chinese authorities have arrested some Kanjutis who were cultivating a small piece of land in Raskam, and have written to the Mir of Hunza that he must not allow his subjects to come there again. We believe that any attempt to incorporate within our frontier either of the zones mentioned by Sir John Ardagh would involve real risk of strained relations with China, and might tend to precipitate the active interposition of Russia in Kashgaria, which it should be our aim to postpone as long as possible.

4. We are unable to concur altogether in Sir John Ardagh's suggestions on military grounds. He advocates an advance beyond the great mountain ranges which we regard as our natural frontier, on the ground that it is impossible to watch the actual watershed. Sir John Ardagh is no doubt right in theory, and the crest of a mountain range does not ordinary form a good military frontier. In the present instance, however, we see no strategic advantage in going beyond mountains over which no hostile advance is ever likely to be attempted. Moreover, the alternative frontiers which Sir John Ardagh proposes practically coincide with the watersheds of other ranges. Our objection is mainly based on the opinion of officers who have visited this region. They unanimously represent the present mountain frontier as perhaps the most difficult and inaccessible country in the world. The country beyond is barren, rugged, and sparsely populated. An advance would interpose between ourselves and our outposts a belt of the most difficult and impracticable country, it would unduly extend and weaken our military position without, in our opinion, securing any corresponding advantage. No invader has ever approached India from this direction where nature has placed such formidable barriers.

We have the honour to be,

MY LORD,

Your Lordship's most obedient, humble servants,

(Signed) ELGIN.

G. S. WHITE.

J. WESTLAND.

M. D. CHALMERS.

E. H. H. COLLEN.

A. C. TREVOR.

C. M. RIVAZ.

(F.O./17/1373)

Sir C. MacDonald to the Tsung-li Yamên

Peking.

MM. les Ministres,   14th March 1899.

        I have the honour, by direction of Her Majesty's Government, to address your Highness and your Excellencies on the subject of the boundary between the Indian State of Cashmere and the new dominion of Chinese Turkestan.

    In the year 1891 the Indian Government had occasion to repress by force of arms certain rebellious conduct on the part of the Ruler of the State of Kanjut, a tributary of Cashmere. The Chinese Government then laid claim to the allegiance of Kanjut by virtue of a tribute of $1\frac{1}{2}$ ounces of gold dust paid by its Ruler each year to the Governor of the new dominion, who gave in return some pieces of silk.

    It appears that the boundaries of the State of Kanjut with China have never been clearly defined. The Kanjutis claim an extensive tract of land in the Tagdumbash Pamir, extending as far north as Tashkurgan, and they also claim the district known as Raskam to the south of Sarikol. The rights of Kanjut over part of the Tagdumbash Pamir were *admitted* by the Taotai of Kashgar in a letter to the Mir of Hunza, dated February 1896, and last year the question of the Raskam district was the subject of negotiations between Kanjut and the officials of the new dominion, in which the latter admitted that some of the Raskam land should be given to the Kanjutis.

    It is now proposed by the Indian Government that for the sake of avoiding any dispute or uncertainty in the future, a clear understanding should be come to with the Chinese Government as to the frontier between the two States. To obtain this clear understanding, it is necessary that China should relinquish her shadowy claim to suzerainty over the State of Kanjut. The Indian Government, on the other hand, will, on behalf of Kanjut, reliquish her claims to most of the Tagdumbash and Raskam districts.

    It will not be necessary to mark out the frontier. The natural frontier is the crest of a range of mighty mountains, a great part of which is quite inaccessible. It will be sufficient if the two Governments will enter into an agreement to recognise the frontier as laid down by its clearly marked geographical features. The line proposed by the Indian Government is briefly as follows: It may be seen by reference to the map of the Russo-Chinese frontier brought by the late Minister, Hung Chun, from St. Petersburg, and in possession of the Yamên.

    Commencing on the Little Pamir, from the peak at which the Anglo-Russian Boundary Commission of 1895 ended their work, it runs south-east, crossing the Karachikar stream at Mintaka Aghazi; thence proceeding in the same direction it joins at the Karchenai Pass the crest of the main ridge of the

Mustagh range. It follows this to the south, passing by the Kunjerab Pass, and continuing southwards to the peak just north of the Shimshal Pass. At this point the boundary leaves the crest and follows a spur running east approximately parallel to the road from the Shimshal to the Hunza post at Darwaza. The line turning south through the Darwaza post crosses the road from the Shimshal Pass at that point, and then ascends the nearest high spur, and regains the main crests which the boundary will again follow, passing the Mustagh, Gusherbrun, and Saltoro Passes by the Karakoram. From the Karakoram Pass the crests of the range run east for about half a degree (100 *li*), and then turn south to a little below the thirty-fifth parallel of north latitude. Rounding then what in our maps is shown as the source of the Karakash, the line of hills to be followed runs north-east to a point east of Kizil Gilga, and from there in a south-easterly direction follows the Lak Tsung Range until that meets the spur running south from the K'un-lun range, which has hitherto been shown on our maps as the eastern boundary of Ladakh. This is a little east of 80° east longitude.

Your Highness and your Excellencies will see by examining this line that a large tract of country to the north of the great dividing range shown in Hung Chun's map as outside the Chinese boundary will be recognised as Chinese territory.

I beg your Highness and your Excellencies to consider the matter, and to favour me with an early reply.

I avail, &c.,

(Signed)   CLAUDE M. MACDONALD.

APPENDIX 8

(P.S.F. 1910/1918 p. 1)

From The Secretary to the Government of India in the Foreign Department,

To, Major-General H. Bower, C.B., Commanding the Abor Expeditionary Force

Dated Simla, the 25th September 1911.

SIR,

Its continuation of the instructions issued for your guidance by His Excellency the Commander-in-Chief, I am directed to forward, for your information, a copy of the marginally cited despatch* outlining the policy which, subject to the approval of His Majesty's Government, the Government of India propose to follow on the north-east frontier, and to convey to you the following instructions regarding the political aspect of the punitive expedition against the Abors which will be under your command.

2. The Governor-General in Council is pleased to vest you with full political control during the progress of military operations, and Messrs. Bentinck and Dundas have been appointed as Assistant Political Officers to accompany the expedition, and as such will give you every possible assistance in political matters. Your authority and responsibility will, however, be complete.

You should address all communications on political questions to the Government of Eastern Bengal and Assam, repeating them to the Government of India in the Foreign Department and the Chief of the General Staff, noting in each case that this has been done.

3. The objects of the expedition are –

(1) to exact severe punishment and reparation for the murder of Mr. Williamson, Dr. Gregorson, and their party in March last; and, by establishing our military superiority in the estimation of the tribe, to endeavour to compel the Minyongs to surrender the chief instigators and perpetrators of the massacre;

(2) to visit as many of the Minyong villages as possible, and to make the tribe clearly understand that, in future, they will be under our control, which, subject to good behaviour on their part, will for the present be of a loose political nature;

(3) to visit the Bor Abor or Padam village of Damroh, which the expedition of 1893-94 failed to reach. Provided that the Padam Abors behave themselves, the visit to their country will not be of a punitive nature. (They have already sent in word that they wish to be friends and have proposed to send in a deputation to Sadiya. Orders have been issued to Mr. Dundas, the Assistant Political Officer, Sadiya, to receive the deputation, if it is a representative one, and to inform the Padam Abors that there is no desire to attack them, povided that

* To His Majesty's Secretary of State for India, No. 105 (Secret-External), dated September 21, 1911.

they conduct themselves in a friendly manner, but that a friendly visit will be paid to Damroh);

(4) if during the course of the expedition Chinese officials or troops are met, endeavour should be made to maintain amicable relations. If, however, such officials or troops be met within the territory of tribes on this side of recognised Tibetan-Chinese limits, they should be invited to withdraw into recognised Tibetan-Chinese limits, and, if necessary, should be compelled to do so;

(5) to explore and survey★ as much of the country as possible, visiting, if practicable, the Pemakoi falls and incidentally settling the question of the identity of the Tsangpo and Brahmaputra rivers; and

(6) to submit proposals for a suitable frontier line between India and Tibet in general conformity with the line indicated in paragraph 6 of the despatch enclosed. No boundary must, however, be settled on the ground without the orders of Government except in cases where the recognised limits of the Tibetan-Chinese territory are found to conform approximately to the line indicated above, and to follow such prominent physical features as are essential for a satisfactory strategic and well-defined boundary line. A memorandum by the General Staff on the subject is enclosed for your guidance.

4. I am to add that instructions will be issued to the officer in charge of the Mishmi Mission, which will explore and survey the country to the east of the scene of your operations, to endeavour to get into touch with the expedition, and to connect his results with yours; and, in the event of the sanction of His Majesty's Government to the despatch of a mission to the Miri and Dafla country being received, similar instructions will be issued to the officer in charge of that mission.

I have the honour to be,

Sir,

Your most obedient servant,

A. H. McMahon,

Secretary to the Government of India.

★ A survey party will be attached to the expedition consisting of – 2 British officers, 2 Surveyors, 26 Khalasis, With reserve at base of – 2 Surveyors. 10 Khalasis.

(Annexure F. P.S.F. 1910/1918/Pt 2 Register 3057ª)

Confidential Note by Chief of General Staff

NOTE ON NORTH-EAST FRONTIER

1. Although the survey and exploration work of the past season has not been so fruitful in results as might have been hoped for, and much yet remains to be done before we shall be in a position accurately to define our frontier with China, much useful geographical and political information has been gained from which an indication can be given of the line the frontier should take.

Taking the area section by section as dealt with by the various Missions during the past season, *i.e.*, Miri, Abor, Mishmi and Hkamti Sections, the politico-geographical information will be summarised, a rough definition made of the proposed frontier line, recommendations put forward for the completion of the work, and past errors discussed with a view to profiting in future by the experience gained.

A rough sketch map of the whole area, the latest survey sheets of the Abor and Mishmi work are attached.

2. *The Miri Section.* The Mission did not penetrate far enough to examine or survey a suitable frontier line and the information gathered is not complete nor definite, but the survey parties were able to fix a few peaks by triangulation and these, together with points previously fixed, and evidence obtained through the tribesmen and from observation and deduction, lead to fairly positive conclusions regarding the existence of a continuous range of snowy mountains which would serve as a suitable frontier line in this section.

Starting from the east this range may be described thus:

From about Long. 94°, Lat. 28° 25′ to Long. 93°, Lat. 28° 20′, a high range varying in height from 13,000 to 16,000 feet was seen, and peaks in it fixed. It appeared to be without a break and to form a well-defined barrier. Immediately west of Long. 93°, there appeared to be a knot of high peaks from which a lofty range, in which peaks had been previously fixed, ran in a south-westerly direction towards Tawang. This range was also apparently without a break, the two thus forming a continuous mountain barrier.

Regarding the rivers draining this area, all evidence tends to show that the Subansiri and Kamla both rise south and east of the range and do not pierce it, while the evidence to the same effect is almost equally strong in the case of the Khru river. The Nia chu is said to flow north of the range into the Tsang po.

In the Miri country only two passes appear to cross the range; one towards the eastern end at the head of a tributary of the Subansiri, from all accounts not difficult and much used by the Miris to cross into Tibet for salt: the other leads from the Khru valley into Tibet, is high, difficult and little frequented. The small amount of trade carried on between the western Miris and Tibet appears to cross by a pass in Daphla country.

The first named pass is the most important connection with Tibet throughout this section, it affords the easiest and most direct line by which any effort could be made from Tibet to influence the Miris.

The Northern Miris are in no way under Tibetan influence.

The mountain barrier above-mentioned would therefore appear to be a suitable frontier line but more definite information is necessary, especially as regards the Khru river, and it is important that the pass from the Subansiri in the eastern part of the section should be reconnoitred.

The direction of the frontier line about Tawang requires careful consideration. The present boundary (demarcated) is south of Tawang, running westwards along the foothills from near Odalguri to the southern Bhutan border, and thus a dangerous wedge of territory is thrust in between the Miri country and Bhutan. A comparatively easy and much used trade route traverses this wedge from north to south by which the Chinese would be able to exert influence of pressure on Bhutan, while we have no approach to this salient from a flank, as we have in the case of the Chumbi salient. A rectification of the boundary here is therefore imperative, and an ideal line would appear to be one from the knot of mountains near Long. 93°, Lat. 28° 20′ to the Bhutan border north of Chona Dzong in a direct east and west line with the northern frontier of Bhutan. There appears to be a convenient watershed for it to follow.

Future exploration. The conflict with the Miris at Tali is reported to have had a great effect throughout the whole country of the Miris and neighbouring tribes. Reports of their losses, greatly exaggerated, spread rapidly over the country, causing a great impression. There is little sympathy with the Tali people over the punishment they have received, and there is a general appreciation of the fact that those who receive us well have little to fear from us. The probability is that future expeditions will have a friendly reception, and the chances of opposition have decreased instead of increased.

Recommendations. It is very desirable to obtain exact information of the pass north of Mara, and the extent of communication carried out across it, to discover whether the range observed is the main range, and to put beyond question of doubt the courses of the rivers Subansiri, Kamla, Khru and Nia chu. The months in which the best weather is enjoyed are November and December, and allowing for the best transport and supply services, and a start being made from the base at the earliest possible date after the monsoon, it is improbable that exploration and survey work could be commenced on the higher hills till about the beginning of December in the case of the Subansiri, and the middle of December in the case of the Kamla.

There is reason to believe, however, that a considerable stretch of the Subansiri river is navigable above the Subansiri-Sidan confluence, and if this is so the difficulties of supply on this line will be considerably lessened.

It is recommended that an exploring party and two survey parties with escort should proceed to Mara in the Subansiri valley, whence small parties should be sent up to the pass north of Mara, and up the main valley of the Subansiri. That a similar party be sent through the Daphla country to the upper waters of the Khru river.

To give the parties a good chance of success, early arrangements should be made in the hot weather and supplies collected at the bases (the furthest points accessible by water) by 15th October. To ensure this, arrangements should be commenced in August at the latest.

The difficulties of reaching the northern ranges by the Kamla and Subansiri routes at a season when snowfall has not rendered high altitudes inaccessible, suggests the possibility of using a route which would give access to points whence all doubts could easily be cleared up. Should political considerations admit of a party moving north by the Tawang route, this line appears to offer a solution of the difficulty. Leading, as it does, at once into high country, where the summer rainfall is light, operations might be undertaken in the hot weather. By a move eastwards from about the Se la, north of Chona Dzong, the courses of the rivers, and the existence, or otherwise, of a line of mountains north of Lat. 28° 20′ affording a better frontier line, would be ascertained.

3. *The Abor Section*. At about Long. 95° 10′, Lat. 29° 35′, near the Tibetan district of Pemakoi a very high peak, altitude 25,700 has been fixed – we may call this 'Pemakoi Peak'. From this peak a lofty snowy range runs in a south-westerly direction and, from, evidence obtained locally and the conclusions of survey officers, it is said to be highly improbable that any river breaks through this range, *i.e.*, west of Pemakoi peak. It is therefore probable that this range joins that mentioned in the Miri Section and is the main range of the Himalayahs. The range continues to the east of the Dihang, but its direction and peaks in it have not been observed. At the eastern base of Pemakoi peak the Dihang breaks through by a deep gorge with many windings.

North of the Yamne river a minor snowy range lies east and west at about Lat. 28° 45′, and this is joined to the main range to the north by a low lying range on the east bank of the Dihang. The Yamne river rises south of the minor snow range, and only small tributaries of the Dihang rise on the west of the latter, lowlying range. No rivers pierce either range.

Abors state that north of Pemakoi a large rapid river runs into the Tsang po from the north-east. This river they call the Yigrung, and say that it flows out of the Po country, and that it was this river that caused the great flood in the Dihang in 1899, and bodies of Pobas were washed down by it. The Nagong chu has also been called the Nyagrong chu,★ a name sufficiently like Yigrung to support the idea that this river does not drain into the Dibang, but becomes the Yigrung and drains into the Tsang po.

East of Jido, the northernmost Abor village on the left bank of the Dihang, Abors state is a hill, whence they can see part of the distance up the gorge of the Dihang, and can also see to the east a large river flowing eastwards, but they have no knowledge of the eventual course the latter takes. The river must either join the Nagong chu and become the Yigrung, or, be one of the head waters of the Dibang river system, or, flow into the Rong Thod chu. The last is the most unlikely course, as it would be difficult then to account for the Dibang river having a larger discharge than the Lohit with a much lesser drainage area.

We can therefore come to the conclusion that there exists either:

★ Tibetan Route Book.

(1) a continuous mountain range running east to south-east from the gorge of the Dihang, joining the Mishmi hills which form the watershed between the Rong Thod chu and the Delei, with the unknown river rising east of Jido flowing into the Dibang;

(2) or, a continuous range from the gorge of the Dihang, formed by the low lying range east of Jido joining the minor snow range north of the Yamne, and continuing on to join the Mishmi hills which form the watershed between the Rong Thod chu and the Delei, with the unknown river east of Jido flowing into the Yigrung and thence into the Tsang po.

It would appear that (1) is the more likely conclusion and that we shall probably find the mountain barrier suitable for our frontier along such a line.

Ethnological evidence also supports the choice. The Tibetans and Abors both recognise the Pemakoi range as the boundary, while Abors state that to the north-east of their country is a region of uninhabited, inhospitable mountains.

North of the Pemakoi range the people are called Menba, and in the snows to the north-west of Abor country are said to dwell a cannibal race called Mimat (the Galongs call them Nyimek). The people are Abors as far as Jido on the left bank of the Dihang, and pure Abors extend nearly as far on the right bank, the last three villages below the gorge being mixed Abor and Menba, who act as trade intermediaries between Tibet and Aborland.

As regards passes. There is no route up the Dihang left bank from Jido, the river must be crossed to the right bank, when the route into Tibet crosses the Doshung la. There is said to be a pass at the head of the Sigon and also at the head of the Siyom river. Kinthup visited a pass on the left bank of the Dihang which he called the Zik la; this is probably at the head of the Sik river shown on the map and leads to the source of the unknown river flowing east. No pass leads northwards from the Yamne river region

The best route to reach the northernmost limits of Abor Territory and Tibet is *viâ* Rotung, across the Dihang to Pongging, thence a short distance up the Yamne, across the Yamne-Dihang watershed to Geku, thence *viâ* Simong and the left bank of the Dihang to Jido. This route, from Pongging onwards, passes through the territory of the Panggi and Simong-Panggi Abors, sections most friendly to us. These sections are cut off from access to the plains of Assam by the Minyongs and Padams on either side, inimical to them; they are very desirous of opening trade relations with India, and welcomed the idea of a post at Rotung and a road through their country accordingly; moreover they are the sections of the Abors who have intercourse with Tibet, the Minyongs and Padams have none. The withdrawal from Rotung is therefore most unfortunate; posts at that place and at Geku would keep open the road to the north and afford an avenue by which information regarding Chinese activities in eastern Tibet could reach us.

Recommendations. Both Simong and Riga have made promises to conduct exploring parties next cold weather into the northern limits of the country.

Mr. Bentinck believes that small parties could now proceed through most parts of the country.

A small exploring and survey party, capable of living on the country, should be sent *viâ* Pongging and Simong to Jido to visit the Doshung la.

N

A similar party, which might be accompanied by a police patrol as far as Dosing if necessary, should proceed *viâ* Riga to explore the sources of the Siyom and Sigon rivers. The Boris, at the head of the Siyom, are friendly.

4. *The Mishmi Section.* The work of the mission has revealed little to solve the riddle of the Dibang. The Dri tributary of this river has been fixed as rising in the southern slopes of a high range to the north in about Long. 95° 52′ Lat. 29° 5′. The source of the main river ,which flows from the east remains undiscovered; one branch of it probably rises north-west of the Glei Dakbru Pass; the river flowing due east from near Jido may take a southerly turn and supply the main waters.

In the Lohit valley the work of the mission has thrown into prominence certain facts which bear closely upon the choice of a frontier line.

As regards Passes –

On the left bank: (1) A comparatively easy route from the Lohit valley runs up the Sa alti valley by an easy gradient, and crosses the Taluk la into Hkamti Long. It is considerably used by Tibetan traders.

(2) From this route another branches off southwards and leads into the Ghalum valley.

(3) A route leads up the Ghalum valley and crosses the Krong Jong pass into Hkamti Long.

On the right bank: (4) A route leads up the Torchu valley over the Dou Dakhru pass and down again to the Lohit by the Dou valley.

(5) A route leads up the Delei valley and, crossing the Glei Dakhru pass, leads to Dri in the Rong Thod chu valley a short distance above Rima. It traverses a thickly populated area, enjoys considerable traffic, and affords, next to the Lohit valley, the best access from Tibet into Mishmi country. It was by this route that the Chinese entered in 1911 and issued passports to the Taroan Mishmis of the Delei valley.

(6) Further west is a less used pass, the Hadigra, connecting the same regions.

(7) Three routes lead from the Delei valley, across passes into the Bebejiya country.

Political and Strategical. The Lohit valley is exceedingly sensitive to interference by any of the above-mentioned routes.

The Chinese are reported to be increasing their garrison and building more barracks at Rima.

The Taroan and Miju Mishmis trade freely between Assam and Tibet, acting the part of middlemen. The Chinese made a determined effort in 1911 to bring the Taroans of the Delei and Dou valleys under their sway, informing the headmen there that they were to look to China for protection, in earnest of which passports were distributed, and in the wording of these passports occurs the expression 'has tendered submission.' Furthermore, they demanded that the Taroans should plant the dragon flag at the confluence of the Delei and Lohit rivers. This is eloquent testimony to Chinese ambitions.

The Tibetans of Zayul are desirous of exchanging the Chinese for the British yoke. This fact is known to the Chinese and renders them suspicious of our intentions. The attitude of the Mishmis, on the other hand, is tinctured with caution, and is non-committal, those of them who have migrated to Zayul have been well treated by the Chinese, provided with land, and their taxes remitted. They have seen our columns winding laboriously over their rugged paths at the rate of 5 or 6 miles a day, and realise that some time must elapse before an appeal for assistance could be answered. Their period of greatest danger from the Chinese is when the passes are open in May, June and July, and this is precisely the season when we are least able to help them, a roadless tract and unbridged torrents separate us from them.

The Glei Dakhru pass can be reached from Rima in 5 days, and it is 20 marches from Sadiya.

One of the first necessities therefore is the construction of a graded and bridged road up the valley of the Lohit which will be open throughout the year.

Frontier Posts. It is necessary to establish posts in the Mishmi country for the following reasons.

(1) The Mishmi mountains impose a screen behind which the progress of the policy and movements of the Chinese near our vulnerable north-east salient cannot be observed from within our administrative border, and it is imperative that we should be in a position to watch this progress. Native information, necessarily unreliable, would often arrive too late to be of value.

(2) A wrong construction will be placed, both by the Mishmis and the Chinese, upon our failure to establish posts after the withdrawal of the Mission. The fact that the mission started on its return journey just at a time when a considerable concentration of Chinese troops was taking place at Rima, will be given undue significance, and the Chinese are skilful in turning such matters to account.

(3) The Taroans of the Delei valley, who were induced to surrender their Chinese passports to us, will find themselves in a false position if the Chinese demand an explanation, were we not in a position to support them.

(4) The difficulty of future negotiations with China will be much enhanced by an apparent renunciation of territory by us, and our failure to set up boundary marks or occupy any position will be construed to mean that we are not justified in regarding the country as under our control, and acquiesce in the Chinese demarcation.

(5) Mishmis of all clans are anxious to obtain firearms. They have been informed that they cannot expect them from India. The establishment of posts in their country will minimise the danger of their obtaining them from the Chinese.

(6) Advantage should be taken of the present friendly attitude and primitive armament of the Mishmis to consolidate our position.

Sites for Frontier Posts. Menilkrai, the spot where the Chinese planted their dragon flags to mark their southernmost limits in the Lohit valley, affords no indication of a line of frontier and has been chosen by them with the evident intention of denying to us the only suitable site in the valley for a frontier post – Walong* – an ideal site, in an elevated situation, commanding the valley to the north on either bank, lending itself to the construction of defensible post and offering little difficulty in the matter of watter-supply, as three streams flow through the elevated plateau on which it stands.

* See map showing ground in the vicinity of Walong.

Frontier Line. It is imperative to deny to the Chinese access to the routes up the Sa alti into Hkamti Long and up the Torchu valley into the Dou valley; the frontier line should therefore cross the Lohit valley at some point north of where these two routes leave the valley and from which it would rise by convenient spurs to the mountain chains on either side, and it should also include the Glei Dakhru pass on our side. The point of crossing should therefore be a few miles north of Walong.

Walong was a Mishmi settlement at about the middle of last century and is now a spot where Tibetan herdsmen maintain cattle for Mishmi owners. Three Tibetan hamlets on the left bank of the Lohit, Kahao, Dong and Tinai, of one or two houses each, would then have to be included on our side of the border and their section would have to be arranged for. The two last mentioned are recent settlements, and have existed on sufferance. The inhabitants, of all three, who in the aggregate do not exceed 50 persons, are employed by the Mijus to assist in keeping and pasturing their cattle.

Recommendations. (1) A matter of the first importance is the construction of a road up the Lohit valley as far as Walong. This should be a cart road in the plains section (constructed by the Public Works Department) and in the hill section a good bridle path, with permenent bridges above flood level over the Tidding, Delei and Dou rivers.

For this work the employment of 2 Companies, Sappers and Miners and 2 double Companies Pioneers is recommended, the whole under an Engineer Major of experience in such work. The question of the economical strength of the party resolves itself into one of supply and transport. The above party is the minmum that could hope to complete the work in one season, and the maximum for which supplies, together with the bridging material, etc., could be forwarded. Half the strength of the above party, with a road survey party should advance from Sadiya on 15th September to commence preliminary work from the terminus of the Public Works Department cart track, in order to facilitate supply matters. The remainder of the party should leave Sadiya on 1st November, and at once commence work on the bridges.

An early decision on this point is necessary in order that the officer in charge may be appointed at once, that the details of the scheme may be worked out and the arrangements for supplies and materials made betimes. For a proper economy of time and money all supplies and materials should be delivered at rail head by 15th August:

(2) The construction of Military Police Posts at Walong, Minzang and near the mouth of the Delei river.

(3) Later on, tracks up the Delei river to the Glei Dakhru pass, and up the Ghalum river to the Krong Jong pass should be improved, and a bridge thrown across the Lohit river near Minzang.

(4) An exploring party, accompanied by a survey party, should proceed up the Delei valley to the top of the Glei Dakhru pass. Last season the Mission only penetrated as far as Tajobum in this valley, and the position of the Glei Dakhru pass does not appear to have been correctly fixed, according to tribal evidence It is necessary to determine the configuration of the watershed proposed as a frontier line in this region.

(5) An exploring and survey party should proceed up the Dibang valley to determine the course of the main river and configuration of the mountain ranges.

5. *The Hkamti Long Section.* Very little of the information gathered by the recent Mission to Hkamti is yet to hand, but Captain Pritchard, on his return from his journey of exploration, has been able to supply a great deal of essential matter. The results of the survey work received to date are shown approximately on the accompanying sketch map.

Captain Pritchard has furnished the following information:

Geographical. There are four known passes over the Salween-Irrawaddy watershed from Sachangbum to Lat. 27° 25'.

There is no natural feature up to this Latitude, other than this watershed, which would make a satisfactory frontier line.

The upper reaches of the Tamai, the Taziwang and Taron remain unknown, as do the passes over the snow clad ranges separating them, but Captain Bailey crossed one or two of these rivers in their northernmost reaches, if not indeed at their actual sources.

Political. Excepting the incursion of Chinese and tribesmen from Tenkeng in 1911, there is not a trace of Chinese influence up the valley of the N'mai, and north of the Mekh confluence Chinese are almost unheard of. It is significant that while a few Chinese petty traders are said to come annually down the valley of the Laking, they never cross by the existing passes north of Sachangbum, nor do they use the Mekh valley route, the reason being that by the Laking route Lisus are not met with, whereas these passes, as well as the Mekh valley route lead through Lisu country. This emphasises the importance of the Hpimaw-Laking-N'mai-Hkamti route from the Chinese point of view, enabling them, as it would, to avoid Lisu country.

The Chinese are said to be subduing the Lisus on the Salween, and their main object in so doing must be presumed to be the extension of their influence further west.

We should take steps to prevent their activity furnishing us with another Hpimaw incident further north.

Up to Lat. 27° 25', the people of the N'mai valley are Marus; the Naingvaws, hitherto miscalled black Marus, are merely an isolated clan of the Maru tribe; their southern boundary is the Laking valley. North of this Latitude the people are known as Nungs or Khanungs identical in reality with the Naingvaws, but there is now no communication between them. North of the Khanungs again are the Kinungs, who are probably the Lutze described by Prince Henri d'Orleans. The Naingvaws of some of the N'mai villages paytribute in kind toi Lisus residing both east and west of the Salween, and they suffer greatly from their depredations. Several influential Naingvaws openly asked that we should definitely take over their country, but the majority were afraid to express this sentiment, though they shared it, fearing the subsequent vengeance of the Lisus.

These Lisus have been attracted from their original abode in the valley of the Salween by the gold found at the Mekh-N'mai confluence and further up the N'mai as well, and many of their villages are to be found up the valley of the

Akhyang and on the left bank of the N'mai above the confluence of these two rivers. Some of this gold is exported to China through the Lisu country by the valley of the Akhyang, while some of it goes to that country by the Laking-Hpimaw route. (It is worthy of note that the Lisus dig for gold and do not merely wash for it.)

Except for the almost ridiculous tribute of monkey skins and bees-wax, said to be gathered by the headman of Ze-chi (on the Mekong) among the Khanungs and Kinungs in the valley of the Taron, or similar tribute paid by these tribes to Tibetans further north, the Chinese cannot be said to have any influence, direct or indirect, in the valleys of those rivers which go to form the N'mai. This is probably the case almost up to the Latitude where Captain Bailey crossed the upper waters of these tributaries.

Frontier Line. There are therefore political, ethnological and geographical grounds to support our claim for a frontier line running from some point north of the Taluk la, along the Zayul chu-Irrawaddy watershed, to the junction of this range with the Salween-Irrawaddy watershed in the vicinity of Menkong, and thence in a southerly direction down this watershed, and so branching off along the offshoot from the main range to Pangseng chet.

On further exploration of the extreme apex of the north-east salient and the main tributaries of the N'mai, strategical and geographical considerations may come to light which may render it expedient to align our frontier along one of the inner-lying ranges separating these tributaries. Should this be the case we hold in our hands a handle for negotiation if we claim, as we should in the first instance, the main watersheds described above.

Recommendations. (1) The despatch of a couple of officers, accompanied by a surveyor, is recommended to explore the routes leading from the Lohit into Hkamti Long, and thence to carry out the exploration of the upper reaches of the Nam Tamai, Taziwang and Taron rivers, more particularly to report on any routes leading from China into this territory south of the line traversed by Captain Bailey in 1911, and on routes over the snow clad ranges separating the above rivers. This officer to be also accompanied, if possible, by Maung Chit su, the Burman Myok, who was with Mr. Bernard.

Appointment orders could be issued by these officers to all villages to which Chinese or Tibetan influence has not yet extended. This might be done by pushing Hkamti influence beyond its present limits.

(2) That the Civil Officer at Laukhaung should tour up the N'mai valley at least as far as the Akhyang confluence with a sufficient escort to permit of the detachment of an officer to visit the Lisus of the Akhyang, and another to visit the Lisus on the left bank of the N'mai south of latitude 27° 40', with the object of issuing appointment orders to these Lisus, and warning them that they are under British protection and are not to enter into any relations with the Chinese.

A Public Works Department Officer might accompany to prospect on an alignment for a mule road.

The gold, reported at the N'mai-Mekh confluence, the silver mine said to be at Ritjaw, and the mineral wealth of Hkamti (Shan-'gold land'), might repay the despatch of an officer of the Geological Department to these regions.

(3) The despatch of two survey parties, to survey the country west of the Salween-Irrawaddy watershed, including the range itself, to complete the work eastwards of the surveyor who accompanied Captain Pritchard.

It is important that the Mekh and Akhyang rivers should be traced to their sources.

(4) The time appears to be propitious, owing to the success of the Hkamti Mission, for the despatch of a friendly mission into the Hukawng valley from Burma, to further British influence there and gather information regarding routes from that valley into Hkamti Long.

No recommendations as to situations for frontier posts can be made until fuller information is available, but the valley of the N'mai at about Lat. 27° 40′ or that vicinity, appears to be indicated for the location of a post whence the activities of the Chinese towards the North-East salient could be watched.

6. *The proposed Frontier line.* Subject to alteration which may be necessitated as our knowledge increases, the proposed frontier can be described as a line following the watersheds of:

The Subansiri river, with its tributaries the Kamla and the Khru,

the Dihang as far as the gorge in about Long. 95° 10′ Lat. 29° 40′ and all its tributaries south of that point,

the Dibang and all its tributaries,

the Lohit and all its tributaries south of about Lat. 28° 20′,

thence along the Zayulchu-Irrawaddy watershed to its junction with the Salween-Irrawaddy watershed, which latter it will follow southwards to about Lat. 25° 50′, from which point it will follow the Nam Ti and Taping-N'mai-hka watershed to Pang-seng-chet.

This line is shown by a red chain-dotted line on the accompanying sketch map, and corresponds very closely with the line proposed in paragraph 6 of Government of India letter No. 105 of 1911.

7. *Weak points in the past season's work.* It was in the operations of the Miri Mission chiefly that weaknesses in the preliminary arrangements militated against the successful accomplishment of the task allotted, entailing extra expenditure in the endeavour to remedy them at a later stage, and it was in the supply and transport work that the main errors occurred. The following are some of the points brought to light:

The coolies were in many cases of unsuitable classes, unfitted for the work and insufficient in number.

An estimate of the transport required in a difficult and unknown country can only be made out by an experienced officer who is put in possession of all existing information and the objectives of the expedition. It would be advisable to utilise the services of a skilled Supply and Transport or other military officer.

To ensure proper control over supply depôts and along a line of communications and to prevent waste of supplies and of transporting power, a small staff of Non-Commissioned Officers from the Indian Army (preferably Gurkhas on this frontier) should be employed with one or more officers to command, and an organisation similar to a coolie corps on a military expedition adopted.

In order that Supplies may be sent forward in the correct proportions, a British Supply Subordinate should be placed in control of supplies at the base.

The collection of supplies should be commenced at a very early date so that the expedition may start directly weather conditions are favourable.

The Officer Commanding the escort should have command of the whole Supply and Transport Staff and control of these arrangements. This officer is responsible for the safety of the expedition and that safety is intimately bound up with the Supply and Transport question and the organisation of the line of communication.

A Medical Officer should accompany an expedition of any size where opposition is a possibility.

8. Throughout this note the assumption is made that the pertinacity of the Chinese will not long permit of their acquiescence in the present state of affairs in Tibet. Although their activity on our frontier may have received a temporary check on account of the Revolution, history proves that succeeding a Revolution, as a rule, a period of national vigour and expansion follows. A renewal of activity may therefore be expected. Moreover the Republican Government has revealed its intention of making the new China a Military Power, and we have received news that the Chinese are already sending parties to align the frontier with the Republican flag on the borders of Assam.

There is therefore no time to be lost in declaring to the Chinese in unmistakeable terms the line the frontier is to follow, in making our occupation of that line effective in so far as placing ourselves in positions whence we can watch developments and prevent further encroachments is concerned, and in improving communications on our side. By reason of the effect produced by the expeditions of last season – *although the effect may have been discounted to some extent, in the case of the Abors, by the withdrawal from Rotung* –, the present time is a propitious one to carry on and complete the work of survey and exploration throughout these regions. It is therefore worth while to make the effort now; if we delay, the necessity for so doing may, later on, be forced on us at a greater expenditure of force and money.

9. It is obviously dangerous to attempt to delimit a frontier on incomplete geographical knowledge, and the time for demarcation may come before many years are past. When that time comes we should endeavour to avoid the heavy pecuniary loss which has occurred in past demarcations in other parts of the world owing to inexact geographical expression in the definition of the frontier, and consequent delay and constant reference of points of dispute, by being ready with such complete geographical information that vague definition will not occur and that technical accuracy of expression will be assured.

10. To sum up, the recommendations for next season's work are:

In the Miri Section. (1) An exploring and Survey party with escort to proceed to Mara in the Subansiri valley and explore the pass and upper waters of the valley.

(2) A similar party through the Daphla country to the upper waters of the Khru river.

In the Abor Section. (3) Exploring and Survey parties to the Doshung la and to the head waters of the Siyom and Sigon rivers.

In the Mishmi Section. (4) The employment of 2 Sapper Companies and 2 double companies of Pioneers in the construction of a bridged bridle track up the Lohit valley to Walong.

(5) The construction of Military Police Posts at Walong, Minzang and near the mouth of the Delei river.

(6) The exploration and survey of the Delei valley to the top of the Glei Dakhru pass.

(7) The exploration and survey of the upper waters of the Dibang.

The Hkamti Long Section. (8) The despatch of a couple of officers with a surveyor to explore the passes from the Lohit into Hkamti Long and the upper waters of the northern tributaries of the N'mai hka, *i.e.,* the Nam Tamai, Taziwang and Taron.

(9) Tour by the Civil Officer, Laukhaung up the N'mai valley to visit the Lisus in that valley and tributary valleys.

(10) The despatch of Survey parties to complete the survey east of the N'mai and west of the Salween-Irrawaddy watershed.

(11) The despatch of a friendly Mission into the Hukawng valley.

Dated 1st June 1912.

APPENDIX 10

(F.O. 535/15. No. 193 and P.E.F. 1912/69 No. 3460/12)

*Extract from Memorandum communicated to Wai-chiao Pu by
Sir J. Jordan, 17 August 1912*

His Majesty's Government consider it to be in the interest of harmonious relations that they should now state clearly their policy in regard to Thibet. His Majesty's Minister had the honour to inform his Excellency Yuan Shih-kai that a communication in this respect would shortly be submitted to the Chinese Government, and he now begs, under instructions from Sir Edward Grey, to make following definite statement of that policy:

1. His Majesty's Government, while they have formally recognised the 'suzerain rights' of China in Thibet, have never recognised, and are not prepared to recognise, the right of China to intervene actively in the internal administration of Thibet, which should remain, as contemplated by the treaties, in the hands of the Thibetan authorities, subject to the right of Great Britain and China, under Article 1 of the Convention of the 27th April 1906, to take such steps as may be necessary to secure the due fulfilment of treaty stipulations.
2. On these grounds His Majesty's Government must demur altogether to the conduct of the Chinese officers in Thibet during the last two years in assuming all administrative power in the country, and to the doctrine propounded in Yuan Shih-kai's presidential order of the 21st April 1912, that Thibet is to be 'regarded as on an equal footing with the provinces of China proper,' and that 'all administrative matters' connected with that country 'will come within the sphere of internal administration.'
His Majesty's Government formally decline to accept such a definition of the political status of Thibet, and they must warn the Chinese Republic against any repetition by Chinese officers of the conduct to which exception has been taken.
3. While the right of China to station a representative, with a suitable escort, at Lhassa, with authority to advise the Thibetans as to their foreign relations, is not disputed, His Majesty's Government are not prepared to acquiesce in the maintenance of an unlimited number of Chinese troops either at Lhassa or in Tibet generally.
4. His Majesty's Government must press for the conclusion of a written agreement on the foregoing lines as a condition precedent to extending their recognition to the Chinese Republic.
5. In the meantime all communication with Thibet *viâ* India must be regarded as absolutely closed to the Chinese, and will only be reopened on such conditions as His Majesty's Government may see fit to impose when an agreement has been concluded on the lines indicated above.

This does not apply to the withdrawal of the present Chinese garrison at Lhassa, who, as Yuan Shih-kai has already been informed, are at liberty to return to China *via* India if they wish to do so.

Sir John Jordan has the honour to request the Wai-chiao Pu to favour him with a reply to this Memorandum.

APPENDIX II

(Simla Conference Report F.O. 371/1931)

India-Tibet Frontier (1914). Exchange of Notes between the British and Tibetan Plenipotentiaries

To
  Lönchen Shatra,
  Tibetan Plenipotentiary.

In February last you accepted the India-Tibet frontier from the Isu Razi Pass to the Bhutan frontier, as given in the map (two sheets)*, of which two copies are herewith attached, subject to the confirmation of your Government and the following conditions:

(*a*) The Tibetan ownership in private estates on the British side of the frontier will not be disturbed.

(*b*) If the sacred places of Tso Karpo and Tsari Sarpa fall within a day's march of the British side of the frontier, they will be included in Tibetan territory and the frontier modified accordingly.

I understand that your Government have now agreed to this frontier subject to the above two conditions. I shall be glad to learn definitely from you that this is the case.

You wished to know whether certain dues now collected by the Tibetan Government at Tsöna Jong and in Kongbu and Kham from the Monpas and Lopas for articles sold may still be collected. Mr. Bell has informed you that such details will be settled in a friendly spirit, when you have furnished to him the further information, which you have promised.

The final settlement of this India-Tibet frontier will help to prevent causes of future dispute and thus cannot fail to be of great advantage to both Governments.

DELHI,   A. H. McMAHON,
24th March 1914   *British Plenipotentiary.*

★ This map (eight miles to the inch) was first published in 'An Altas of the Northern Frontier of India', by the Ministry of External Affairs, New Delhi, 1960.

TRANSLATION

To
   Sir Henry McMahon,
   British Plenipotentiary to the China-Tibet Conference.

As it was feared that there might be friction in future unless the boundary between India and Tibet is clearly defined, I submitted the map, which you sent to me in February last, to the Tibetan Government at Lhasa for orders. I have now received orders from Lhasa, and I accordingly agree to the boundary as marked in red in the two copies of the maps signed by you subject to the conditions, mentioned in your letter, dated the 24th March, sent to me through Mr. Bell. I have signed and sealed the two copies of the maps. I have kept one copy here and return herewith the other.

Sent on the 29th day of the 1st Month of the Wood-Tiger year (25th March 1914) by Lonchen Shatra, the Tibetan Plenipotentiary.

[Seal of Lonchen Shatra].

(F.O. 371/1931)

Convention between Great Britain, China and Tibet (1914)

His Majesty the King of the United Kingdom of Great Britain and Ireland and of the British Dominions beyond the Seas, Emperor of India, His Excellency the President of the Republic of China, and His Holiness the Dalai Lama of Tibet, being sincerely desirous to settle by mutual agreement various questions concerning the interests of their several States on the Continent of Asia, and further to regulate the relations of their several Governments, have resolved to conclude a Convention on this subject and have nominated for this purpose their respective Plenipotentiaries, that is to say:

His Majesty the King of the United Kingdom of Great Britain and Ireland and of the British Dominions beyond the Seas, Emperor of India, Sir Arthur Henry McMahon, Knight Grand Cross of the Royal Victorian Order, Knight Commander of the Most Eminent Order of the Indian Empire, Companion of the Most Exalted Order of the Star of India, Secretary to the Government of India, Foreign and Political Department;

His Excellency the President of the Republic of China, Monsieur Ivan Chen, Officer of the Order of the Chia H O;

His Holiness the Dalai Lama of Tibet, Lonchen Ga-den Shatra Pal-jor Dorje; who having communicated to each other their respective full powers and finding them to be in good and due form have agreed upon and concluded the following Convention in eleven Articles:

ARTICLE I

The Conventions specified in the Schedule to the Present Convention shall, except in so far as they may have been modified by, or may be inconsistent with or repugnant to, any of the provisions of the present Convention, continue to be binding upon the High Contracting Parties.

ARTICLE 2

The Governments of Great Britain and China recognising that Tibet is under the suzerainty of China, and recognising also the autonomy of Outer Tibet, engage to respect the territorial integrity of the country, and to abstain from interference in the administration of Outer Tibet (including the selection and installation of the Dalai Lama), which shall remain in the hands of the Tibetan Government at Lhasa.

The Government of China engages not to convert Tibet into a Chinese province. The Government of Great Britain engages not to annex Tibet or any portion of it.

ARTICLE 3

Recognising the special interest of Great Britain, in virtue of the geographical position of Tibet, in the existence of an effective Tibetan Government, and in the maintenance of peace and order in the neighbourhood of the frontiers of

India and adjoining States, the Government of China engages, except as provided in Article 4 of this Convention, not to send troops into Outer Tibet, nor to station civil or military officers, nor to establish Chinese colonies in the country. Should any such troops or officials remain in Outer Tibet at the date of the signature of this Convention, they shall be withdrawn within a period not exceeding three months.

The Government of Great Britain engages not to station military or civil officers in Tibet (except as provided in the Convention of September 7, 1904, between Great Britain and Tibet) nor troops (except the Agents' escorts), nor to establish colonies in that country.

ARTICLE 4

The foregoing Article shall not be held to preclude the continuance of the arrangement by which, in the past, a Chinese high official with suitable escort has been maintained at Lhasa, but it is hereby provided that the said escort shall in no circumstances exceed 300 men.

ARTICLE 5

The Governments of China and Tibet engage that they will not enter into any negotiations of agreements regarding Tibet with one another, or with any other Power, excepting such negotiations and agreements between Great Britain and Tibet as are provided for by the Convention of September 7, 1904, between Great Britain and Tibet and the Convention of April 27, 1906, between Great Britain and China.

ARTICLE 6

Article 3 of the Convention of April 27, 1906, between Great Britain and China is hereby cancelled, and it is understood that in Article 9(d) of the Convention of September 7, 1904, between Great Britain and Tibet the term 'Foreign Power' does not include China.

Not less favourable treatment shall be accorded to British commerce than to the commerce of China or the most favoured nation.

ARTICLE 7

(a) The Tibet Trade Regulations of 1893 and 1908 are hereby cancelled.

(b) The Tibetan Government engages to negotiate with the British Government new Trade Regulations for Outer Tibet to give effect to Articles 2, 4 and 5 of the Convention of September 7, 1904, between Great Britain and Tibet without delay; provided always that such Regulations shall in no way modify the present Convention except with the consent of the Chinese Government.

ARTICLE 8

The British Agent who resides at Gyantse may visit Lhasa with his escort whenever it is necessary to consult with the Tibetan Government regarding matters arising out of the Convention of September 7, 1904, between Great Britain and Tibet, which it has been found impossible to settle at Gyantse by correspondence or otherwise.

ARTICLE 9

For the purpose of the present Convention the borders of Tibet, and the boundary between Outer and Inner Tibet, shall be as shown in red and blue respectively on the map attached hereto.

Nothing in the present Convention shall be held to prejudice the existing rights of the Tibetan Government in Inner Tibet, which include the power to select and appoint the high priests of monasteries and to retain full control in all matters affecting religious institutions.

ARTICLE 10

The English, Chinese and Tibetan texts of the present Convention have been carefully examined and found to correspond, but in the event of there beng any difference of meaning between them the English text shall be authoritative.

ARTICLE 11

The present Convention will take effect from the date of signature.

In token whereof the respective Plenipotentiaries have signed and sealed this Convention, three copies in English, three in Chinese and three in Tibetan.

Done at Simla this third day of July, A.D., one thousand nine hundred and fourteen, corresponding with the Chinese date, the third day of the seventh month of the third year of the Republic, and the Tibetan date, the tenth day of the fifth month of the Wood-Tiger year.

INITIAL* OF THE LONCHEN SHATRA.   (INITIALLED) A.H.M.
Seal of the   *Seal of the*
Lonchen Shatra.   *British Plenipotentiary.*

SCHEDULE

(1) Convention between Great Britain and China relating to Sikkim and Tibet, signed at Calcutta the 17th March 1890.

(2) Convention between Great Britain and Tibet, signed at Lhasa the 7th September 1904.

(3) Convention between Great Britain and China respecting Tibet, signed at Peking the 27th April 1906.

The notes exchanged are to the following effect:

(1) It is understood by the High Contracting Parties that Tibet forms part of Chinese territory.

(2) After the selection and installation of the Dalai Lama by the Tibetan Government, the latter will notify the installation to the Chinese Government, whose representative at Lhasa will then formally communicate to His Holiness the titles consistent with his dignity, which have been conferred by the Chinese Government.

(3) It is also understood that the selection and appointment of all officers in Outer Tibet will rest with the Tibetan Government.

(4) Outer Tibet shall not be represented in the Chinese Parliament or in any other similar body.

(5) It is understood that the escorts attached to the British Trade Agencies in Tibet shall not exceed seventy-five per centum of the escort of the Chinese Representative at Lhasa.

* Owing to it not being possible to write initials in Tibetan, the mark of the Lönchen at this place is his signature.

(6) The Government of China is hereby released from its engagements under Article 3 of the Convention of March 17, 1890, between Great Britain and China to prevent acts of aggression from the Tibetan side of the Tibet-Sikkim frontier.

(7) The Chinese high official referred to in Article 4 will be free to enter Tibet as soon as the terms of Article 3 have been fulfilled to the satisfaction of representatives of the three signatories to this Convention, who will investigate and report without delay.

INITIAL* OF LONCHEN SHATRA	(INITIALLED) A.H.M.
Seal of the	*Seal of the British*
Lonchen Shatra	*Plenipotentiary.*

* Owing to it not being possible to write initials in Tibetan, the mark of the Lonchen at this place is his signature.

(Aitchison's Treaties, XIV (1929) pp. 39–41)

Whereas by Article 7 of the Convention concluded between the Governments of Great Britain, China and Tibet on the third day of July, A.D., 1914, the Trade Regulations of 1893 and 1908 were cancelled and the Tibetan Government engaged to negotiate with the British Government new Trade Regulations for Outer Tibet to give effect to Articles 2, 4 and 5 of the Convention of 1904;

His Majesty the King of the United Kingdom of Great Britain and Ireland, and of the British Dominions beyond the Seas, Emperor of India, and His Holiness the Dalai Lama of Tibet have for this purpose named as their Plenipotentiaries, that is to say:

His Majesty the King of Great Britain and Ireland and of the British Dominions beyond the Seas, Emperor of India, Sir, A. H. McMahon, G.C.V.O., K.C.I.E., C.S.I.;

His Holiness the Dalai Lama of Tibet – Lonchen Ga-den Shatra Pal-jor Dorje;

And whereas Sir A. H. McMahon and Lonchen Ga-den Shatra Pal-jor Dorje have communicated to each other since their respective full powers and have found them to be in good and true form, the following Regulations have been agreed upon:

(1) The area falling within a radius of three miles from the British Trade Agency site will be considered as the area of such Trade Mart.

It is agreed that British subjects may lease lands for the building of houses and godowns at such Marts. This arrangement shall not be held to prejudice the right of British subjects to rent houses and godowns outside the Marts for their own accommodation and the storage of their goods. British subjects desiring to lease building sites shall apply through the British Trade Agent to the Tibetan Trade Agent. In consultation with the British Trade Agent the Tibetan Trade Agent will assign such or other suitable building sites without unnecessary delay. They shall fix the terms of the leases in conformity with the existing laws and rates.

(2) The administration of the Trade Marts shall remain with the Tibetan authorities, with the exception of the British Trade Agency sites and compounds of the rest-houses, which will be under the exclusive control of the British Trade Agents.

The Trade Agents at the Marts and Frontier Officers shall be of suitable rank, and shall hold personal intercourse and correspondence with one another on terms of mutual respect and friendly treatment.

(3) In the event of disputes arising at the Marts or on the routes to the Marts between British subjects and subjects of other nationalities, they shall be enquired into and settled in personal conference between the British and Tibetan Trade Agents at the nearest Mart. Where there is a divergence of view the law of the country to which the defendant belongs shall guide.

All questions in regard to rights, whether of property or person, arising between British subjects, shall be subject to the jurisdiction of the British Authorities.

British subjects, who may commit any crime at the Marts or on the routes to the Marts, shall be handed over by the Local Authorities to the British Trade Agent at the Mart nearest to the scene of offence, to be tried and punished according to the laws of India, but such British subjects shall not be subjected by the Local Authorities to any ill-usage in excess of necessary restraint.

Tibetan subjects, who may be guilty of any criminal act towards British subjects, shall be arrested and punished by the Tibetan Authorities according to law.

Should it happen that a Tibetan subject or subjects bring a criminal complaint against a British subject or subjects before the British Trade Agent, the Tibetan Authorities shall have the right to send a representative or representatives of suitable rank to attend the trial in the British Trade Agent's Court. Similarly in cases in which a British subject or subjects have reason to complain against a Tibetan subject or subjects, the British Trade Agent shall have the right to send a representative or representatives to the Tibetan Trade Agent's Court to attend the trial.

(4) The Government of India shall retain the right to maintain the telegraph lines from the Indian frontier to the Marts. Tibetan messages will be duly received and transmitted by these lines. The Tibetan Authorities shall be responsible for the due protection of the telegraph lines from the Marts to the Indian frontier, and it is agreed that all persons damaging the lines or interfering with them in any way or with the officials engaged in the inspection or maintenance thereof shall at once be severely punished.

(5) The British Trade Agents at the various Trade Marts now or hereafter to be established in Tibet may make arrangements for the carriage and transport of their posts to and from the frontier of India. The couriers employed in conveying these posts shall receive all possible assistance from the Local Authorities, whose districts they traverse, and shall be accorded the same protection and facilities as the persons employed in carrying the despatches of the Tibetan Government.

No restrictions whatever shall be placed on the employment by British officers and traders of Tibetan subjects in any lawful capacity. The persons so employed shall not be exposed to any kind of molestation or suffer any loss of civil rights, to which they may be entitled as Tibetan subjects, but they shall not be exempted from lawful taxation. If they be guilty of any criminal act, they shall be dealt with by the Local Authorities according to law without any attempt on the part of their employer to screen them.

(6) No rights of monopoly as regards commerce or industry shall be granted to any official or private company, institution, or individual in Tibet. It is of course understood that companies and individuals, who have already received such monopolies from the Tibetan Government previous to the conclusion of this agreement shall retain their rights and privileges until the expiry of the period fixed.

(7) British subjects shall be at liberty to deal in kind or in money, to sell their goods to whomsoever they please, to hire transport of any kind, and to conduct

in general their business transactions in conformity with local usage and without any vexations, restrictions or oppressive exactions whatever. The Tibetan Authorities will not hinder the British Trade Agents or other British subjects from holding personal intercourse or correspondence with the inhabitants of the country.

It being the duty of the Police and the Local Authorities to afford efficient protection at all times to the persons and property of the British subjects at the Marts and along the routes to the Marts, Tibet engages to arrange effective police measures at the Marts and along the routes to the Marts.

(8) Import and Export in the following Articles:
arms ammunition, military stores, liquors and intoxicating or narcotic drugs

may at the option of either Government be entirely prohibited, or permitted only on such conditions as either Government on their own side may think fit to impose.

(9) The present Regulations shall be in force for a period of ten years reckoned from the date of signature by the two Plenipotentiaries; but, if no demand for revision be made on either side within six months after the end of the first ten years the Regulations shall remain in force for another ten years from the end of the first ten year; and so it shall be at the end of each successive ten years.

(10) The English and Tibetan texts of the present Regulations have been carefully compared, but in the event of there being any difference of meaning between them the English text shall be authoritative.

(11) The present Regulations shall come into force from the date of signature.

Done at Simla this third day of July, A.D., one thousand nine hundred and fourteen, corresponding with the Tibetan date, the tenth day of the fifth month of the Wood-Tiger year.

Seal of the Dalai Lama.

Signature of the Lonchen Shatra.   A. HENRY McMAHON,
                                                                      British Plenipotentiary.
Seal of the   *Seal of the*
Lonchen   *British*
Shatra.   *Plenipotentiary.*

Seal of the	*Seal of the*	*Seal of the*	*Seal of the*
Drepung	*Sera*	*Gaden*	*National*
Monastery.	*Monastery.*	*Monastery.*	*Assembly.*

APPENDIX 14

(White Paper I. pp. 98–101)

Agreement between the Republic of India and the People's Republic of China on Trade and Intercourse between Tibet Region of China and India (1954)

The Government of the Republic of India and the Central People's Government of the People's Republic of China.

Being desirous of promoting trade and cultural intercourse between Tibet Region of China and India and of facilitating pilgrimage and travel by the peoples of China and India.

Have resolved to enter into the present Agreement based on the following principles:

(1) mutual respect for each other's territorial integrity and sovereignty,
(2) mutual non-aggression,
(3) mutual non-interference in each other's internal affairs,
(4) equality and mutual benefit, and
(5) peaceful co-existence.

And for this purpose have appointed as their respective Plenipotentiaries:

The Government of the Republic of India, H.E. Nedyam Raghavan, Ambassador Extraordinary and Plenipotentiary of India accredited to the People's Republic of China; the Central People's Government of the People's Republic of China, H.E. Chang Han-fu, Vice-Minister of Foreign Affairs of the Central People's Government, who, having examined each other's credentials and finding them in good and due form, have agreed upon the following:

ARTICLE 1

The High Contracting Parties mutually agree to establish Trade Agencies:

(1) The Government of India agrees that the Government of China may establish Trade Agencies at New Delhi, Calcutta and Kalimpong.
(2) The Government of China agrees that the Government of India may establish Trade Agencies at Yatung, Gyantse and Gartok.

The trade Agencies of both Parties shall be accorded the same status and same treatment. The Trade Agents of both Parties shall enjoy freedom from arrest while exercising their functions, and shall enjoy in respect of themselves, their wives and children who are dependent on them for livelihood freedom from search.

The Trade Agencies of both Parties shall enjoy the privileges and immunities for couriers, mail-bags and communications in code.

ARTICLE 2

The High Contracting Parties agree that traders of both countries known to be customarily and specifically engaged in trade between Tibet Region of China and India may trade at the following places:

(1) The Government of China agrees to specify (1) Yatung, (2) Gyantse and (3) Phari as markets for trade. The Government of India agrees that trade may be carried on in India, including places like (1) Kalimpong, (2) Siliguri and (3) Calcutta, according to customary practice.

(2) The Government of China agrees to specify (1) Gartok, (2) Pulanchung (Taklakot), (3) Gyanima-Khargo, (4) Gyanima-Charkra, (5) Rampura, (6) Dongbra, (7) Puling-Sumdo, (8) Nabra, (9) Shangtse and (10) Tashigong as markets for trade; the Government of India agrees that in future, when in accordance with the development and need of trade between the Ari District of Tibet Region of China and India, it has become necessary to specify markets for trade in the corresponding district in India adjacent to the Ari District of Tibet Region of China, it will be prepared to consider on the basis of equality and reciprocity to do so.

ARTICLE 3

The High Contracting Parties agree that pilgrimage by religious believers of the two countries shall be carried on in accordance with the following provisions:

(1) Pilgrims from India of Lamaist, Hindu and Buddhist faiths may visit Kang Rimpoche (Kailas) and Mavam Tso (Manasarovar) in Tibet Region of China in accordance with custom.

(2) Pilgrims from Tibet Region of China of Lamaist and Buddhist faiths may visit Banaras, Sarnath, Gaya and Sanchi in India in accordance with custom.

(3) Pilgrims customarily visiting Lhasa may continue to do so in accordance with custom.

ARTICLE 4

Traders and pilgrims of both countries may travel by the following passes and route:

(1) Shipki La Pass, (2) Mana Pass, (3) Niti Pass, (4) Kungri Bingri Pass, (5) Darma Pass, and (6) Lipu Lekh Pass.

Also, the customary route leading to Tashigong along the valley of the Shangatsangpu (Indus) River may continue to be traversed in accordance with custom.

ARTICLE 5

For travelling across the border, the High Contracting Parties agree that diplomatic personnel, officials and nationals of the two countries shall hold passports issued by their own respective countries and visaed by the other Party except as provided in Paragraphs 1, 2, 3 and 4 of this Article.

(1) Traders of both countries known to be customarily and specifically engaged in trade between Tibet Region of China and India, their wives and children who are dependent on them for livelihood and their attendants will be allowed entry for purposes of trade into India or Tibet Region of China, as the case may be, in accordance with custom on the production of certificates duly issued by the local government of their own country or by its duly authorised agents and examined by the border checkposts of the other Party.

(2) Inhabitants of the border districts of the two countries who cross the border to carry on petty trade or to visit friends and relatives may proceed to the border districts of the other Party as they have customarily done heretofore and need not be restricted to the passes and route specified in Article 4 above and shall not be required to hold passports, visas or permits.

(3) Porters and mule-team drivers of the two countries who cross the border to perform necessary transportation services need not hold passports issued by their own country, but shall only hold certificates good for a definite period of time (three months, half a year or one year) daily issued by the local government of their own country or by its duly authorised agents and produce them for registration at the border checkposts of the other Party.

(4) Pilgrims of both countries need not carry documents of certification but shall register at the border checkposts of the other Party and receive a permit for pilgrimage.

(5) Notwithstanding the provisions of the foregoing paragraphs of this Article, either Government may refuse entry to any particular person.

(6) Persons who enter the territory of the other Party in accordance with the foregoing paragraphs of this Article may stay within its territory only after complying with the procedures specified by the other Party.

ARTICLE 6

The present Agreement shall come into effect upon ratification by both Governments and shall remain in force for eight (8) years. Extension of the present Agreement may be negotiated by the two Parties if either Party requests for it six (6) months prior to the expiry of the Agreement and the request is agreed to by the other Party.

Done in duplicate in Peking on the twentyninth day of April, 1954, in the Hindi, Chinese and English languages, all texts being equally valid.

(SD.) NEDYAM RAGHAVAN,
    Plenipotentiary of the
    Government of the
    Republic of China.

(SD.) CHANG HAN-FU,
    Plenipotentiary of the
    Central People's Government,
    People's Republic of China.

APPENDIX 15

(Hsinhua News Agency, 30 April 1960)

Chou En-lai's Press Conference, April 30, 1960

Saturday, April 30, 1960   *Supplement No. 42*
042942 – Full Proceedings of Premier Chou's press conference in New Delhi.

New Delhi, April twenty-ninth (Hsinhua) – following is the report of the full proceedings of Premier Chou En-lai's press conference in New Delhi:

Premier Chou En-lai gave a press conference in Rashtrapati Bhavan in India from ten thirty p.m. April twenty-fifth to zero one zero zero a.m. April twenty-sixth. More than one hundred fifty correspondents of India and from other countries attended the press conference. Premier Chou En-lai first issued a written statement (which was released on April twenty-fifth). He then said that he was willing to answer any question put by the correspondents. However, he expressed the hope that the newspapers or news agencies would publish the full proceedings or the full text of their respective questions and the answers to them. The major Chinese newspapers would also publish the proceedings in full and the English language *Peking Review* would also print them so that a copy would be made available to everyone of them. Following are the questions and answers:

Question (K. Sabarwel, an Indian correspondent for Press Syndicate of Japan): Your Excellency has invited Prime Minister Nehru to visit China. Has Nehru accepted the invitation?

Answer: Prime Minister Nehru told me that he would consider according to how the work between the officials of the two sides proceeds.

Question (C. Raghavan of the Press Trust of India): In India, your letters to Prime Minister Nehru have all been published in full. But the Chinese newspapers have not published Prime Minister Nehru's letters to you. Speaking about freedom of speech, would you also take steps to publish the letters sent by our Prime Minister in the Chinese press?

Answer: This gentleman has probably not read Chinese newspapers. The Chinese papers long ago published in full Prime Minister Nehru's letters to me and my replies to him.

Question (Mahesh Chandra of *The Statesman*, India): What has prevented you to return to the *Status quo ante*, that is the position of the border as obtained one or two years ago? For it was one or two years ago that actions were taken.

Answer: On the part of China, in the last one or two years as well as in the past, the Chinese Government has never taken action to change the existing state of the border.

Question (K. Rangaswami of Hindu, India): In which sector in the talks did the two Prime Ministers find the greatest difference?

Answer: There are disputes both with regard to the eastern sector and the western sector. As regards the middle sector, the dispute is comparatively small.

Regarding the eastern sector: the boundary line which appears on our maps is to the south of the boundary line one Indian maps. The area included in India on Indian maps had long been under Chinese administrative jurisdiction. Since its independence, India has gradually moved forward up to the line delineated on its present maps. The Indian Government asks us to recognise this line which it sometimes even openly said is the McMahon Line. We absolutely cannot recognise this line, because it was illegally delineated through an exchange of secret notes by British imperialism with the Tibetan local authorities of China, and the successive Chinese Governments have never recognised it. Nevertheless, pending a settlement of the Sino-Indian boundary question, we are willing to maintain the present state and will not cross this line; in negotiations on the Boundary question, too, we have not put forward territorial claims as pre-conditions. Since we have adopted such an attitude of understanding and conciliation, it appears that comparatively less time has been spent on discussions of the eastern sector of the boundary.

With regard to the western sector: the way of delineation of the boundary on Chinese maps is different from that on Indian maps. Despite small discrepancies which exist in the delineations of this sector on past Chinese maps, these maps are in the main consistent. The Indian maps, however, have changed many times. China has always exercised administrative jurisdiction in accordance with the line on Chinese maps, that is, the line which runs from the Karakoram pass southeastward roughly along the watershed of the Karakoram Mountain to the Kongka Pass, then turns southward from the Kongka Pass and extends to the vicinity of the Pare river. The border area to the north and east of this line has historically been under the jurisdiction of China. The greater part of it, including the Aksai Chin area, is under the jurisdiction of Sinkiang of China, and the smaller part under the jurisdiction of Tibet of China. We have many historical documents and materials to prove this historical administrative jurisdiction. Since the founding of New China, it has always exercised juris-diction in this area as the main communication artery linking southern Sinkiang and the Ari area of Tibet. With regard to this area, the delineation of the boundary on Indian maps before the middle of the nineteenth century was approximate to that on Chinese maps. During the period from eighteen sixty-five to nineteen forty-three, the more important maps of India were quite vague with regard to the delineation of this sector of the buondary. The official Indian map of nineteen fifty used colour shades to indicate an outline of this sector of the Boundary as is now advocated by India. Nevertheless, this map still marked the area as undelimited. Finally, in nineteen fifty-four, the line, just like the eastern sector of the boundary, became as if it had been formally delineated as shown on the map you now see in Indian newspapers. Therefore, even the changes of the Indian maps during the past one hundred years and more can also fully prove that the boundary in this area is undelimited. We have asked the Indian Government to adopt an attitude towards this area similar to the attitude of the Chinese Government towards the area of the eastern sector, that is, it may keep its own stand, while agreeing to conduct negotiations and not to cross the line of China's administrative jurisdiction as shown on Chinese maps. The Indian Government has not entirely agreed to this. Therefore, there exists a relatively bigger dispute and the two Prime

Ministers have spent a particularly long period of time on discussions in this connection.

With regard to the middle sector: there are also disputes, but they are questions concerning individual places.

Question (B. G. Verghese of the *Times of India*): What are the Chinese claims in regard to Bhutan?

Answer: I am sorry to disappoint you. We have no claim with regard to Bhutan, nor do we have any dispute with it. You may recall that in its letters to the Indian Government, the Chinese Government twice mentioned that China has no boundary dispute with Sikkim and Bhutan and that China respects India's proper relations with Sikkim and Bhutan.

Question (S. G. Roy of *Pakistan Times*): Prime Minister Koirala of Nepal said that China laid claim to Mt. Jolmo Longma. What is the situation?

Answer: Thank you for reminding us of this question. Tomorrow we are going to Nepal. I believe that we shall be able to settle this question in a friendly manner.

Question (Telang of the Press Trust of India): I mean to ask P. M. whether it is true that China regards that mountain as its own.

Answer: The course of events is not like what you have learned. Since this is a question of foreign relations, I do not intend to disclose the detailed contents of the talks between the Prime Ministers of our two countries.

Question (L. P. Atkinson of the British *Daily Mail*): Is the Chinese Prime Minister pleased with his talks in Delhi inasmuch as he has not given an inch to India? It is to be remembered in this connection that India's basis for these talks is that China should vacate aggression.

Answer: China has never committed agression against the territory of any country. Moreover, China in its history has always suffered from agression by others. Even now, we still have territory, Taiwan for instance, which has been invaded and occupied by others. I am very glad that both the Chinese and Indian Prime Ministers in their talks fully agreed that territorial claims should not be made by either side as pre-conditions for negotiations. This proves that the talks have proceeded on a friendly basis, Speaking about aggression against others' territory, since this gentleman represents a British newspaper, he of course knows what Chinese territory Britain is still occupying up till now.

Question (J. P. Chaturvedi of the Hindi Daily *Aj* of Banaras): when the Indian Government drew the attention of the Chinese Government to Chinese maps, the Chinese Government said that they were drawn during the period of the Kuomintang without systematic and careful surveys and that they would be adjusted once careful surveys are made. Is this true? Why didn't you raise the question of the maps during your first and second talks with Nehru? And why do you now want to press forward Chinese claim on the basis of the Chinese history while you want us to forget about the things which happened during the British period?

Answer: Chinese maps have been drawn according to the situation which has prevailed throughout history. At some places there are differences between these maps and the actual state of jurisdiction. And this is what we have always been saying. The same holds true not only between China and India, but also between China and other neighbouring countries. To put it the other way around, such a situation also exists on the maps of other countries with regard to the areas bordering on China. Therefore, we have for many times told Prime Minister Nehru that in connection with the Chinese maps, after both sides conduct surveys and delimit the boundary, we shall revise our respective maps in accordance with the agreement between both sides. Regarding this point, you gentlemen can find proof in the boundary agreement between China and Burma. That is to say, once we have signed a Sino-Burmese boundary treaty, both sides will revise their respective maps. However, pending the survey and delimitation through negotiations, certainly neither side can unilaterally impose its maps on the other side and ask the other side to revise maps according to its demands. This is not a friendly attitude, nor a fair attitude. Therefore we cannot do it this way.

Question (S. V. Bedi of the Weekly magazine *Link*): What is the position of Longju?

Answer: Longju lies to the north of the so-called McMahon Line and this is proved by historical materials. The Indian Government, however, alleges that it is to the south of the so-called McMahon Line and within its jurisdiction.

Question (Anand Swarup of *The Hindustan Times*): During your talks with Indian leaders and after, are you carrying the impression that great changes have taken place in India and that the friendship and faith of the Indian people towards the Chinese people are changing? And what drastic steps are you taking to change this situation?

Answer: I do not share your views. I have already said in my written statement that the friendship between the Chinese and the Indian peoples was immortal and that the disputes over the boundary question were temporary. The two governments, in the course of negotiating a settlement, may meet with temporary barriers. However, as a result of the talks this time, the understanding between the two sides has been further enhanced. I believe that the dark clouds hovering for the time being will disappear, because there is no conflict of fundamental interests between the Chinese and Indian peoples. We have been friendly to each other in the past and shall remain so for thousands and tens of thousands of years to come. I would like to tell you, and particularly the broad masses of the Indian people, that the Chinese people and government do not claim any territory from India or any of our neighbouring countries. We will never commit aggression against a single inch of territory of any country. And of course we will never tolerate aggression by others against us. As for the relations between China and India, I firmly believe that the temporary disputes over the boundary can be settled, that the peoples of the two countries will remain friends forever, and that on the part of the overwhelming majority of the Indian people their ideas of friendship with China have not changed. This was shown by the fact that the broad masses of the Indian people appreciated and attached importance to the Chinese agricultural exhibition held not long ago in Delhi. I would like to avail myself of this opportunity to express through you our thanks to the broad masses of the Indian people. My colleagues and I of course can do some work in promoting Sino-Indian friendship, but the most important thing is the solidarity of the one thousand million people of the two great countries which cannot be undermined by any forces of reaction.

Question (Miss Elaine Shepard of the North America News Alliance and Women's News Service): Would you consider inviting President Eisenhower to visit Peking provided it does not involve recognizing Red China?

Answer: Your good wishes are annulled by the condition you put forward. Since the United States does not recognize New China, how could China invite President Eisenhower, the head of the state of the U.S., to visit Peking?

Question (Elaine Shepard): Now my second question which I ask on behalf of the Women's News Service. The Prime Minister looks exceptionally fit for his sixty-two years of age. How does he look after his health? Does he maintain a particular diet or does he always exercise?

Answer: Thank you. I am an oriental and I follow an oriental way of life.

Question (Charles Wheeler, B.B.C. correspondent in Delhi): In your consultations with the Indian leaders, was there any suggestion from these leaders that China committed aggression against India? How did you remove such a basic difference in your talks? And how could the officials of the two countries remove such a difference in view of the fact that you and Prime Minister Nehru failed to do so?

Answer: This is an idea entertained by western imperialists. During our talks this time, this question has not been raised. If the leaders of the Indian government bring up such a question, it would not only be out of keeping with objective reality, but would also be extremely unfriendly. I would only say that our two friendly countries have no intention to satisfy the desire of the western countries in this regard.

Question (K. N. Sharma of *Assam Tribune*): In view of the fact that negotiations about such a tiny spot as Bara Hoti went on for three years without a settlement, have the two Prime Ministers agreed on some special instructions to be given to the officials so that their forthcoming negotiations may be expedited?

Answer: With regard to Bara Hoti which we call Wu-Je in China, although the dispute has existed for a long time, it has never led to clashes, and, moreover, it will eventually be resolved. As for the terms of reference of the meetings of officials, they have been made public in the joint communiqué. Of course, to facilitate their work, the two governments will respectively give them further instructions. The communiqué has expressed the hope that the work of the officials of the two countries will be helpful to the two governments in their further consideration of a settlement of the boundary question.

Question (Inder Jit of *The Times of India*): You said that no country should impose its map on the other country. Does it not follow in the interests of the immortal friendship as you said that you should agree, as Prime Minister Nehru suggested, to neutralise the disputed area of Ladakh?

Answer: During the talks this time, Prime Minister Nehru did not insist on such a demand. If Prime Minister Nehru should ask China to withdraw from the Aksai Chin area, that is what you call Ladakh, the Chinese government similarly could also ask India to withdraw from the area in the eastern sector, that is, from the area in the eastern sector where the delineations on Indian and Chinese maps show very great discrepancies. How could the Indian Government accept this? Of course the Chinese Government has not raised such a demand.

Question (Bedi of the weekly magazine *Link*): Could one observe any shift in the position taken by you before you started the talk?

Answer: China's position is to find a friendly, reasonable and fair settlement of the border disputes between the two countries, and first to reach an agreement in principle. This position has not changed. As for specific questions, we have not been able to touch upon many of them during these talks.

Question (B. B. Saxena of the Hindi daily *Nai Duniya*): Did the two Prime Ministers, apart from the boundary question, touch on any other grievances, like the Tibet question, political asylum for the Dalai Lama, observance of the five principles of peaceful coexistence. Did the Indian people or government take any action which offended your sentiment?

Answer: Speaking about the Tibet question, the Dalai Lama and mainly his followers started the rebellion in order to maintain the system of serfdom in Tibet. But the rebellion failed and they fled to India and in India they were given political asylum. This is normal international practice and we have no objection to it. However, their activities after they came to India have gone beyond that limit. The Indian Government has repeatedly told the Chinese Government that it would not allow the Dalai Lama and his followers to carry out in India any political activity against New China. But the Dalai Lama and his followers have on quite a few occasions carried out within and without India, activities against China. We feel regret over this.

Tibet is a part of China and this is what the Indian Government has recognised. I can tell this gentleman that the overwhelming majority of the Tibetan people have now been freed from serfdom. Land has been distributed among them and democratic reform has been carried out. The economy in Tibet will continuously develop and the population there will grow. Tibet will forever be a member of the great family of the various nationalities of China. Any act of foreign interference in China's internal affairs is doomed to failure. Such an act is in itself a violation of the five principles jointly initiated by China and India.

Question (Walter Friendenberg of the *Chicago Daily News*): In your formal statement this evening, in the fifth point, it is said that pending a settlement by the two sides, they may keep to the line of actual control. If no settlement can be made, would it be your suggestion that both sides keep to that line of control?

Answer: This line of actual control exists not only in the eastern sector, but also in the western sector and the middle sector. For both sides, to keep to this line of actual control and stop patrolling along all sectors of the boundary will avoid border clashes and facilitate the proceeding of negotiations. This is what we insist on.

Question (Dusab Ruppeldt of the Czechoslovak Broadcasting Corporation): In the joint communiqué it was mentioned that the two parties discussed the World situation. Could you tell us some of the contents of the talks in this respect and especially China's attitude to the Summit Conference?

Answer: In the joint communiqué it was already said that we held hopes for the forthcoming conference of the Big Powers, hoping that it would help to ease international tension, to prohibit nuclear weapons and promote disarmament. As for the attitude of the Chinese Government, it has repeatedly stated its full support for the Soviet Government's propositions with regard to general disarmament, the Berlin question and a number of other questions.

Question (S. G. Roy of the *Pakistan Times*): You find Prime Minister the same as in nineteen fifty-six or a little different?

Answer: Prime Minister Nehru and myself alike have expressed the common desire to maintain Sino-Indian friendship. On the boundary question, we have expounded our respective views and stands and devoted more time in our talks to it.

Question (Roderick Macfarquhar of the British *Daily Telegraph*): when the Dalai Lama came to India the Chinese Government issued a statement suggesting that he was under duress and forced to come to India by his followers. Presumably bearing this in mind when you created the new government in Tibet, the seat of chairman was left for the Dalai Lama to occupy. In your answer to a question just now you stated that the Dalai Lama and his followers had been carrying out certain political activities against China. It would appear from this that the Dalai Lama is a free and independent agent in India. I therefore ask: One. What made the Chinese government change its earlier view? Two. What action is taken by you to describe to the Chinese people the Dalai Lama as carrying on in India activities against the Chinese Government? Three. Is the position of the head of the autonomous region of Tibet still open for the Dalai Lama?

Answer: The three letters written by the Dalai Lama to the Chinese authorities at the time before he left Lhasa proved that he was held under duress by those persons surrounding him. After he came to India, the Dalai Lama also admitted that he wrote those three letters. The Chinese people left room for the Dalai Lama, reserving for him not only the chairmanship of the preparatory committee for the Tibet autonomous region, but also the vice-chairmanship of the standing committee of the National People's Congress. The persons surrounding the Dalai Lama, however, have made him go farther and farther, pushing him into betrayal of the Motherland and trying their utmost to prevent his return to the fold of the Motherland. As to how much free will the Dalai Lama can now exercise, I cannot answer the question because I have not seen him.

Question (D. G. Kulkarni of the Tamil daily *Dina Seithi*): Besides inviting Prime Minister Nehru, did you invite any other ministers to visit China?

Answer: When we met the other ministers of the Indian Government, we expressed the wish to invite them to visit China. Of course formal invitations have yet to be sent by the Chinese Government.

Question (Kulkarni of *Dina Seithi*). Did you invite all the ministers?

Answer: We have not invited all the ministers. If they would like to visit China, they are welcome.

Question (K. R. Malkani of the *Organizer*): What would follow if the officials of the two sides do not agree as the Prime Ministers have not agreed?

Answer: I would not take such a pessimistic view. We have confidence in the friendship between China and India and events after all will develop in a favourable direction. Of course this will take some time. If we did not have sincere desire and confidence, we wouldn't have come to Delhi. I myself or someone else would come to Delhi again for the sake of the friendship of the great Chinese and Indian peoples, END ITEM.

APPENDIX 16

(White Paper IX)

Colombo Proposals together with clarifications (in italics) offered to the Government of India on behalf of the Colombo Conference by representatives of Ceylon, United Arab Republic and Ghana during talks in Delhi between January 11 and 13, 1963

'1. The Conference considers that the existing *de facto* cease fire period is a good starting point for a peaceful settlement of the Indian-Chinese conflict.

'2. (a) With regard to the WESTERN SECTOR, the Conference would like to make an appeal to the Chinese Government to carry out their 20 kilometres withdrawal of their military posts as has been proposed in the letter of Prime Minister Chou En-lai to Prime Minister Nehru on November 21 and November 28, 1962.

(b) The Conference would make an appeal to the Indian Government to keep their existing military position.

(c) Pending a final solution of the border dispute, the area vacated by the Chinese military withdrawals will be a demilitarised zone to be administered by civilian posts of both sides to be agreed upon, without prejudice to the rights of the previous presence of both India and China in that area.

CLARIFICATION

(i) The withdrawal of Chinese forces proposed by the Colombo Conference will be 20 kilometres as proposed by Prime Minister Chou En-lai to Prime Minister Nehru in the statement of the Chinese Government dated 21st November and in Prime Minister Chou En-lai's letter of 28th November, 1962, i.e., from the line of actual control between the two sides as of November 7, 1959, as defined in Maps III and V circulated by the Government of China.

(ii) The existing military posts which the forces of the Government of India will keep to will be on and up to the line indicated in (i) above.

(iii) The demilitarised zone of 20 kilometres created by Chinese military withdrawals will be administered by civilian posts of both sides. This is a substantive part of the Colombo Conference proposals. It is as to the location, the number of posts and their composition that there has to be an agreement between the two Governments of India and China.

'3. With regard to the EASTERN SECTOR, the Conference considers that the line of actual control in the areas recognised by both the Governments could serve as a cease fire line to their respective positions. Remaining areas in this sector can be settled in their future discussion.

CLARIFICATION

The Indian forces can, in accordance with the Colombo Conference proposals, move right up to the south of the line of actual control, i.e., the McMahon Line, except for the two areas on which there is difference of opinion between the Governments of India and China. The Chinese forces similarly can move right up to the north of the McMahon

Line except for these two areas. The two areas referred to as the remaining areas in the Colombo Conference proposals, arrangements in regard to which are to be settled between the Governments of India and China according to the Colombo Conference proposals, are Che Dong or the Thagla ridge area and the Longju area, in which cases there is a difference of opinion as to the line of actual control between the two Governments.

'4. With regard to the problems of the MIDDLE SECTOR, the Conference suggests that they will be solved by peaceful means, without resorting to force.

CLARIFICATION

The Colombo Conference desired that the status quo in this sector should be maintained and neither side should do anything to disturb the status quo.

'5. The Conference believes that these proposals, which could help in consolidating the cease fire, once implemented, should pave the way for discussions between representatives of both parties for the purpose of solving problems entailed in the case fire position.

'6. This Conference would like to make it clear that a positive response for the proposed appeal will not prejudice the position of either of the two Governments as regards its conception of the final alignment of the boundaries.'

(Sino-Pakistan 'Agreement'
March 2, 1963. By External Publicity Division M.E.A. New Delhi pp. 18–19)

*Note given by the Ministry of External Affairs, New Delhi to the High Commission of
Pakistan in India, 10 May 1962*

The Ministry of External Affairs present their compliments to the High Commission of Pakistan in India and have the honour to state that according to a
communiqué issued by the Government of Pakistan on 3rd May 1962, the
Governments of Pakistan and China have agreed to enter into negotiations to
locate and align that portion of boundary between India and China west
of the Karakoram Pass which is presently under Pakistan's unlawful occupation.

When earlier reports about these proposed negotiations appeared in the
Pakistan press, the Acting High Commissioner of India had, in his letters Nos.
CH/CO/9/61 dated 4th May 1961 and HC/180/61 dated 12th June 1961 to the
Foreign Secretary to the Government of Pakistan, conveyed the surprise and
concern of the Government of India and pointed out that these reports were
confusing as Pakistan and China had no common boundary between them.
The Acting High Commissioner of India had also taken the precaution to warn
the Government of Pakistan that the Government of India would not be bound
by the results of any such bilateral discussions between Pakistan and the People's
Republic of China, should these discussions concern the boundaries of the State
of Jammu & Kashmir.

Despite numerous reports in the press and the Pakistan Government's refusal
to provide the clarification sought from them, the Government of India had all
this time been disinclined to believe that the Government of Pakistan would in
fact enter into negotiations with China in respect of the territory of the State of
Jammu & Kashmir which forms an integral pert of the Indian Union. The
Government of Pakistan are obviously not entitled to negotiate with China or
any other country about territory that is not their own.

As the Government of Pakistan are aware the international boundary alignment in the sector west of the Karakoram Pass of the boundary of Jammu &
Kashmir State of India follows well-known natural features, has been recognised in history for all these years, and does not require fresh delimitation. The
position regarding this boundary was made clear in the Note given to the
Pakistan Government at the time of Indian Prime Minister's visit to Pakistan in
Setpember 1960. The Government of India will never agree to any arrangements,
provisional or otherwise, between the Governments of China and Pakistan
regarding territory which constitutes an inalienable part of the Indian Union.

The Government of India lodge an emphatic protest with the Government of
Pakistan and warn them of the grave consequences of their action.

The Ministry of External Affairs avail themselves of the opportunity to renew
to the High Commission of Pakistan the assurances of their highest consideration.

o

17 (b)

(Ibid. pp. 20–21)

Note given by the High Commission of Pakistan in India to the Ministry of External Affairs, New Delhi, 9 August 1962

The High Commission of Pakistan presents its compliments to the Ministry of External Affairs of the Government of India and has the honour to refer to the Note of the Ministry of External Affairs of 10th May, 1962 on the subject of Sino-Pakistan border negotiations as announced in the Government of Pakistan communiqué of 3rd May, 1962.

The High Commission has been instructed to state that the Government of India's 'emphatic protest' against the forthcoming border negotiations between the Governments of Pakistan and China is based on their claim to the territory of the State of Jammu and Kashmir as constituting 'an integral' and 'inalienable part of the Indian Union'. This claim, as the Government of India must be only too well aware, has never been recognised by Pakistan nor by the United Nations. The Government of India has been left in no doubt about the stand of Pakistan with regard to the status of the State of Jammu and Kashmir. According to the relevant Security Council and UNCIP resolutions which constitute an international agreement between Pakistan and India under the aegis of the United Nations Security Council, the State of Jammu and Kashmir cannot be considered to be 'an integral' or 'inalienable part of the Indian Union'. The State is a territory in dispute between Pakistan and India, the question of whose accession to Pakistan or to India is to be decided in accordance with the freely expressed wishes of the people of the State through an impartial plebiscite to be held under the auspices of the United Nations.

Accordingly, the High Commission of Pakistan has been instructed to advise the Government of India that the Government of Pakistan consider the Note of protest of the External Affairs Ministry of 10th May, 1962 to be totally unjustified and must, therefore, reject it.

In that Note the Government of India have considered it fit to warn the Government of Pakistan of the 'grave consequences of their action' with reference to the decision of the Government of the Pakistan to enter into negotiations with the Government of the People's Republic of China with a view to reaching an agreed understanding of the location and alignment of the border between the Chinese province of Sinkiang and the contiguous areas the defence of which is under the control of Pakistan and, to sign on this basis, an agreement of a provisional nature.

Such an agreement can in no way prejudice a peaceful and just settlement of the dispute between Pakistan and India over Kashmir – a dispute which remains unsettled since 1947 due solely to the refusal of the Government of India to honour their solemn pledge to the people of Kashmir, to Pakistan and to the world, to respect the right of the people of Kashmir to self-determination. It is strange that the Government of India should first obstruct and frustrate the attempts of the United Nations and of Pakistan, over the past fourteen years, to settle by peaceful procedures the status of the territory of the State of Jammu and Kashmir and then proceed to question the right of Pakistan to enter into negotiations with China to reach an understanding on the alignment of that portion of the territory for the defence of which Pakistan is responsible.

The High Commission is instructed to state that in proposing to enter into negotiations of this kind, the Government of Pakistan is motivated by its declared and accepted policy of settling all border questions with its neighbours peacefully and by negotiation and to remove any factors which may tend to create any misunderstandings or friction with its neighbours. The conclusion of an agreement of a provisional nature, embodying an agreed understanding of the common border between Pakistan and China, would be a positive contribution to the strengthening of peace in Asia. Therefore, the threat of 'grave consequences' to which the Indian Note refers, would appear to be not only gratuitous and wholly unnecessary, but calculated to threaten or intimidate and to to prevent Pakistan from pursuing its steadfast policy of removing any possible causes of friction or tension between states by recourse to the peaceful procedure of negotiations in accordance with the Charter of the United Nations.

The High Commission of Pakistan avails itself of this opportunity to renew to the Ministry of External Affairs the assurances of its highest consideration.

APPENDIX 18

(Ibid. p. 22)

Note given by the Ministry of External Affairs, New Delhi to the Embassy of China in India December 31, 1962

The Ministry of External Affairs presents its compliments to the Embassy of the People's Republic of China and has the honour to refer to the communiqué issued by the Chinese and Pakistan Governments on 26th December on their agreement in principle on the alignment of the border between China (Sinkiang) and the territory of Kashmir illegally occupied by Pakistan.

In their note of 30th June 1962, the Government of India had drawn attention to the attempts of the Chinese Government to exploit, for its own ends, the differences on Kashmir between the Indian and Pakistan Governments. Despite the assertion by the Chinese Government that it does not wish to get involved in the dispute, the calculated release of this communiqué at a time when delegations from India and Pakistan were attempting to resolve their differences on Kashmir and related matters is clear evidence of China's desire to exploit Indo-Pakistan differences for its own selfish and expansionist designs.

The joint communiqué is a brazen attempt at legitimisation of the gains of aggression in the hope that the Chinese Government will thereby secure Pakistan support to Chinese aggression on India and the gains of this aggression.

The Government of India protest strongly against this aggressive and expansionist move by the Government of China. They repudiate firmly the validity of any agreement involving Indian territory between parties who have no legal or constitutional *locus standi* whatever in respect of this territory.

The Ministry of External Affairs avails itself of this opportunity to renew to the Embassy of the People's Republic of China the assurances of its highest consideration.

APPENDIX 19

(Ibid. pp. 24–28)

Text of the Agreement signed by China and Pakistan in Peking on 2 March 1963

The Government of the People's Republic of China and the Government of Pakistan;

Having agreed, with a view to ensuring the prevailing peace and tranquillity on the border, to formally delimit and demarcate the boundary between China's Sinkiang and the contiguous areas the defence of which is under the actual control of Pakistan, in a spirit of fairness, reasonableness, mutual understanding and mutual accommodation, and on the basis of the ten principles as enunciated in the Bandung conference;

Being convinced that this would not only give full expression to the desire of the peoples of China and Pakistan for the development of good-neighbourly and friendly relations, but also help safeguard Asian and world peace.

Have resolved for this purpose to conclude the present agreement and have appointed as their respective plenipotentiaries the following:

For the Government of the People's Republic of China Chen Yi, Minister of Foreign Affairs;

For the Government of Pakistan; Mr. Zulfikar Ali Bhutto, Minister of External Affairs;

Who, having mutually examined their full powers and found them to be in good and due form, have agreed upon the following:

Article 1

In view of the fact that the boundary between China's Sinkiang and the contiguous areas the defence of which is under the actual control of Pakistan has never been formally delimited, two parties agree to delimit it on the basis of the traditional customary boundary line including natural features and in a spirit of equality, mutual benefit and friendly co-operation.

Article 2

In accordance with the principle expounded in Article 1 of the present agreement, the two parties have fixed, as follows the alignment of the entire boundary line between China's Sinkiang and the contiguous areas the defence of which is under the actual control of Pakistan:

(1) Commencing from its north-western extremity at height 5,630 metres (a peak, the reference coordinates of which are approximately longitude 74 degrees 34 minutes east and latitude 37 degrees 03 minutes north), the boundary line runs generally eastward and then southeastward strictly along the main watershed between the tributaries of the Tashkurgan river of the Tarim river system on the one hand and the tributaries of the Hunza river of the Indus river system on the other hand, passing through the Kilik Daban (Dawan), the Mintake Daban (pass), the Kharchanai Daban (named on the Chinese map only), the Mutsjilga Daban (named on the Chinese map only), and the Parpik Pass (named on the Pakistan map only), and reaches the Khunjerab (Yutr) Daban (Pass).

(2) After passing through the Khunjerab (Yutr) Daban (pass), the boundary line runs generally southward along the above-mentioned main watershed upto a mountain-top south of this Daban (pass), where it leaves the main watershed to follow the crest of a spur lying generally in a southeasterly direction, which is the watershed between the Akjilga river (a nameless corresponding river on the Pakistan map) on the one hand, and the Taghumbash (Oprang) river and the Koliman Su (Oprang Jilga)on the other hand.

According to the map of the Chinese side, the boundary line, after leaving the southeastern extremity of this spur, runs along a small section of the middle line of the bed of the Keliman Su to reach its confluence with the Elechin river. According to the map of the Pakistan side, the boundary line, after leaving the southeastern extremity of this spur, reaches the sharp bend of the Shaksgam or Muztagh river.

(3) From the aforesaid point, the boundary line runs up the Kelechin river (Shaksgam or Muztagh river) along the middle line of its bed to its confluence (reference co-ordinates approximately longitude 76 degrees 02 minjtes east and latitude 36 degrees 26 minutes north) with the Shorbulak Daria (Shimshal river or Braldu river).

Main watershed

(4) From the confluence of the aforesaid two rivers. the boundary line, according to the map of the Chinese side, ascends the crest of a spur and runs along it to join the Karakoram range main watershed at a mountain-top (reference co-ordinates approximately longitude 75 degrees 54 minutes east and latitude 36 degrees 15 minutes north) which on this map is shown as belonging to the Shorgulak mountain. According to the map of the Pakistan side, the boundary line from the confluence of the above-mentioned two rivers ascends the crest of a corresponding spur and runs along it, passing through height 6,520 metres (21,390 feet) till it joins the Karakoram range main watershed at a peak (reference co-ordinates approximately longitude 75 degrees 57 minutes east and latitude 36 degrees 03 minutes north).

(5) Thence, the boundary line, running generally southward and then eastward, strictly follows the Karakoram range main watershed which separates the Tarim river drainage system from the Indus river drainage system, passing through the east Mustagh pass (Muztagh pass), the top of the Chogri peak (K-2), the top of the broad peak, the top of the Gasherbrum mountain (8,068), the Indirakoli pass (names on the Chinese maps only) and the top of the Teram Kankri peak, and reaches its southeastern extremity at the Karakoram pass.

(Two) The alignment of the entire boundary line as described in section one of this article, has been drawn on the one million scale map of the Chinese side in Chinese and the one million scale map of the Pakistan side in English which are signed and attached to the present agreement.

(Three) In view of the fact that the maps of the two sides are not fully identical in their representation of topographical features the two parties have agreed that the actual features on the ground shall prevail, so far as the location and alignment of the boundary described in Section one is concerned, and that they will be determined as far as possible by joint survey on the ground.

ARTICLE 3

The two parties have agreed that:

(1) Wherever the boundary follows a river, the middle line of the river bed shall be the boundary line; and that

Wherever the boundary passes through a deban (pass), the water-parting line thereof shall be the boundary line.

ARTICLE 4

One: The two parties have agreed to set up, as soon as possible, a joint boundary demarcation commission. Each side will appoint a chairman, one or more members and a certain number of advisers and technical staff. The joint boundary demarcation commission is charged with the responsibility, in accordance with the provisions of the present agreement, to hold concrete discussions on and carry out the following tasks jointly:

(1) To conduct necessary surveys of the boundary area on the ground, as stated in Article 2 of the present agreement, so as to set up boundary markers at places considered to be appropriate by the two parties and to delineate the boundary line of the jointly prepared accurate maps.

(2) To draft a protocol setting forth in detail the alignment of the entire boundary line and the location of all the boundary markers and prepare and get printed detailed maps, to be attached to the protocol, with the boundary line and the location of the boundary markers shown on them.

Two: The aforesaid protocol, upon being signed by the representatives of the Governments of the two countries, shall become an annex to the present agreement, and the detailed maps shall replace the maps attached to the present agreement.

Three: Upon the conclusion of the above-mentioned protocol, the tasks of the joint boundary demarcation commission shall be terminated.

ARTICLE 5

The two parties have agreed that any dispute concerning the boundary which may arise after the delimitation of the boundary line actually existing between the two countries shall be settled peacefully by the two parties through friendly consultations.

ARTICLE 6

The two parties have agreed that after the settlement of the Kashmir dispute between Pakistan and India, the sovereign authority concerned will reopen negotiations with the Government of the people's Republic of China on the boundary, as described in Article Two of the present agreement, so as to sign a formal boundary treaty to replace the present agreement, provided that in the event of that sovereign authority being Pakistan, the provisions of the present agreement and of the aforesaid protocol shall be maintained in the formal boundary treaty to be signed between the Peoples Republic of China and Pakistan.

ARTICLE 7

The present agreement shall come into force on the date of its signature.

Done in duplicate in Peking on the second day of March, 1963, in the Chinese and English languages, both texts being equally authentic.

('Tashkent Declaration'
Externel Publicity Division, Government of India, pp. 1–4)

Text of Tashkent Agreement January 10, 1966

The Prime Minister of India and the President of Pakistan having met at Tashkent and having discussed the existing relations between India and Pakistan, hereby declare their firm resolve to restore normal and peaceful relations between the countries and to promote understanding and friendly relations between their peoples. They consider the attainment of these objectives of vital importance for the welfare of the 600 million people of India and Pakistan.

The Prime Minister of India and the President of Pakistan agree that both sides will exert all efforts to create good neighbourly relations between India and Pakistan in accordance with the United Nations Charter. They reaffirm their obligations under the Charter not to have recourse to force and to settle their disputes through peaceful means.

They consider the interests of peace in their region and particularly in the Indo-Pakistan subcontinent and indeed the interests of the peoples of India and Pakistan, were not served by continuance of tension between the two countries. It was against this background that Jammu and Kashmir was discussed and each of the sides set forth its respective position.

The Prime Minister of India and the President of Pakistan have agreed that all armed personnel of the two countries shall be withdrawn, not later than February 25, 1966, to the positions they held prior to August 5, 1965, and both sides shall observe the cease-fire terms on the cease-fire line.

The Prime Minister of India and the President of Pakistan have agreed that the relations between India and Pakistan shall be based on the principle of non-interference in the internal affairs of each other.

The Prime Minister of India and the President of Pakistan have agreed that both sides will discourage any propaganda directed against the other country and will encourage propaganda which promotes the development of friendly relations between the two countries.

The Prime Minister of India and the President of Pakistan have agreed that the High Commissioner of India to Pakistan and the High Commissioner of Pakistan to India will return to their posts and that the normal functioning of diplomatic missions will be restored. Both Governments shall observe the Vienna Convention of 1961 on diplomatic intercourse.

The Prime Minister of India and the President of Pakistan have agreed to consider measures towards the restoration of economic and trade relations, communications as well as cultural exchanges between India and Pakistan and to take measures to implement the existing agreements between India and Pakistan.

The Prime Minister of India and the President of Pakistan have agreed that they give instructions to their respective authorities to carry out the repatriation of the prisoners of war.

The Prime Minister of India and the President of Pakistan have agreed that both sides will continue the discussion of questions relating to the problems of refugees and eviction of illegal immigrants. They also agreed that both sides will create conditions which will prevent the exodus of people. They further agreed to discuss the return of the property and assets taken over by either side in connection with the conflict.

The Prime Minister of India and the President of Pakistan have agreed that both sides will continue meetings both at the highest and at other levels on matters of direct concern to both countries. Both sides have recognised the need to set up joint India-Pakistan bodies which will report to their Governments in order to decide what further steps should be taken.

The Prime Minister of India and the President of Pakistan record their feelings of deep appreciation and gratitude to the leaders of the Soviet Union, the Soviet Government and personally to the Chairman of the Council of Ministers of the USSR for their constructive friendly and noble part in bringing about the present meeting which has resulted in mutually satisfactory result.

They also express to the Government and friendly people of Uzbekistan their sincere thankfulness for their overwhelming reception and generous hospitality. They invite the Chairman of the Council of Ministers of the USSR to witness this declaration.

(Aitchison's Treaties Vol. XII. 1931. pp. 66–67)

Convention between Great Britain and China relating to Sikkim and Tibet (1890)

Whereas Her Majesty the Queen of the United Kingdom of Great Britain and Ireland, Empress of India, and His Majesty the Emperor of China, are sincerely desirous to maintain and perpetuate the relations of friendship and good understanding which now exists between their respective Empires; and whereas recent occurrences have tended towards a disturbance of the said relations, and it is desirable to clearly define and permanently settle certain matters connected with the boundary between Sikkim and Tibet, Her Britannic Majesty and His Majesty the Emperor of China have resolved to conclude a Convention on this subject and have, for this purpose, named Plenipotentiaries, that is to say:

Her Majesty the Queen of Great Britain and Ireland, His Excellency the Most Hon'ble Henry Charles Keith Petty Fitzmaurice, G.M.S.I., G.C.M.G., G.M.I.E., Marquess of Landsdowne, Viceroy and Governor-General of India.

And His Majesty the Emperor of China, His Excellency Shêng Tai, Imperial Associate Resident in Tibet, Military Deputy Lieutenant-Governor.

Who having met and communicated to each other their full powers, and finding these to be in proper form, having agreed upon the following Convention in eight Articles:

(1) The boundary of Sikkim and Tibet shall be the crest of the mountain range separating the waters flowing into the Sikkim Teesta and its affluents from the waters flowing into the Tibetan Mochu and northwards into other rivers of Tibet. The line commences at Mount Gipmochi on the Bhutan frontier and follows the abovementioned water-parting to the point where it meets Nepal territory.

(2) It is admitted that the British Government, whose protectorate over the Sikkim State is hereby recognised, has direct and exclusive control over the internal administration and foreign relations of the State, and except through and with the permission of the British Government, neither the Ruler of the State nor any of its officers shall have official relations of any kind, formal or informal, with any other country.

(3) The Government of Great Britain and Ireland and the Government of China engage reciprocally to respect the boundary as defined in Article (1), and to prevent acts of aggression from their respective sides of the frontier.

(4) The question of providing increased facilities for trade across the Sikkim-Tibet frontier will hereafter be discussed with a view to a mutually satisfactory arrangement by the High Contracting Powers.

(5) The question of pasturage on the Sikkim side of the frontier is reserved for further examination and future adjustment.

(6) The High Contracting Powers reserve for discussion and arrangement the

method in which official communications between the British authorities in India and the authorities in Tibet shall be conducted.

(7) Two Joint Commissioners shall, within six months from the ratification of this Convention, be appointed, one by the British Government in India, the other by the Chinese Resident in Tibet. The said Commissioners shall meet and discuss the questions which by the last three preceding Articles have been reserved.

(8) The present Convention shall be ratified, and the ratifications shall be exchanged in London as soon as possible after the date of the signature thereof.

In witness whereof the respective negotiators have signed the same and affixed thereunto the seals of their arms.

Done in quadruplicate at Calcutta this seventeenth day of March in the year of our Lord one thousand eight hundred and ninety, corresponding with the Chinese date the twenty-seventh day of the second moon of the sixteenth year of Kuang Hsü.

LANSDOWNE
Chinese Seal and Signature

Index